empowered ™

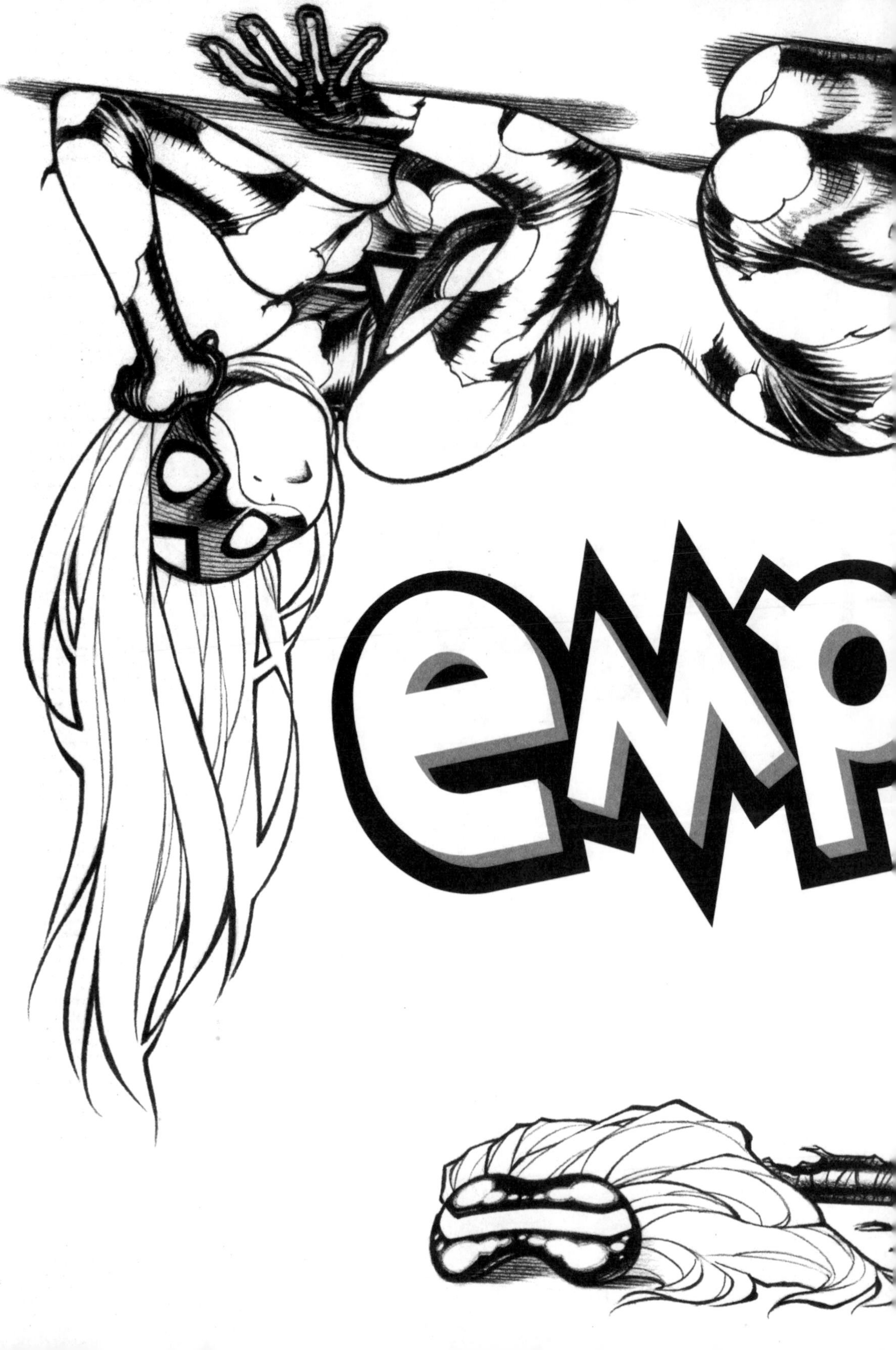
emp

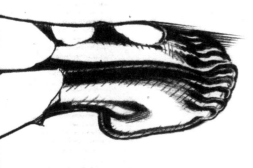

volume **6**

oWered

by ADAM WARREN

cover colors and yaoi story (page 69) by EMILY WARREN yaoi story (page 67) by JO CHEN

back-cover colors by JOCHEN WELTJENS for GURUeFX

linguistic assistance (pages 130-131) by MARC MIYAKE empowered logo by EUGENE WANG

DARK HORSE BOOKS®

publisher
Mike Richardson

editor
Chris Warner

designer
Josh Elliott

art director
Lia Ribacchi

EMPOWERED VOLUME 6

Dark Horse Books
A division of Dark Horse Comics, Inc.
10956 SE Main Street
Milwaukie, OR 97222

darkhorse.com

To find a comics shop in your area, call the Comic Shop
Locator Service toll-free at 1-888-266-4226

First edition: September 2010
ISBN 978-1-59582-391-5

1 3 5 7 9 10 8 6 4 2

Printed by Transcontinental Gagné, Louiseville, QC, Canada.

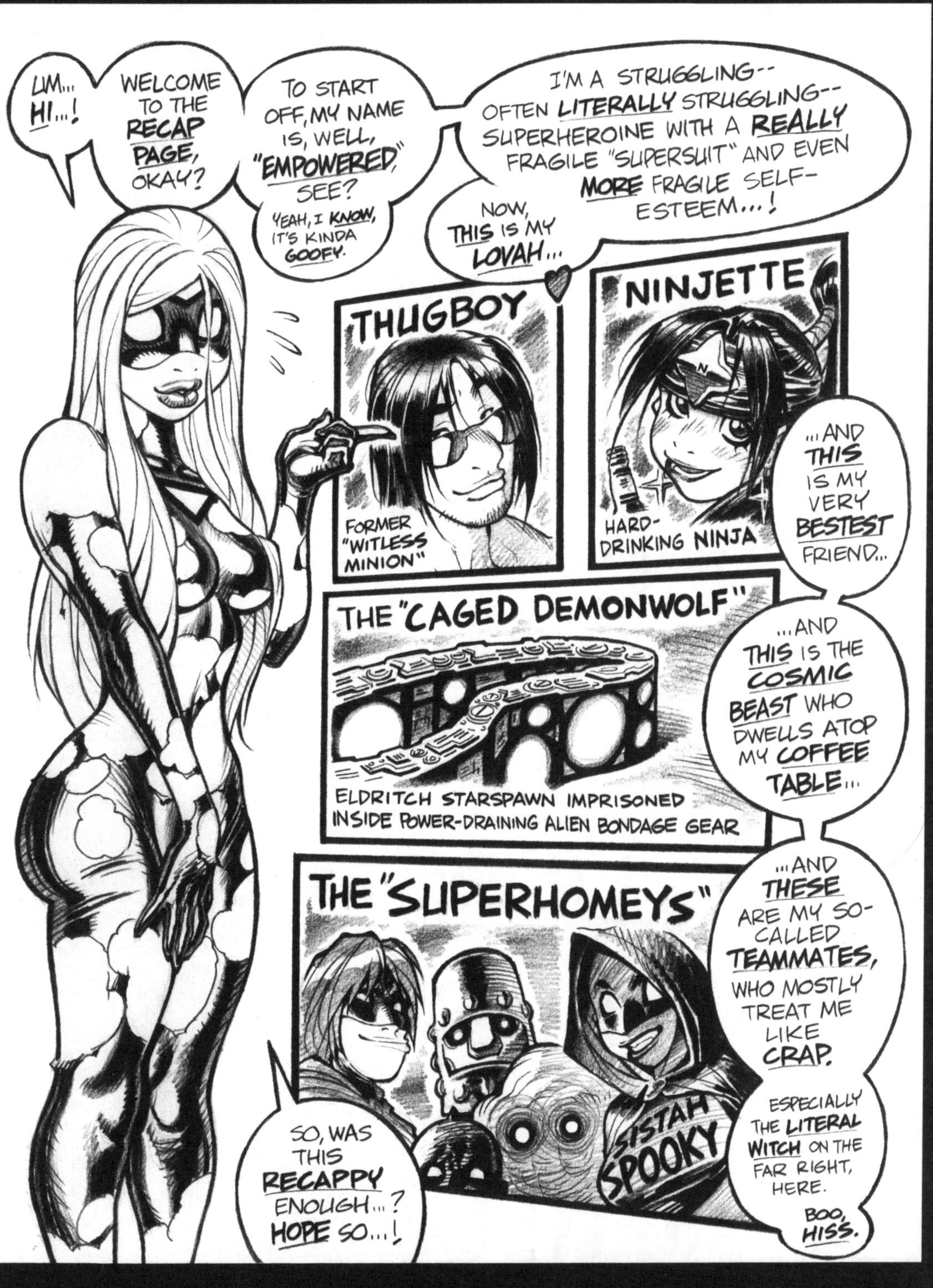

UM... HI...!
WELCOME TO THE RECAP PAGE, OKAY?
TO START OFF, MY NAME IS, WELL, "EMPOWERED," SEE?
YEAH, I KNOW, IT'S KINDA GOOFY.
I'M A STRUGGLING-- OFTEN LITERALLY STRUGGLING-- SUPERHEROINE WITH A REALLY FRAGILE "SUPERSUIT" AND EVEN MORE FRAGILE SELF-ESTEEM...!
NOW, THIS IS MY LOVAH...
THUGBOY
FORMER "WITLESS MINION"
NINJETTE
HARD-DRINKING NINJA
...AND THIS IS MY VERY BESTEST FRIEND...
THE "CAGED DEMONWOLF"
ELDRITCH STARSPAWN IMPRISONED INSIDE POWER-DRAINING ALIEN BONDAGE GEAR
...AND THIS IS THE COSMIC BEAST WHO DWELLS ATOP MY COFFEE TABLE...
THE "SUPERHOMEYS"
SISTAH SPOOKY
...AND THESE ARE MY SO-CALLED TEAMMATES, WHO MOSTLY TREAT ME LIKE CRAP.
ESPECIALLY THE LITERAL WITCH ON THE FAR RIGHT, HERE.
BOO, HISS.
SO, WAS THIS RECAPPY ENOUGH...? HOPE SO...!

OKAY. LEMME THINK OF WHAT YOU NEED TO KNOW FOR **THIS** PARTICULAR VOLUME... **HRMM.**

FOR **ONE** THING, MY REAL NAME IS **ELISSA MEGAN POWERS.** "**EMP**," GET IT?

AND **NINJETTE'S** REAL NAME IS **KOZUE KABURAGI.**

OR, UM, "**KABURAGI KOZUE**" IN PROPER JAPANESE FASHION... NOT THAT SHE'S **ACTUALLY** JAPANESE.

LONG STORY.

かぶらぎ こずえ
鏑木 梢

TURNS OUT THAT SHE'S A **WHITE-GIRL NINJA** FROM **NEW JERSEY** -- I KNOW, I **KNOW** -- WHO HAPPENS TO HAVE A JAPANESE NAME.

A WHILE BACK, A BUNCH OF **BOUNTY-HUNTING NINJAS** TRIED TO CAPTURE HER AND TAKE HER BACK TO THE NINJA CLAN SHE **RAN AWAY** FROM.

OOPS, JUST ENDED A SENTENCE WITH A **PREPOSITION**... SORRY 'BOUT THAT.

BUT **YOURS TRULY** SHOWED UP IN THE PROVERBIAL **NICK,** AND ZAPPED 'EM INTO NINJA-SCENTED **VAPOR.** YAY, **ME.**

MY **SUPERSUIT** SPROUTED SOME WEIRD, UM, **WINGS** IN THE PROCESS... WHICH I **DIDN'T** SEEM TO NOTICE, FOR SOME REASON...

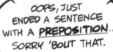

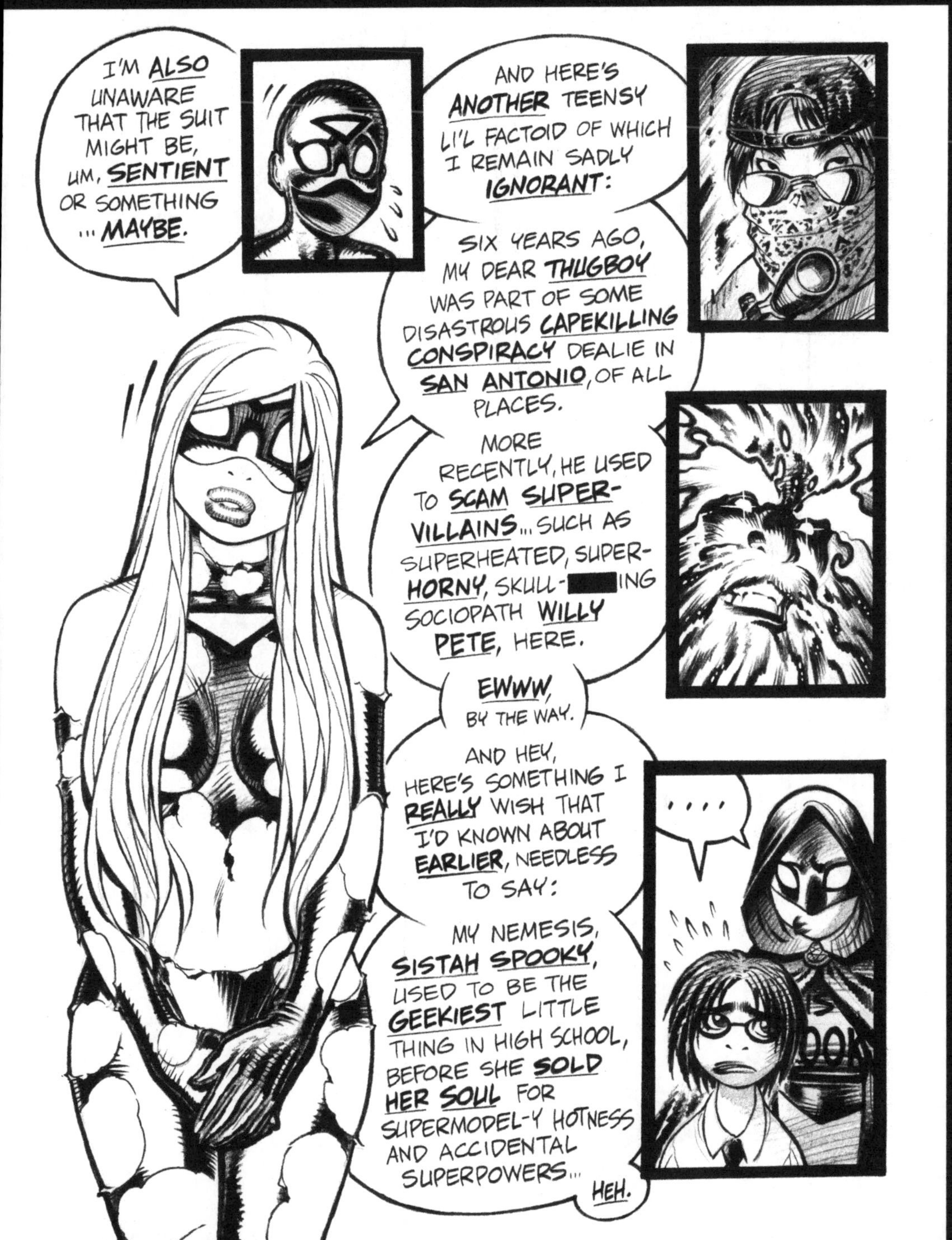

I'M ALSO UNAWARE THAT THE SUIT MIGHT BE, UM, SENTIENT OR SOMETHING ... MAYBE.
AND HERE'S ANOTHER TEENSY LI'L FACTOID OF WHICH I REMAIN SADLY IGNORANT:
SIX YEARS AGO, MY DEAR THUGBOY WAS PART OF SOME DISASTROUS CAPEKILLING CONSPIRACY DEALIE IN SAN ANTONIO, OF ALL PLACES.
MORE RECENTLY, HE USED TO SCAM SUPER-VILLAINS... SUCH AS SUPERHEATED, SUPER-HORNY, SKULL-[redacted]ING SOCIOPATH WILLY PETE, HERE.
EWWW, BY THE WAY.
AND HEY, HERE'S SOMETHING I REALLY WISH THAT I'D KNOWN ABOUT EARLIER, NEEDLESS TO SAY:
MY NEMESIS, SISTAH SPOOKY, USED TO BE THE GEEKIEST LITTLE THING IN HIGH SCHOOL, BEFORE SHE SOLD HER SOUL FOR SUPERMODEL-Y HOTNESS AND ACCIDENTAL SUPERPOWERS... HEH.
....

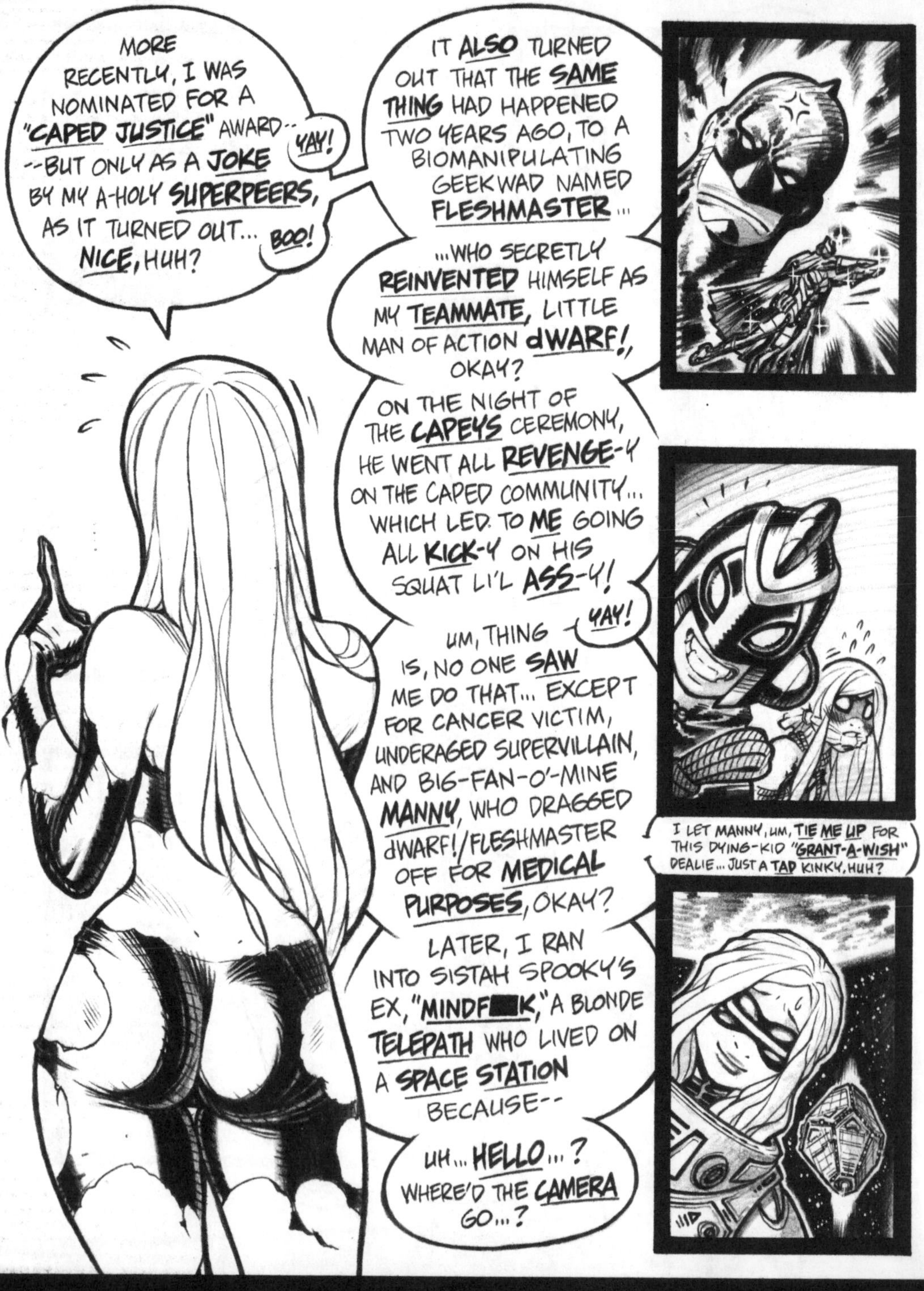
MORE RECENTLY, I WAS NOMINATED FOR A "CAPED JUSTICE" AWARD...
YAY!
--BUT ONLY AS A JOKE BY MY A-HOLY SUPERPEERS, AS IT TURNED OUT...
BOO!
NICE, HUH?
IT ALSO TURNED OUT THAT THE SAME THING HAD HAPPENED TWO YEARS AGO, TO A BIOMANIPULATING GEEKWAD NAMED FLESHMASTER...
...WHO SECRETLY REINVENTED HIMSELF AS MY TEAMMATE, LITTLE MAN OF ACTION dWARF!, OKAY?
ON THE NIGHT OF THE CAPEYS CEREMONY, HE WENT ALL REVENGE-Y ON THE CAPED COMMUNITY... WHICH LED TO ME GOING ALL KICK-Y ON HIS SQUAT LI'L ASS-Y!
YAY!
UM, THING IS, NO ONE SAW ME DO THAT... EXCEPT FOR CANCER VICTIM, UNDERAGED SUPERVILLAIN, AND BIG-FAN-O'-MINE MANNY, WHO DRAGGED dWARF!/FLESHMASTER OFF FOR MEDICAL PURPOSES, OKAY?
I LET MANNY, UM, TIE ME UP FOR THIS DYING-KID "GRANT-A-WISH" DEALIE... JUST A TAD KINKY, HUH?
LATER, I RAN INTO SISTAH SPOOKY'S EX, "MINDF[redacted]K," A BLONDE TELEPATH WHO LIVED ON A SPACE STATION BECAUSE--
UH... HELLO...? WHERE'D THE CAMERA GO...?

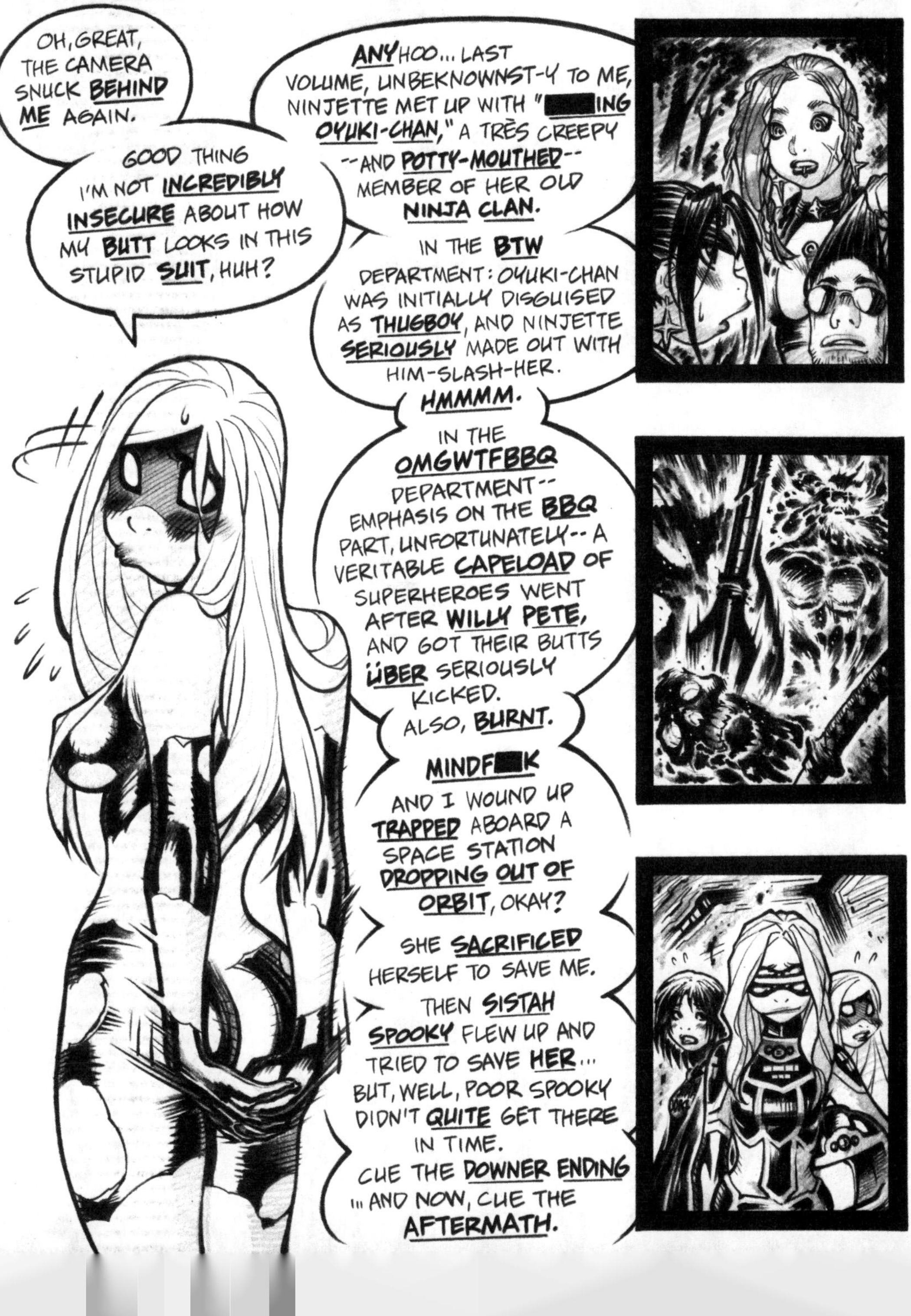
OH, GREAT, THE CAMERA SNUCK BEHIND ME AGAIN.
GOOD THING I'M NOT INCREDIBLY INSECURE ABOUT HOW MY BUTT LOOKS IN THIS STUPID SUIT, HUH?
ANYHOO... LAST VOLUME, UNBEKNOWNST-Y TO ME, NINJETTE MET UP WITH "[redacted]ING OYUKI-CHAN," A TRÈS CREEPY --AND POTTY-MOUTHED-- MEMBER OF HER OLD NINJA CLAN.
IN THE BTW DEPARTMENT: OYUKI-CHAN WAS INITIALLY DISGUISED AS THUGBOY, AND NINJETTE SERIOUSLY MADE OUT WITH HIM-SLASH-HER.
HMMMM.
IN THE OMGWTFBBQ DEPARTMENT-- EMPHASIS ON THE BBQ PART, UNFORTUNATELY-- A VERITABLE CAPELOAD OF SUPERHEROES WENT AFTER WILLY PETE, AND GOT THEIR BUTTS ÜBER SERIOUSLY KICKED.
ALSO, BURNT.
MINDF[redacted]K AND I WOUND UP TRAPPED ABOARD A SPACE STATION DROPPING OUT OF ORBIT, OKAY?
SHE SACRIFICED HERSELF TO SAVE ME.
THEN SISTAH SPOOKY FLEW UP AND TRIED TO SAVE HER... BUT, WELL, POOR SPOOKY DIDN'T QUITE GET THERE IN TIME.
CUE THE DOWNER ENDING
... AND NOW, CUE THE AFTERMATH.

Empowered™

The What-the-F[redacted]kiest Five Minutes of My Career So Far

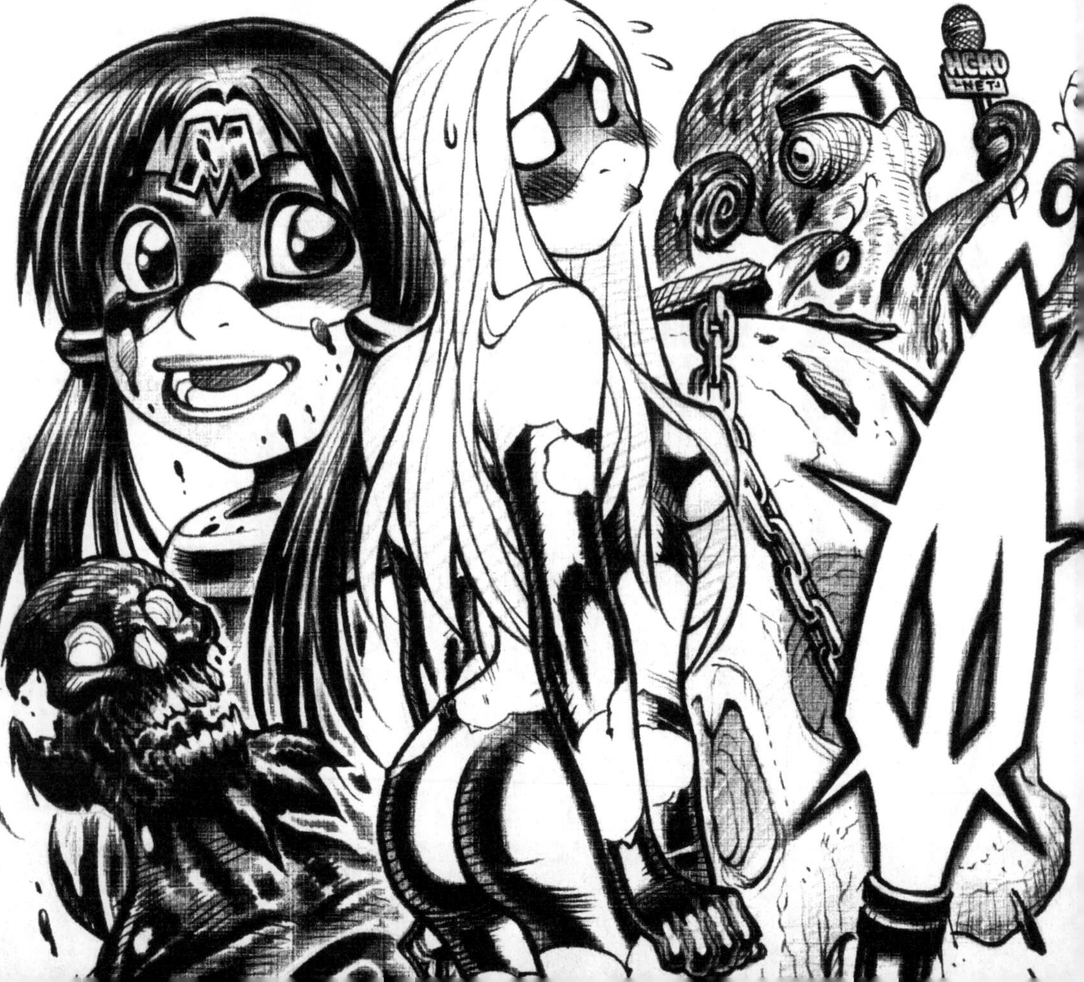
HERO NET

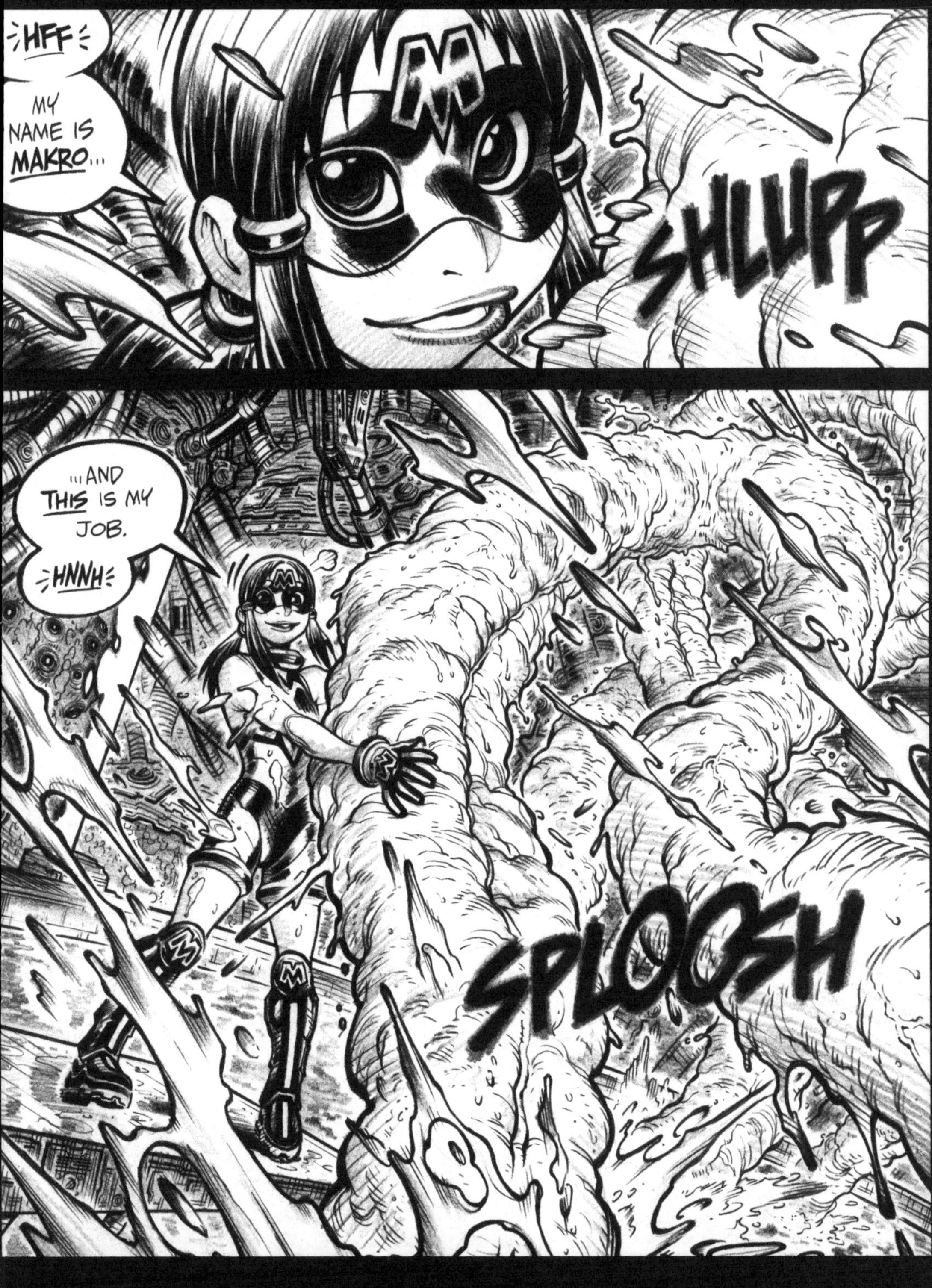
HFF
MY NAME IS MAKRO...
SHLUPP
...AND THIS IS MY JOB.
HNNH
SPLOOSH

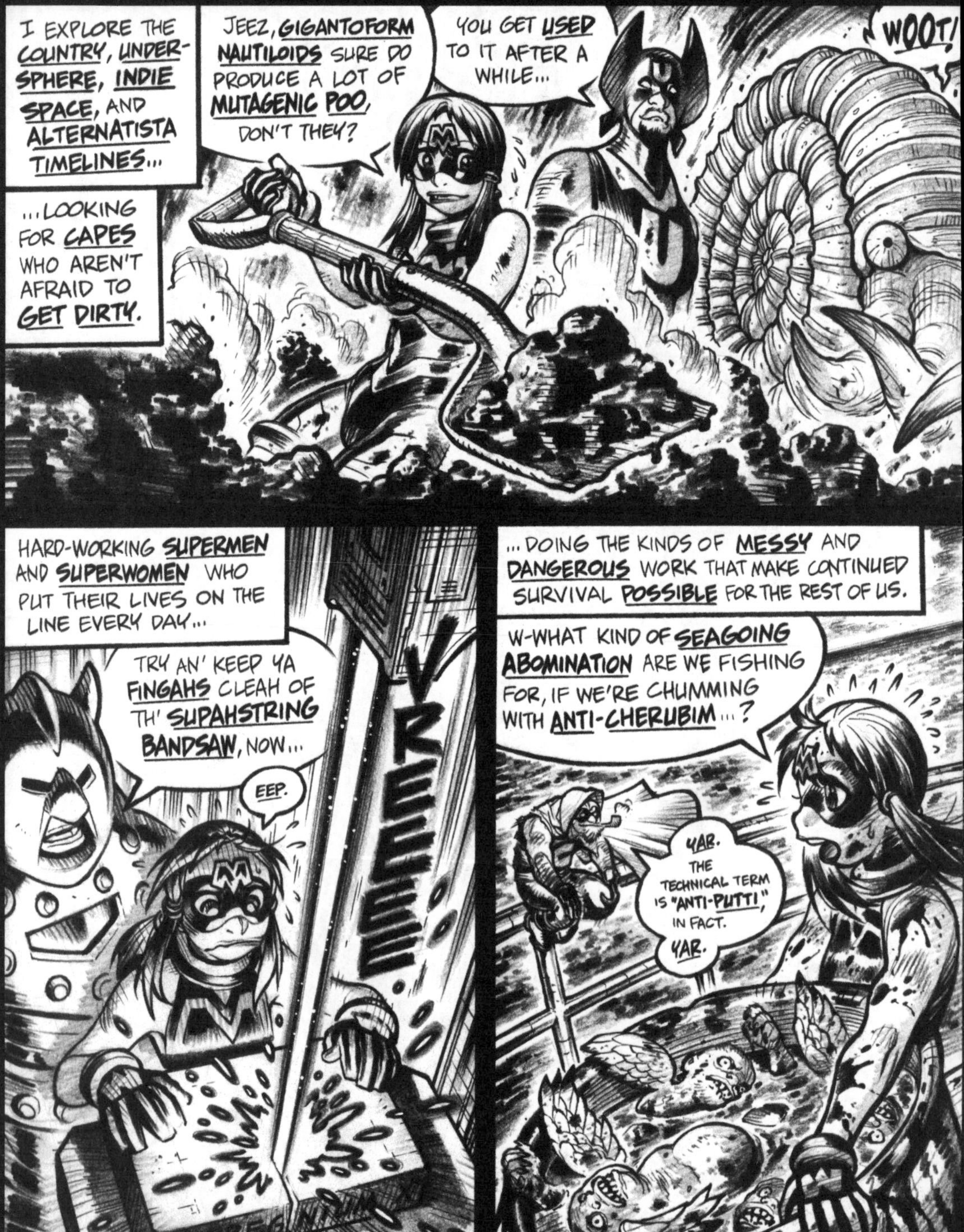
I EXPLORE THE COUNTRY, UNDER-SPHERE, INDIE SPACE, AND ALTERNATISTA TIMELINES...
JEEZ, GIGANTOFORM NAUTILOIDS SURE DO PRODUCE A LOT OF MUTAGENIC POO, DON'T THEY?
YOU GET USED TO IT AFTER A WHILE...
WOOT!
...LOOKING FOR CAPES WHO AREN'T AFRAID TO GET DIRTY.
HARD-WORKING SUPERMEN AND SUPERWOMEN WHO PUT THEIR LIVES ON THE LINE EVERY DAY...
TRY AN' KEEP YA FINGAHS CLEAH OF TH' SUPAHSTRING BANDSAW, NOW...
EEP.
VREEEEE...
...DOING THE KINDS OF MESSY AND DANGEROUS WORK THAT MAKE CONTINUED SURVIVAL POSSIBLE FOR THE REST OF US.
W-WHAT KIND OF SEAGOING ABOMINATION ARE WE FISHING FOR, IF WE'RE CHUMMING WITH ANTI-CHERUBIM...?
YAR. THE TECHNICAL TERM IS "ANTI-PUTTI," IN FACT. YAR.

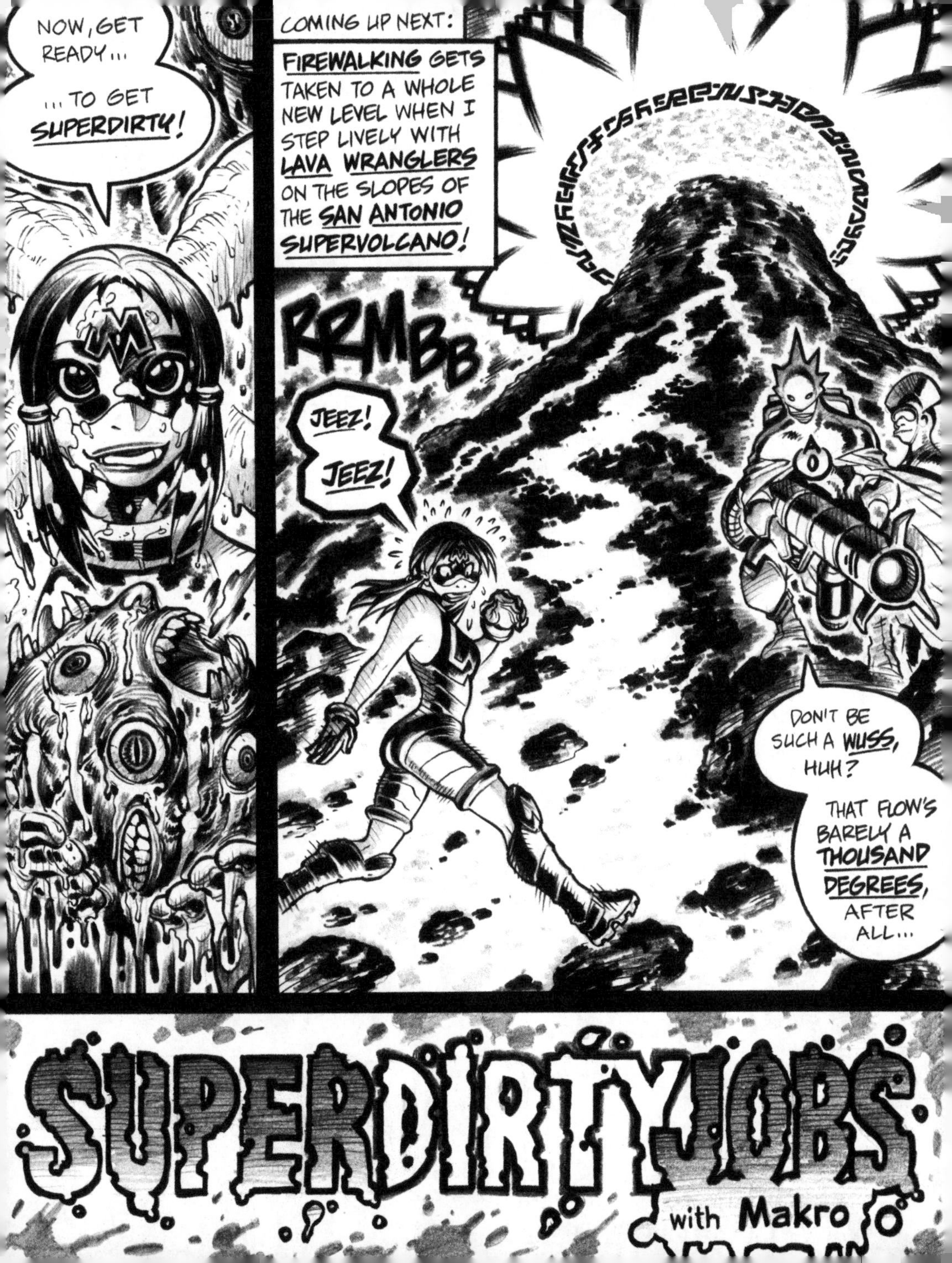
NOW, GET READY...
...TO GET SUPERDIRTY!
COMING UP NEXT:
FIREWALKING GETS TAKEN TO A WHOLE NEW LEVEL WHEN I STEP LIVELY WITH LAVA WRANGLERS ON THE SLOPES OF THE SAN ANTONIO SUPERVOLCANO!
RRMBB
JEEZ!
JEEZ!
DON'T BE SUCH A WUSS, HUH?
THAT FLOW'S BARELY A THOUSAND DEGREES, AFTER ALL...
SUPERDIRTYJOBS
with Makro

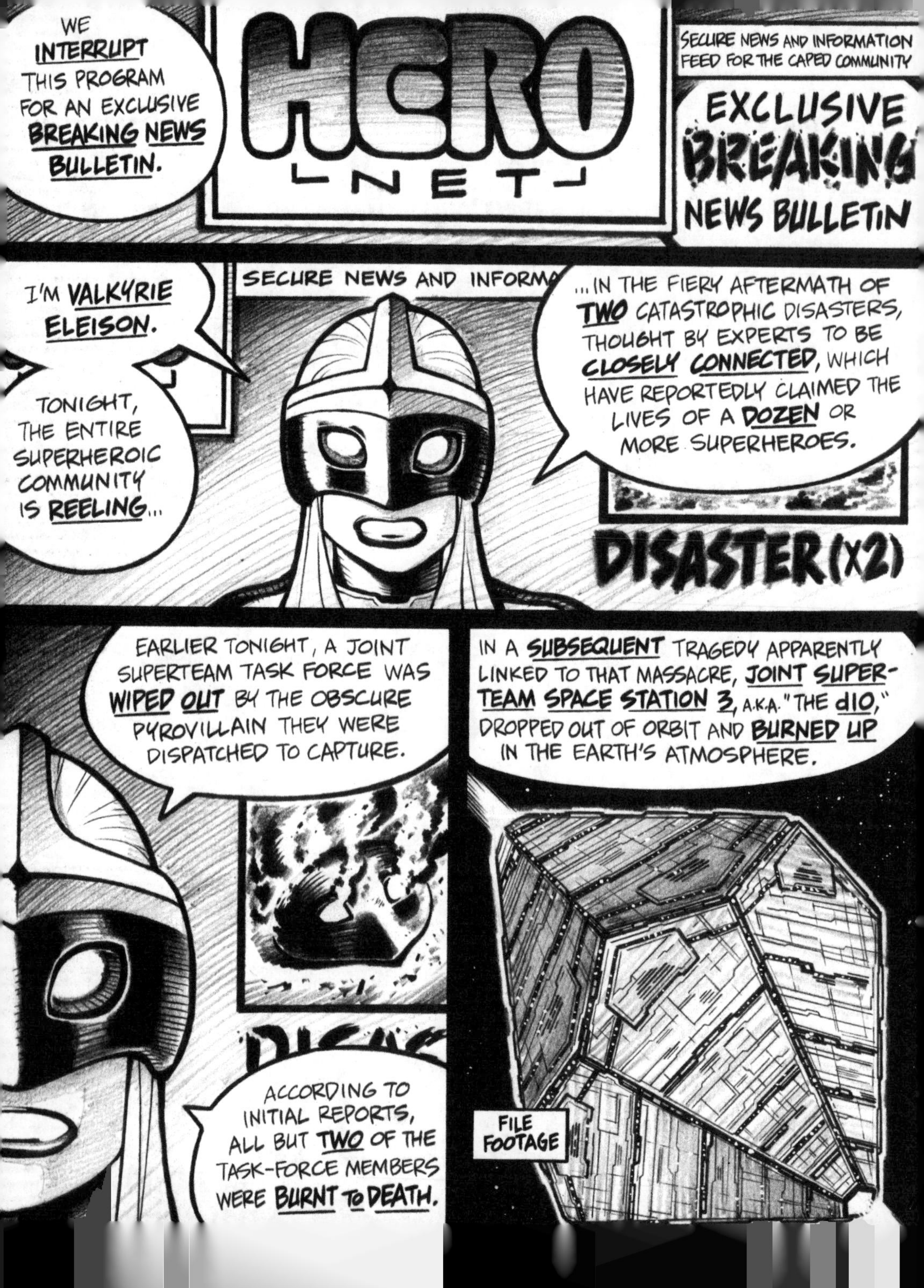
WE INTERRUPT THIS PROGRAM FOR AN EXCLUSIVE BREAKING NEWS BULLETIN.
HERO NET
SECURE NEWS AND INFORMATION FEED FOR THE CAPED COMMUNITY
EXCLUSIVE BREAKING NEWS BULLETIN
I'M VALKYRIE ELEISON.
TONIGHT, THE ENTIRE SUPERHEROIC COMMUNITY IS REELING...
SECURE NEWS AND INFORMA
...IN THE FIERY AFTERMATH OF TWO CATASTROPHIC DISASTERS, THOUGHT BY EXPERTS TO BE CLOSELY CONNECTED, WHICH HAVE REPORTEDLY CLAIMED THE LIVES OF A DOZEN OR MORE SUPERHEROES.
DISASTER (X2)
EARLIER TONIGHT, A JOINT SUPERTEAM TASK FORCE WAS WIPED OUT BY THE OBSCURE PYROVILLAIN THEY WERE DISPATCHED TO CAPTURE.
ACCORDING TO INITIAL REPORTS, ALL BUT TWO OF THE TASK-FORCE MEMBERS WERE BURNT TO DEATH.
IN A SUBSEQUENT TRAGEDY APPARENTLY LINKED TO THAT MASSACRE, JOINT SUPER-TEAM SPACE STATION 3, A.K.A. "THE d10," DROPPED OUT OF ORBIT AND BURNED UP IN THE EARTH'S ATMOSPHERE.
FILE FOOTAGE

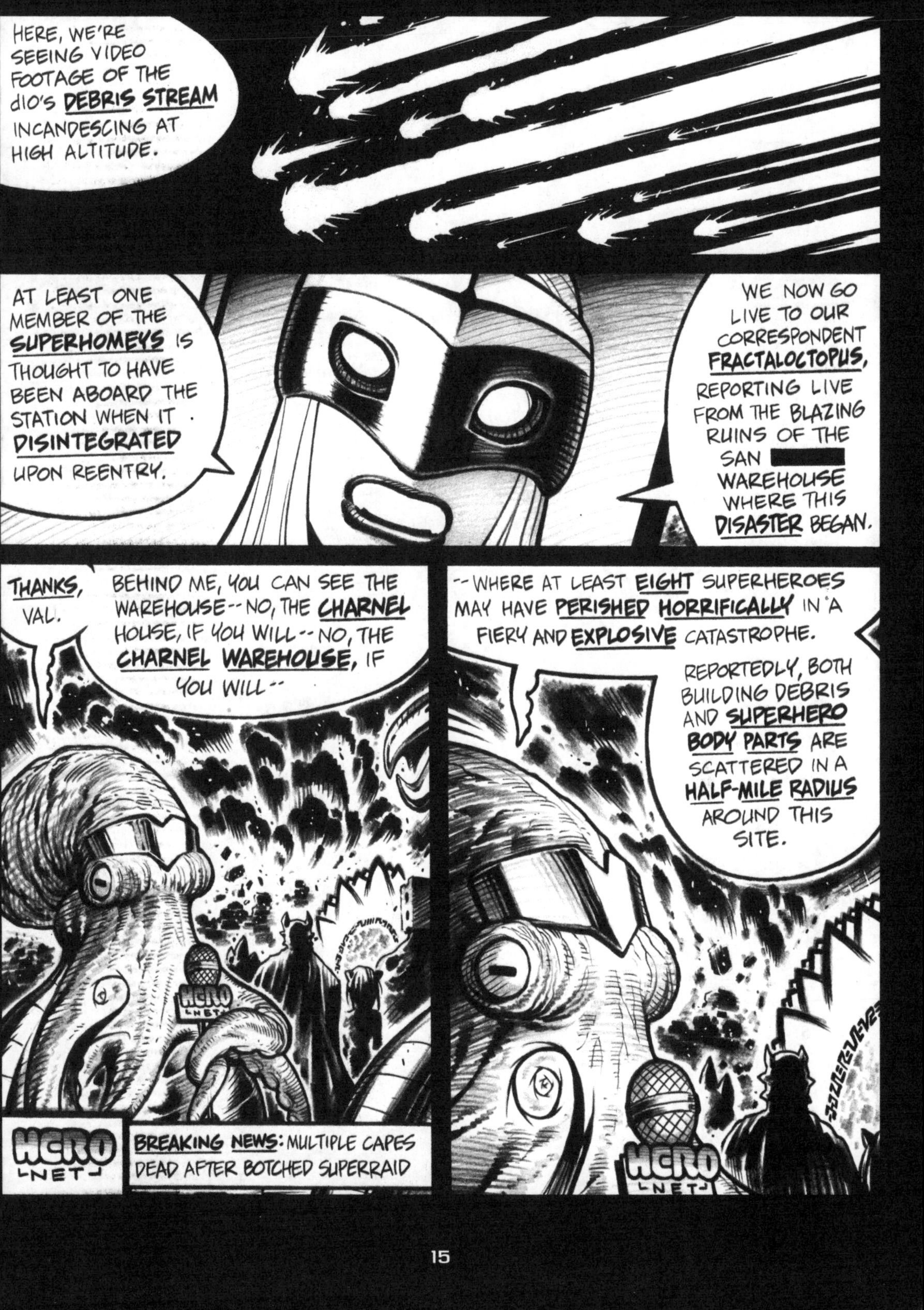
HERE, WE'RE SEEING VIDEO FOOTAGE OF THE dIO'S DEBRIS STREAM INCANDESCING AT HIGH ALTITUDE.
AT LEAST ONE MEMBER OF THE SUPERHOMEYS IS THOUGHT TO HAVE BEEN ABOARD THE STATION WHEN IT DISINTEGRATED UPON REENTRY.
WE NOW GO LIVE TO OUR CORRESPONDENT FRACTALOCTOPUS, REPORTING LIVE FROM THE BLAZING RUINS OF THE SAN [redacted] WAREHOUSE WHERE THIS DISASTER BEGAN.
THANKS, VAL.
BEHIND ME, YOU CAN SEE THE WAREHOUSE--NO, THE CHARNEL HOUSE, IF YOU WILL--NO, THE CHARNEL WAREHOUSE, IF YOU WILL--
HERO NET
BREAKING NEWS: MULTIPLE CAPES DEAD AFTER BOTCHED SUPERRAID
--WHERE AT LEAST EIGHT SUPERHEROES MAY HAVE PERISHED HORRIFICALLY IN A FIERY AND EXPLOSIVE CATASTROPHE.
REPORTEDLY, BOTH BUILDING DEBRIS AND SUPERHERO BODY PARTS ARE SCATTERED IN A HALF-MILE RADIUS AROUND THIS SITE.
HERO NET

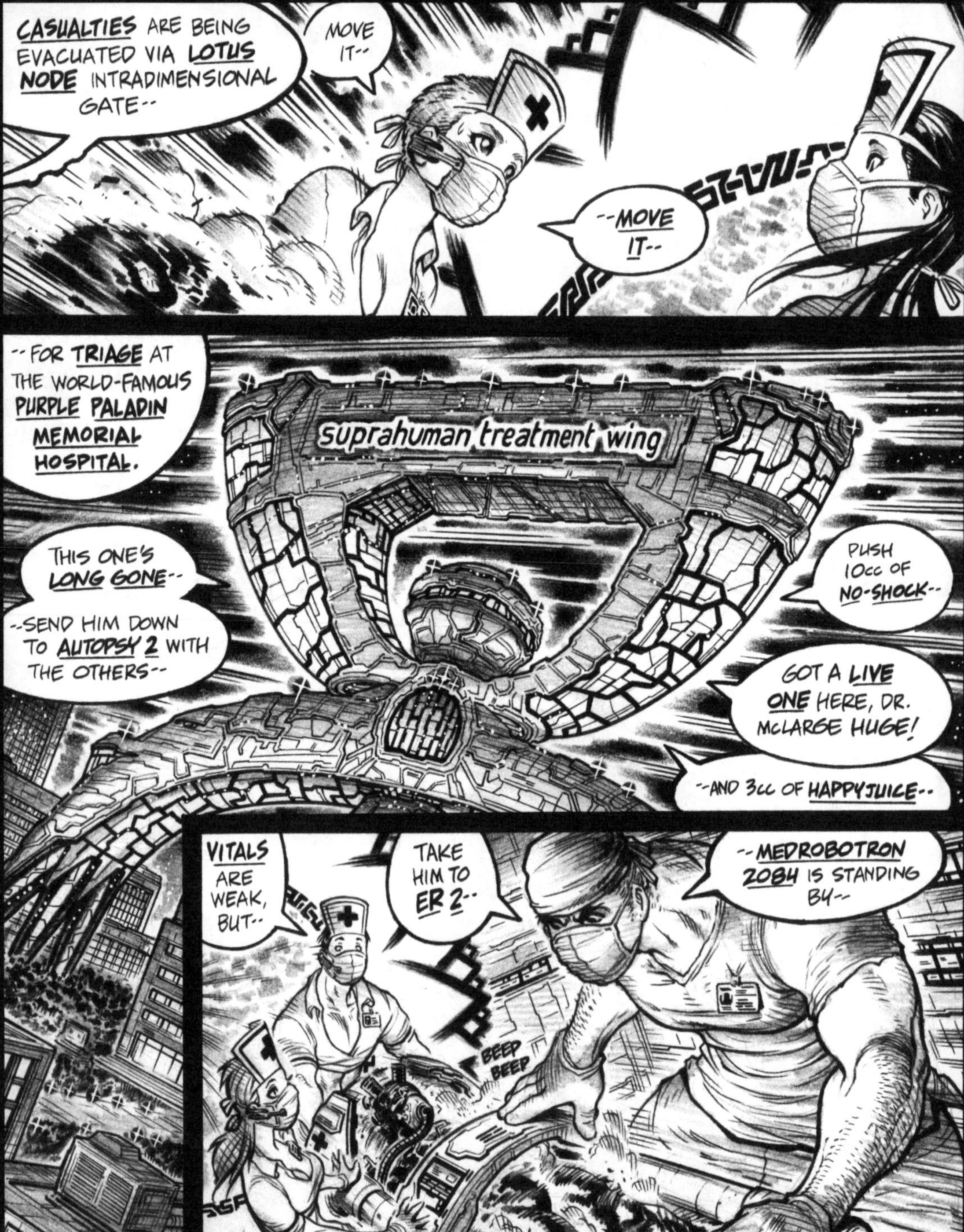
CASUALTIES ARE BEING EVACUATED VIA LOTUS NODE INTRADIMENSIONAL GATE--
MOVE IT--
--MOVE IT--
--FOR TRIAGE AT THE WORLD-FAMOUS PURPLE PALADIN MEMORIAL HOSPITAL.
suprahuman treatment wing
THIS ONE'S LONG GONE--
--SEND HIM DOWN TO AUTOPSY 2 WITH THE OTHERS--
PUSH 10cc OF NO-SHOCK--
GOT A LIVE ONE HERE, DR. McLARGE HUGE!
--AND 3cc OF HAPPYJUICE--
VITALS ARE WEAK, BUT--
TAKE HIM TO ER 2--
--MEDROBOTRON 2084 IS STANDING BY--
BEEP BEEP

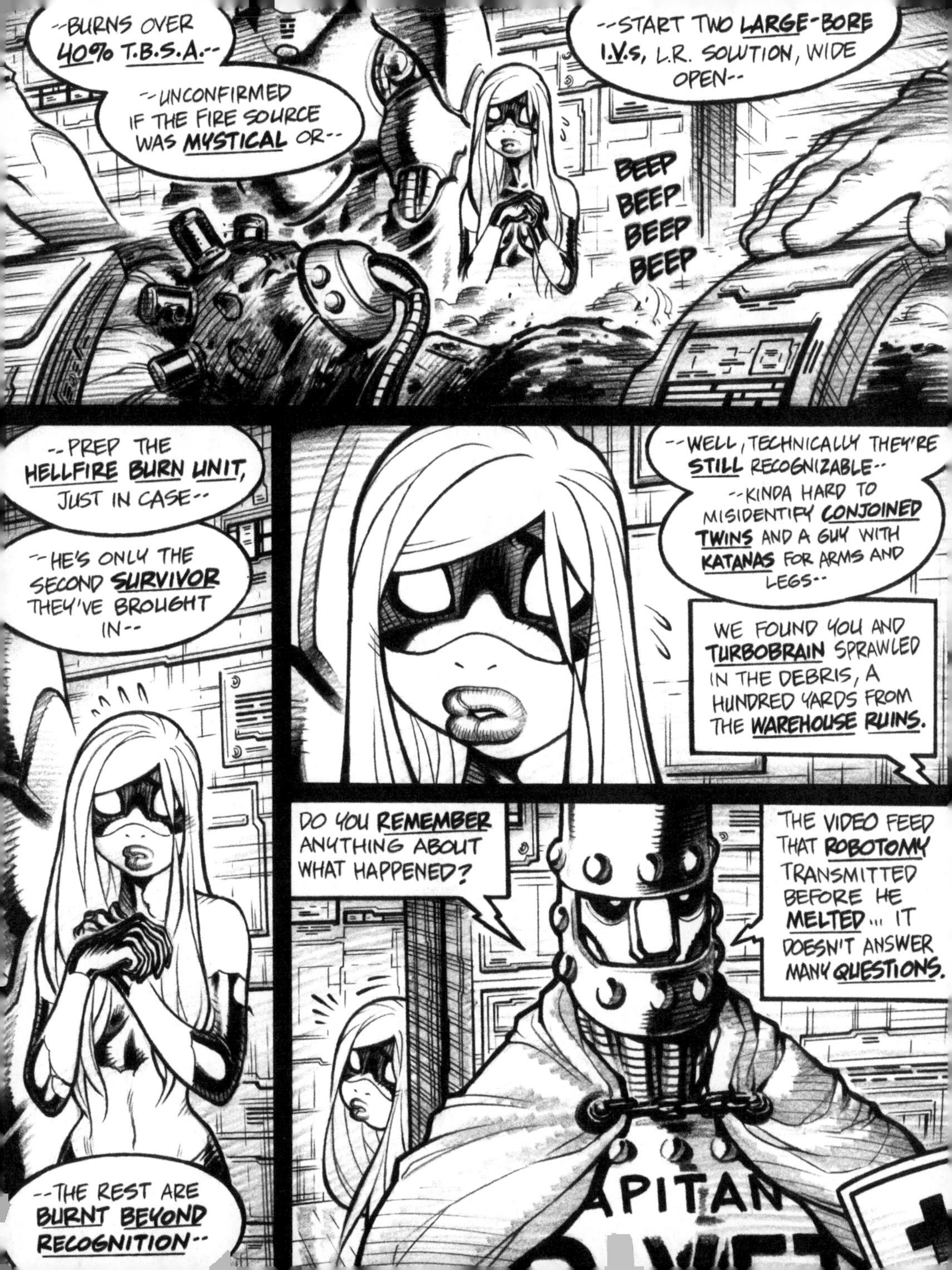
--BURNS OVER 40% T.B.S.A.--
--UNCONFIRMED IF THE FIRE SOURCE WAS MYSTICAL OR--
--START TWO LARGE-BORE I.V.s, L.R. SOLUTION, WIDE OPEN--
BEEP BEEP BEEP BEEP
--PREP THE HELLFIRE BURN UNIT, JUST IN CASE--
--HE'S ONLY THE SECOND SURVIVOR THEY'VE BROUGHT IN--
--THE REST ARE BURNT BEYOND RECOGNITION--
--WELL, TECHNICALLY THEY'RE STILL RECOGNIZABLE--
--KINDA HARD TO MISIDENTIFY CONJOINED TWINS AND A GUY WITH KATANAS FOR ARMS AND LEGS--
WE FOUND YOU AND TURBOBRAIN SPRAWLED IN THE DEBRIS, A HUNDRED YARDS FROM THE WAREHOUSE RUINS.
DO YOU REMEMBER ANYTHING ABOUT WHAT HAPPENED?
THE VIDEO FEED THAT ROBOTOMY TRANSMITTED BEFORE HE MELTED... IT DOESN'T ANSWER MANY QUESTIONS.

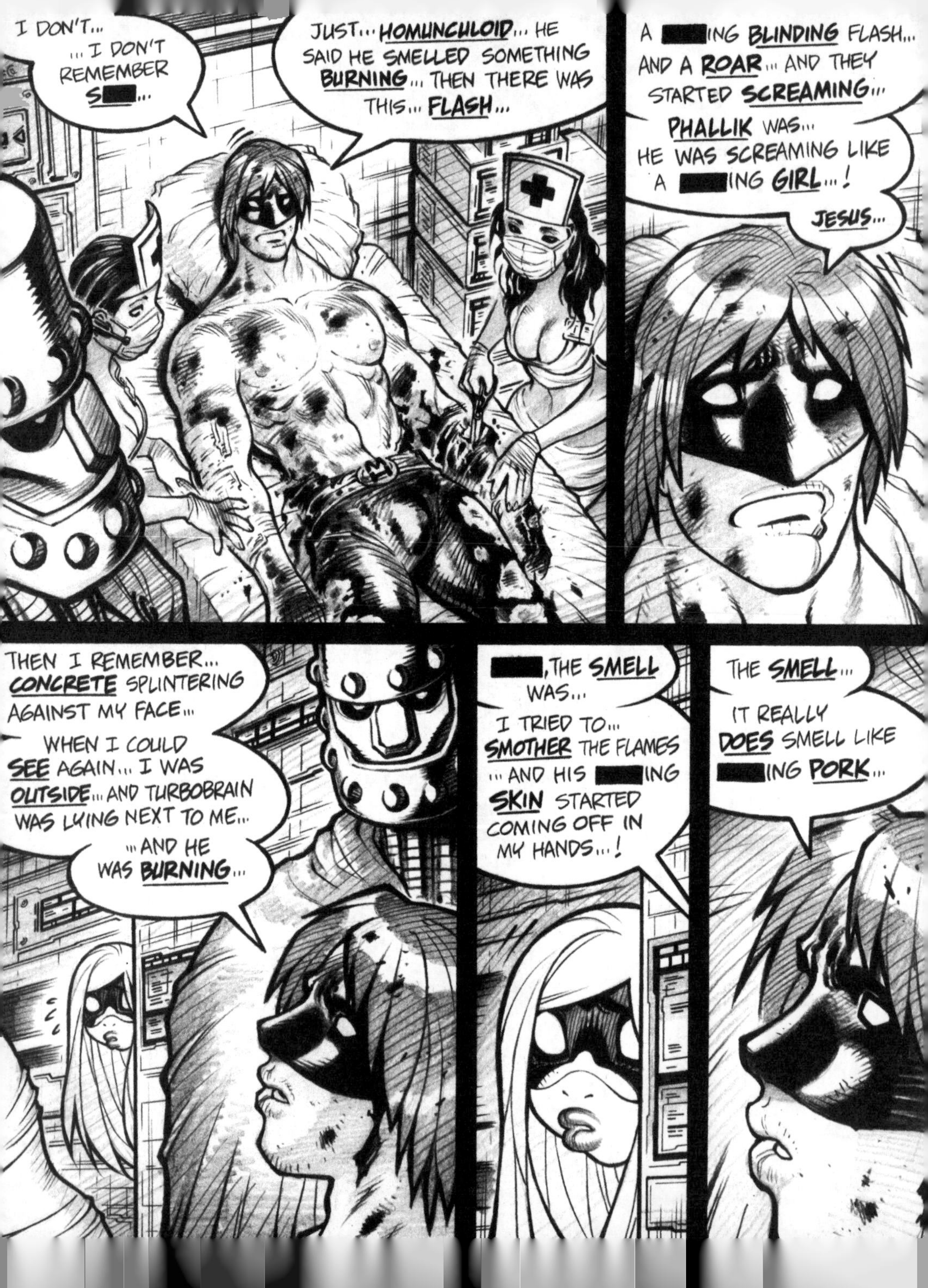
I DON'T... ...I DON'T REMEMBER S[redacted]...
JUST... HOMUNCULOID... HE SAID HE SMELLED SOMETHING BURNING... THEN THERE WAS THIS... FLASH...
A [redacted]ING BLINDING FLASH... AND A ROAR... AND THEY STARTED SCREAMING...
PHALLIK WAS... HE WAS SCREAMING LIKE A [redacted]ING GIRL...!
JESUS...
THEN I REMEMBER... CONCRETE SPLINTERING AGAINST MY FACE...
WHEN I COULD SEE AGAIN... I WAS OUTSIDE... AND TURBOBRAIN WAS LYING NEXT TO ME...
...AND HE WAS BURNING...
[redacted], THE SMELL WAS...
I TRIED TO... SMOTHER THE FLAMES ...AND HIS [redacted]ING SKIN STARTED COMING OFF IN MY HANDS...!
THE SMELL...
IT REALLY DOES SMELL LIKE [redacted]ING PORK...

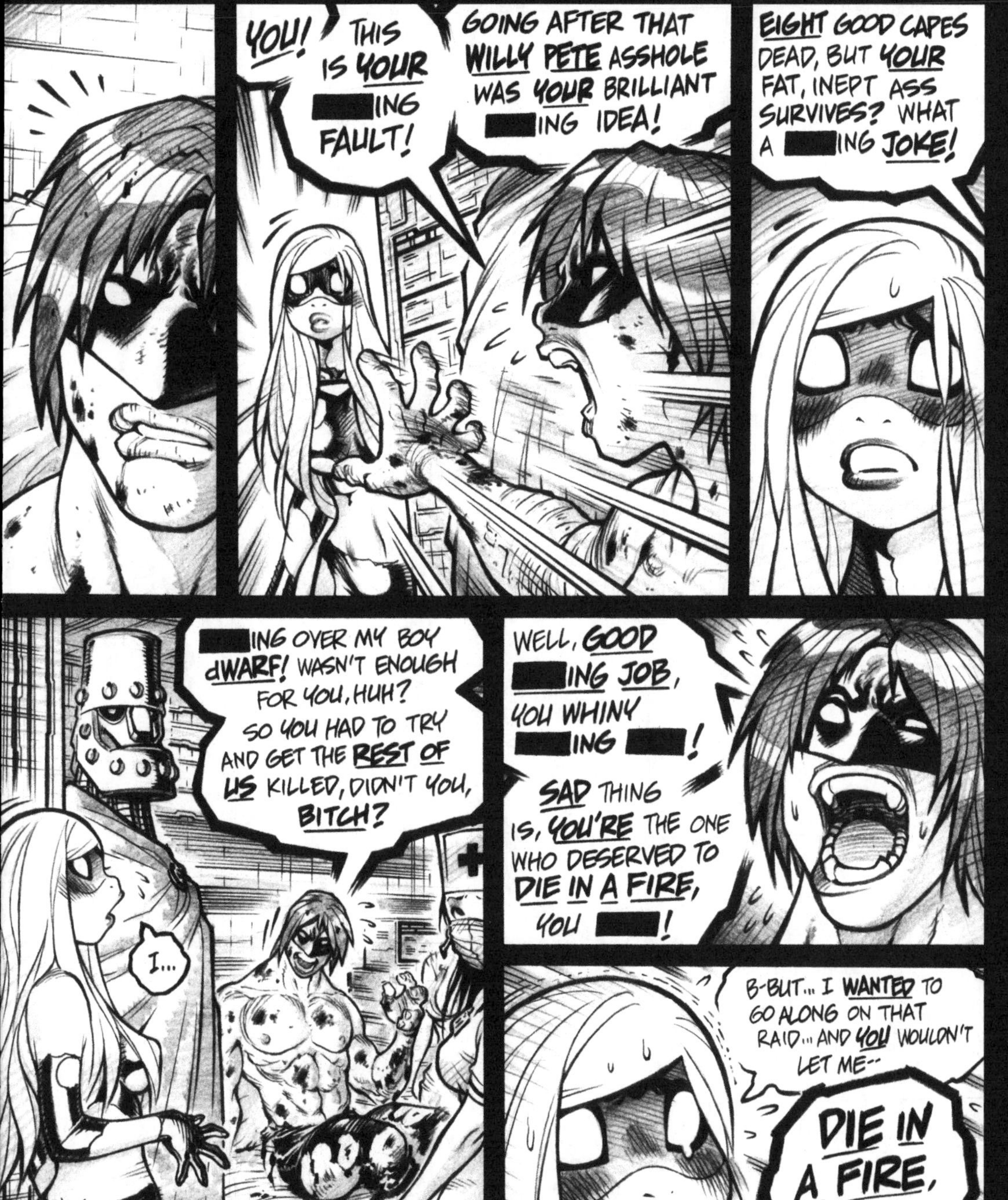
YOU! THIS IS YOUR [redacted]ING FAULT!
GOING AFTER THAT WILLY PETE ASSHOLE WAS YOUR BRILLIANT [redacted]ING IDEA!
EIGHT GOOD CAPES DEAD, BUT YOUR FAT, INEPT ASS SURVIVES? WHAT A [redacted]ING JOKE!
[redacted]ING OVER MY BOY dWARF! WASN'T ENOUGH FOR YOU, HUH? SO YOU HAD TO TRY AND GET THE REST OF US KILLED, DIDN'T YOU, BITCH?
I...
...I DIDN'T...
WELL, GOOD [redacted]ING JOB, YOU WHINY [redacted]ING [redacted]!
SAD THING IS, YOU'RE THE ONE WHO DESERVED TO DIE IN A FIRE, YOU [redacted]!
B-BUT... I WANTED TO GO ALONG ON THAT RAID... AND YOU WOULDN'T LET ME--
DIE IN A FIRE, [redacted]!

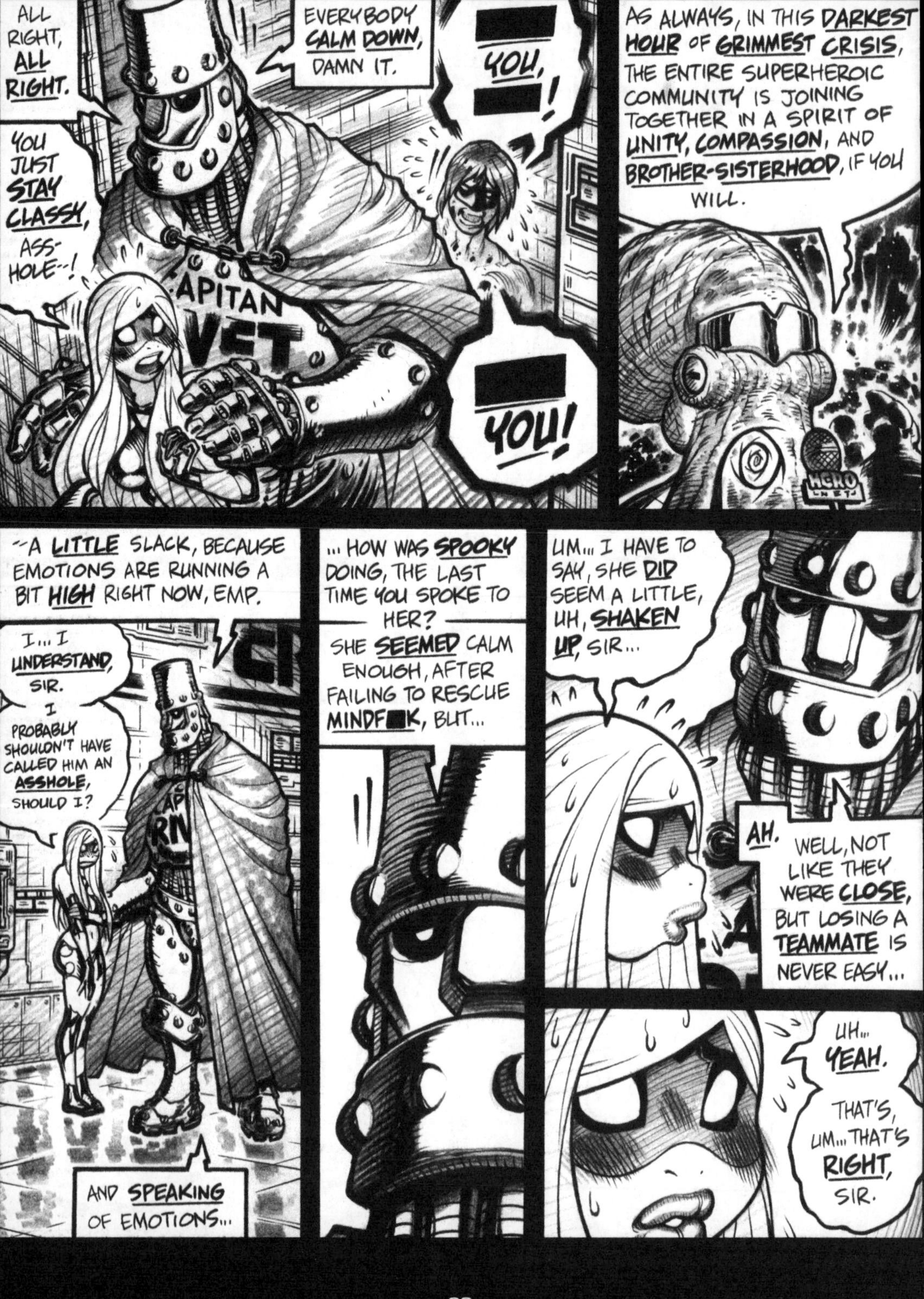

ALL RIGHT, ALL RIGHT.
EVERYBODY CALM DOWN, DAMN IT.
YOU JUST STAY CLASSY, ASS-HOLE--!
[redacted] YOU, [redacted]!
APITAN
VET
[redacted] YOU!
AS ALWAYS, IN THIS DARKEST HOUR OF GRIMMEST CRISIS, THE ENTIRE SUPERHEROIC COMMUNITY IS JOINING TOGETHER IN A SPIRIT OF UNITY, COMPASSION, AND BROTHER-SISTERHOOD, IF YOU WILL.
HERO
--A LITTLE SLACK, BECAUSE EMOTIONS ARE RUNNING A BIT HIGH RIGHT NOW, EMP.
I... I UNDERSTAND, SIR.
I PROBABLY SHOULDN'T HAVE CALLED HIM AN ASSHOLE, SHOULD I?
AND SPEAKING OF EMOTIONS...
... HOW WAS SPOOKY DOING, THE LAST TIME YOU SPOKE TO HER?
SHE SEEMED CALM ENOUGH, AFTER FAILING TO RESCUE MINDF[redacted]K, BUT...
UM... I HAVE TO SAY, SHE DID SEEM A LITTLE, UH, SHAKEN UP, SIR...
AH.
WELL, NOT LIKE THEY WERE CLOSE, BUT LOSING A TEAMMATE IS NEVER EASY...
UH... YEAH.
THAT'S, UM... THAT'S RIGHT, SIR.

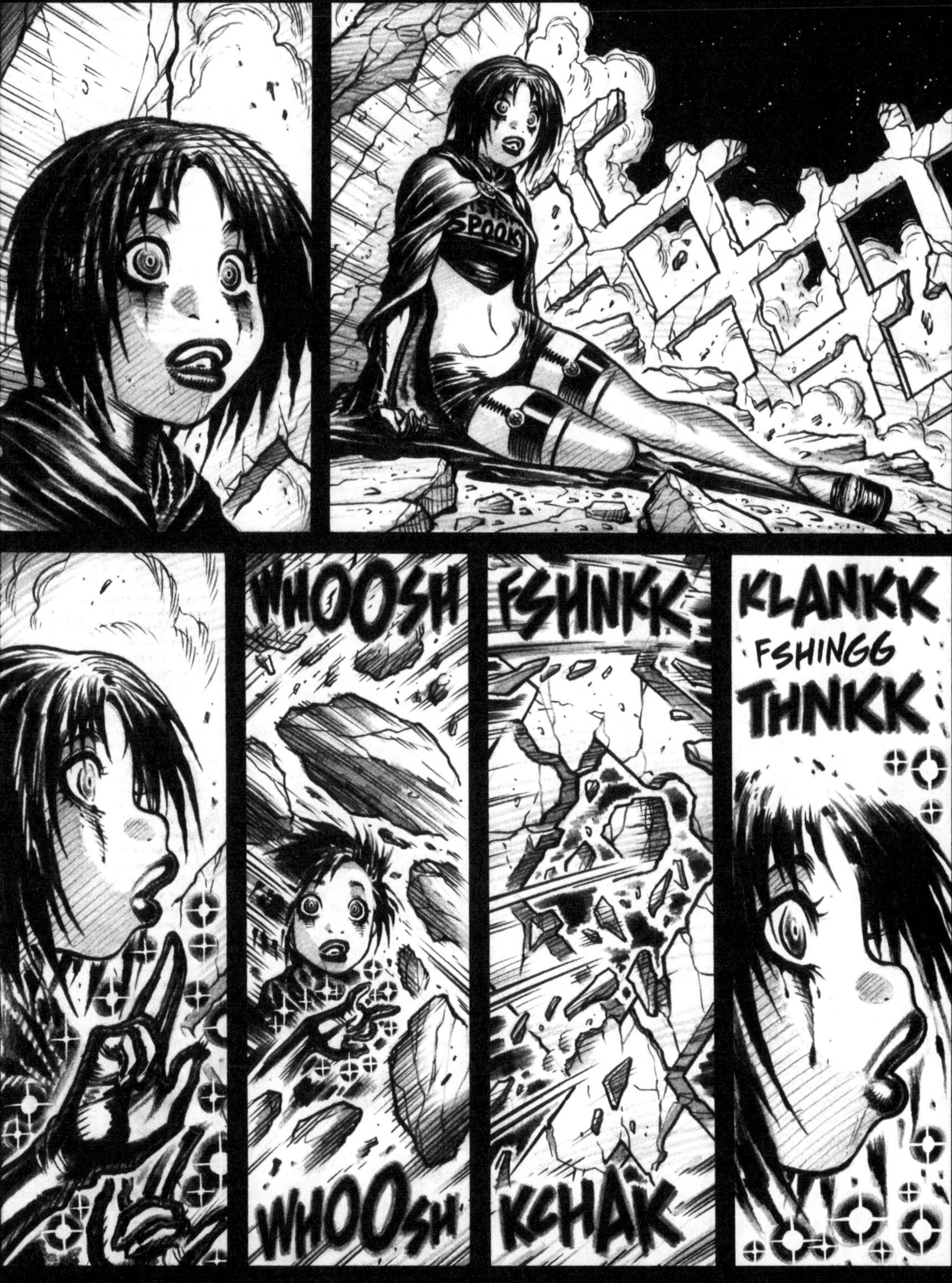
SPOOKS
WHOOSH
WHOOSH
FSHNKK
KCHAK
KLANKK
FSHINGG
THNKK

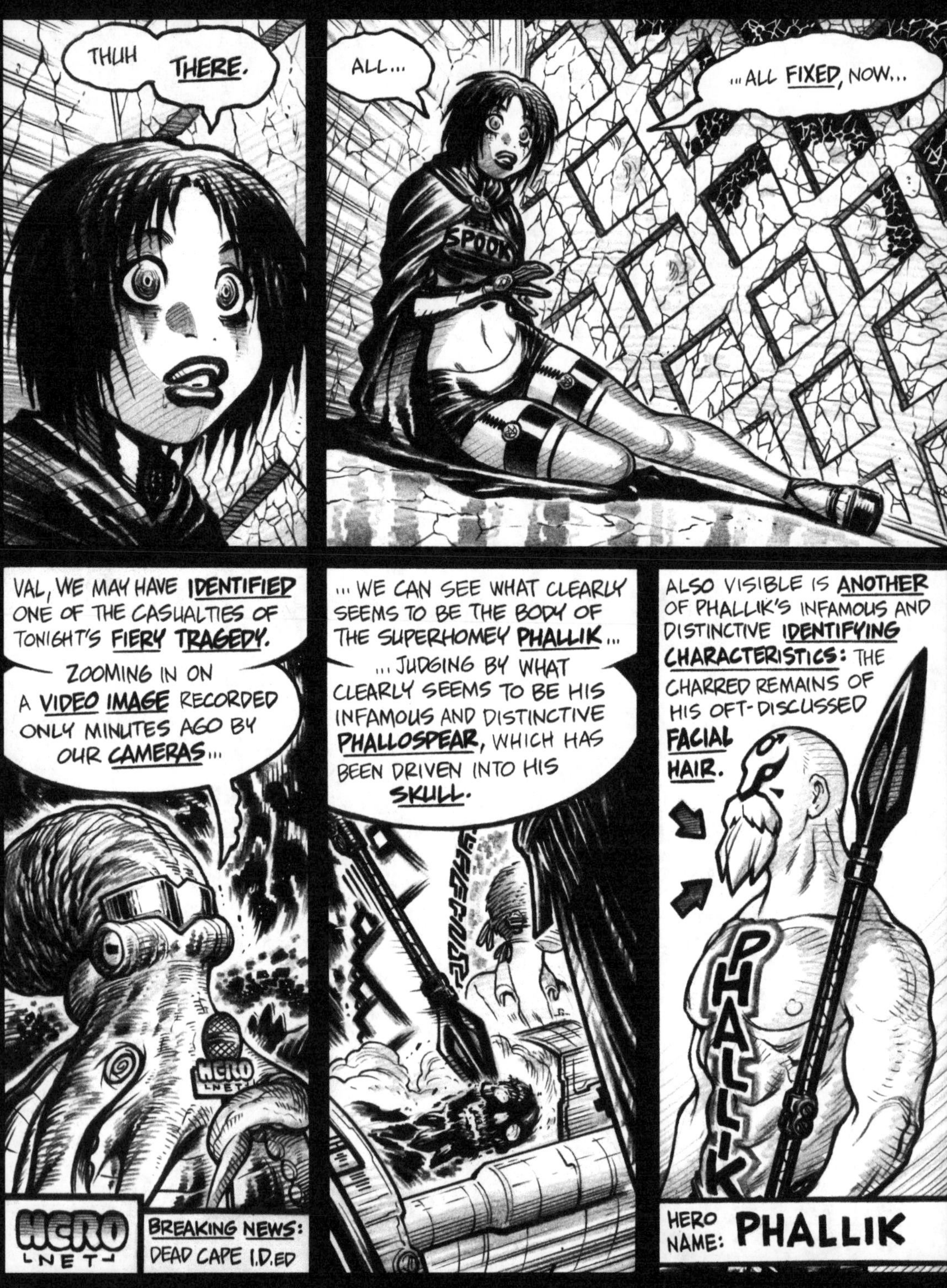
THUH THERE.
ALL...
...ALL FIXED, NOW...
VAL, WE MAY HAVE IDENTIFIED ONE OF THE CASUALTIES OF TONIGHT'S FIERY TRAGEDY.
ZOOMING IN ON A VIDEO IMAGE RECORDED ONLY MINUTES AGO BY OUR CAMERAS...
...WE CAN SEE WHAT CLEARLY SEEMS TO BE THE BODY OF THE SUPERHOMEY PHALLIK...
...JUDGING BY WHAT CLEARLY SEEMS TO BE HIS INFAMOUS AND DISTINCTIVE PHALLOSPEAR, WHICH HAS BEEN DRIVEN INTO HIS SKULL.
ALSO VISIBLE IS ANOTHER OF PHALLIK'S INFAMOUS AND DISTINCTIVE IDENTIFYING CHARACTERISTICS: THE CHARRED REMAINS OF HIS OFT-DISCUSSED FACIAL HAIR.
SPOOK
HERO NET
PHALLIK
HERO NET
BREAKING NEWS: DEAD CAPE I.D.ED
HERO NAME: PHALLIK

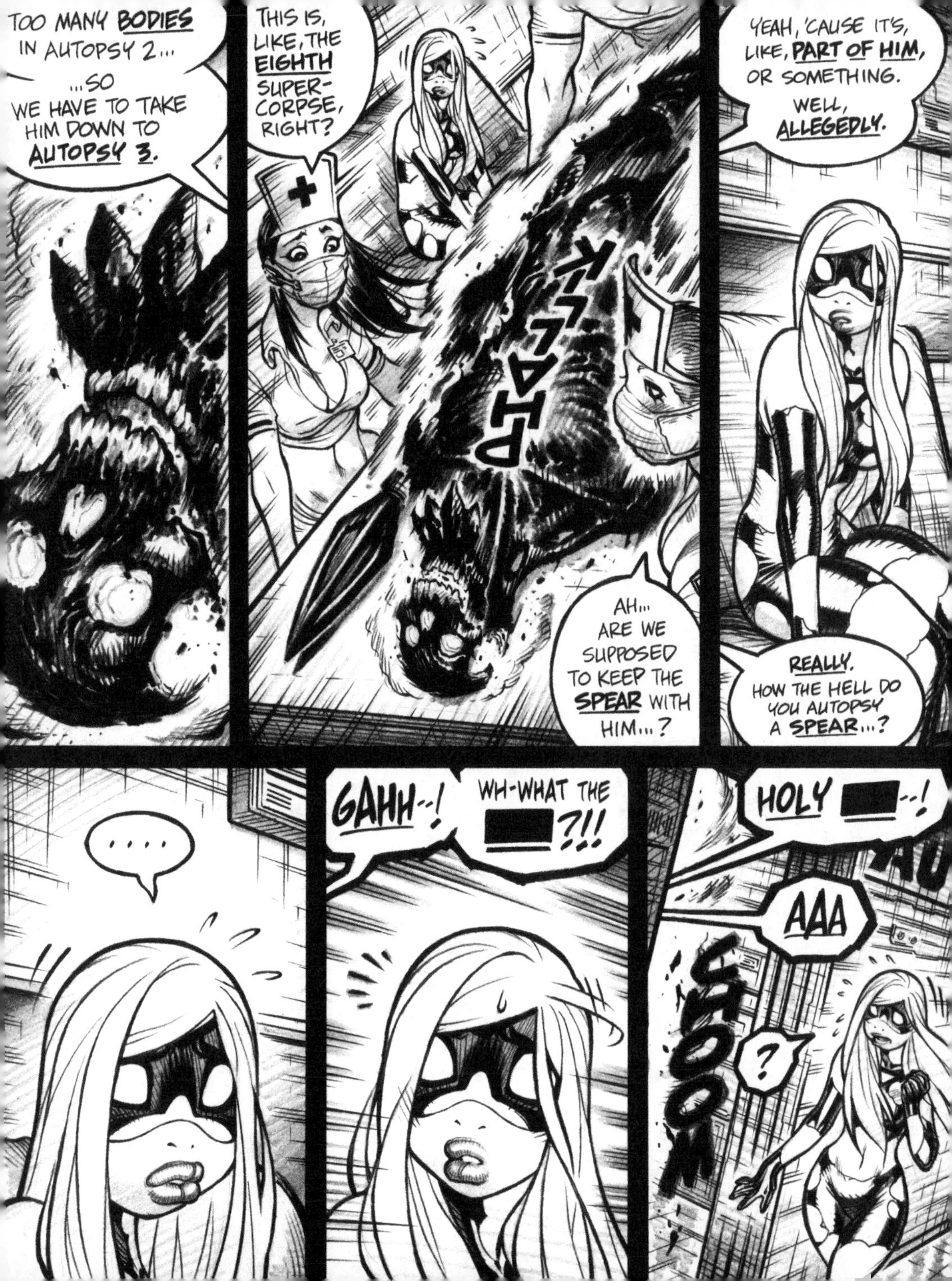
TOO MANY BODIES IN AUTOPSY 2...
...SO WE HAVE TO TAKE HIM DOWN TO AUTOPSY 3.
THIS IS, LIKE, THE EIGHTH SUPER-CORPSE, RIGHT?
AH... ARE WE SUPPOSED TO KEEP THE SPEAR WITH HIM...?
YEAH, 'CAUSE IT'S, LIKE, PART OF HIM, OR SOMETHING.
WELL, ALLEGEDLY.
REALLY. HOW THE HELL DO YOU AUTOPSY A SPEAR...?
....
GAHH--!
WH-WHAT THE [redacted]?!!
HOLY [redacted]--!
AAA
SHOOM
?

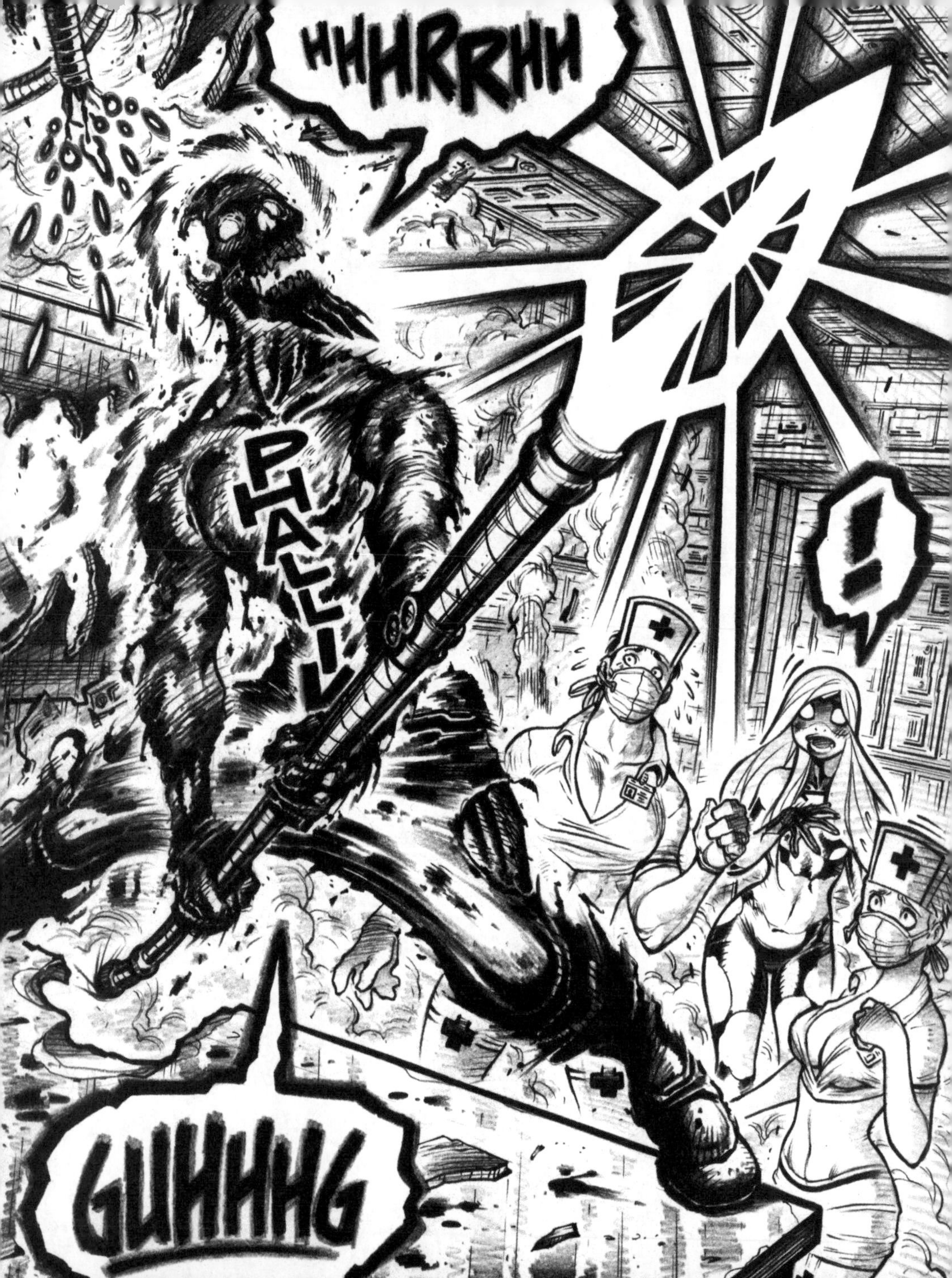
HHHRRHH
PHALLLV
!
GUHHHG

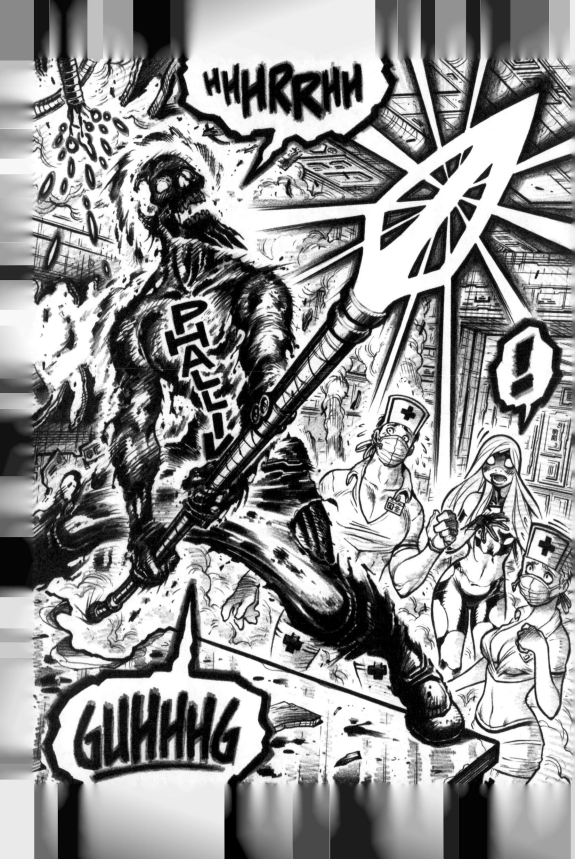

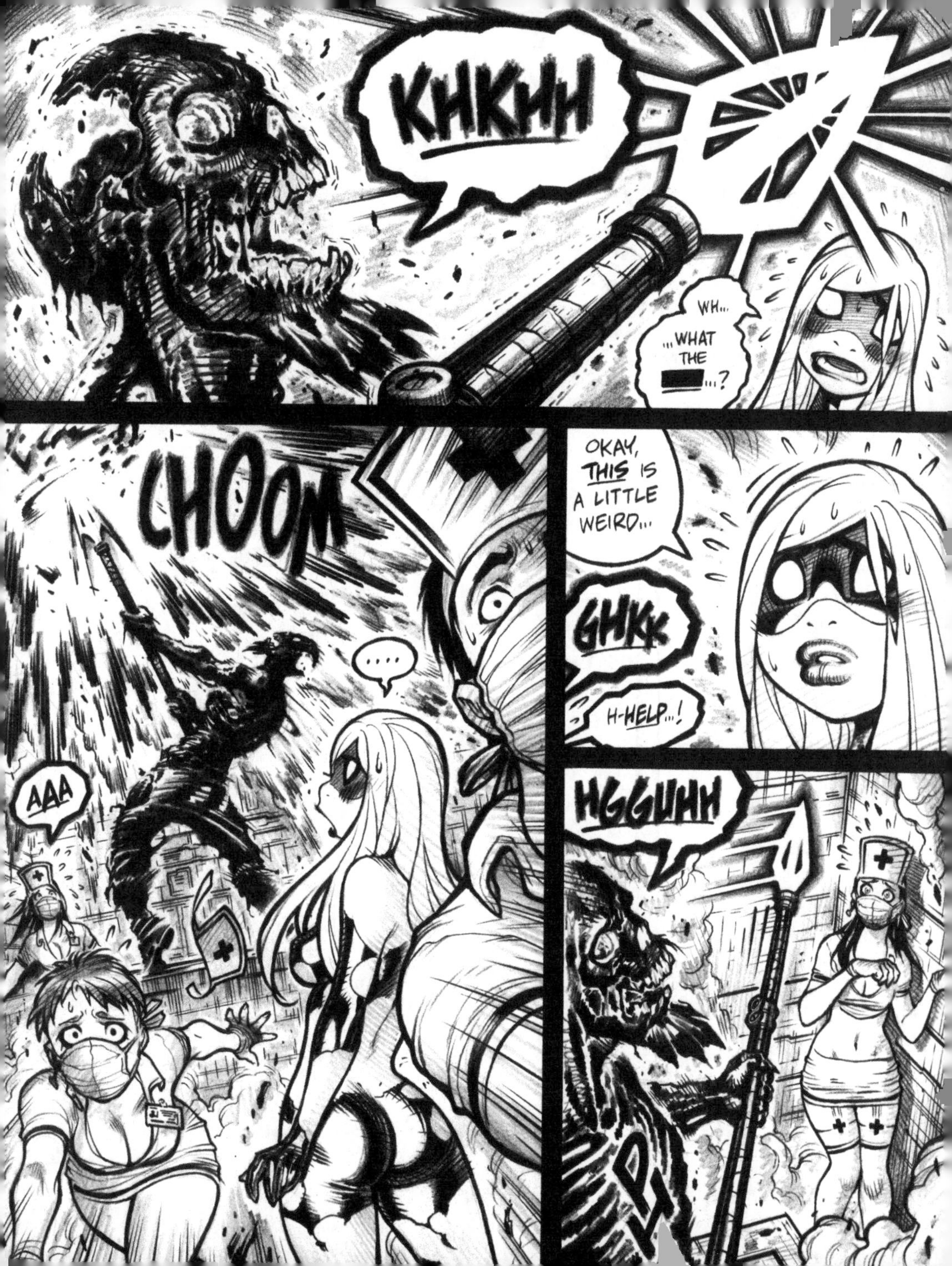
KHKHH
WH...
...WHAT THE [redacted]...?
CHOOM
AAA
....
OKAY, THIS IS A LITTLE WEIRD...
GHKK
H-HELP...!
HGGUHH

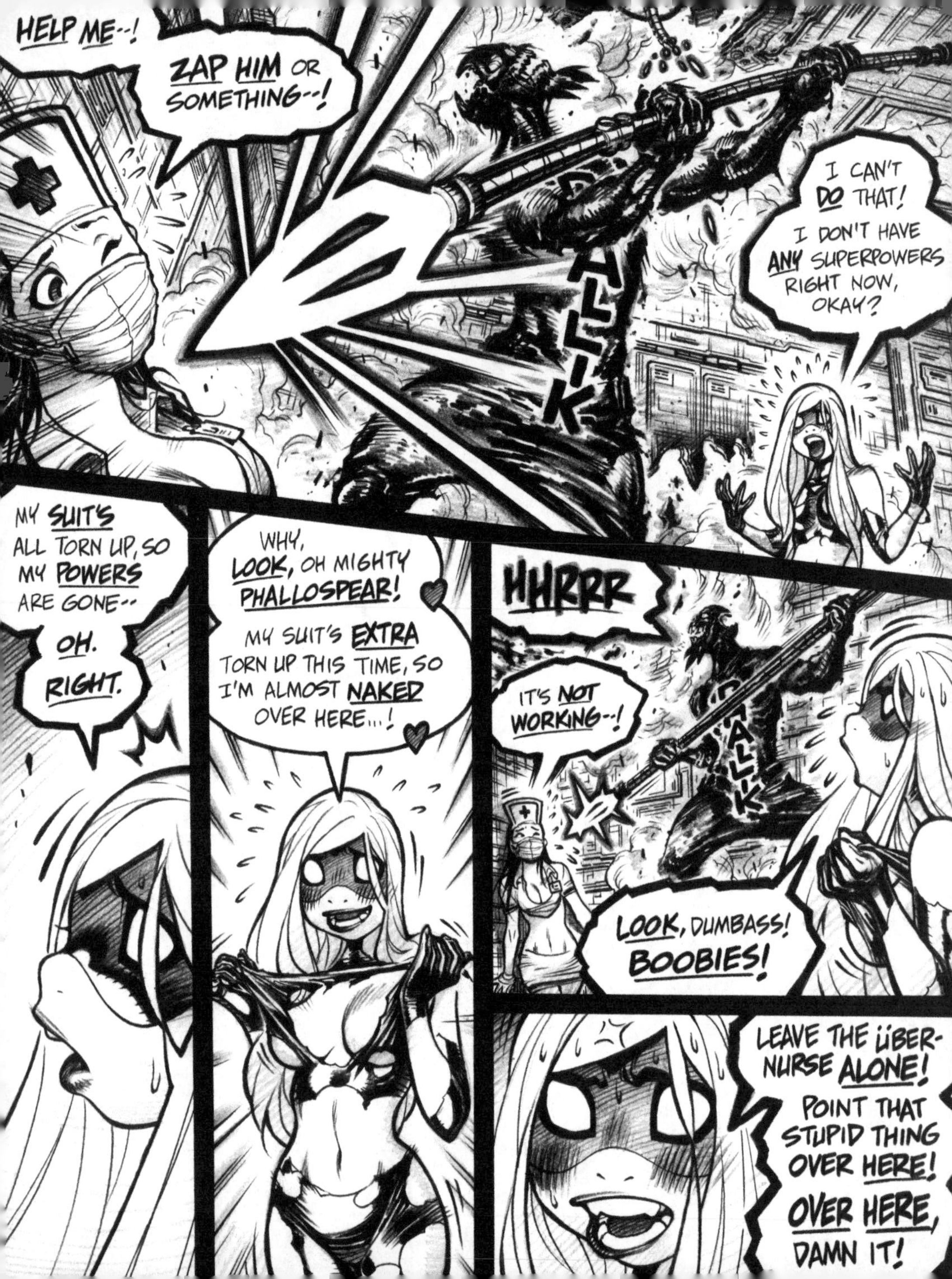
HELP ME--!
ZAP HIM OR SOMETHING--!
I CAN'T DO THAT! I DON'T HAVE ANY SUPERPOWERS RIGHT NOW, OKAY?
PHALLIK
MY SUIT'S ALL TORN UP, SO MY POWERS ARE GONE--
OH. RIGHT.
WHY, LOOK, OH MIGHTY PHALLOSPEAR!
MY SUIT'S EXTRA TORN UP THIS TIME, SO I'M ALMOST NAKED OVER HERE...!
HHRRR
IT'S NOT WORKING--!
PHALLIK
LOOK, DUMBASS! BOOBIES!
LEAVE THE ÜBER-NURSE ALONE!
POINT THAT STUPID THING OVER HERE!
OVER HERE, DAMN IT!

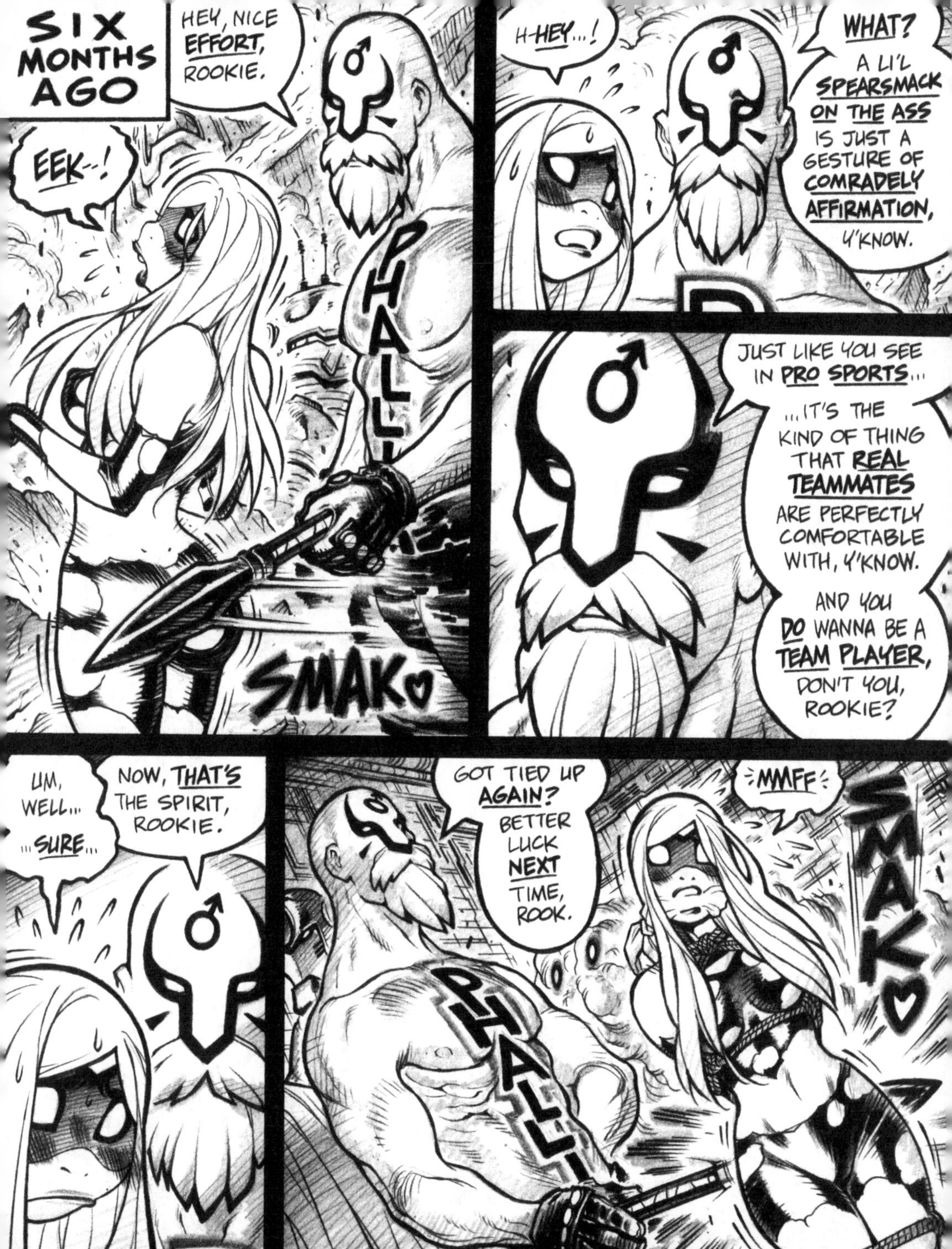

SIX MONTHS AGO
HEY, NICE EFFORT, ROOKIE.
EEK--!
PHALLI
SMAK♡
H-HEY...!
WHAT? A LI'L SPEARSMACK ON THE ASS IS JUST A GESTURE OF COMRADELY AFFIRMATION, Y'KNOW.
JUST LIKE YOU SEE IN PRO SPORTS...
...IT'S THE KIND OF THING THAT REAL TEAMMATES ARE PERFECTLY COMFORTABLE WITH, Y'KNOW.
AND YOU DO WANNA BE A TEAM PLAYER, DON'T YOU, ROOKIE?
UM, WELL... ...SURE...
NOW, THAT'S THE SPIRIT, ROOKIE.
GOT TIED UP AGAIN? BETTER LUCK NEXT TIME, ROOK.
MMFF
PHALLI
SMAK♡

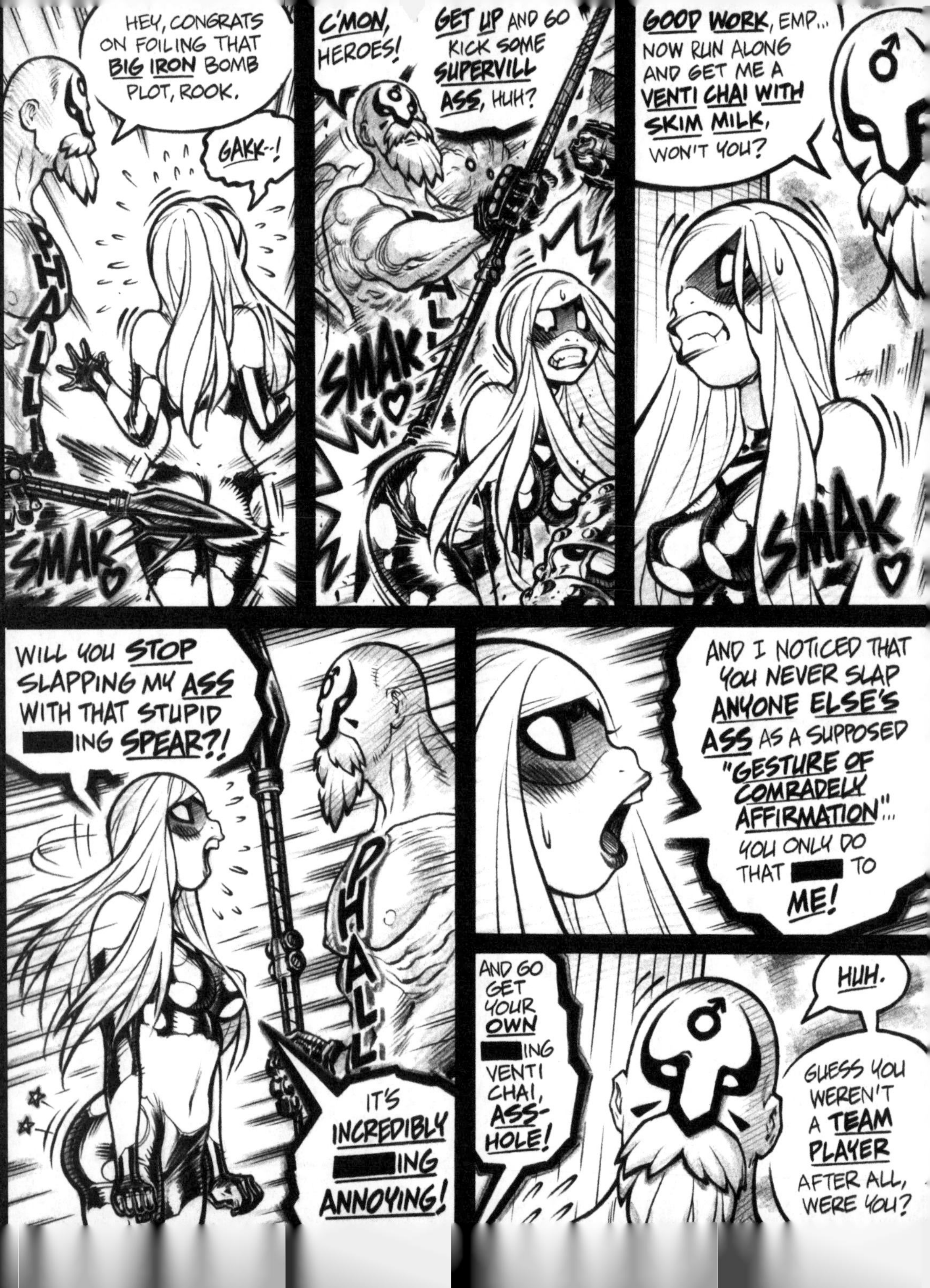
HEY, CONGRATS ON FOILING THAT BIG IRON BOMB PLOT, ROOK.
GAKK--!
SMAK
C'MON, HEROES!
GET UP AND GO KICK SOME SUPERVILL ASS, HUH?
SMAK
GOOD WORK, EMP... NOW RUN ALONG AND GET ME A VENTI CHAI WITH SKIM MILK, WON'T YOU?
SMAK
WILL YOU STOP SLAPPING MY ASS WITH THAT STUPID [redacted]ING SPEAR?!
IT'S INCREDIBLY [redacted]ING ANNOYING!
AND I NOTICED THAT YOU NEVER SLAP ANYONE ELSE'S ASS AS A SUPPOSED "GESTURE OF COMRADELY AFFIRMATION"... YOU ONLY DO THAT [redacted] TO ME!
AND GO GET YOUR OWN [redacted]ING VENTI CHAI, ASS-HOLE!
HUH.
GUESS YOU WEREN'T A TEAM PLAYER AFTER ALL, WERE YOU?

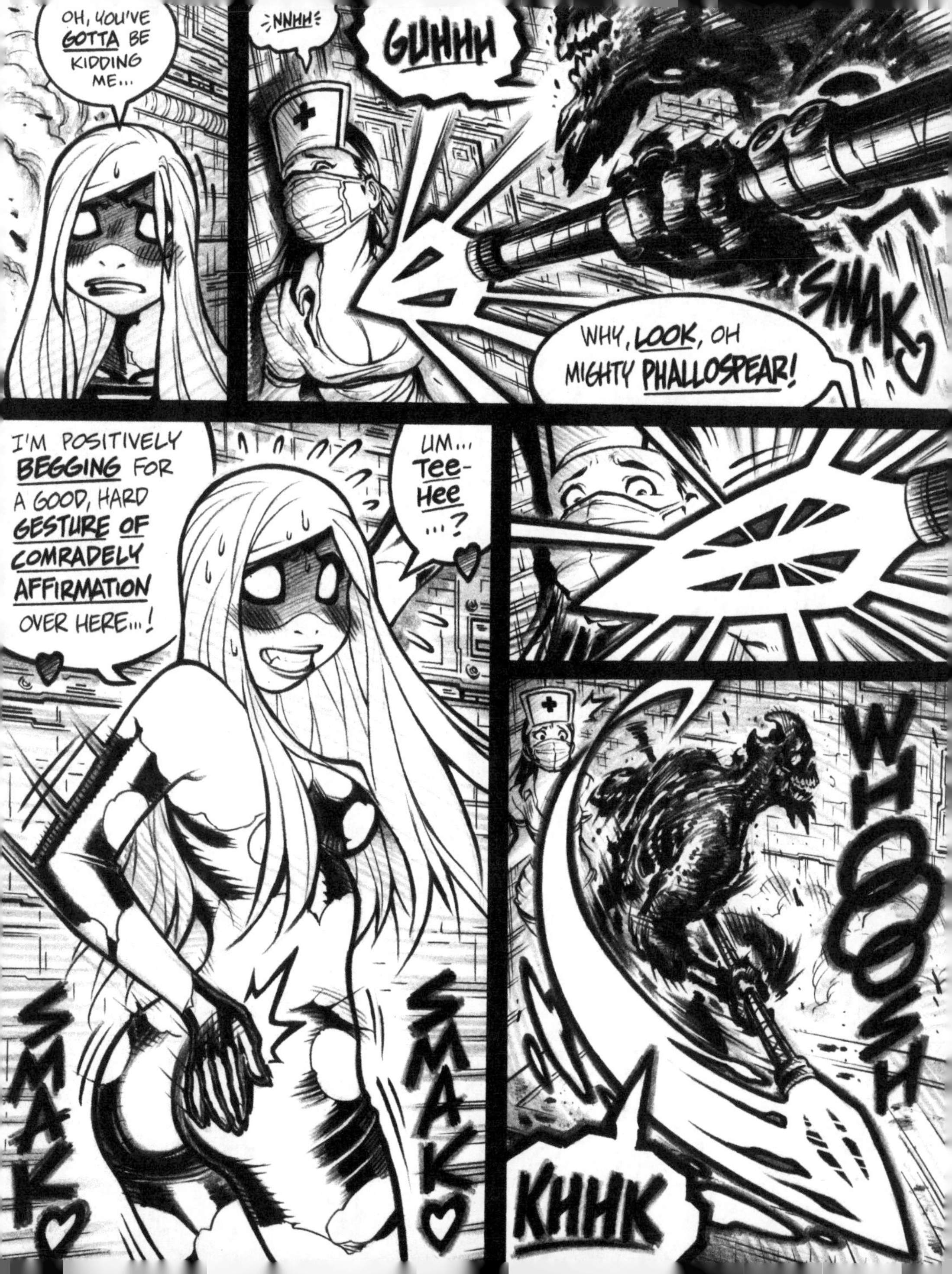
OH, YOU'VE GOTTA BE KIDDING ME...
NNHH
GUHHH
SMAK
WHY, LOOK, OH MIGHTY PHALLOSPEAR!
I'M POSITIVELY BEGGING FOR A GOOD, HARD GESTURE OF COMRADELY AFFIRMATION OVER HERE...!
UM... Tee-Hee ...?
SMAK
SMAK
WHOOOSH
KHHK

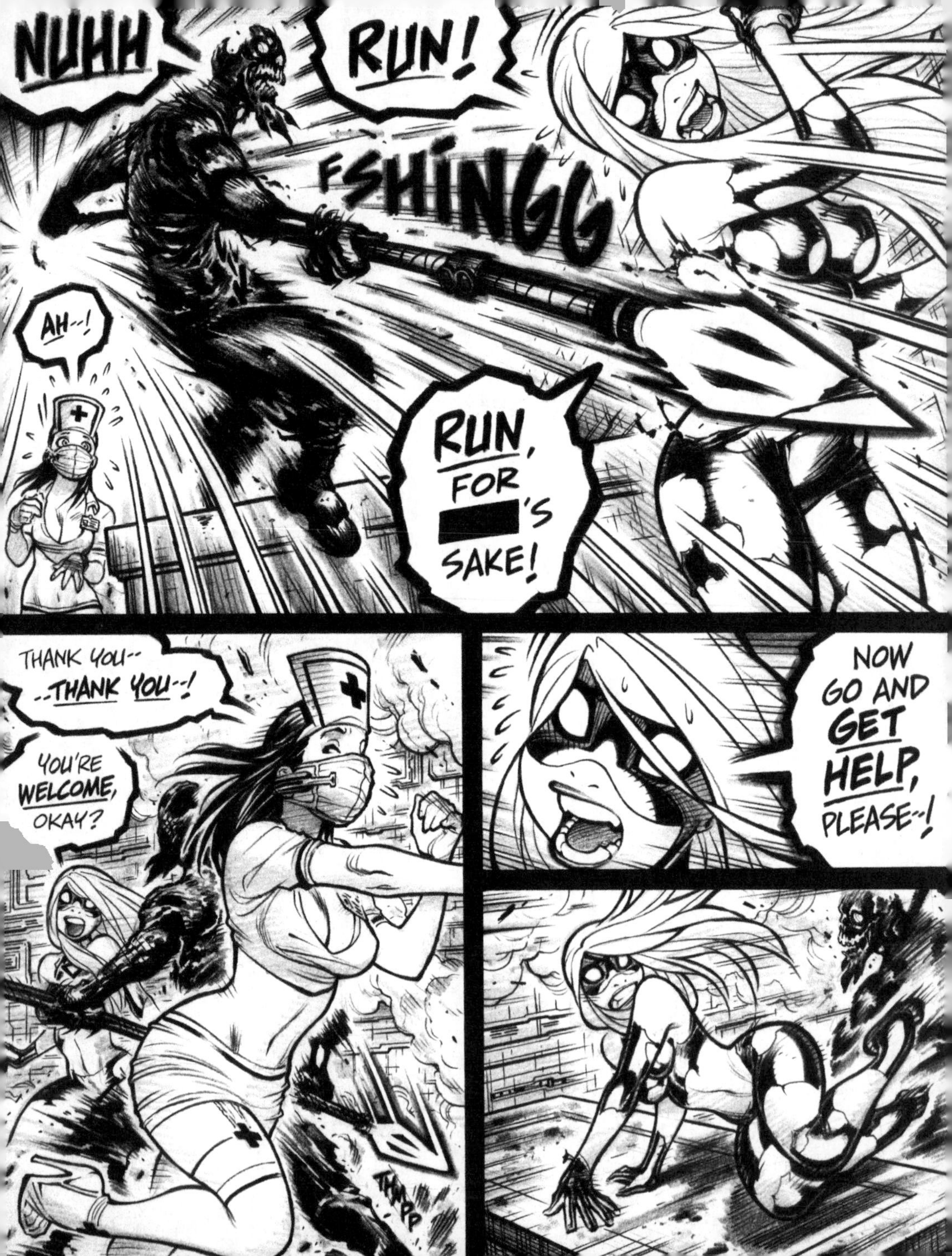
NUHH
RUN!
FSHINGG
AH--!
RUN, FOR [redacted]'S SAKE!
THANK YOU-- --THANK YOU--!
YOU'RE WELCOME, OKAY?
NOW GO AND GET HELP, PLEASE--!
THMPP

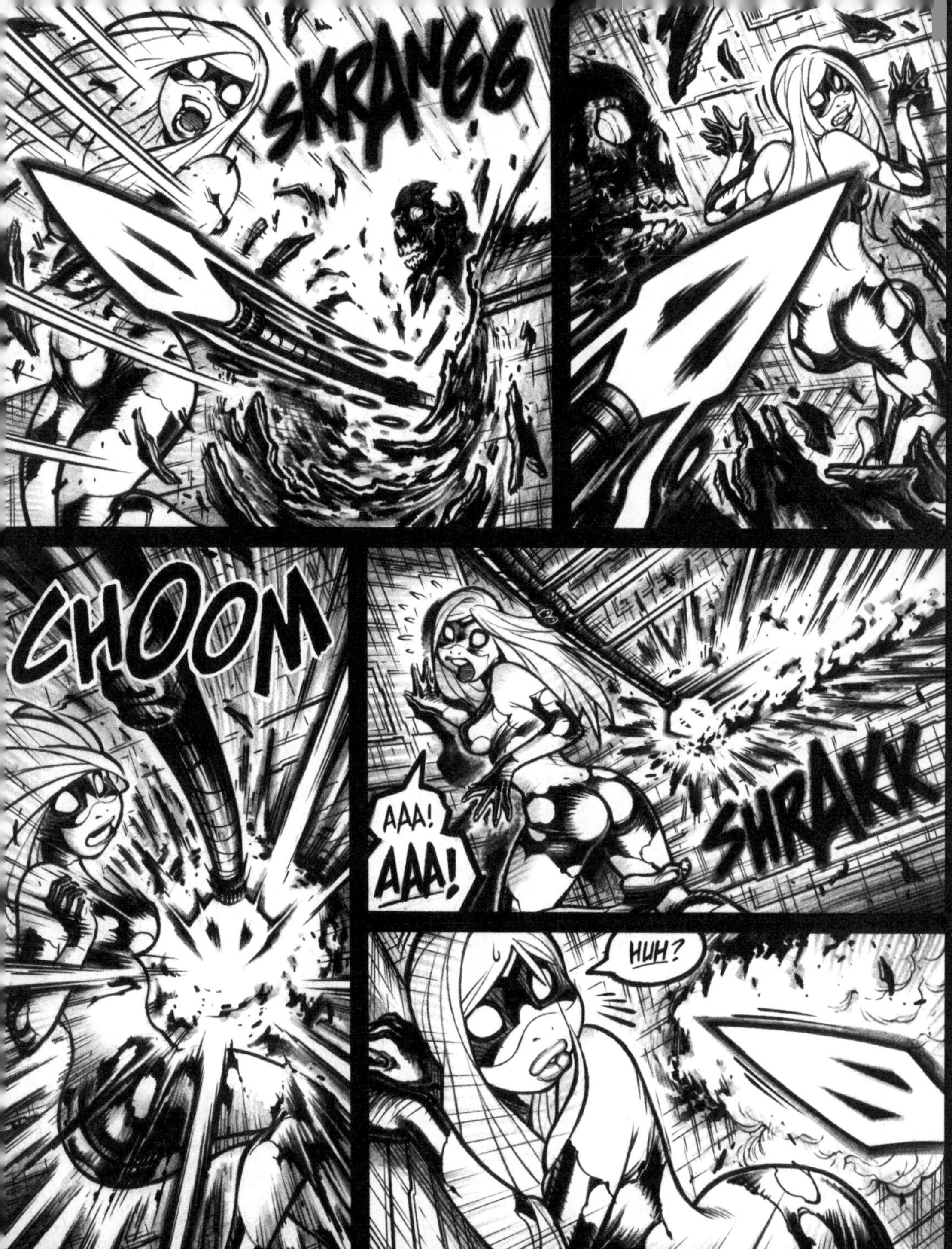
SKRANGG
CHOOM
AAA! AAA!
SHRAKK
HUH?

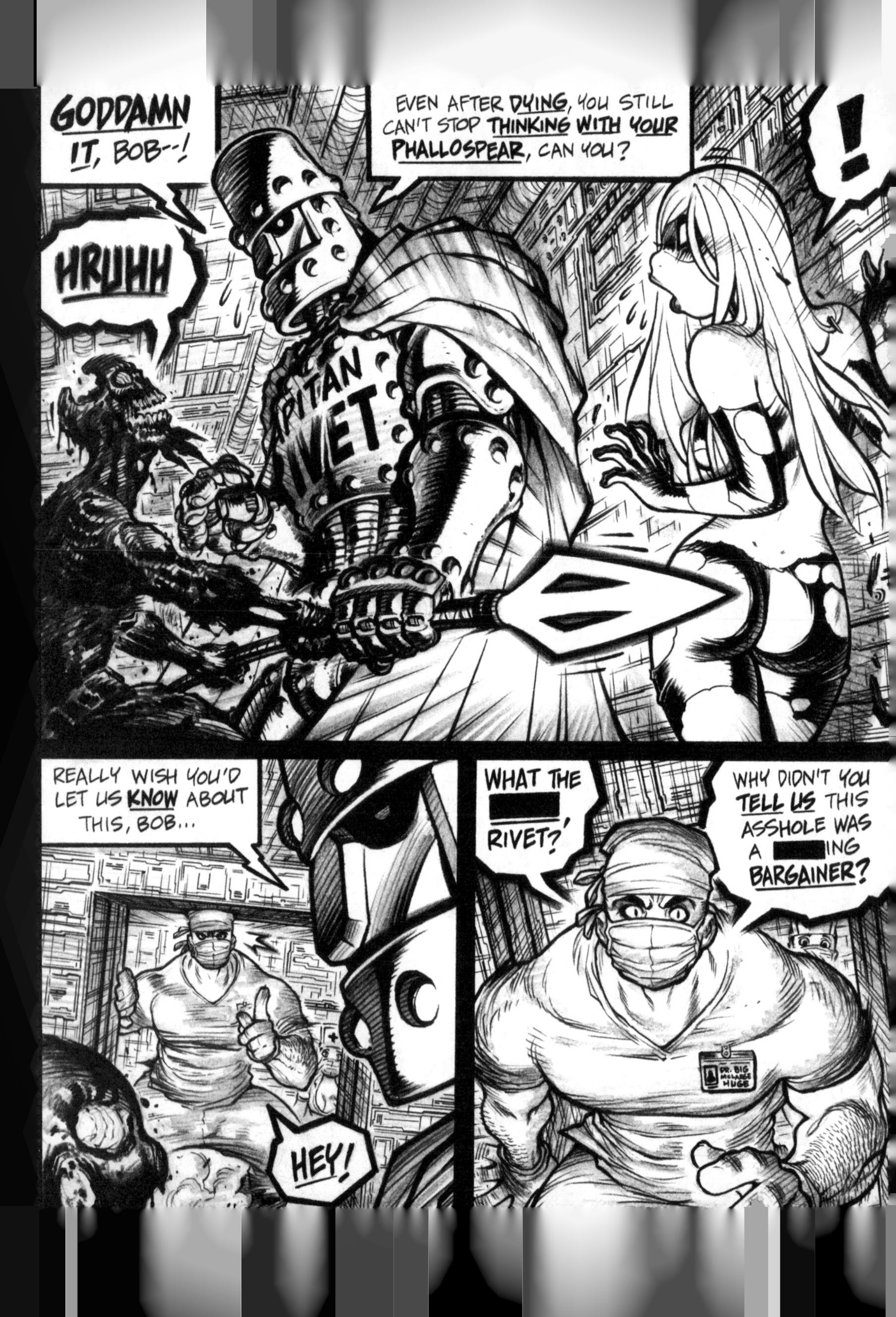
GODDAMN IT, BOB--!
EVEN AFTER DYING, YOU STILL CAN'T STOP THINKING WITH YOUR PHALLOSPEAR, CAN YOU?
!
HRUHH
REALLY WISH YOU'D LET US KNOW ABOUT THIS, BOB...
HEY!
WHAT THE [redacted], RIVET?
WHY DIDN'T YOU TELL US THIS ASSHOLE WAS A [redacted]ING BARGAINER?

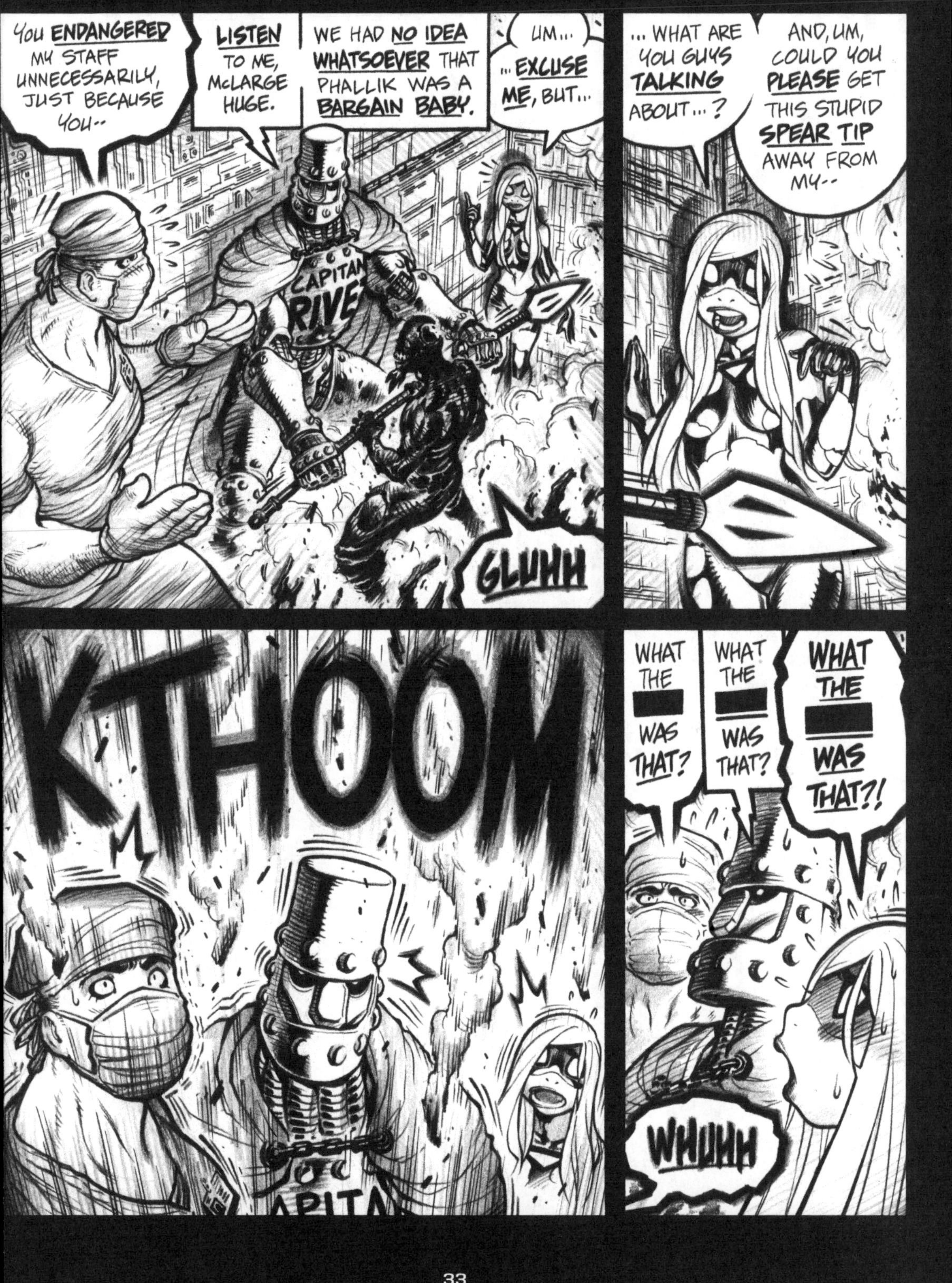

YOU ENDANGERED MY STAFF UNNECESSARILY, JUST BECAUSE YOU--
LISTEN TO ME, McLARGE HUGE.
WE HAD NO IDEA WHATSOEVER THAT PHALLIK WAS A BARGAIN BABY.
UM...
...EXCUSE ME, BUT...
GLUHH
... WHAT ARE YOU GUYS TALKING ABOUT...?
AND, UM, COULD YOU PLEASE GET THIS STUPID SPEAR TIP AWAY FROM MY--
KTHOOM
WHAT THE [redacted] WAS THAT?
WHAT THE [redacted] WAS THAT?
WHAT THE [redacted] WAS THAT?!
WHUHH

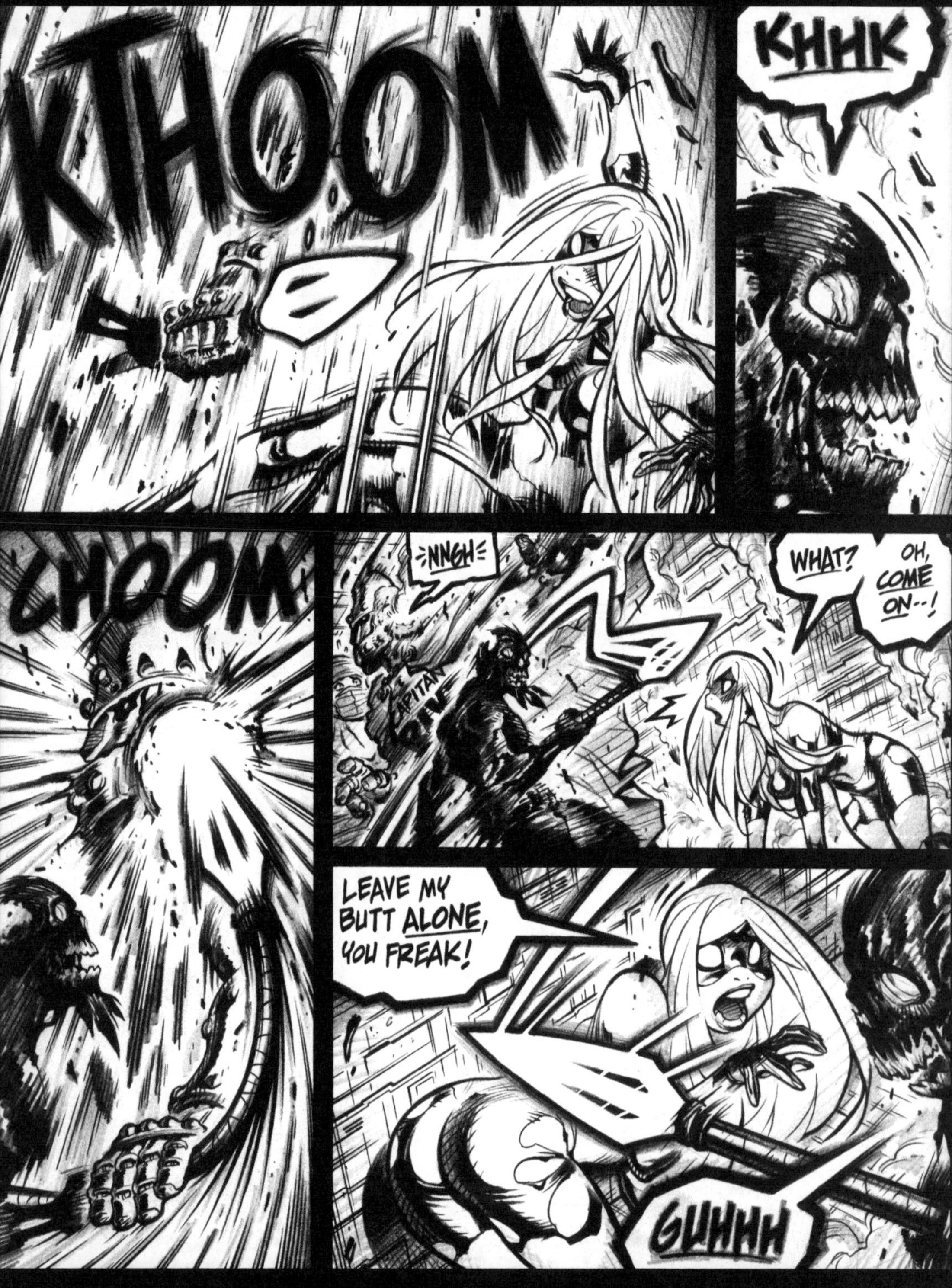
KTHOOM
KHHK
CHOOM
NNGH
WHAT?
OH, COME ON--!
LEAVE MY BUTT ALONE, YOU FREAK!
GUHHH

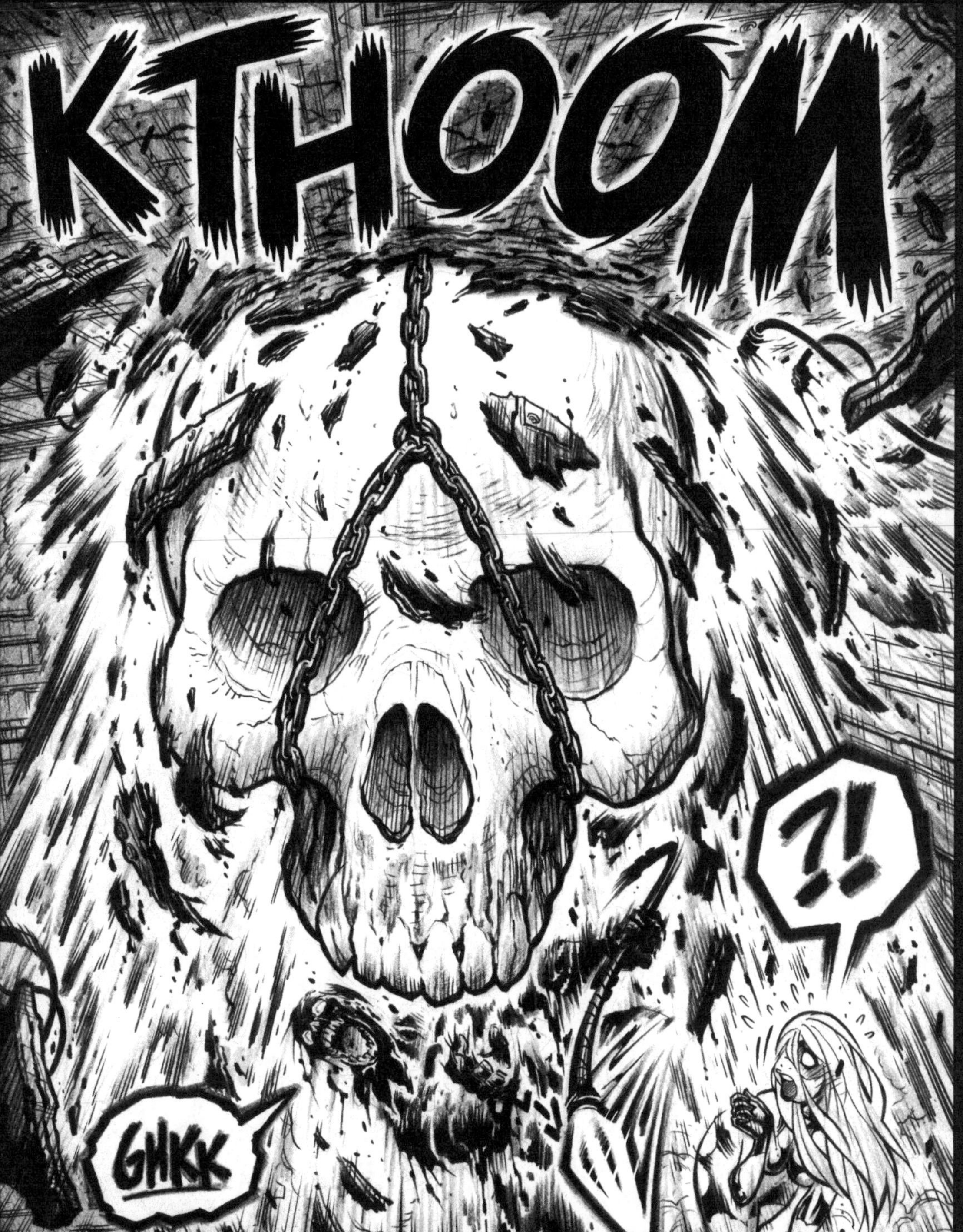
KTHOOM
?!
GHKK

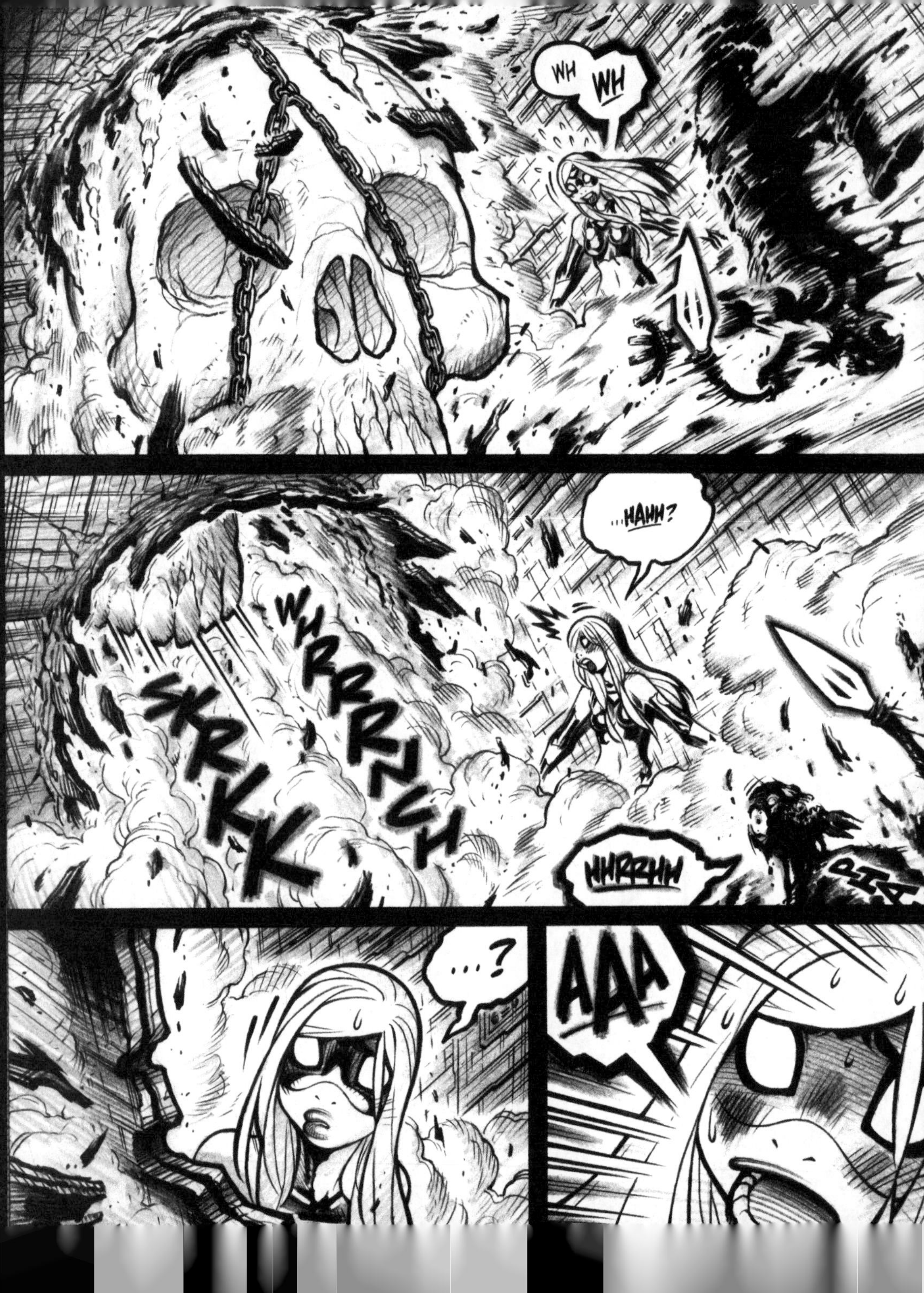
WH WH
...HAHH?
WHRRRRNCH
SKRKKK
MHRRHM
...?
AAA

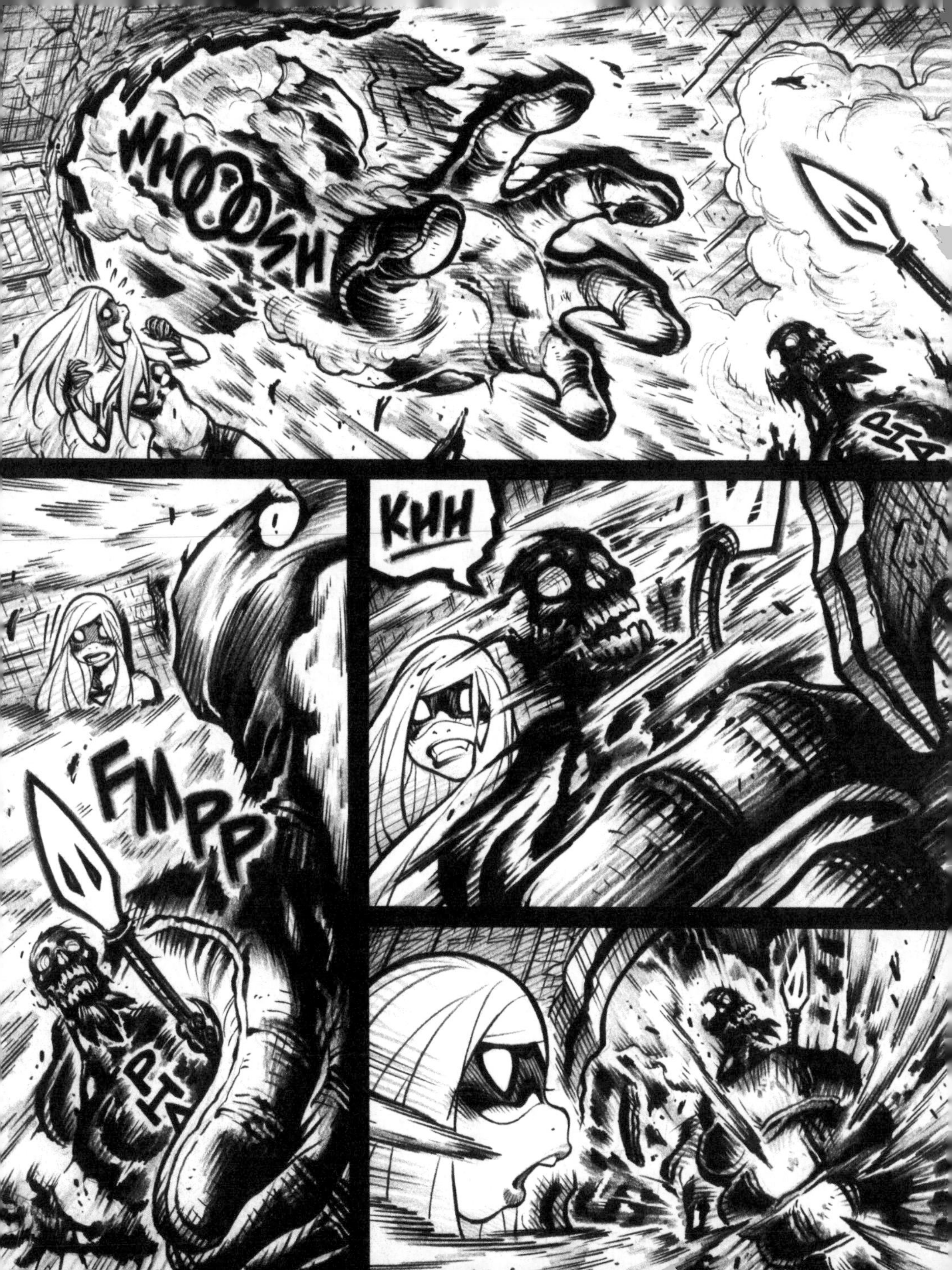
WHOOOSH
!
FMPP
KHH

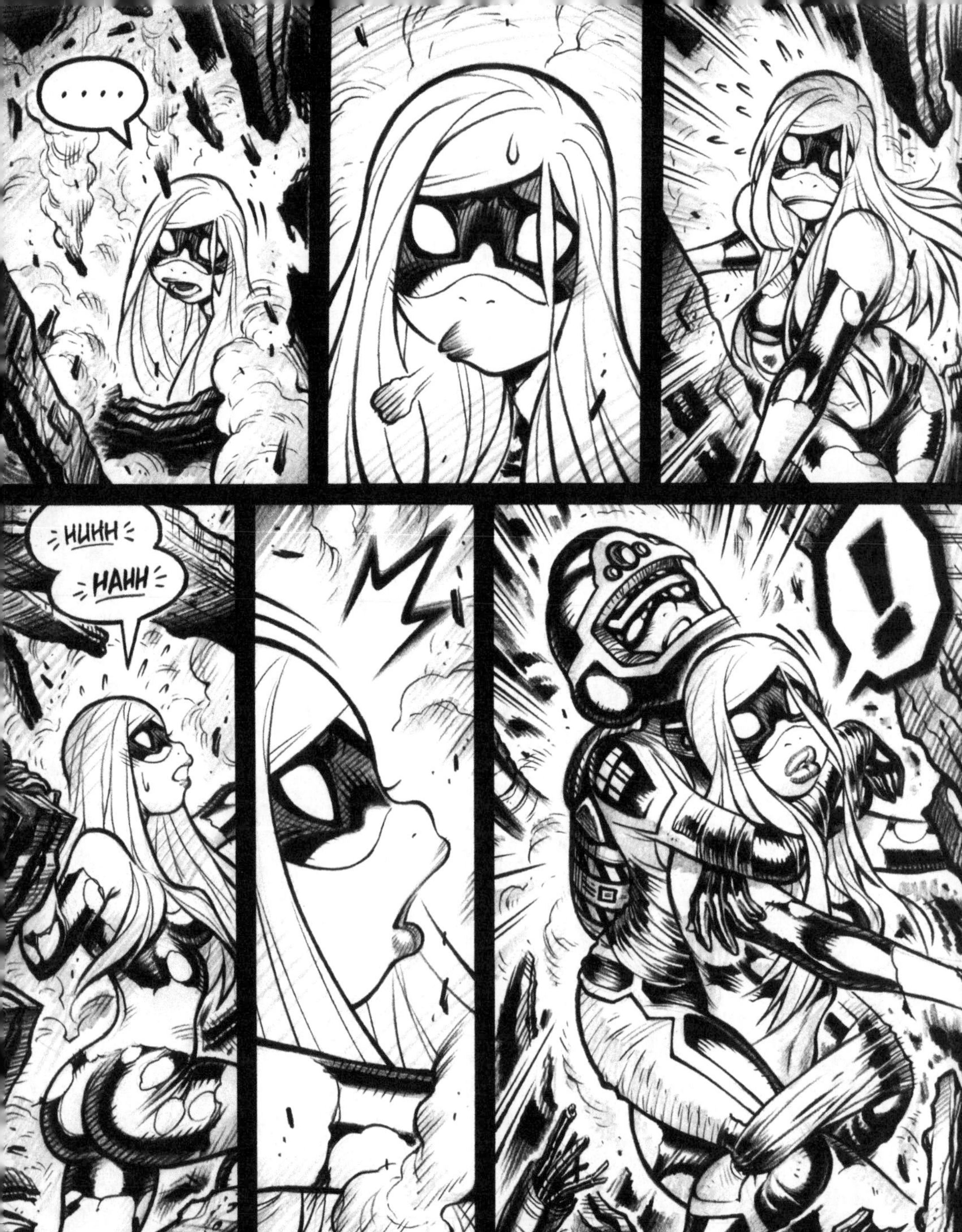

....
HUHH
HAHH
!

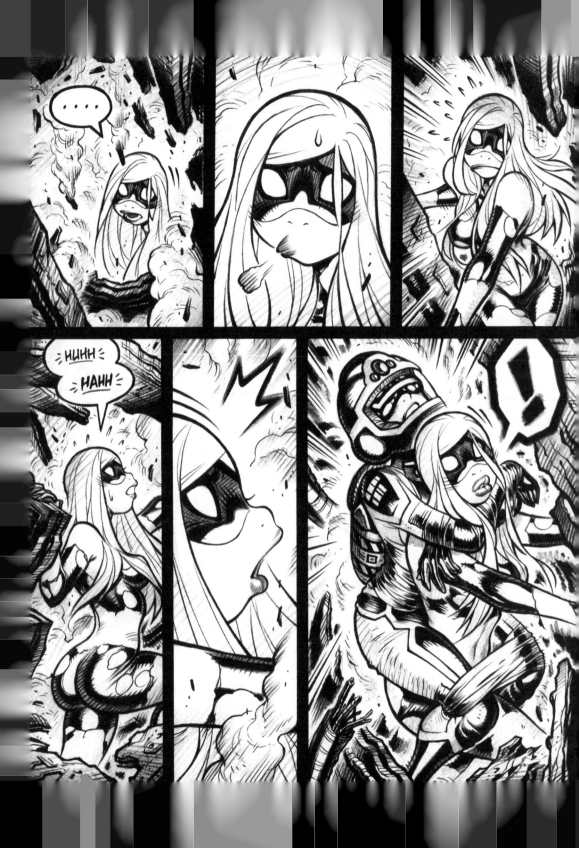

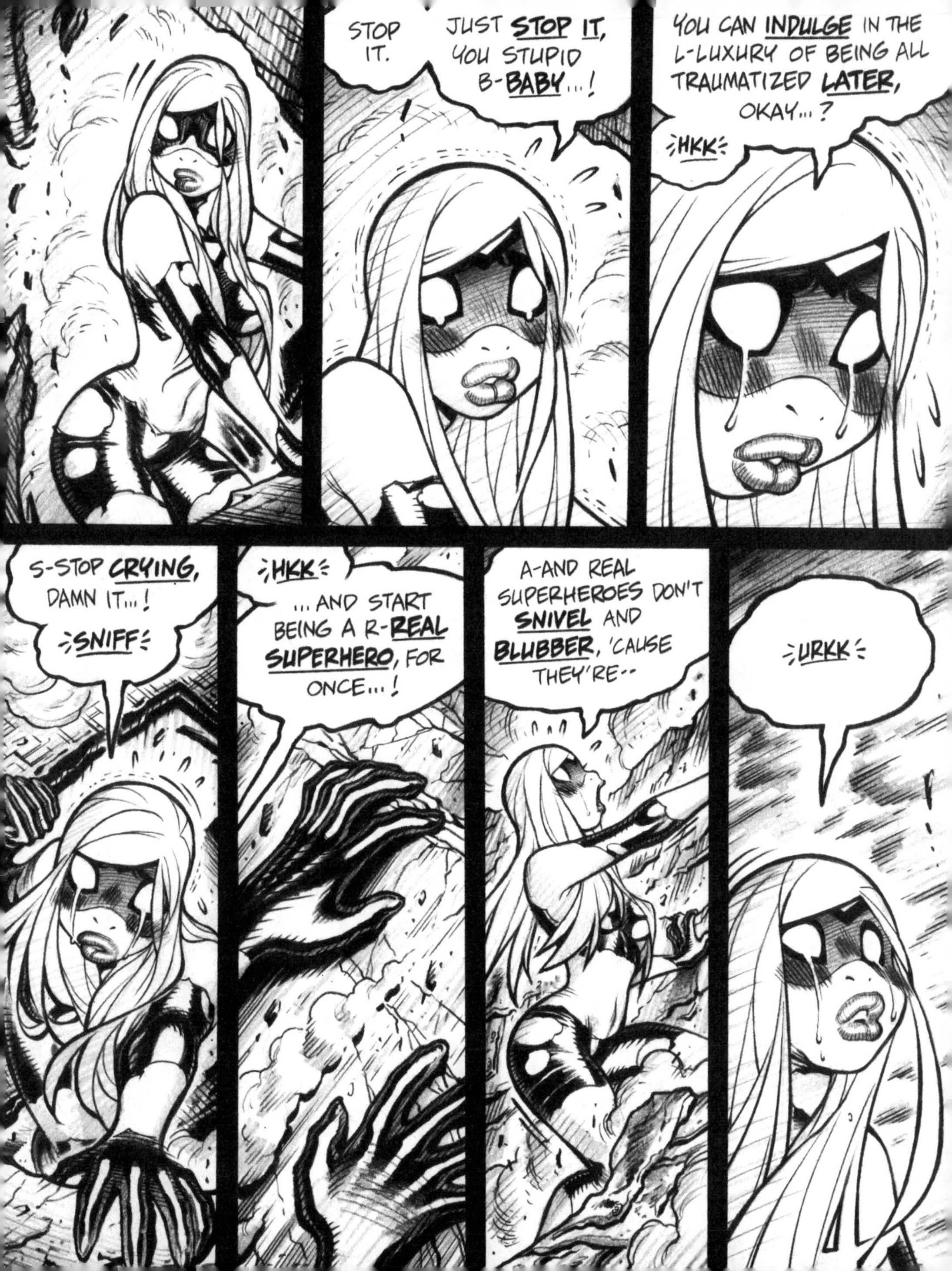
STOP IT.
JUST STOP IT, YOU STUPID B-BABY...!
YOU CAN INDULGE IN THE L-LUXURY OF BEING ALL TRAUMATIZED LATER, OKAY...?
HKK
S-STOP CRYING, DAMN IT...!
SNIFF
HKK
...AND START BEING A R-REAL SUPERHERO, FOR ONCE...!
A-AND REAL SUPERHEROES DON'T SNIVEL AND BLUBBER, 'CAUSE THEY'RE--
URKK

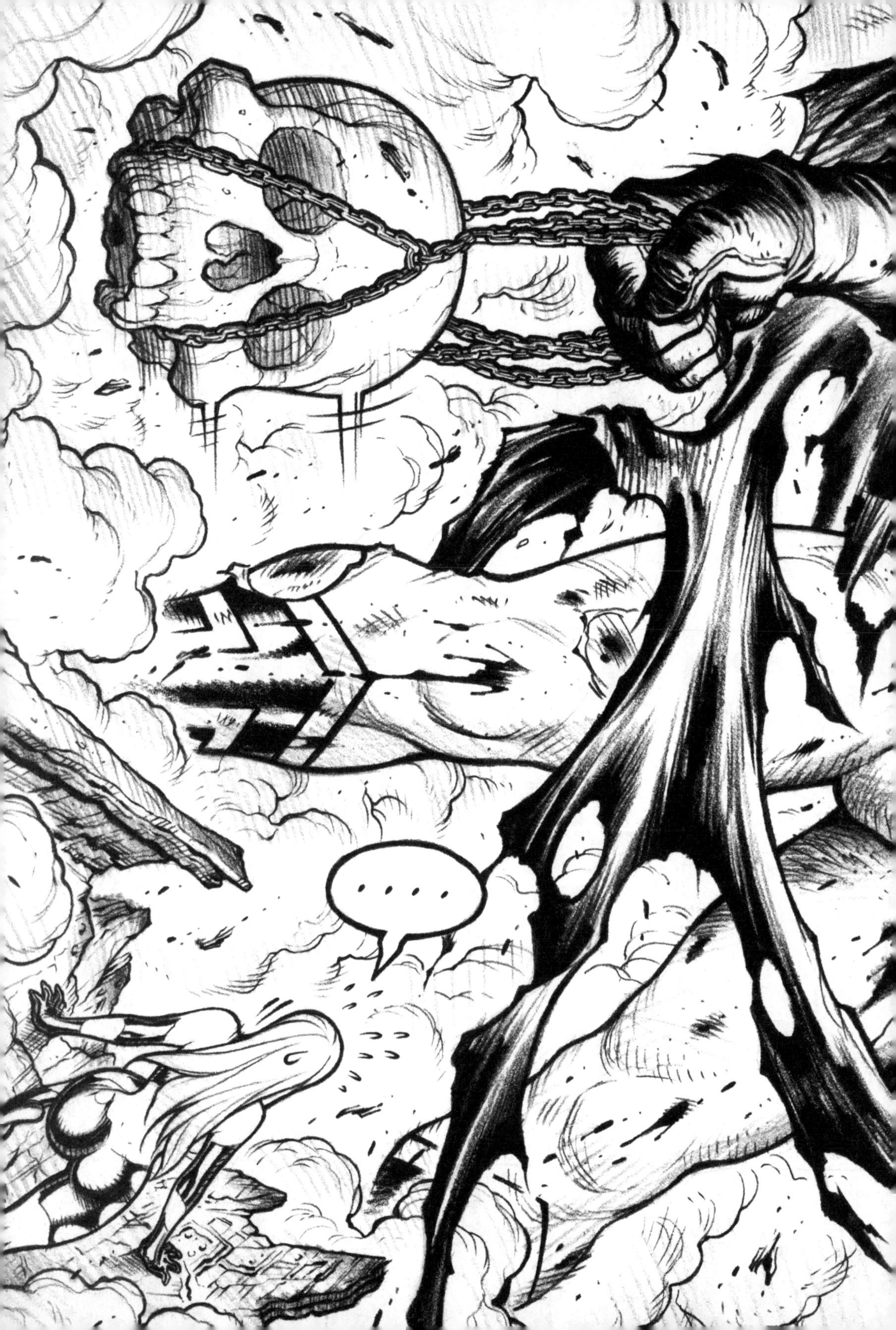
....

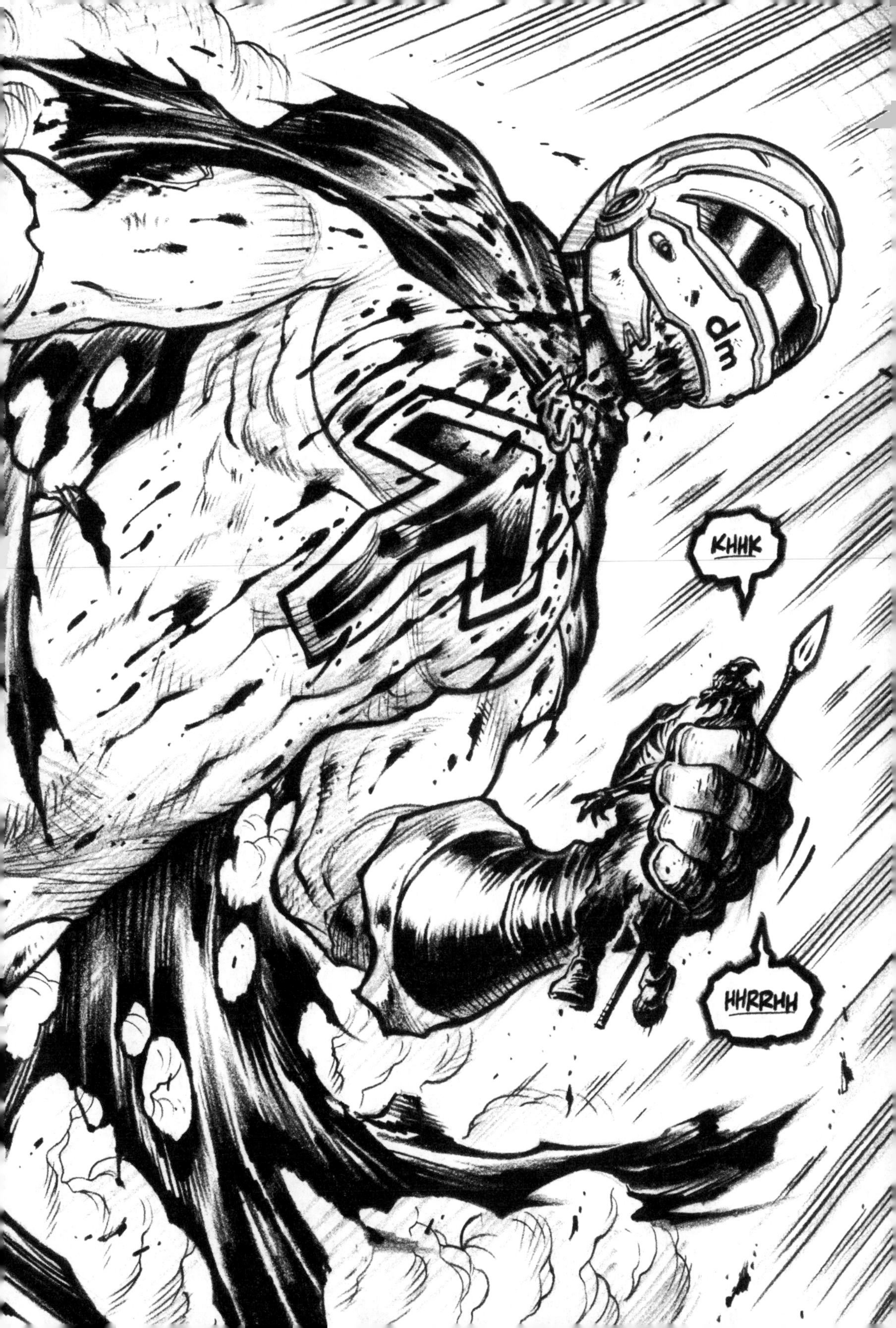
KHHK
HHRRHH

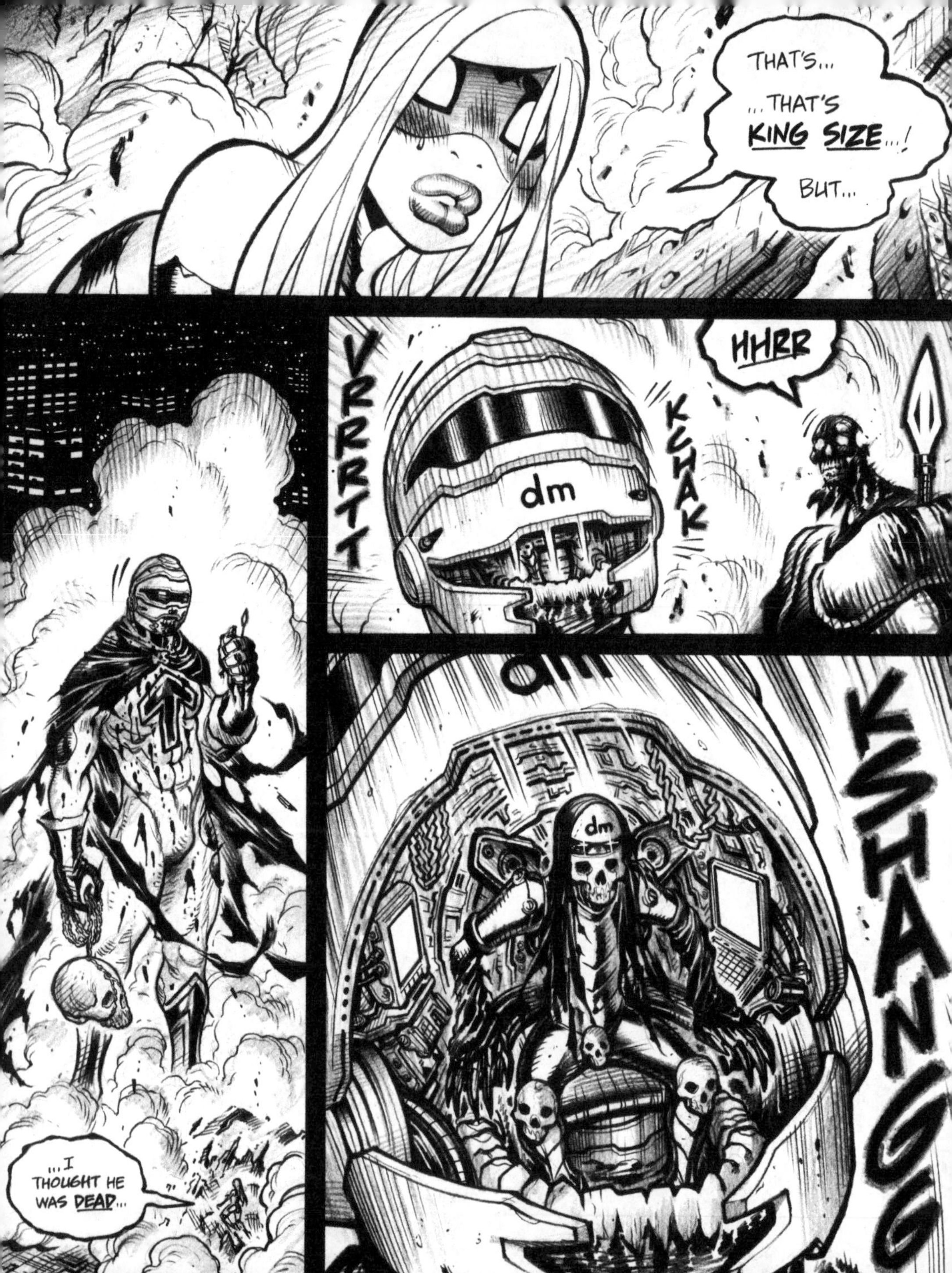
THAT'S...
...THAT'S KING SIZE...!
BUT...
VRRRTT
KCHAK
HHRR
dm
...I THOUGHT HE WAS DEAD...
dm
KSHANGG

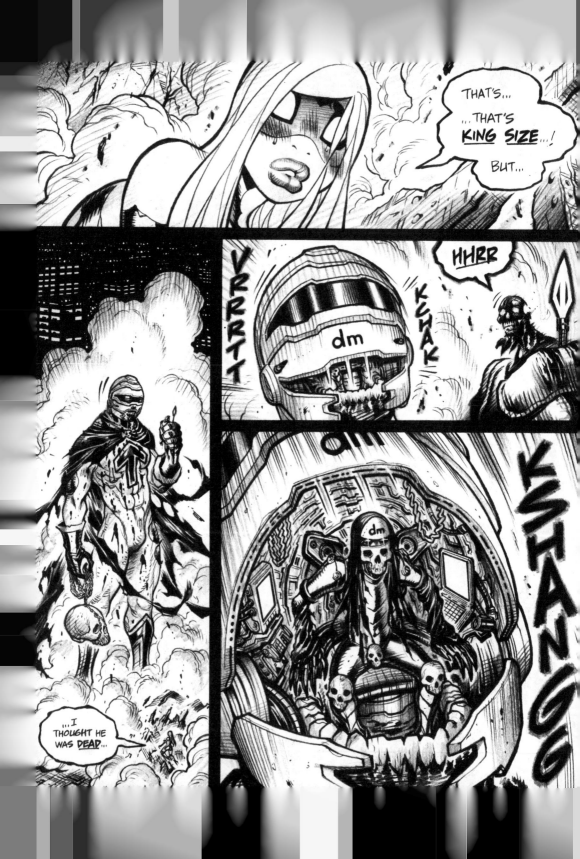

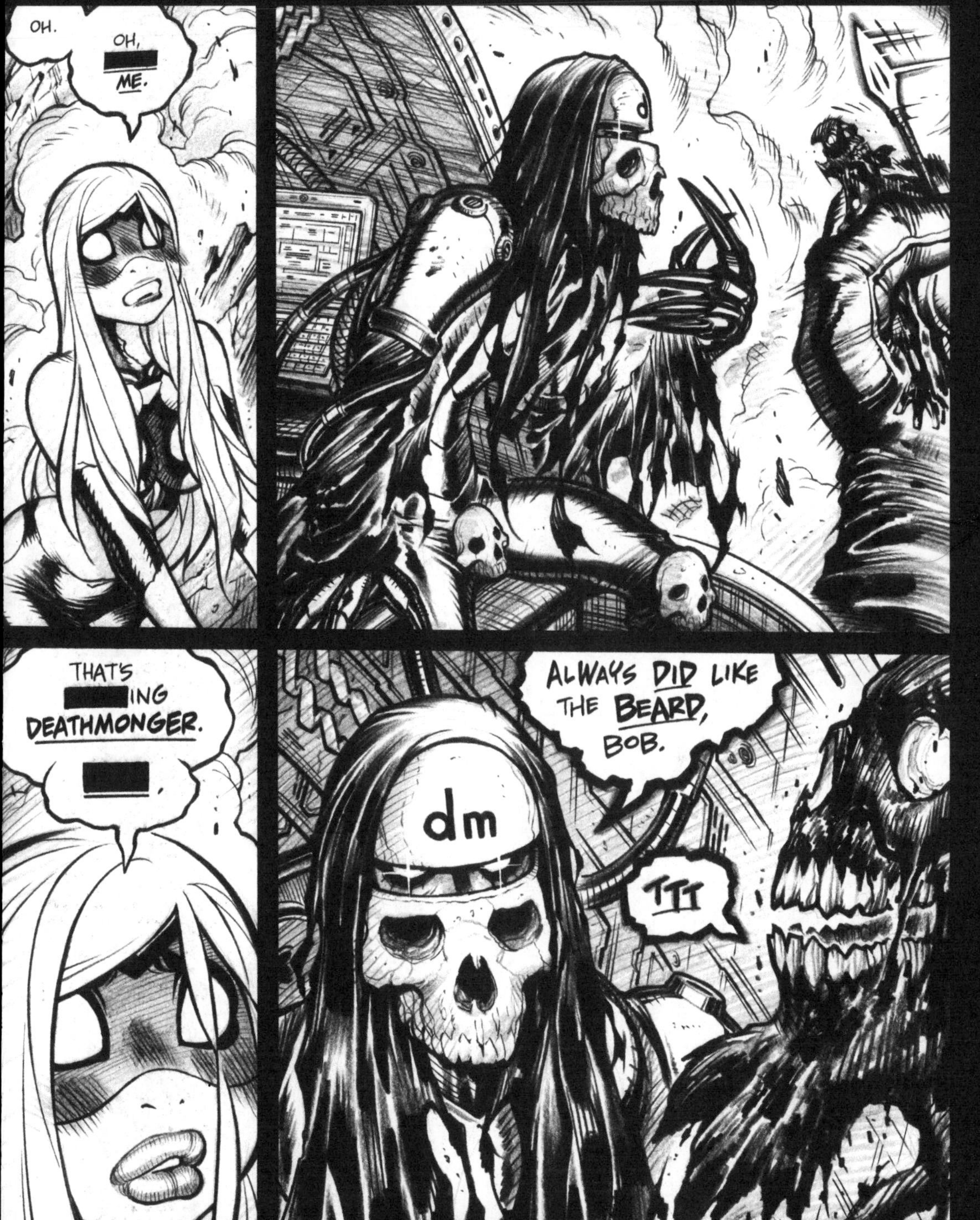
OH.
OH, [redacted] ME.
THAT'S [redacted]ING DEATHMONGER.
[redacted].
dm
ALWAYS DID LIKE THE BEARD, BOB.
TTT

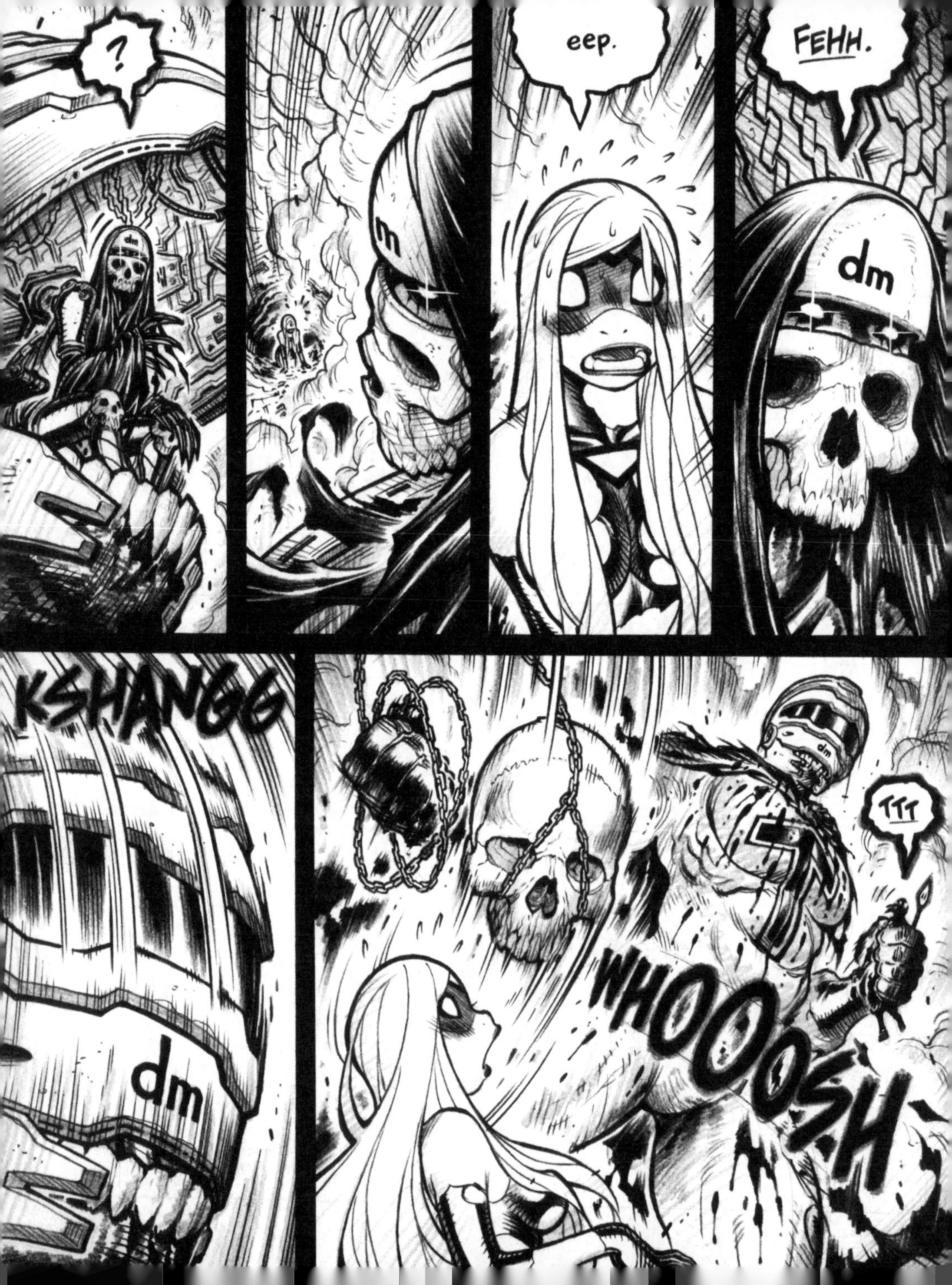
?
eep.
FEHH.
KSHANGG
TTT
WHOOOOSH

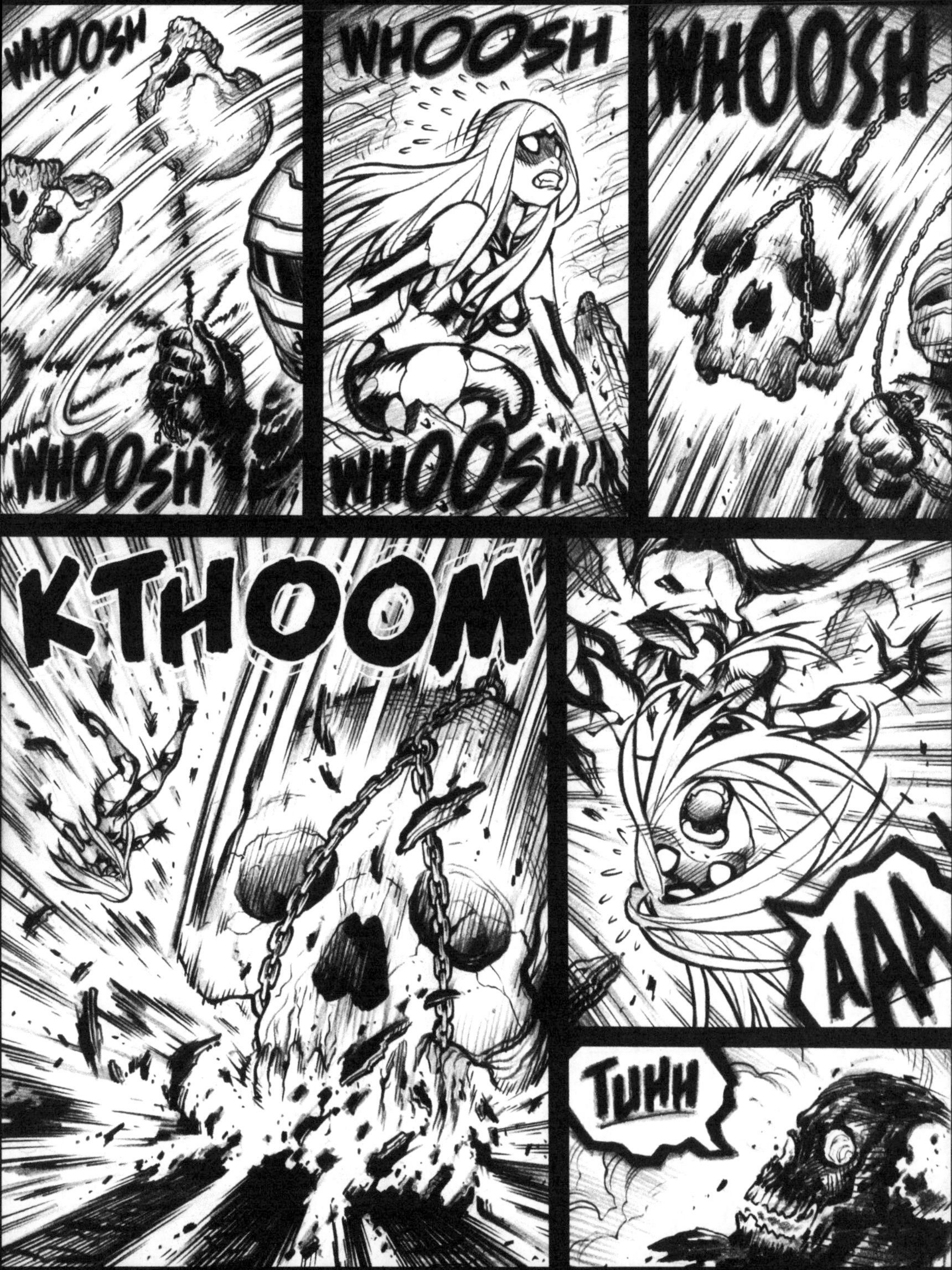
WHOOSH
WHOOSH
WHOOSH
WHOOSH
WHOOSH
KTHOOM
AAA
TUHH

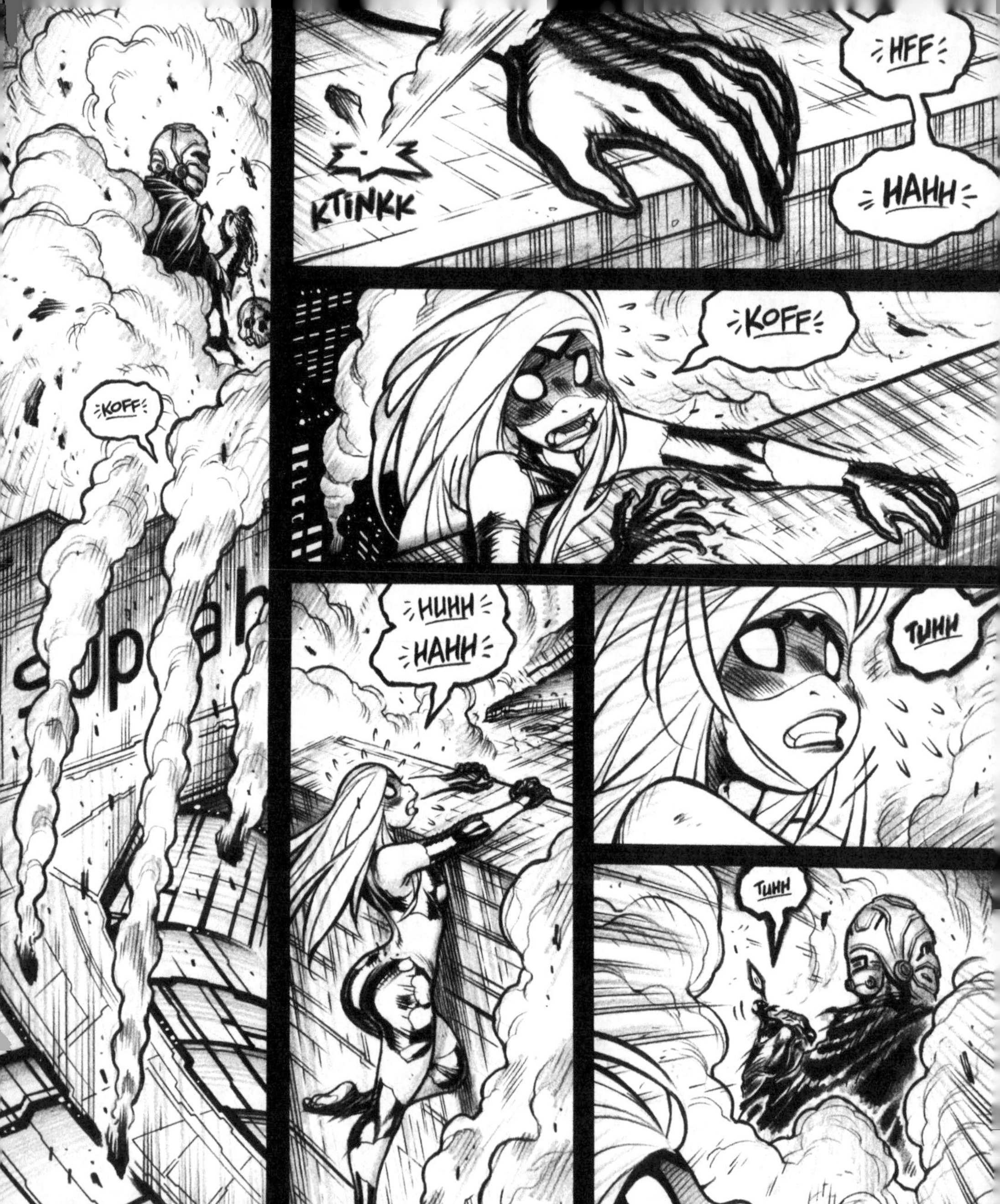
KOFF
KTINKK
HFF
HAHH
KOFF
HUHH
HAHH
TUHH
TUHH

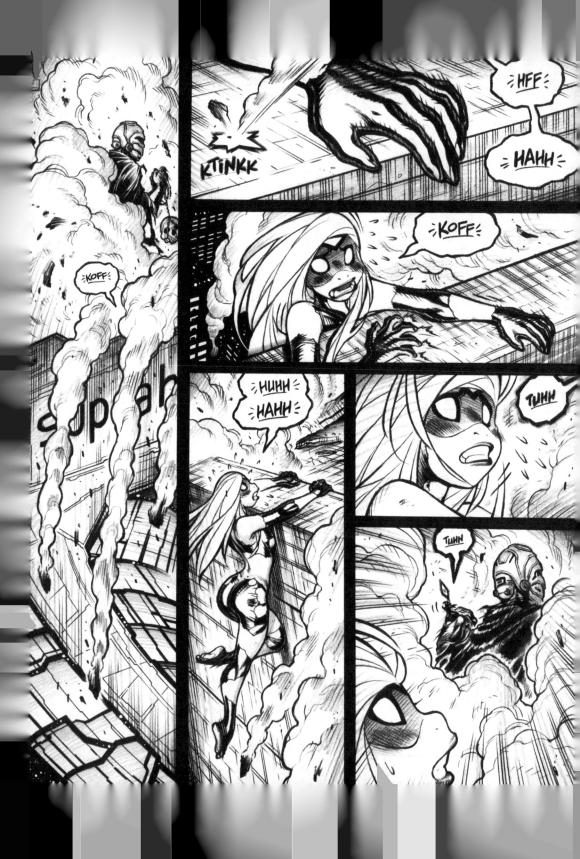

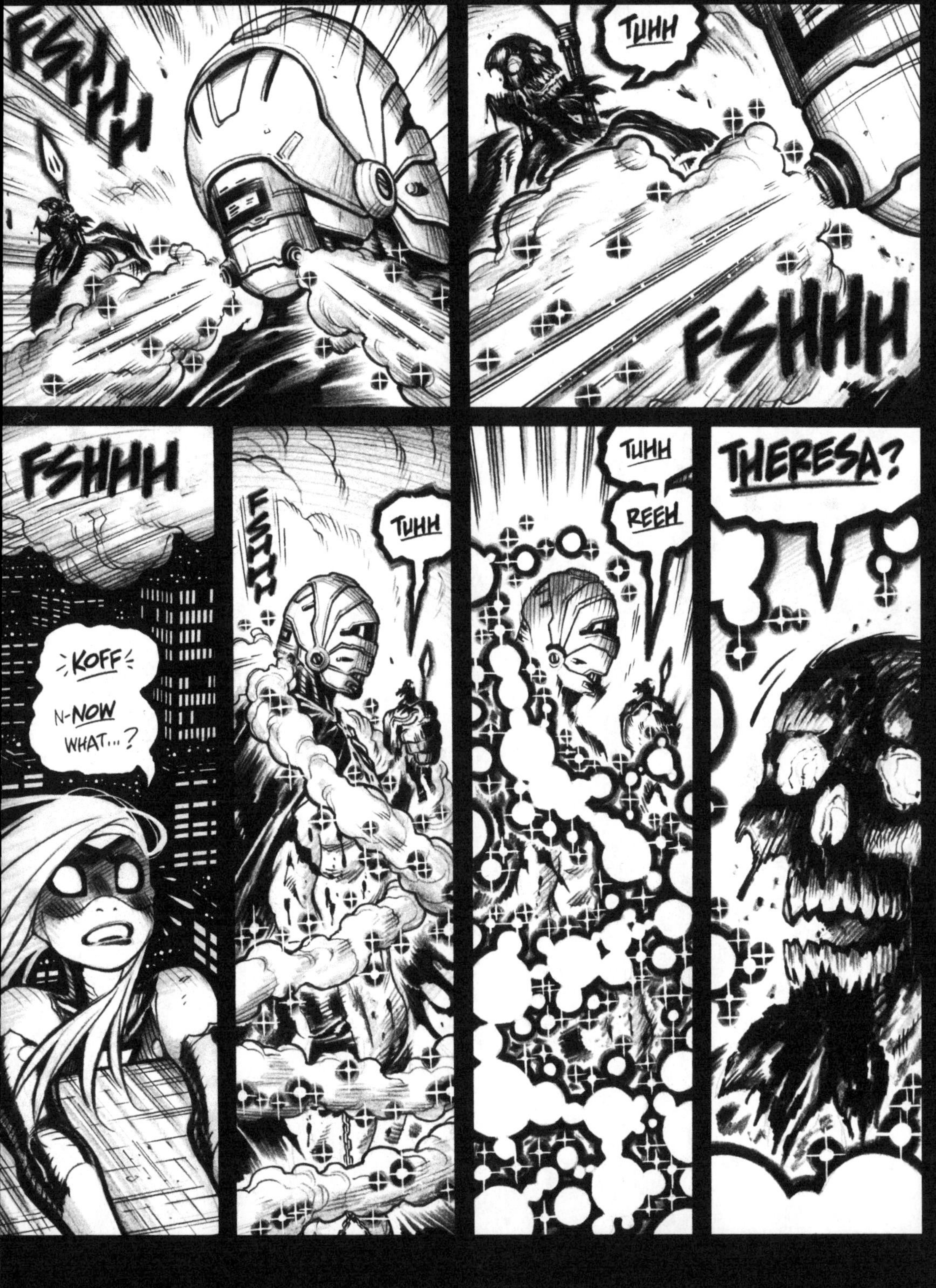
FSHHH
TUHH
FSHHH
FSHHH
KOFF
N-NOW WHAT...?
FSHHH
TUHH
TUHH
REEH
THERESA?

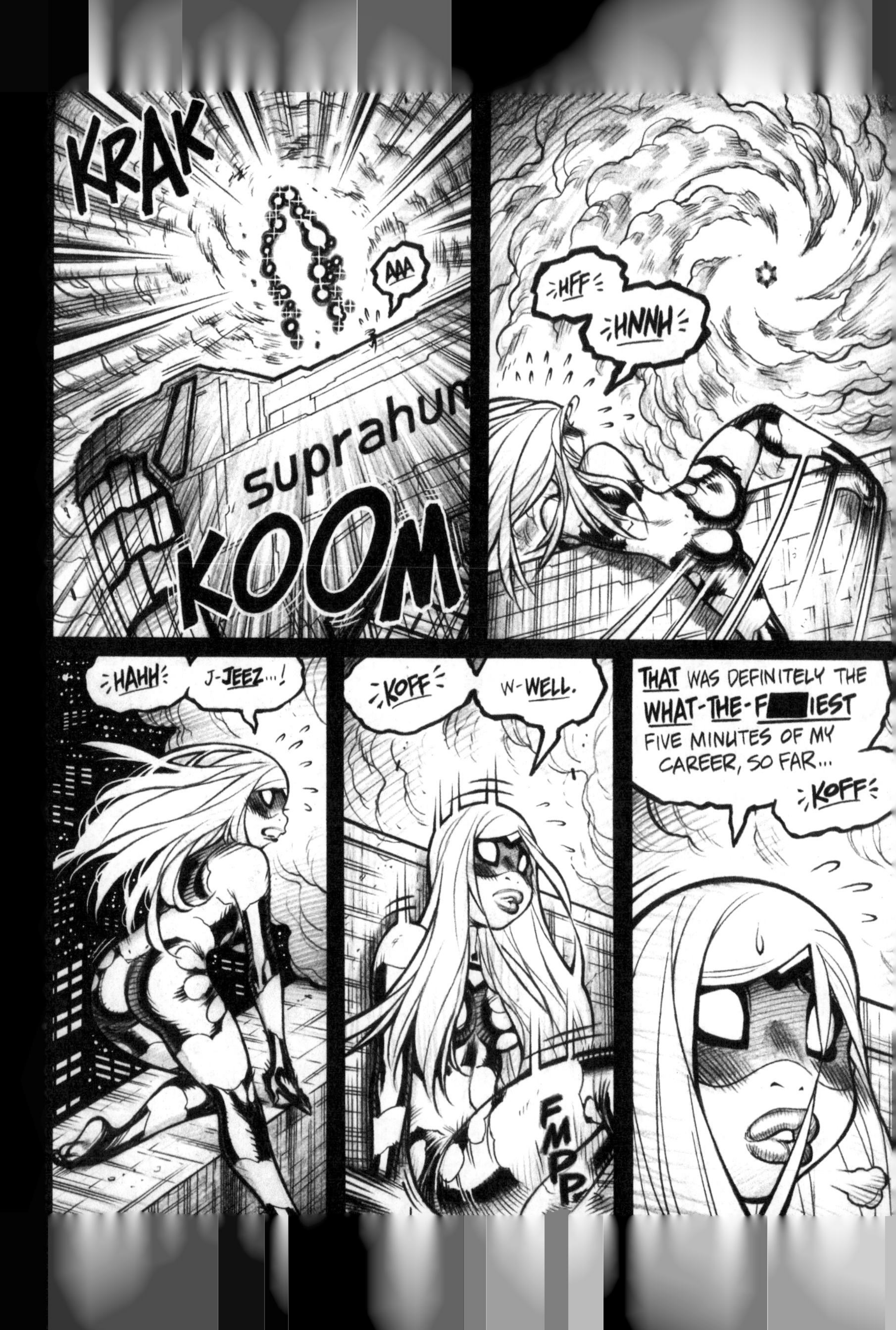
KRAK
AAA
suprahun
KOOM
HFF
HNNH
HAHH
J-JEEZ...!
KOFF
W-WELL.
THAT WAS DEFINITELY THE WHAT-THE-F[redacted]IEST FIVE MINUTES OF MY CAREER, SO FAR...
KOFF
FMPP

Empowered™

Of Clingy Monkeys and Negative Excrescence

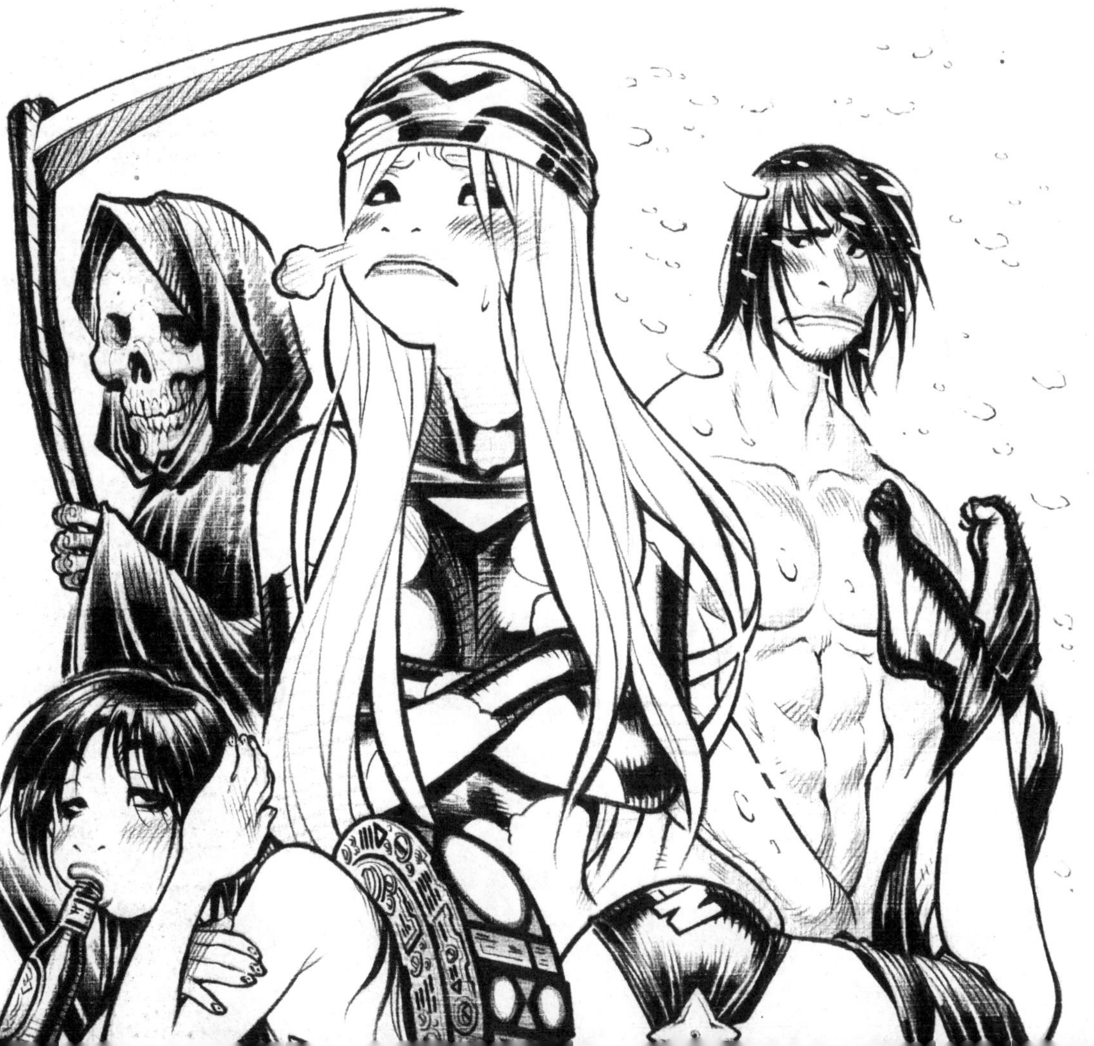

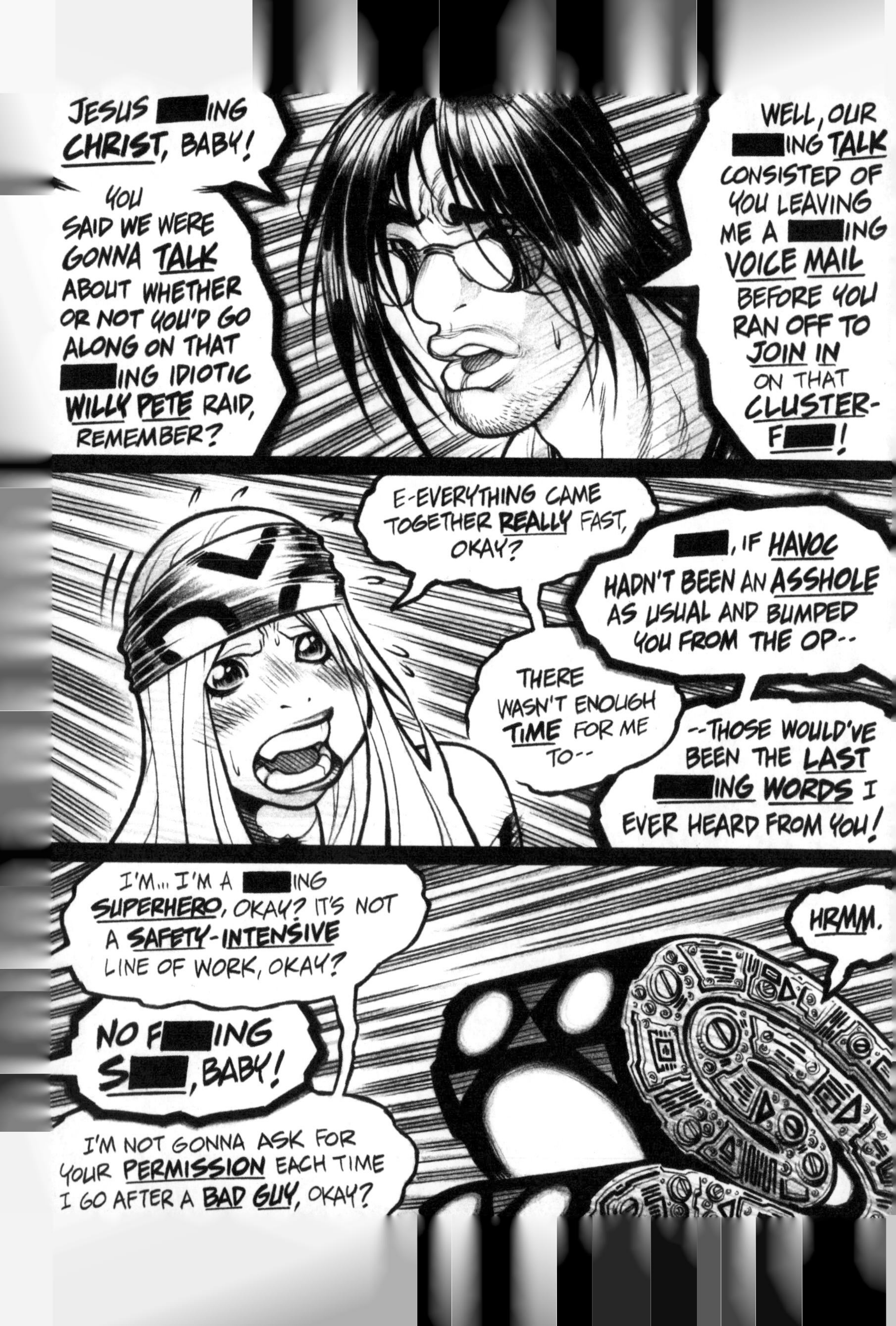
JESUS [redacted]ING CHRIST, BABY!
YOU SAID WE WERE GONNA TALK ABOUT WHETHER OR NOT YOU'D GO ALONG ON THAT [redacted]ING IDIOTIC WILLY PETE RAID, REMEMBER?
WELL, OUR [redacted]ING TALK CONSISTED OF YOU LEAVING ME A [redacted]ING VOICE MAIL BEFORE YOU RAN OFF TO JOIN IN ON THAT CLUSTER-F[redacted]!
E-EVERYTHING CAME TOGETHER REALLY FAST, OKAY?
[redacted], IF HAVOC HADN'T BEEN AN ASSHOLE AS USUAL AND BUMPED YOU FROM THE OP--
THERE WASN'T ENOUGH TIME FOR ME TO--
--THOSE WOULD'VE BEEN THE LAST [redacted]ING WORDS I EVER HEARD FROM YOU!
I'M... I'M A [redacted]ING SUPERHERO, OKAY? IT'S NOT A SAFETY-INTENSIVE LINE OF WORK, OKAY?
NO F[redacted]ING S[redacted], BABY!
I'M NOT GONNA ASK FOR YOUR PERMISSION EACH TIME I GO AFTER A BAD GUY, OKAY?
HRMM.

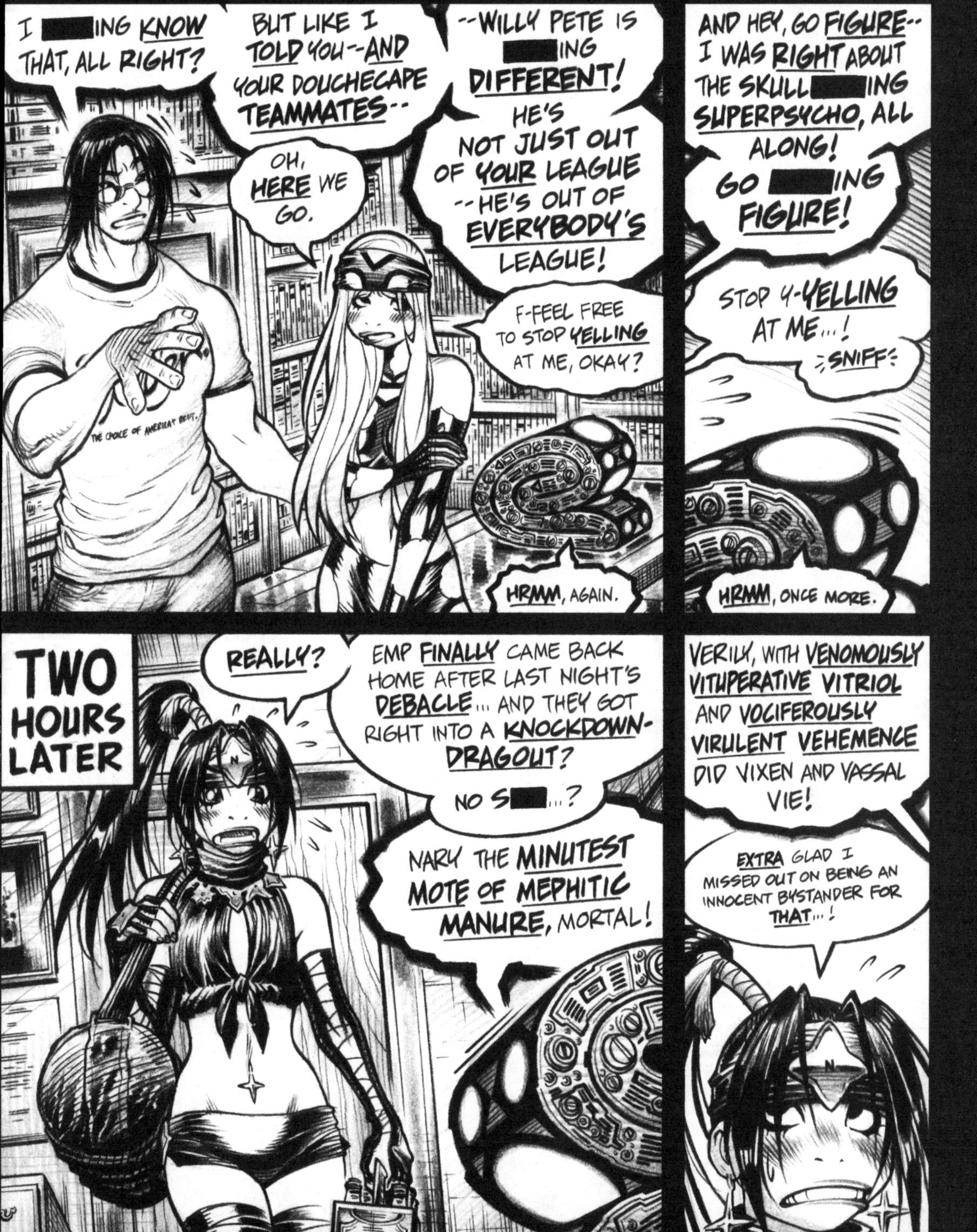
I [redacted]ING KNOW THAT, ALL RIGHT?
BUT LIKE I TOLD YOU--AND YOUR DOUCHECAPE TEAMMATES--
OH, HERE WE GO.
--WILLY PETE IS [redacted]ING DIFFERENT! HE'S NOT JUST OUT OF YOUR LEAGUE --HE'S OUT OF EVERYBODY'S LEAGUE!
F-FEEL FREE TO STOP YELLING AT ME, OKAY?
HRMM, AGAIN.
AND HEY, GO FIGURE-- I WAS RIGHT ABOUT THE SKULL[redacted]ING SUPERPSYCHO, ALL ALONG! GO [redacted]ING FIGURE!
STOP Y-YELLING AT ME...! SNIFF
HRMM, ONCE MORE.
TWO HOURS LATER
REALLY?
EMP FINALLY CAME BACK HOME AFTER LAST NIGHT'S DEBACLE... AND THEY GOT RIGHT INTO A KNOCKDOWN-DRAGOUT?
NO S[redacted]...?
NARY THE MINUTEST MOTE OF MEPHITIC MANURE, MORTAL!
VERILY, WITH VENOMOUSLY VITUPERATIVE VITRIOL AND VOCIFEROUSLY VIRULENT VEHEMENCE DID VIXEN AND VASSAL VIE!
EXTRA GLAD I MISSED OUT ON BEING AN INNOCENT BYSTANDER FOR THAT...!

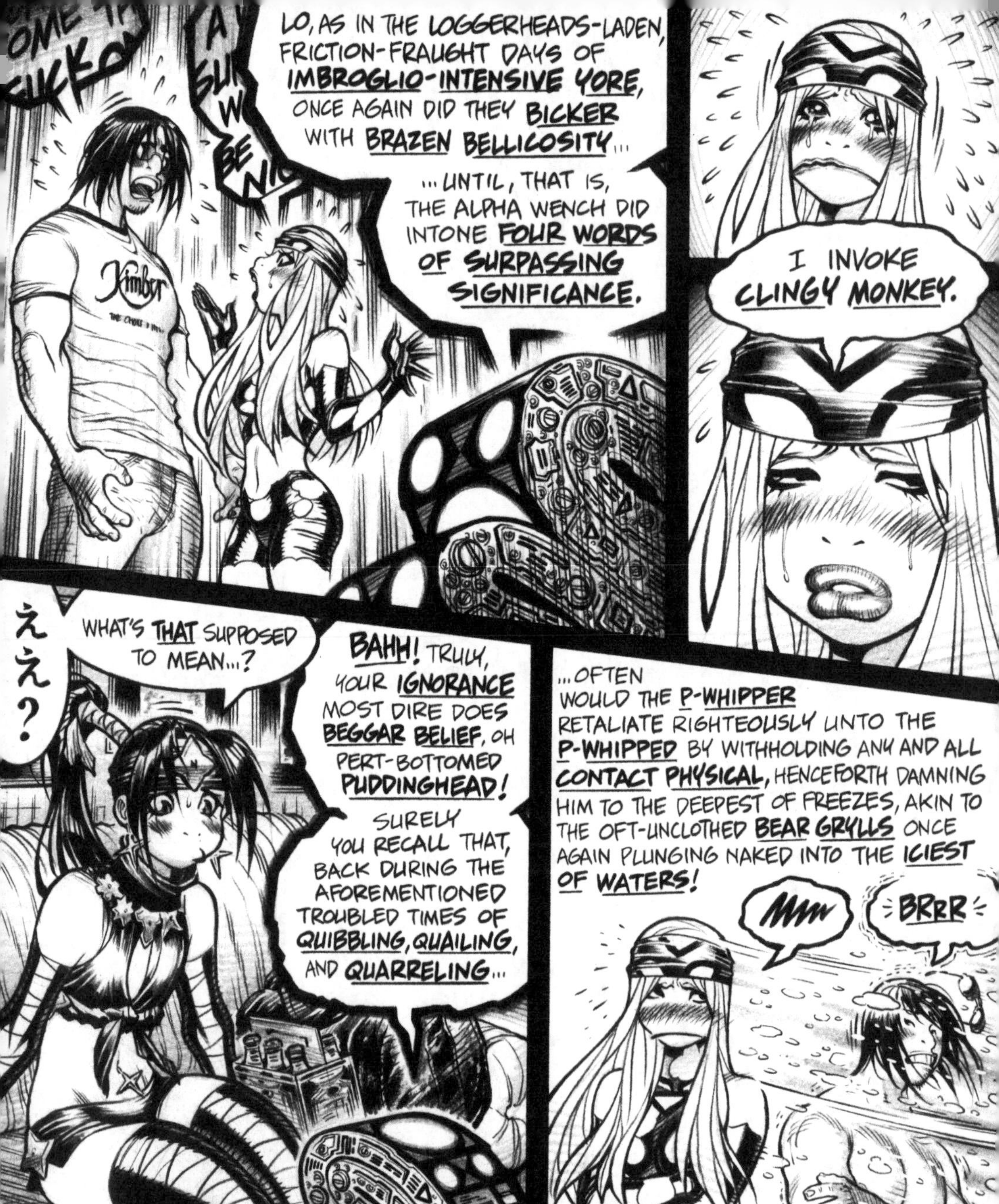
LO, AS IN THE LOGGERHEADS-LADEN, FRICTION-FRAUGHT DAYS OF IMBROGLIO-INTENSIVE YORE, ONCE AGAIN DID THEY BICKER WITH BRAZEN BELLICOSITY...
...UNTIL, THAT IS, THE ALPHA WENCH DID INTONE FOUR WORDS OF SURPASSING SIGNIFICANCE.
I INVOKE CLINGY MONKEY.
ええ？
WHAT'S THAT SUPPOSED TO MEAN...?
BAHH! TRULY, YOUR IGNORANCE MOST DIRE DOES BEGGAR BELIEF, OH PERT-BOTTOMED PUDDINGHEAD!
SURELY YOU RECALL THAT, BACK DURING THE AFOREMENTIONED TROUBLED TIMES OF QUIBBLING, QUAILING, AND QUARRELING...
...OFTEN WOULD THE P-WHIPPER RETALIATE RIGHTEOUSLY UNTO THE P-WHIPPED BY WITHHOLDING ANY AND ALL CONTACT PHYSICAL, HENCEFORTH DAMNING HIM TO THE DEEPEST OF FREEZES, AKIN TO THE OFT-UNCLOTHED BEAR GRYLLS ONCE AGAIN PLUNGING NAKED INTO THE ICIEST OF WATERS!
MMM
BRRR

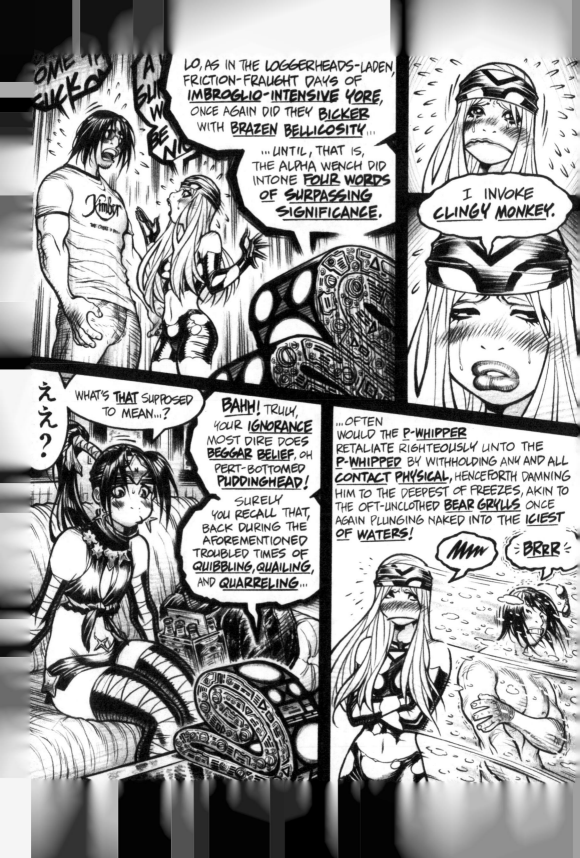

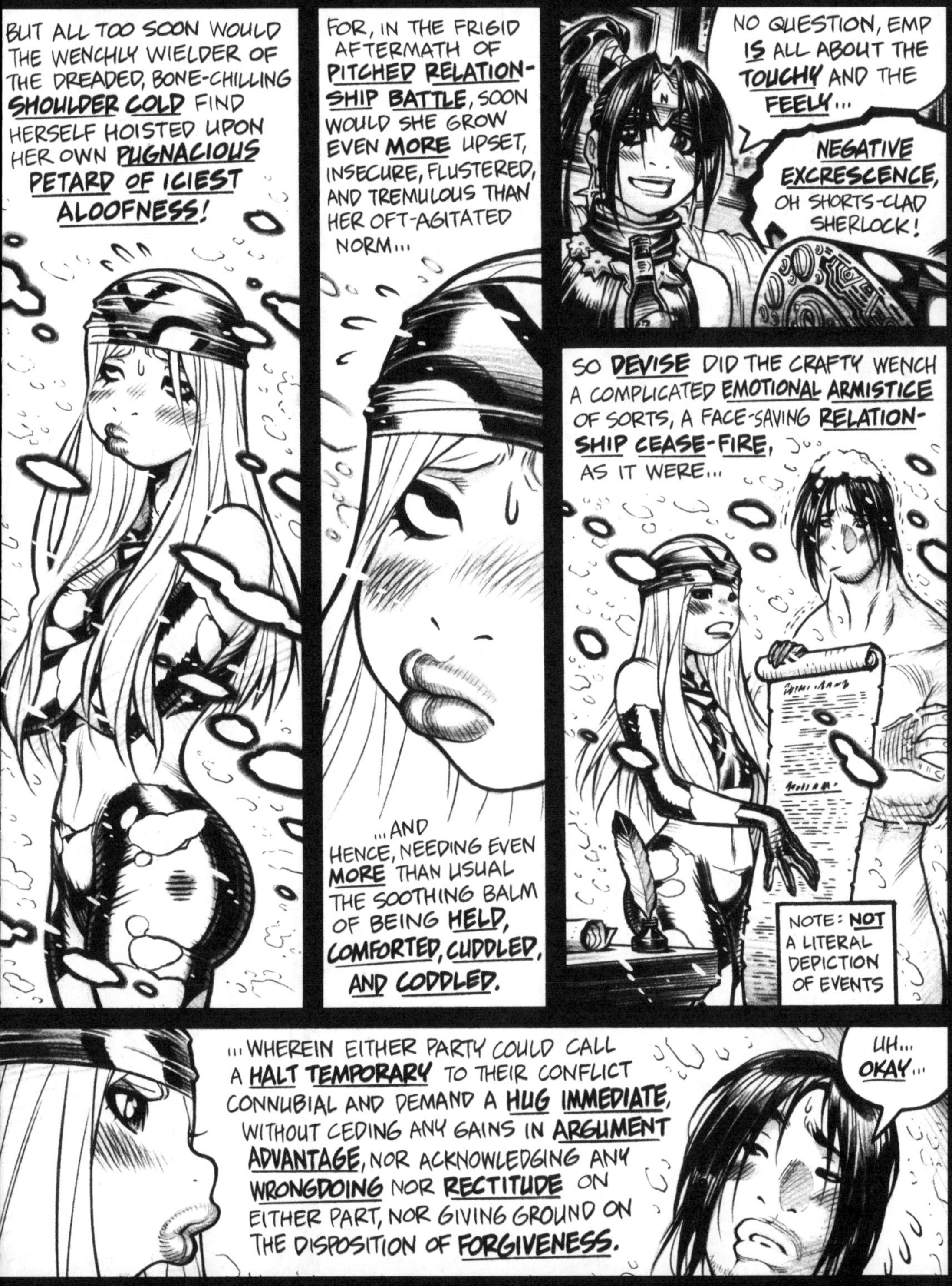
BUT ALL TOO SOON WOULD THE WENCHLY WIELDER OF THE DREADED, BONE-CHILLING SHOULDER COLD FIND HERSELF HOISTED UPON HER OWN PUGNACIOUS PETARD OF ICIEST ALOOFNESS!
FOR, IN THE FRIGID AFTERMATH OF PITCHED RELATIONSHIP BATTLE, SOON WOULD SHE GROW EVEN MORE UPSET, INSECURE, FLUSTERED, AND TREMULOUS THAN HER OFT-AGITATED NORM...
...AND HENCE, NEEDING EVEN MORE THAN USUAL THE SOOTHING BALM OF BEING HELD, COMFORTED, CUDDLED, AND CODDLED.
NO QUESTION, EMP IS ALL ABOUT THE TOUCHY AND THE FEELY...
NEGATIVE EXCRESCENCE, OH SHORTS-CLAD SHERLOCK!
SO DEVISE DID THE CRAFTY WENCH A COMPLICATED EMOTIONAL ARMISTICE OF SORTS, A FACE-SAVING RELATIONSHIP CEASE-FIRE, AS IT WERE...
NOTE: NOT A LITERAL DEPICTION OF EVENTS
...WHEREIN EITHER PARTY COULD CALL A HALT TEMPORARY TO THEIR CONFLICT CONNUBIAL AND DEMAND A HUG IMMEDIATE, WITHOUT CEDING ANY GAINS IN ARGUMENT ADVANTAGE, NOR ACKNOWLEDGING ANY WRONGDOING NOR RECTITUDE ON EITHER PART, NOR GIVING GROUND ON THE DISPOSITION OF FORGIVENESS.
UH... OKAY...

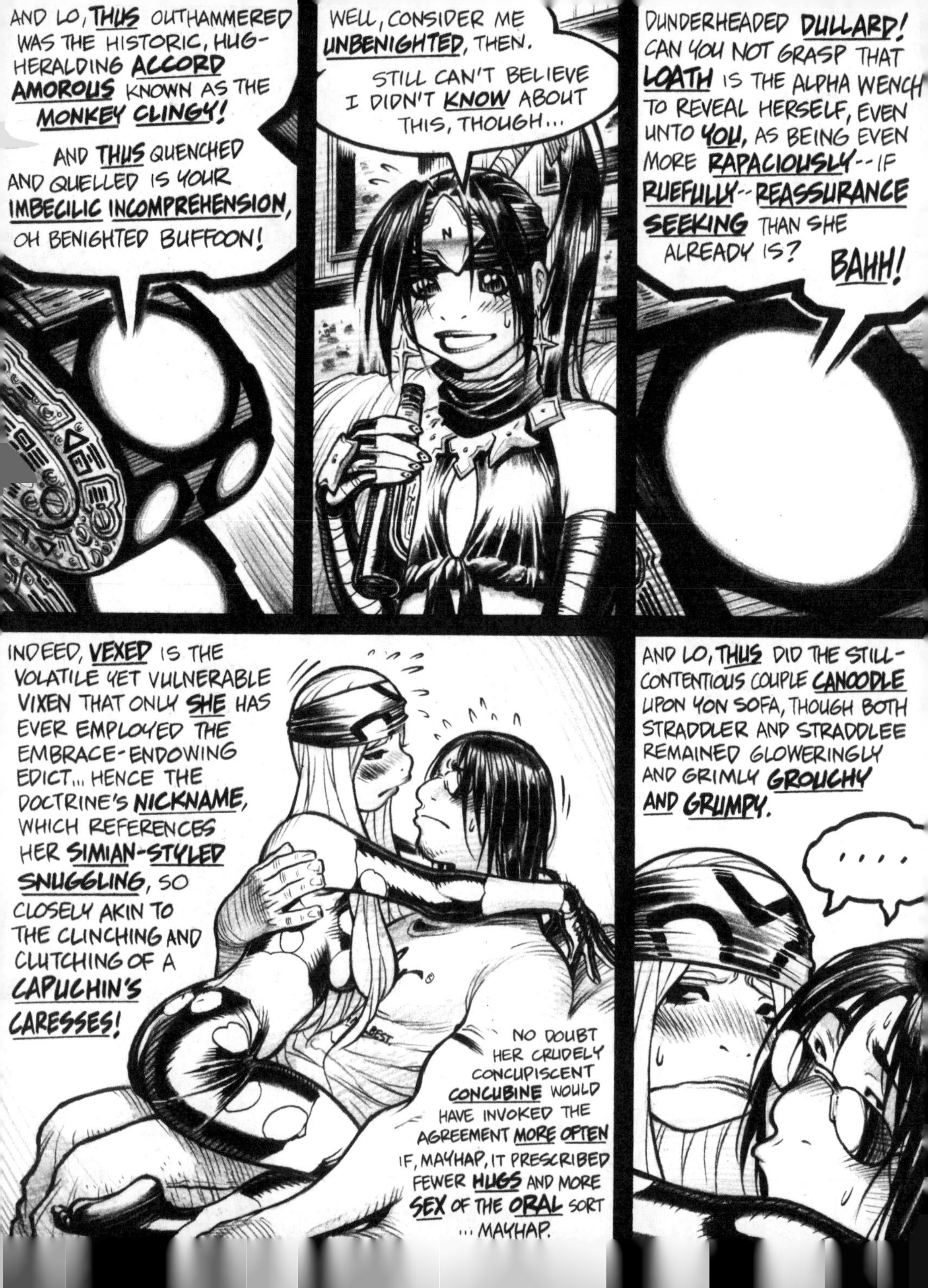
AND LO, THUS OUTHAMMERED WAS THE HISTORIC, HUG-HERALDING ACCORD AMOROUS KNOWN AS THE MONKEY CLINGY!
AND THUS QUENCHED AND QUELLED IS YOUR IMBECILIC INCOMPREHENSION, OH BENIGHTED BUFFOON!
WELL, CONSIDER ME UNBENIGHTED, THEN.
STILL CAN'T BELIEVE I DIDN'T KNOW ABOUT THIS, THOUGH...
DUNDERHEADED DULLARD! CAN YOU NOT GRASP THAT LOATH IS THE ALPHA WENCH TO REVEAL HERSELF, EVEN UNTO YOU, AS BEING EVEN MORE RAPACIOUSLY--IF RUEFULLY--REASSURANCE SEEKING THAN SHE ALREADY IS?
BAHH!
INDEED, VEXED IS THE VOLATILE YET VULNERABLE VIXEN THAT ONLY SHE HAS EVER EMPLOYED THE EMBRACE-ENDOWING EDICT... HENCE THE DOCTRINE'S NICKNAME, WHICH REFERENCES HER SIMIAN-STYLED SNUGGLING, SO CLOSELY AKIN TO THE CLINCHING AND CLUTCHING OF A CAPUCHIN'S CARESSES!
NO DOUBT HER CRUDELY CONCUPISCENT CONCUBINE WOULD HAVE INVOKED THE AGREEMENT MORE OFTEN IF, MAYHAP, IT PRESCRIBED FEWER HUGS AND MORE SEX OF THE ORAL SORT ...MAYHAP.
AND LO, THUS DID THE STILL-CONTENTIOUS COUPLE CANOODLE UPON YON SOFA, THOUGH BOTH STRADDLER AND STRADDLEE REMAINED GLOWERINGLY AND GRIMLY GROUCHY AND GRUMPY.
....

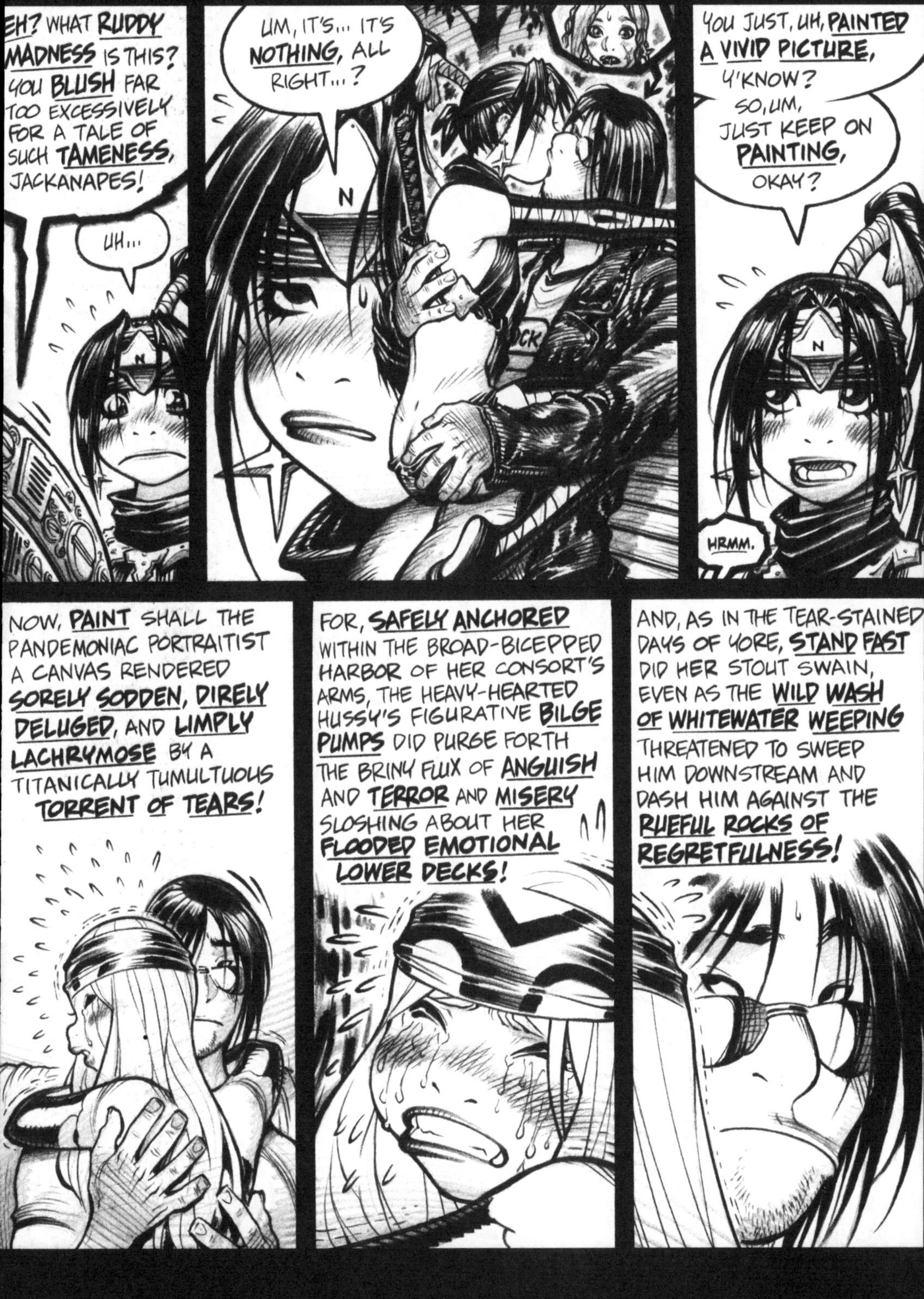
EH? WHAT RUDDY MADNESS IS THIS? YOU BLUSH FAR TOO EXCESSIVELY FOR A TALE OF SUCH TAMENESS, JACKANAPES!
UH...
UM, IT'S... IT'S NOTHING, ALL RIGHT...?
YOU JUST, UH, PAINTED A VIVID PICTURE, Y'KNOW? SO, UM, JUST KEEP ON PAINTING, OKAY?
HRMM.
NOW, PAINT SHALL THE PANDEMONIAC PORTRAITIST A CANVAS RENDERED SORELY SODDEN, DIRELY DELUGED, AND LIMPLY LACHRYMOSE BY A TITANICALLY TUMULTUOUS TORRENT OF TEARS!
FOR, SAFELY ANCHORED WITHIN THE BROAD-BICEPPED HARBOR OF HER CONSORT'S ARMS, THE HEAVY-HEARTED HUSSY'S FIGURATIVE BILGE PUMPS DID PURGE FORTH THE BRINY FLUX OF ANGUISH AND TERROR AND MISERY SLOSHING ABOUT HER FLOODED EMOTIONAL LOWER DECKS!
AND, AS IN THE TEAR-STAINED DAYS OF YORE, STAND FAST DID HER STOUT SWAIN, EVEN AS THE WILD WASH OF WHITEWATER WEEPING THREATENED TO SWEEP HIM DOWNSTREAM AND DASH HIM AGAINST THE RUEFUL ROCKS OF REGRETFULNESS!

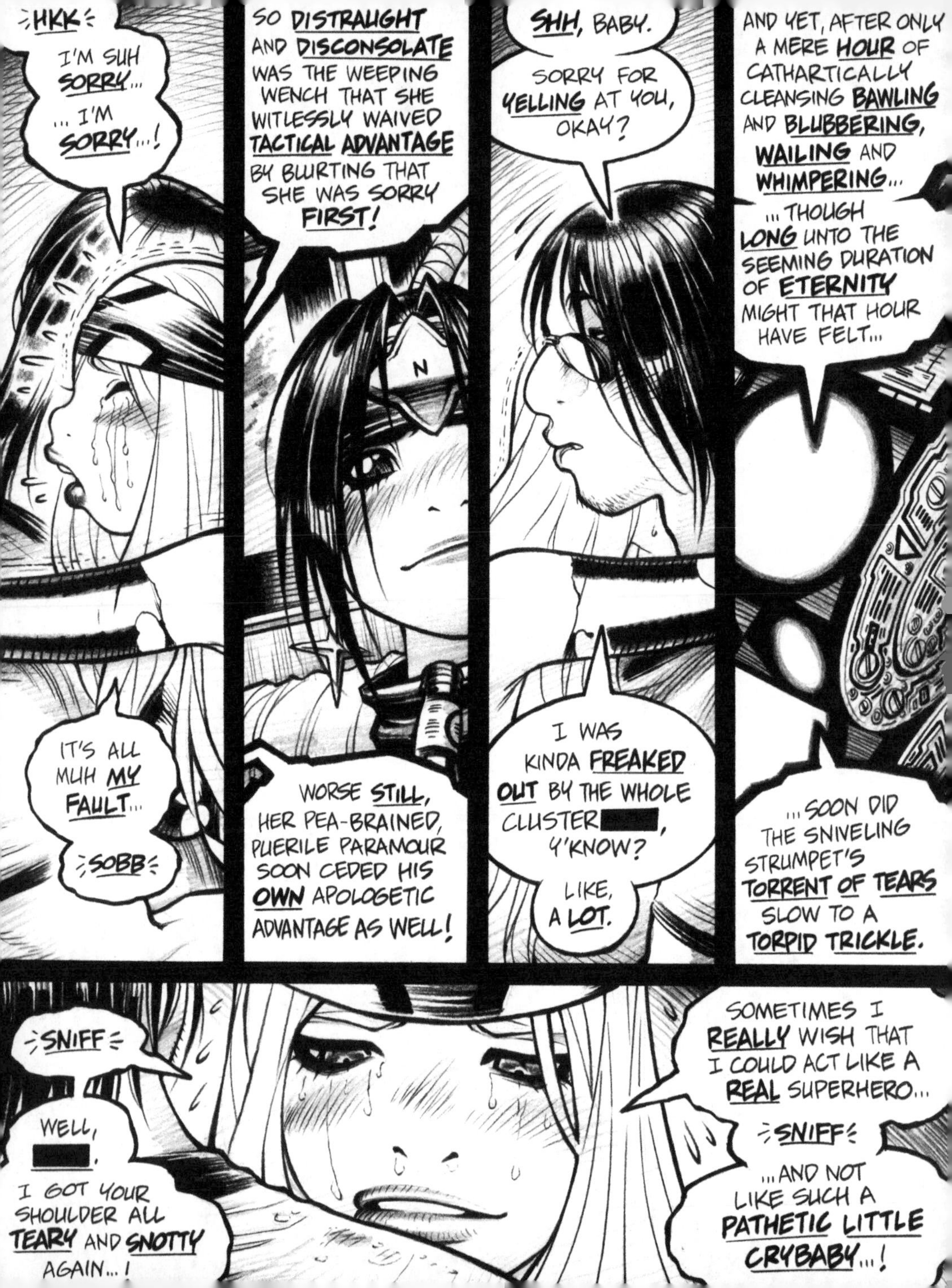
HKK
I'M SUH SORRY...
... I'M SORRY...!
IT'S ALL MUH MY FAULT...
SOBB
SO DISTRAUGHT AND DISCONSOLATE WAS THE WEEPING WENCH THAT SHE WITLESSLY WAIVED TACTICAL ADVANTAGE BY BLURTING THAT SHE WAS SORRY FIRST!
WORSE STILL, HER PEA-BRAINED, PUERILE PARAMOUR SOON CEDED HIS OWN APOLOGETIC ADVANTAGE AS WELL!
SHH, BABY.
SORRY FOR YELLING AT YOU, OKAY?
I WAS KINDA FREAKED OUT BY THE WHOLE CLUSTER[redacted], Y'KNOW?
LIKE, A LOT.
AND YET, AFTER ONLY A MERE HOUR OF CATHARTICALLY CLEANSING BAWLING AND BLUBBERING, WAILING AND WHIMPERING...
... THOUGH LONG UNTO THE SEEMING DURATION OF ETERNITY MIGHT THAT HOUR HAVE FELT...
... SOON DID THE SNIVELING STRUMPET'S TORRENT OF TEARS SLOW TO A TORPID TRICKLE.
SNIFF
WELL, [redacted]. I GOT YOUR SHOULDER ALL TEARY AND SNOTTY AGAIN...!
SOMETIMES I REALLY WISH THAT I COULD ACT LIKE A REAL SUPERHERO...
SNIFF
... AND NOT LIKE SUCH A PATHETIC LITTLE CRYBABY...!

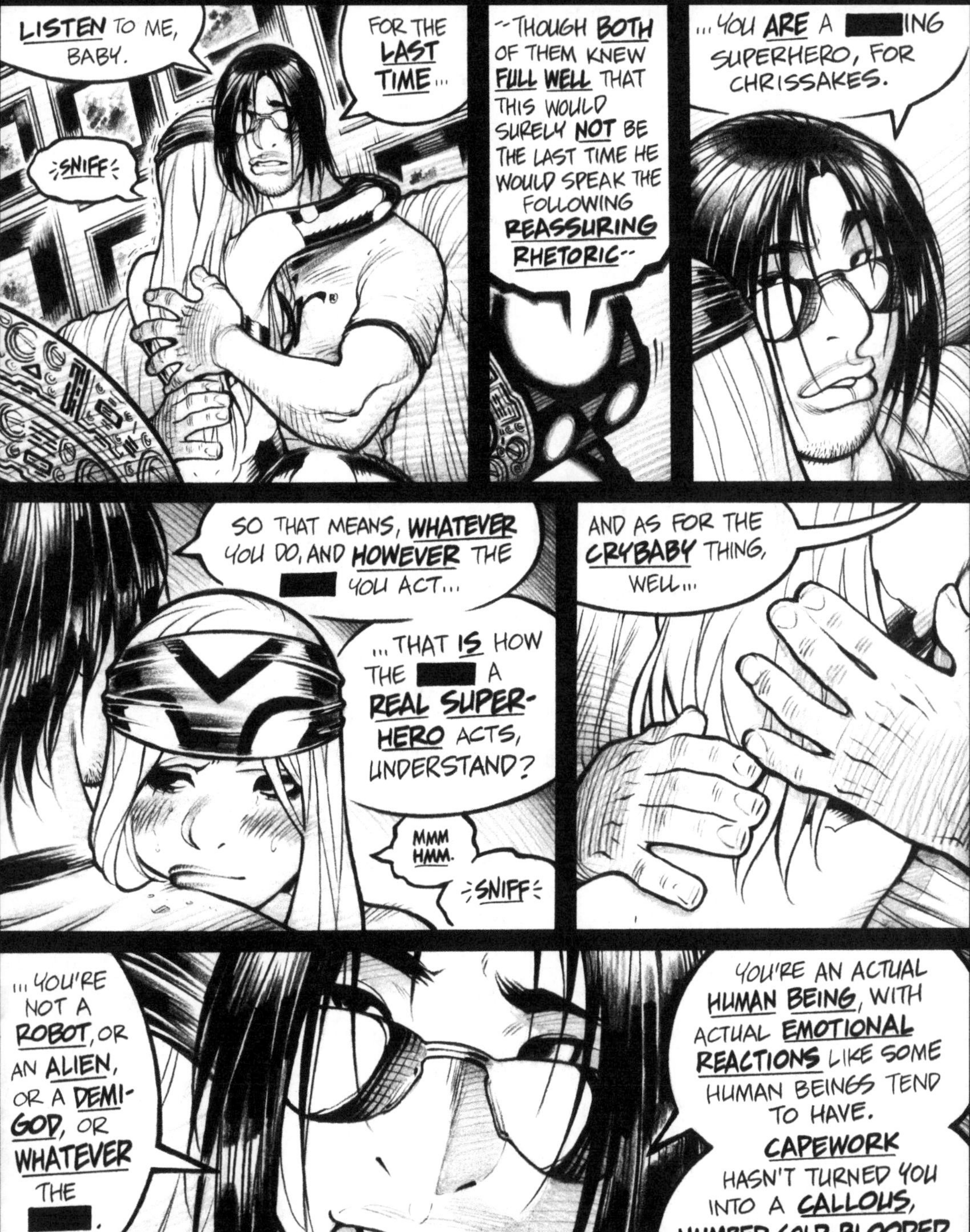
LISTEN TO ME, BABY.
SNIFF
FOR THE LAST TIME...
--THOUGH BOTH OF THEM KNEW FULL WELL THAT THIS WOULD SURELY NOT BE THE LAST TIME HE WOULD SPEAK THE FOLLOWING REASSURING RHETORIC--
...YOU ARE A [redacted]ING SUPERHERO, FOR CHRISSAKES.
SO THAT MEANS, WHATEVER YOU DO, AND HOWEVER THE [redacted] YOU ACT...
...THAT IS HOW THE [redacted] A REAL SUPER-HERO ACTS, UNDERSTAND?
MMM HMM.
SNIFF
AND AS FOR THE CRYBABY THING, WELL...
...YOU'RE NOT A ROBOT, OR AN ALIEN, OR A DEMI-GOD, OR WHATEVER THE [redacted].
YOU'RE AN ACTUAL HUMAN BEING, WITH ACTUAL EMOTIONAL REACTIONS LIKE SOME HUMAN BEINGS TEND TO HAVE.
CAPEWORK HASN'T TURNED YOU INTO A CALLOUS, NUMBED, COLD-BLOODED SUPERMONSTER LIKE THE OTHER CAPES.

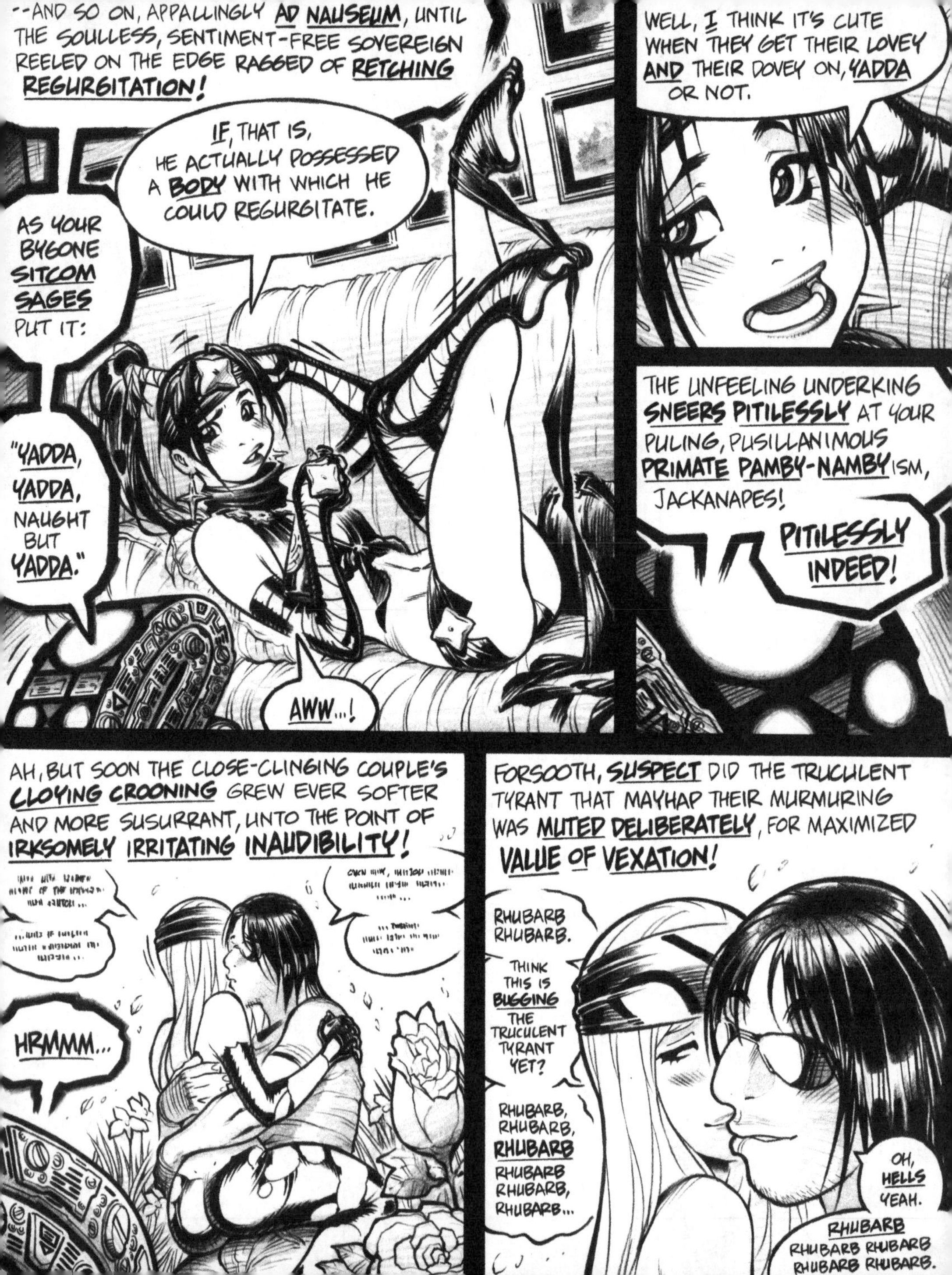
--AND SO ON, APPALLINGLY AD NAUSEUM, UNTIL THE SOULLESS, SENTIMENT-FREE SOVEREIGN REELED ON THE EDGE RAGGED OF RETCHING REGURGITATION!
IF, THAT IS, HE ACTUALLY POSSESSED A BODY WITH WHICH HE COULD REGURGITATE.
AS YOUR BYGONE SITCOM SAGES PUT IT:
"YADDA, YADDA, NAUGHT BUT YADDA."
AWW...!
WELL, I THINK IT'S CUTE WHEN THEY GET THEIR LOVEY AND THEIR DOVEY ON, YADDA OR NOT.
THE UNFEELING UNDERKING SNEERS PITILESSLY AT YOUR PULING, PUSILLANIMOUS PRIMATE PAMBY-NAMBYISM, JACKANAPES!
PITILESSLY INDEED!
AH, BUT SOON THE CLOSE-CLINGING COUPLE'S CLOYING CROONING GREW EVER SOFTER AND MORE SUSURRANT, UNTO THE POINT OF IRKSOMELY IRRITATING INAUDIBILITY!
HRMMM...
FORSOOTH, SUSPECT DID THE TRUCULENT TYRANT THAT MAYHAP THEIR MURMURING WAS MUTED DELIBERATELY, FOR MAXIMIZED VALUE OF VEXATION!
RHUBARB RHUBARB.
THINK THIS IS BUGGING THE TRUCULENT TYRANT YET?
RHUBARB, RHUBARB, RHUBARB RHUBARB RHUBARB, RHUBARB...
OH, HELLS YEAH.
RHUBARB RHUBARB RHUBARB RHUBARB RHUBARB.

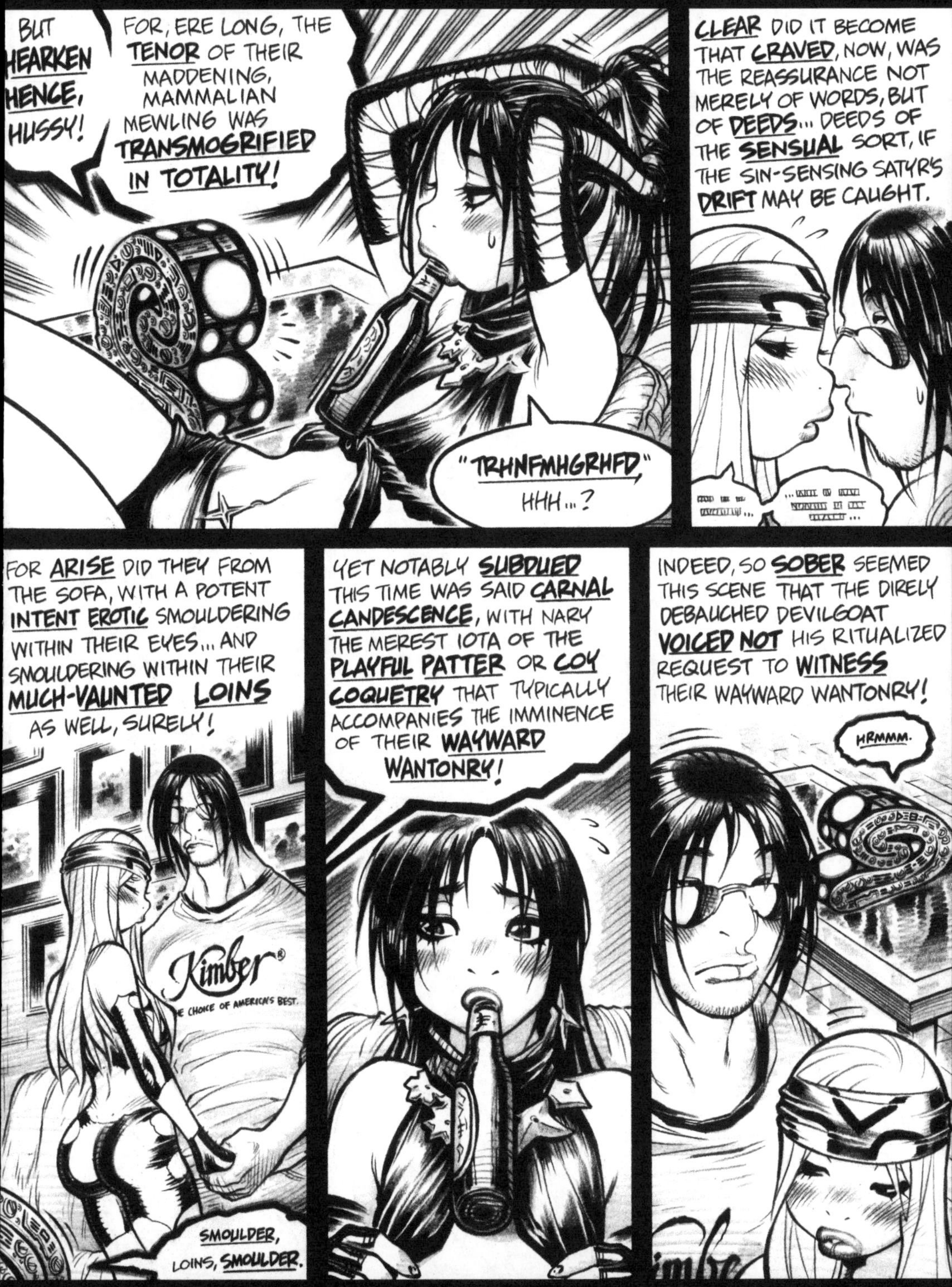
BUT HEARKEN HENCE, HUSSY!
FOR, ERE LONG, THE TENOR OF THEIR MADDENING, MAMMALIAN MEWLING WAS TRANSMOGRIFIED IN TOTALITY!
"TRHNFMHGRHFD," HHH...?
CLEAR DID IT BECOME THAT CRAVED, NOW, WAS THE REASSURANCE NOT MERELY OF WORDS, BUT OF DEEDS... DEEDS OF THE SENSUAL SORT, IF THE SIN-SENSING SATYR'S DRIFT MAY BE CAUGHT.
FOR ARISE DID THEY FROM THE SOFA, WITH A POTENT INTENT EROTIC SMOULDERING WITHIN THEIR EYES... AND SMOULDERING WITHIN THEIR MUCH-VAUNTED LOINS AS WELL, SURELY!
Kimber®
THE CHOICE OF AMERICA'S BEST.
SMOULDER, LOINS, SMOULDER.
YET NOTABLY SUBDUED THIS TIME WAS SAID CARNAL CANDESCENCE, WITH NARY THE MEREST IOTA OF THE PLAYFUL PATTER OR COY COQUETRY THAT TYPICALLY ACCOMPANIES THE IMMINENCE OF THEIR WAYWARD WANTONRY!
INDEED, SO SOBER SEEMED THIS SCENE THAT THE DIRELY DEBAUCHED DEVILGOAT VOICED NOT HIS RITUALIZED REQUEST TO WITNESS THEIR WAYWARD WANTONRY!
HRMMM.

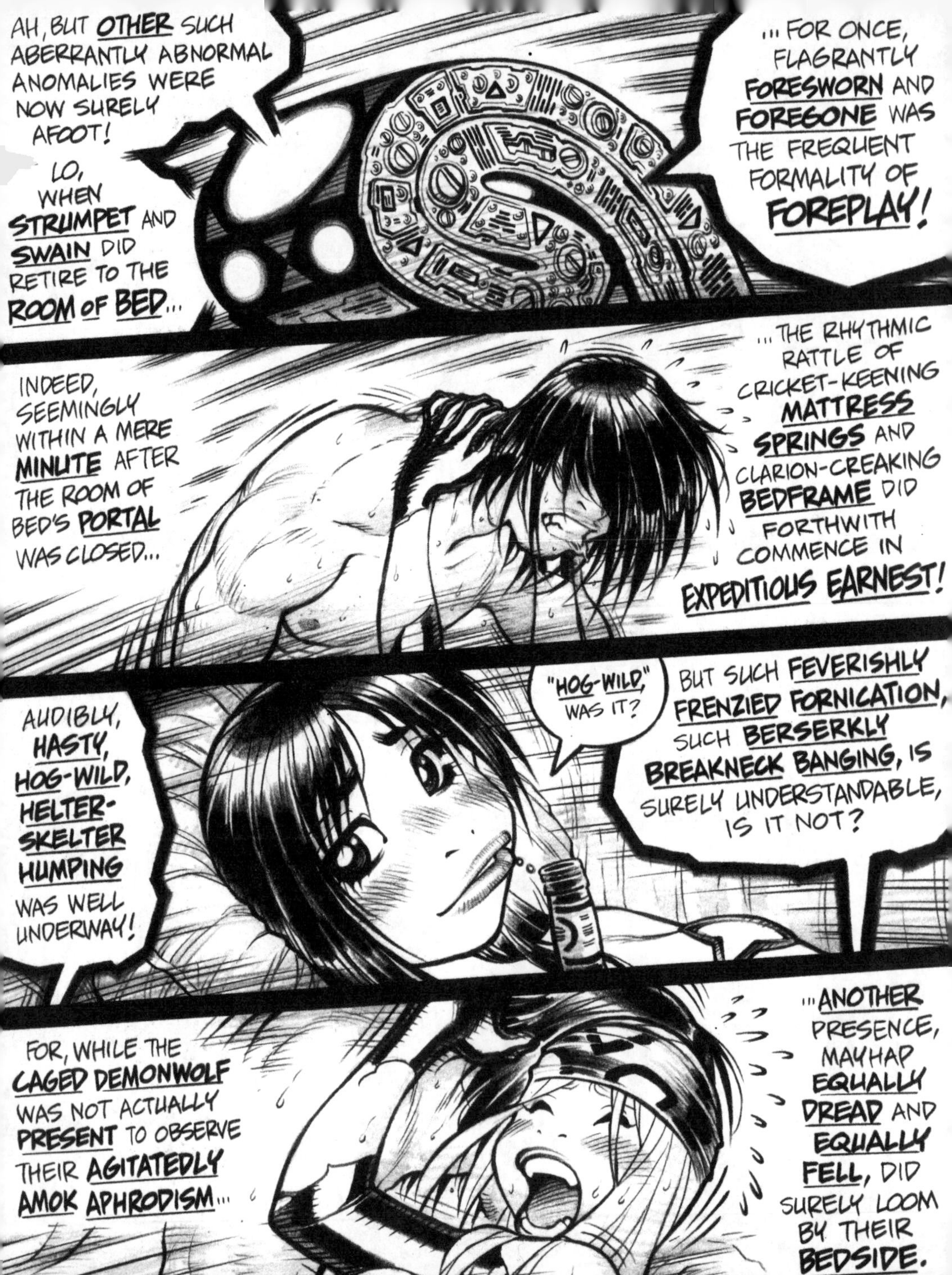
AH, BUT OTHER SUCH ABERRANTLY ABNORMAL ANOMALIES WERE NOW SURELY AFOOT!
LO, WHEN STRUMPET AND SWAIN DID RETIRE TO THE ROOM OF BED...
...FOR ONCE, FLAGRANTLY FORESWORN AND FOREGONE WAS THE FREQUENT FORMALITY OF FOREPLAY!
INDEED, SEEMINGLY WITHIN A MERE MINUTE AFTER THE ROOM OF BED'S PORTAL WAS CLOSED...
...THE RHYTHMIC RATTLE OF CRICKET-KEENING MATTRESS SPRINGS AND CLARION-CREAKING BEDFRAME DID FORTHWITH COMMENCE IN EXPEDITIOUS EARNEST!
AUDIBLY, HASTY, HOG-WILD, HELTER-SKELTER HUMPING WAS WELL UNDERWAY!
"HOG-WILD," WAS IT?
BUT SUCH FEVERISHLY FRENZIED FORNICATION, SUCH BERSERKLY BREAKNECK BANGING, IS SURELY UNDERSTANDABLE, IS IT NOT?
FOR, WHILE THE CAGED DEMONWOLF WAS NOT ACTUALLY PRESENT TO OBSERVE THEIR AGITATEDLY AMOK APHRODISM...
...ANOTHER PRESENCE, MAYHAP EQUALLY DREAD AND EQUALLY FELL, DID SURELY LOOM BY THEIR BEDSIDE.

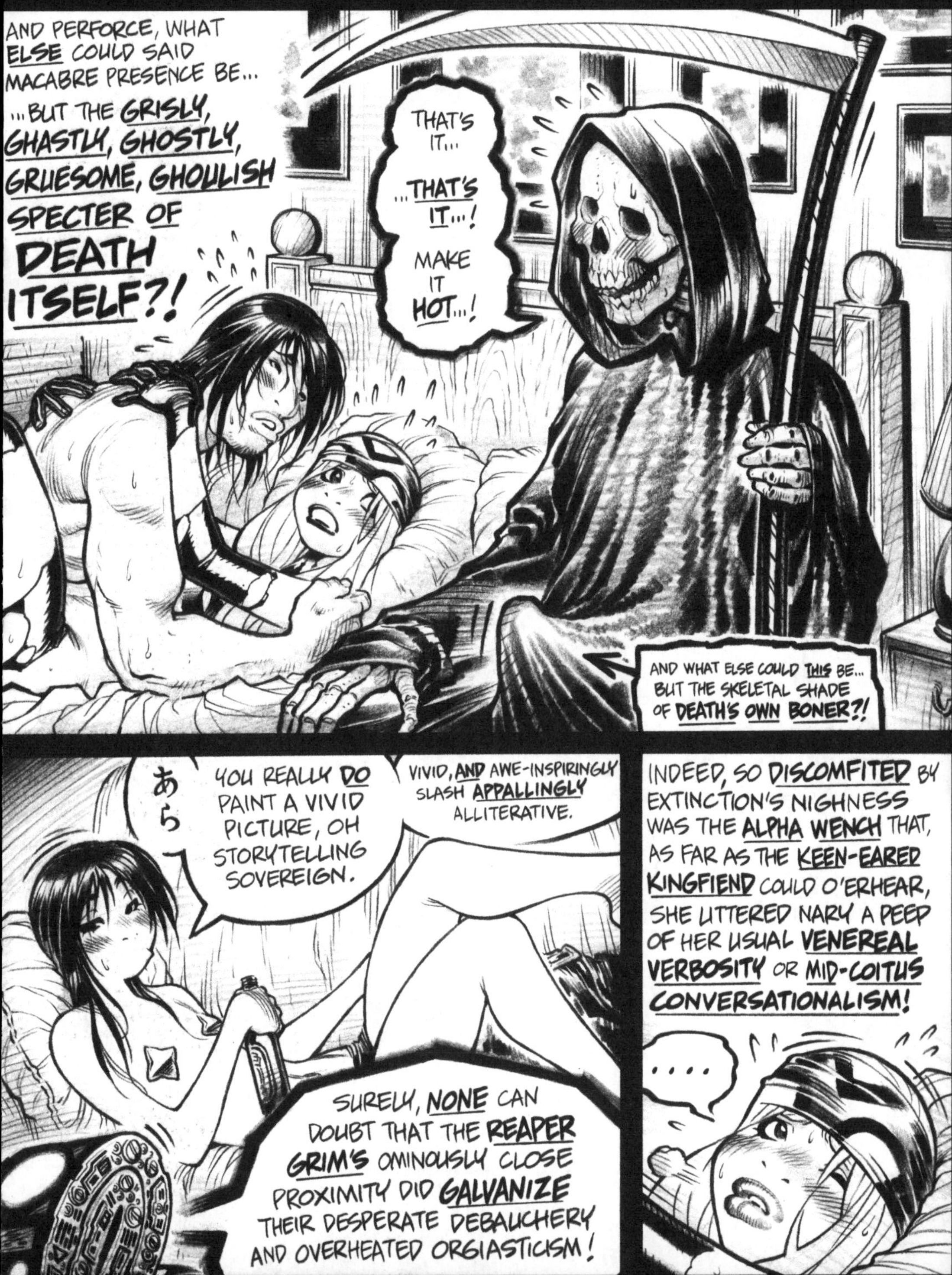
AND PERFORCE, WHAT ELSE COULD SAID MACABRE PRESENCE BE...
...BUT THE GRISLY, GHASTLY, GHOSTLY, GRUESOME, GHOULISH SPECTER OF DEATH ITSELF?!
THAT'S IT...
...THAT'S IT...!
MAKE IT HOT...!
AND WHAT ELSE COULD THIS BE... BUT THE SKELETAL SHADE OF DEATH'S OWN BONER?!
あら
YOU REALLY DO PAINT A VIVID PICTURE, OH STORYTELLING SOVEREIGN.
VIVID, AND AWE-INSPIRINGLY SLASH APPALLINGLY ALLITERATIVE.
SURELY, NONE CAN DOUBT THAT THE REAPER GRIM'S OMINOUSLY CLOSE PROXIMITY DID GALVANIZE THEIR DESPERATE DEBAUCHERY AND OVERHEATED ORGIASTICISM!
INDEED, SO DISCOMFITED BY EXTINCTION'S NIGHNESS WAS THE ALPHA WENCH THAT, AS FAR AS THE KEEN-EARED KINGFIEND COULD O'ERHEAR, SHE UTTERED NARY A PEEP OF HER USUAL VENEREAL VERBOSITY OR MID-COITUS CONVERSATIONALISM!
....

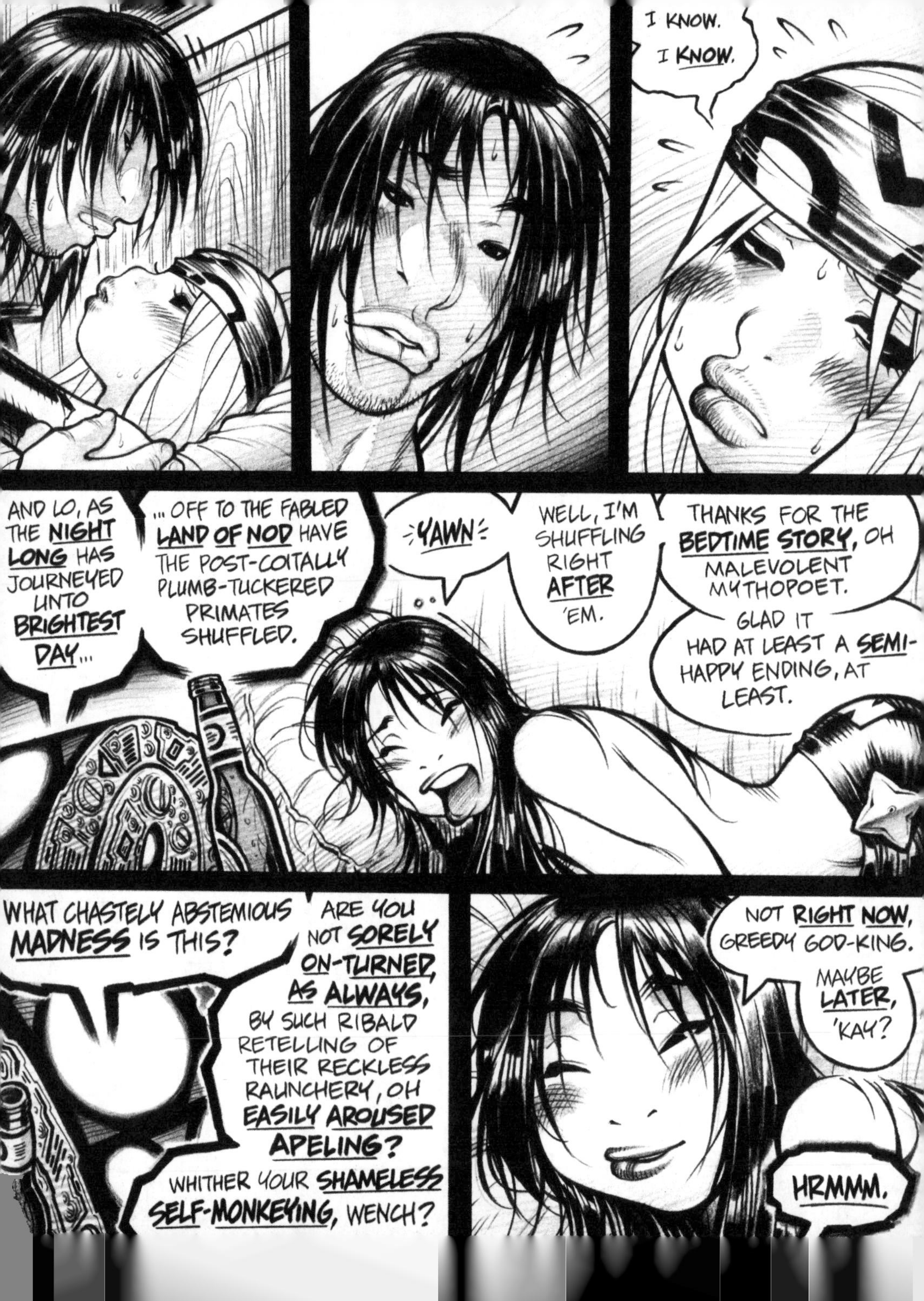

I KNOW.
I KNOW.
AND LO, AS THE NIGHT LONG HAS JOURNEYED UNTO BRIGHTEST DAY...
...OFF TO THE FABLED LAND OF NOD HAVE THE POST-COITALLY PLUMB-TUCKERED PRIMATES SHUFFLED.
YAWN
WELL, I'M SHUFFLING RIGHT AFTER 'EM.
THANKS FOR THE BEDTIME STORY, OH MALEVOLENT MYTHOPOET.
GLAD IT HAD AT LEAST A SEMI-HAPPY ENDING, AT LEAST.
WHAT CHASTELY ABSTEMIOUS MADNESS IS THIS?
ARE YOU NOT SORELY ON-TURNED, AS ALWAYS, BY SUCH RIBALD RETELLING OF THEIR RECKLESS RAUNCHERY, OH EASILY AROUSED APELING?
WHITHER YOUR SHAMELESS SELF-MONKEYING, WENCH?
NOT RIGHT NOW, GREEDY GOD-KING.
MAYBE LATER, 'KAY?
HRMMM.

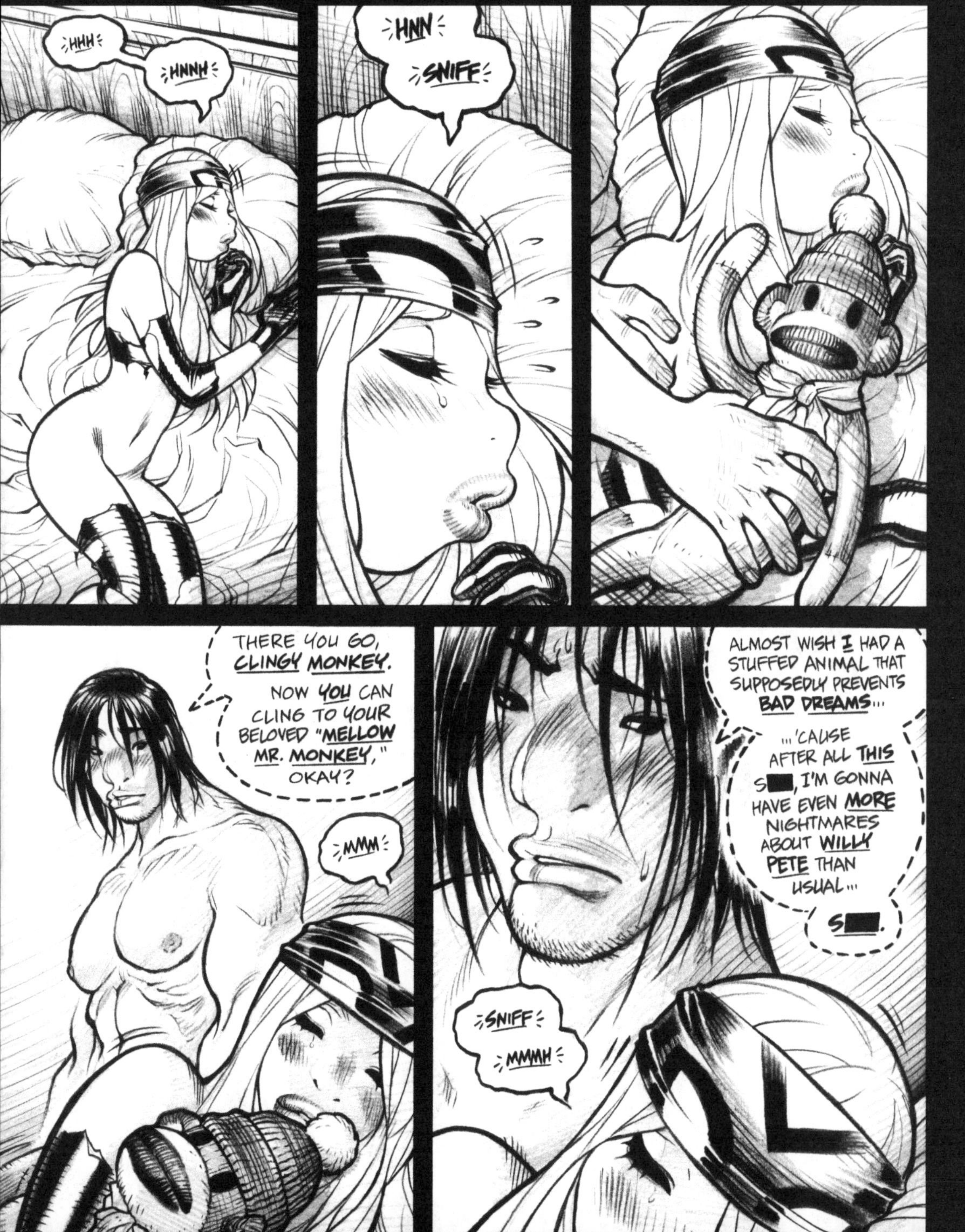
HHH
HNNH
HNN
SNIFF
THERE YOU GO, CLINGY MONKEY.
NOW YOU CAN CLING TO YOUR BELOVED "MELLOW MR. MONKEY," OKAY?
MMM
ALMOST WISH I HAD A STUFFED ANIMAL THAT SUPPOSEDLY PREVENTS BAD DREAMS...
...'CAUSE AFTER ALL THIS S[redacted], I'M GONNA HAVE EVEN MORE NIGHTMARES ABOUT WILLY PETE THAN USUAL...
S[redacted].
SNIFF
MMMH

Empowered

Of Fantasy Points and Aftermathiness

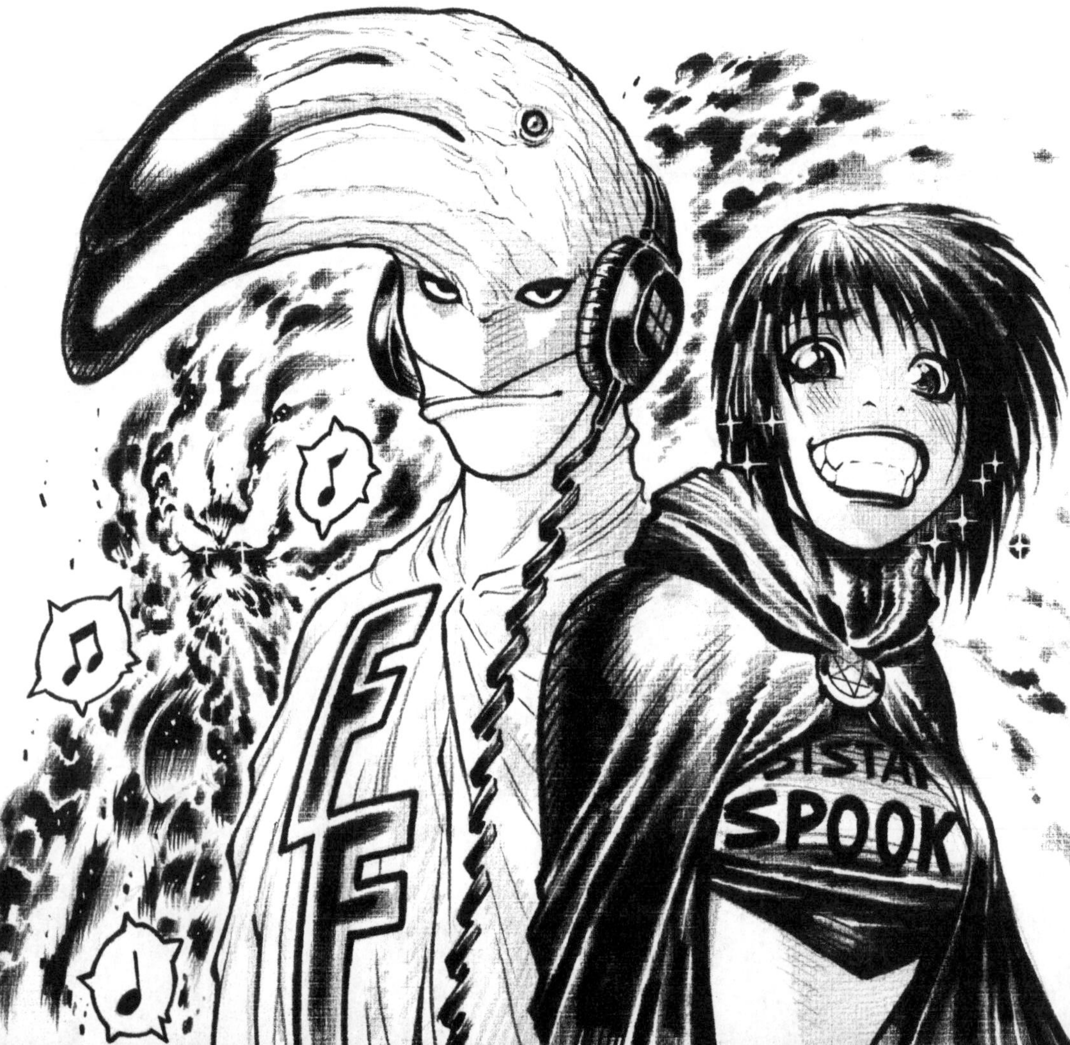
SPOOK

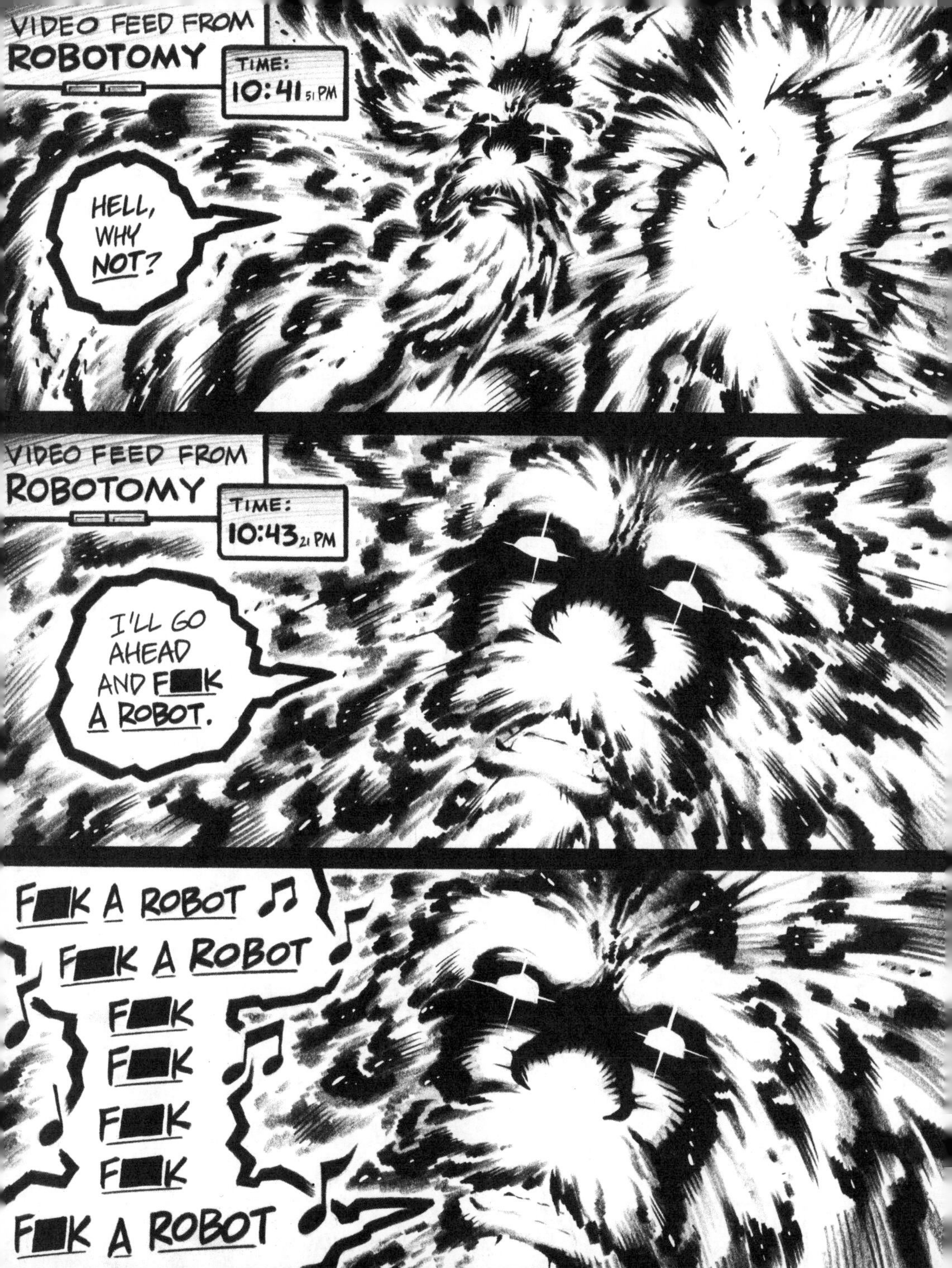
VIDEO FEED FROM ROBOTOMY
TIME: 10:41 51 PM
HELL, WHY NOT?
VIDEO FEED FROM ROBOTOMY
TIME: 10:43 21 PM
I'LL GO AHEAD AND F[redacted]K A ROBOT.
F[redacted]K A ROBOT
F[redacted]K A ROBOT
F[redacted]K
F[redacted]K
F[redacted]K
F[redacted]K
F[redacted]K A ROBOT

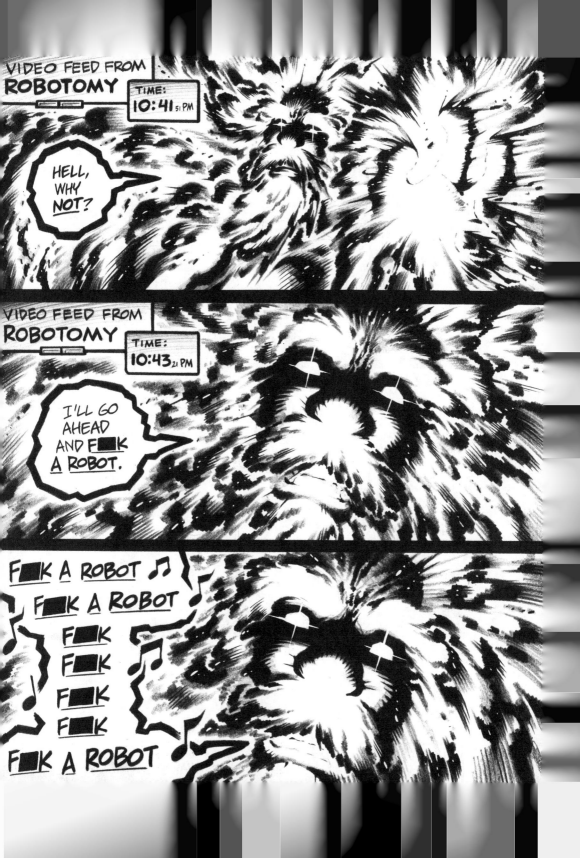

F**K A ROBOT

Willy Pete "Robotf**ka" Remix

00:10

Favorite

AND THAT'S JUST ONE OF **MANY** SUCH GHOULISH VIDEOS THAT HAVE PROLIFERATED ONLINE SINCE **GRISLY FOOTAGE** FROM THE TRAGIC INCIDENT LEAKED OUT EARLIER THIS WEEK.

WHO IS WILLY PETE?

BUT GIVEN THAT **FEW** SUPERVILLAINS, SAVE PERHAPS FOR **DEATHMONGER**, HAVE EVER EXPERIENCED SUCH A DRAMATICALLY SUDDEN, INDEED **EXPLOSIVE**, RISE TO PROMINENCE ON THE SUPRAHUMAN STAGE...

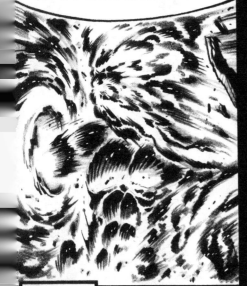

...WE SHOULDN'T BE SURPRISED THAT A PREVIOUSLY **OBSCURE** PYROVILLAIN HAS BECOME SUCH A **CAPE-POP-CULTURE SENSATION** OVERNIGHT.

WE CAN ONLY HOPE THAT **ONE** UNFORTUNATE TREND, THE **TRIVIALIZING OF TRAGEDY**, DOESN'T LEAD TO AN EVEN **WORSE** TREND:

THE **ROMANTICIZING** OF PATHOLOGICAL EVIL.

HERO [NET]

WILLY PETE VAULTS INTO TOP 10 OF RANKED SUPERVILLAINS

ALSO SEIZES #1 RANKING FOR TOP **SUPRAHUMAN FACIAL HAIR**

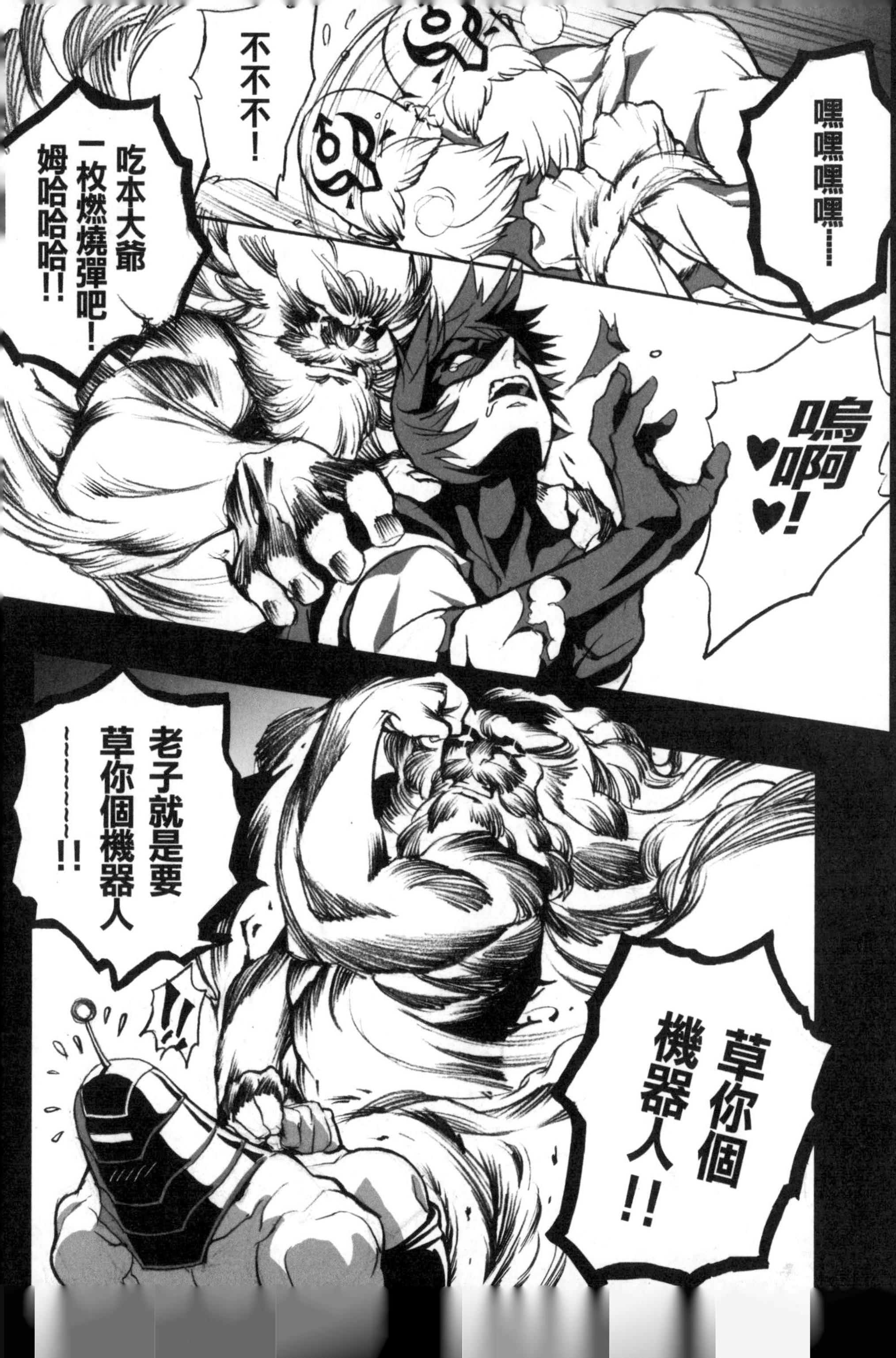

嘿嘿嘿嘿……
不不不不！
吃本大爺一枚燃燒彈吧！姆哈哈哈!!
嗚啊♥♥!
老子就是要草你個機器人~~~~~~!!
草你個機器人!!
!!

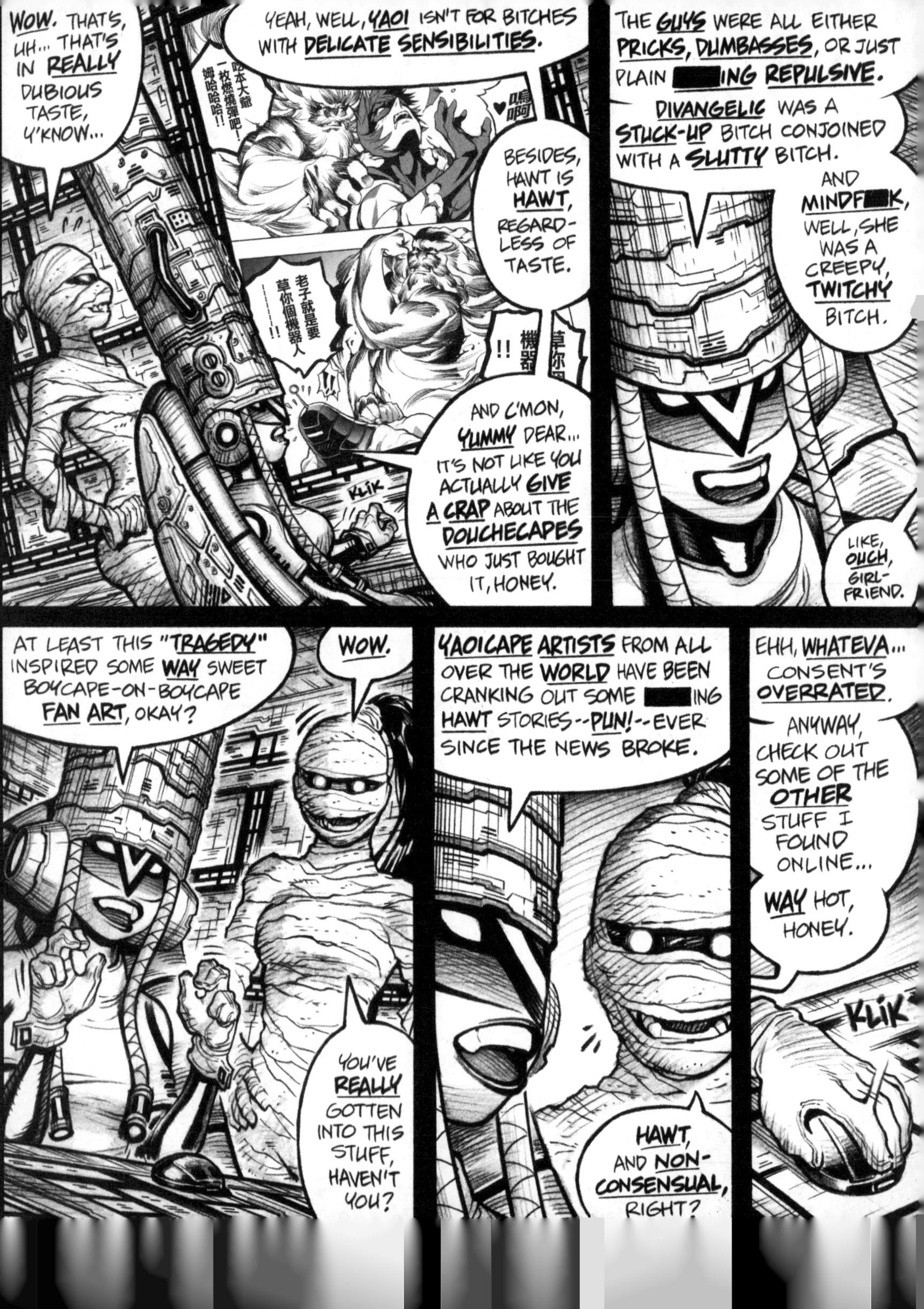
WOW. THAT'S, UH... THAT'S IN REALLY DUBIOUS TASTE, Y'KNOW...
YEAH, WELL, YAOI ISN'T FOR BITCHES WITH DELICATE SENSIBILITIES.
吃本大爺一枚燃燒彈吧!姆哈哈哈!!
嗚啊♥
老子就是要草你個機器人——!!
BESIDES, HAWT IS HAWT, REGARDLESS OF TASTE.
AND C'MON, YUMMY DEAR... IT'S NOT LIKE YOU ACTUALLY GIVE A CRAP ABOUT THE DOUCHECAPES WHO JUST BOUGHT IT, HONEY.
KLIK
THE GUYS WERE ALL EITHER PRICKS, DUMBASSES, OR JUST PLAIN [redacted]ING REPULSIVE.
DIVANGELIC WAS A STUCK-UP BITCH CONJOINED WITH A SLUTTY BITCH.
AND MINDF[redacted]K, WELL, SHE WAS A CREEPY, TWITCHY BITCH.
LIKE, OUCH, GIRL-FRIEND.
AT LEAST THIS "TRAGEDY" INSPIRED SOME WAY SWEET BOYCAPE-ON-BOYCAPE FAN ART, OKAY?
WOW.
YOU'VE REALLY GOTTEN INTO THIS STUFF, HAVEN'T YOU?
YAOICAPE ARTISTS FROM ALL OVER THE WORLD HAVE BEEN CRANKING OUT SOME [redacted]ING HAWT STORIES--PUN!--EVER SINCE THE NEWS BROKE.
HAWT, AND NON-CONSENSUAL, RIGHT?
EHH, WHATEVA... CONSENT'S OVERRATED.
ANYWAY, CHECK OUT SOME OF THE OTHER STUFF I FOUND ONLINE...
WAY HOT, HONEY.
KLIK

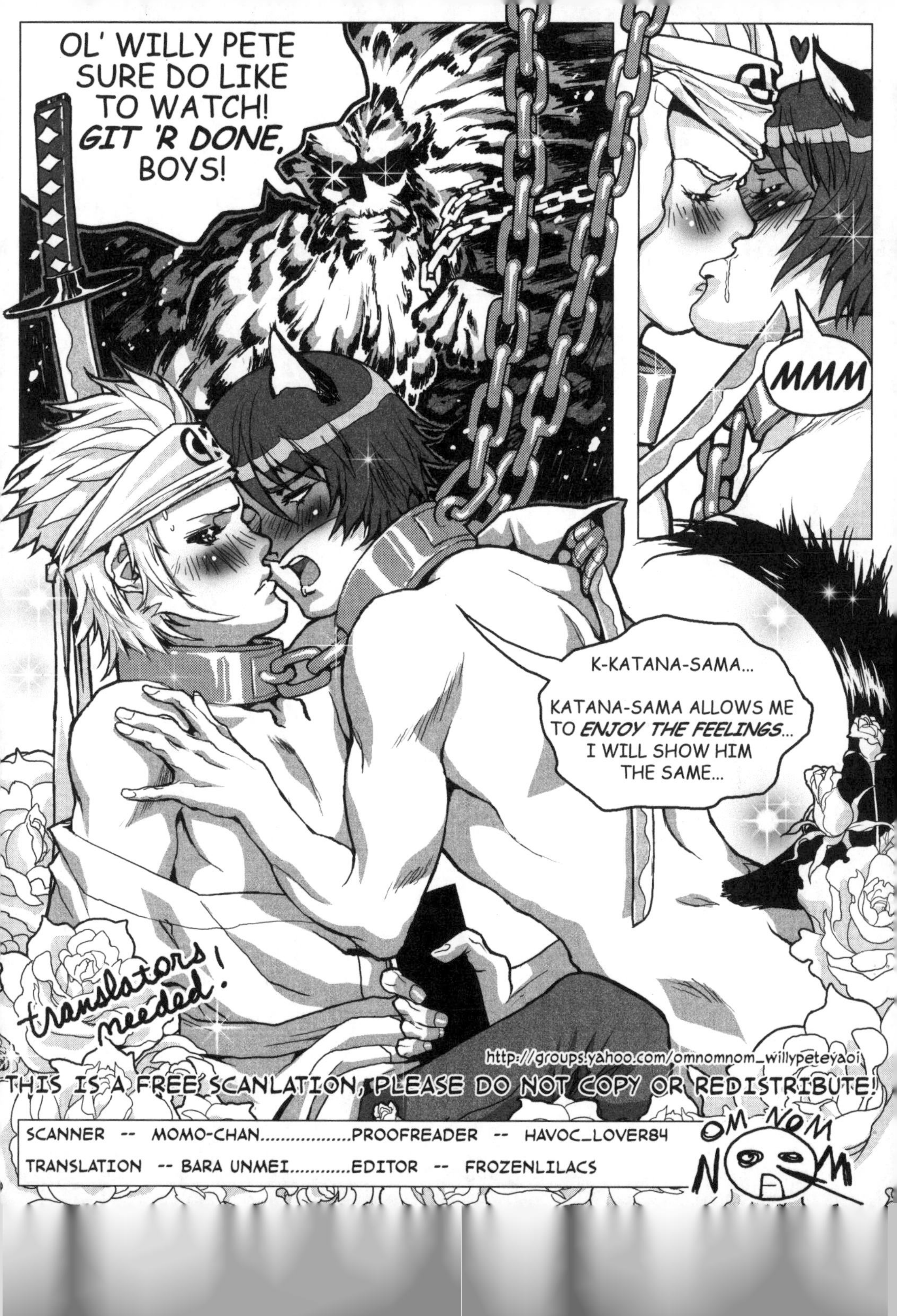
OL' WILLY PETE SURE DO LIKE TO WATCH! GIT 'R DONE, BOYS!
MMM
K-KATANA-SAMA...
KATANA-SAMA ALLOWS ME TO ENJOY THE FEELINGS... I WILL SHOW HIM THE SAME...
translators needed!

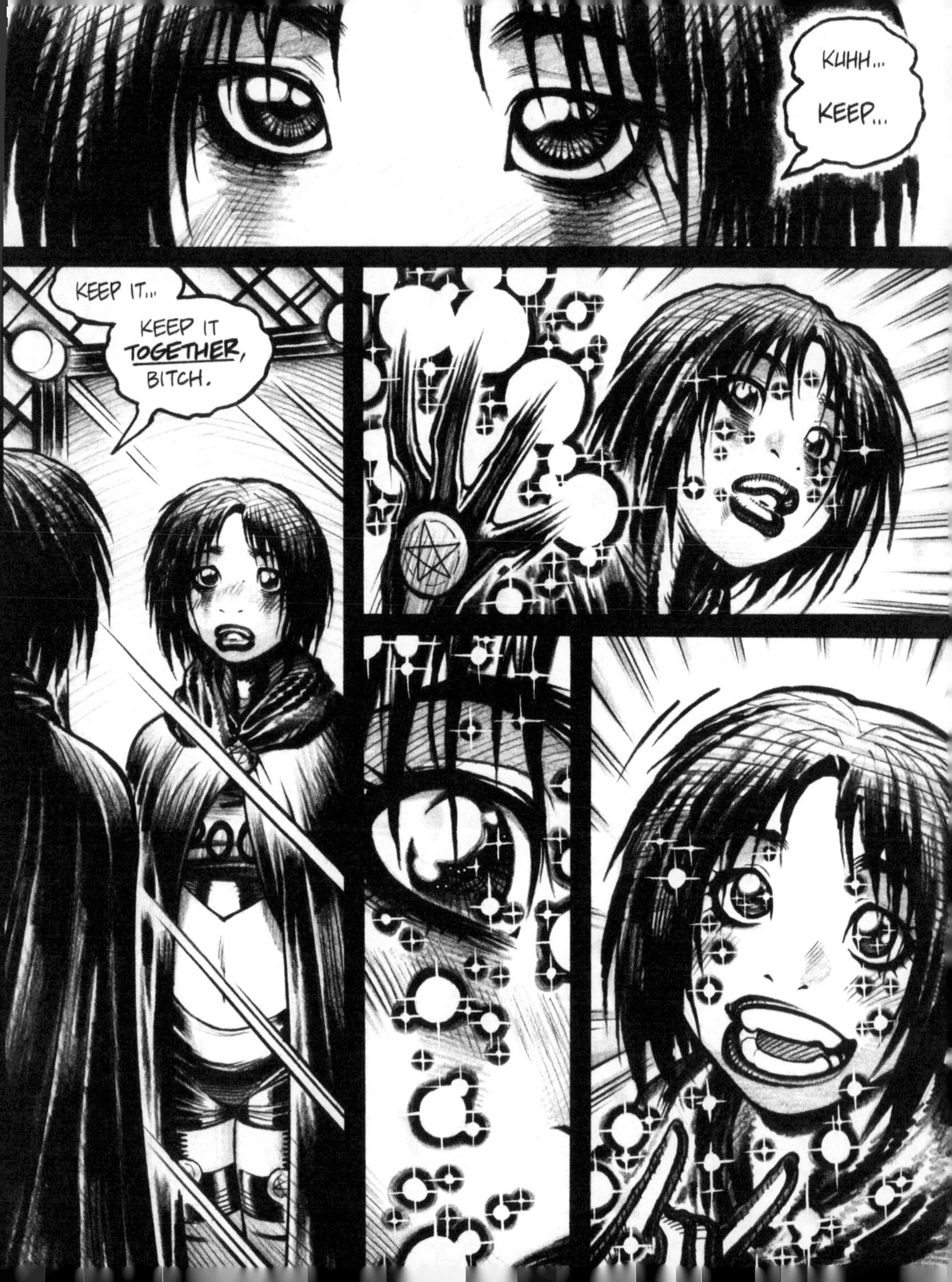
KUHH...
KEEP...
KEEP IT...
KEEP IT TOGETHER, BITCH.

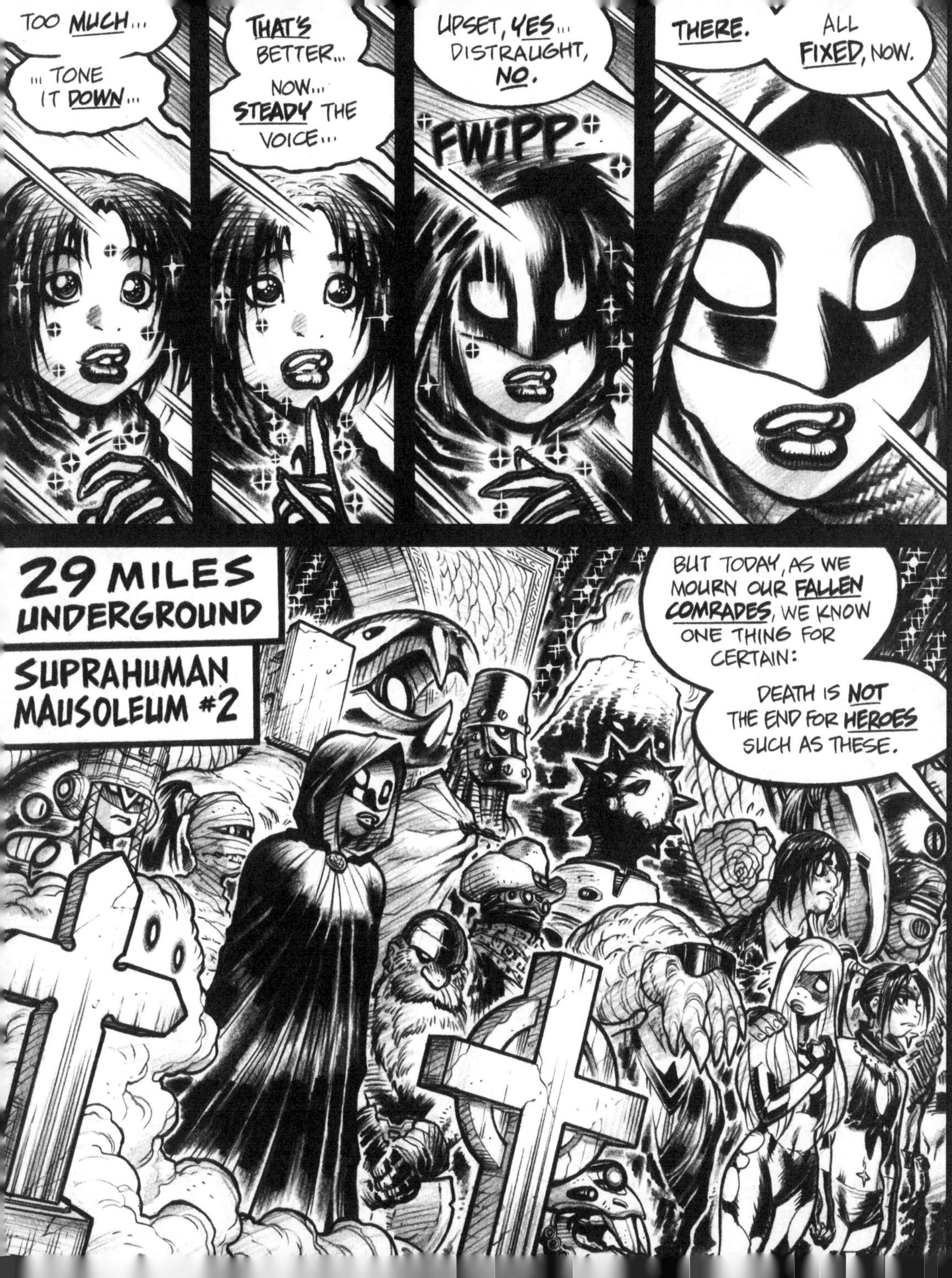TOO MUCH...
... TONE IT DOWN...
THAT'S BETTER...
NOW... STEADY THE VOICE...
UPSET, YES... DISTRAUGHT, NO.
FWIPP
THERE.
ALL FIXED, NOW.
29 MILES UNDERGROUND
SUPRAHUMAN MAUSOLEUM #2
BUT TODAY, AS WE MOURN OUR FALLEN COMRADES, WE KNOW ONE THING FOR CERTAIN:
DEATH IS NOT THE END FOR HEROES SUCH AS THESE.

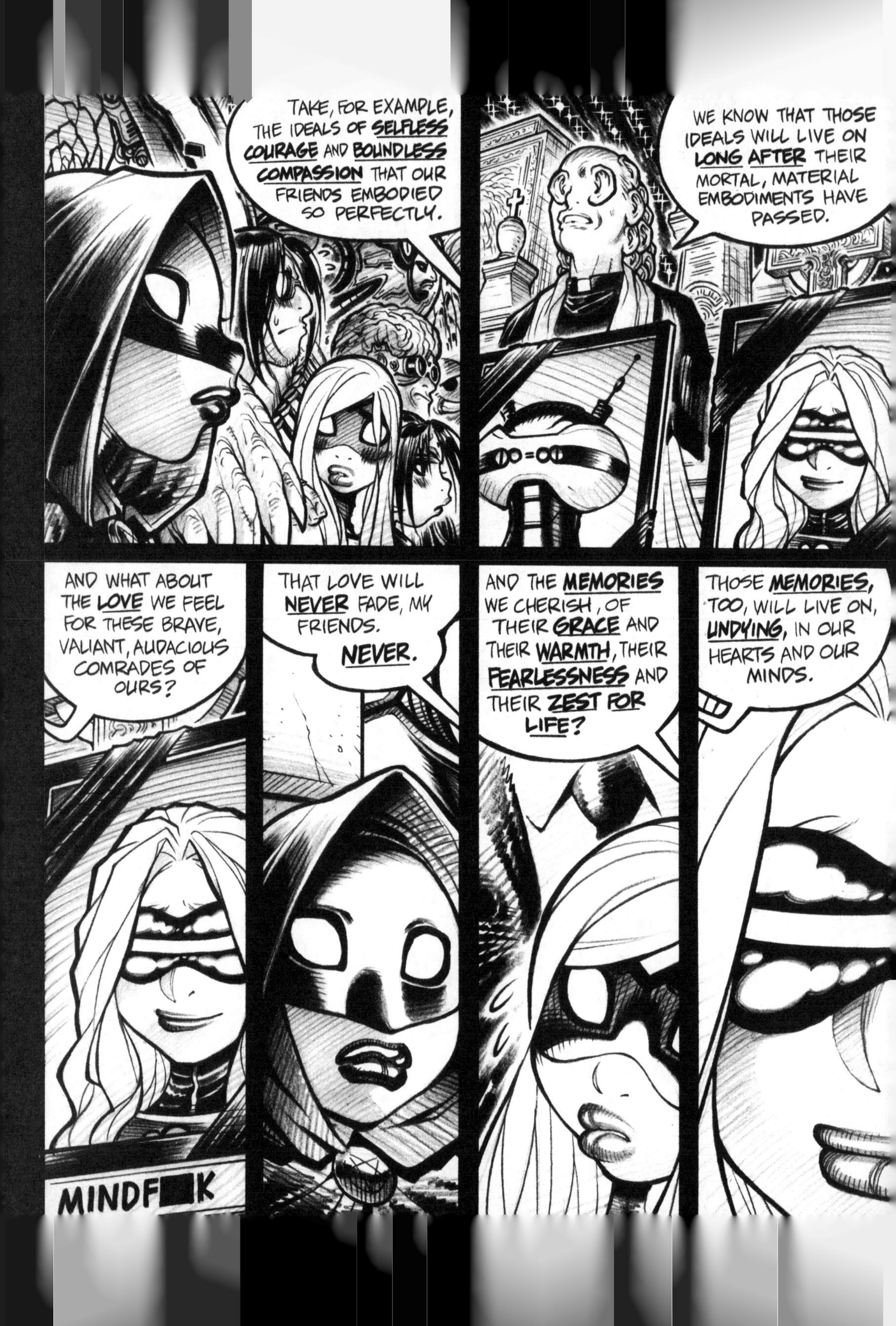
TAKE, FOR EXAMPLE, THE IDEALS OF SELFLESS COURAGE AND BOUNDLESS COMPASSION THAT OUR FRIENDS EMBODIED SO PERFECTLY.
WE KNOW THAT THOSE IDEALS WILL LIVE ON LONG AFTER THEIR MORTAL, MATERIAL EMBODIMENTS HAVE PASSED.
AND WHAT ABOUT THE LOVE WE FEEL FOR THESE BRAVE, VALIANT, AUDACIOUS COMRADES OF OURS?
MINDF[redacted]K
THAT LOVE WILL NEVER FADE, MY FRIENDS.
NEVER.
AND THE MEMORIES WE CHERISH, OF THEIR GRACE AND THEIR WARMTH, THEIR FEARLESSNESS AND THEIR ZEST FOR LIFE?
THOSE MEMORIES, TOO, WILL LIVE ON, UNDYING, IN OUR HEARTS AND OUR MINDS.

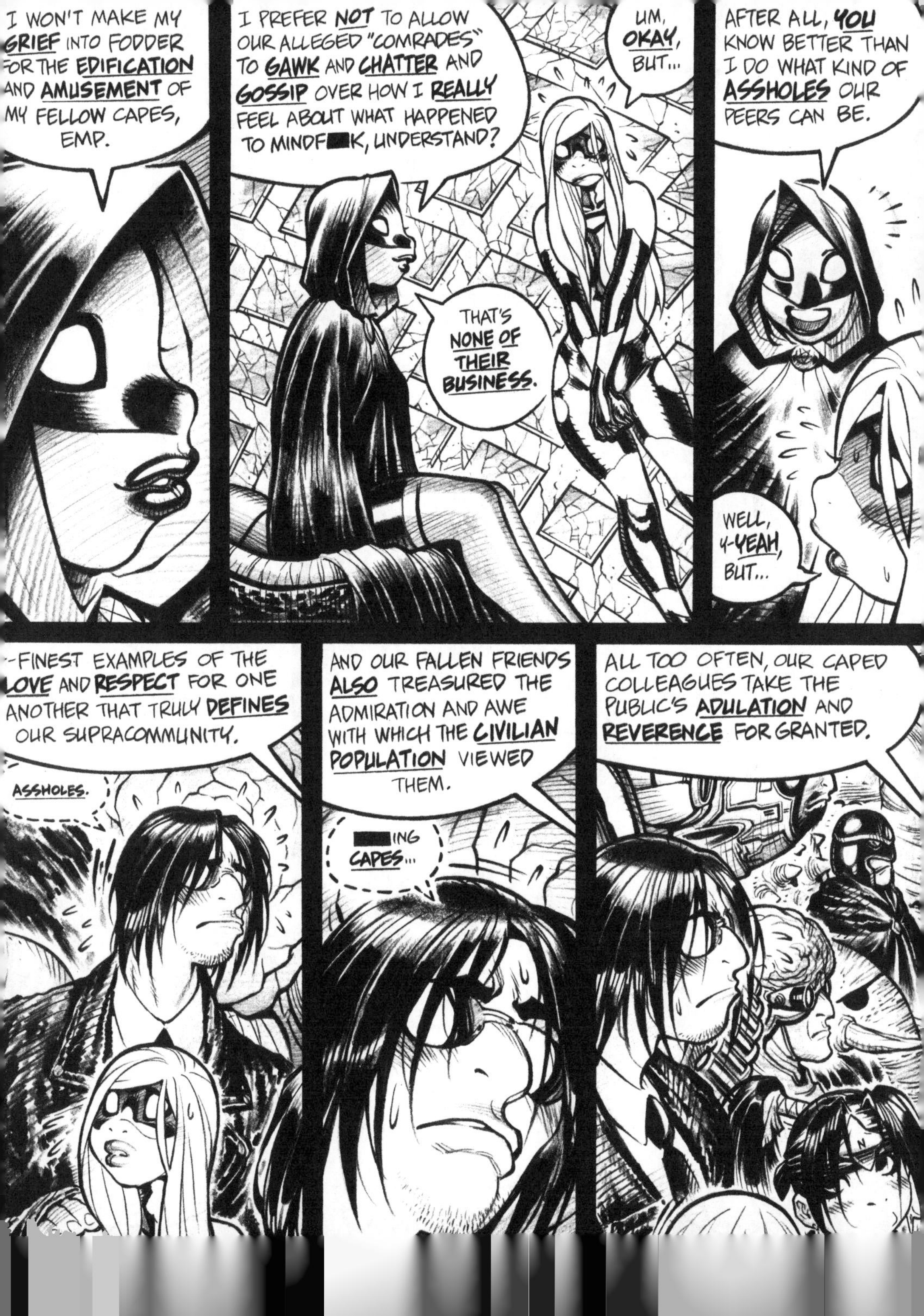
I WON'T MAKE MY GRIEF INTO FODDER FOR THE EDIFICATION AND AMUSEMENT OF MY FELLOW CAPES, EMP.
I PREFER NOT TO ALLOW OUR ALLEGED "COMRADES" TO GAWK AND CHATTER AND GOSSIP OVER HOW I REALLY FEEL ABOUT WHAT HAPPENED TO MINDF[redacted]K, UNDERSTAND?
UM, OKAY, BUT...
THAT'S NONE OF THEIR BUSINESS.
AFTER ALL, YOU KNOW BETTER THAN I DO WHAT KIND OF ASSHOLES OUR PEERS CAN BE.
WELL, Y-YEAH, BUT...
--FINEST EXAMPLES OF THE LOVE AND RESPECT FOR ONE ANOTHER THAT TRULY DEFINES OUR SUPRACOMMUNITY.
ASSHOLES.
AND OUR FALLEN FRIENDS ALSO TREASURED THE ADMIRATION AND AWE WITH WHICH THE CIVILIAN POPULATION VIEWED THEM.
[redacted]ING CAPES...
ALL TOO OFTEN, OUR CAPED COLLEAGUES TAKE THE PUBLIC'S ADULATION AND REVERENCE FOR GRANTED.

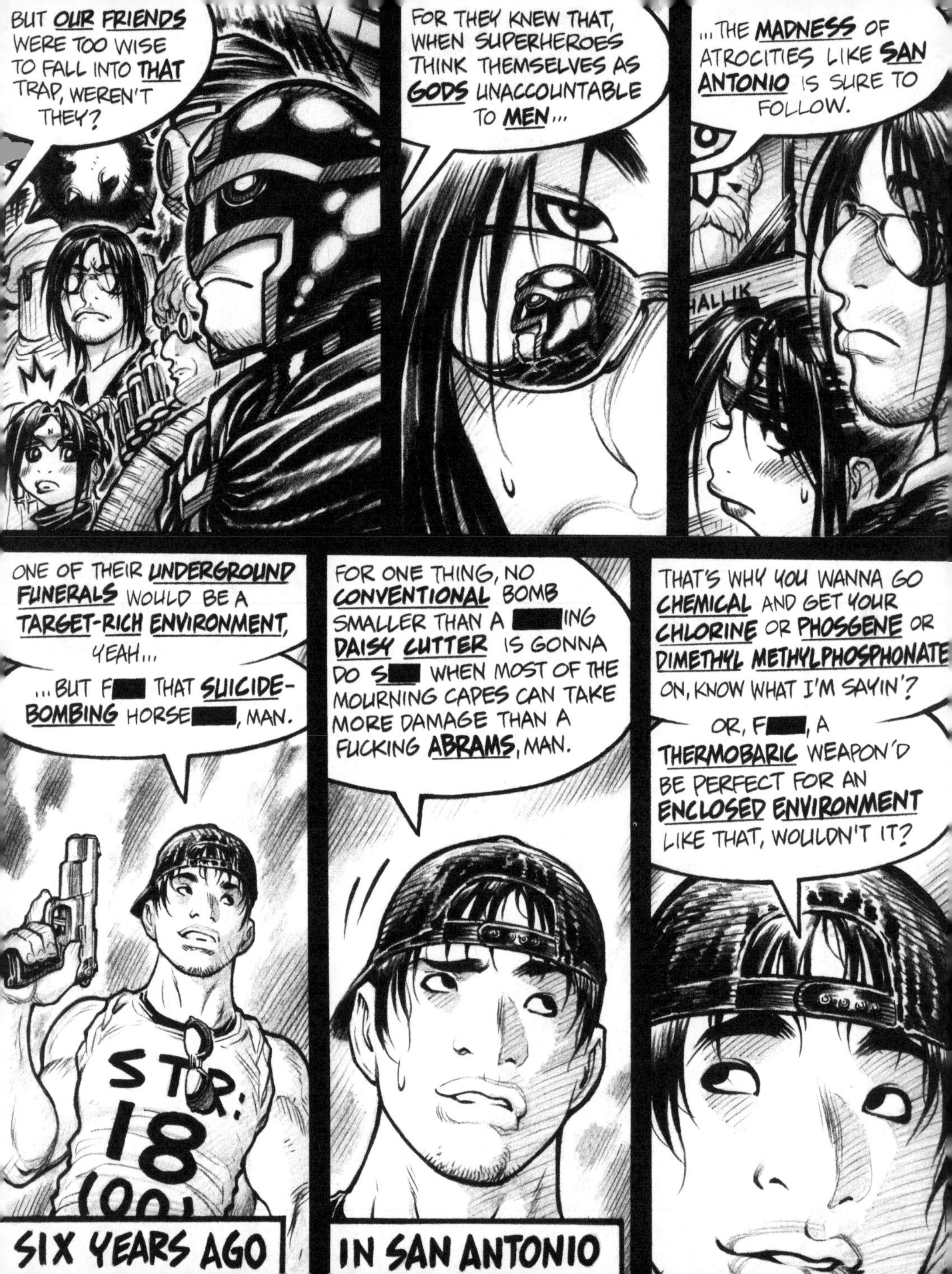
BUT OUR FRIENDS WERE TOO WISE TO FALL INTO THAT TRAP, WEREN'T THEY?
FOR THEY KNEW THAT, WHEN SUPERHEROES THINK THEMSELVES AS GODS UNACCOUNTABLE TO MEN...
...THE MADNESS OF ATROCITIES LIKE SAN ANTONIO IS SURE TO FOLLOW.
HALLIK
ONE OF THEIR UNDERGROUND FUNERALS WOULD BE A TARGET-RICH ENVIRONMENT, YEAH...
...BUT F[redacted] THAT SUICIDE-BOMBING HORSE[redacted], MAN.
STR: 18 (00)
SIX YEARS AGO
FOR ONE THING, NO CONVENTIONAL BOMB SMALLER THAN A [redacted]ING DAISY CUTTER IS GONNA DO S[redacted] WHEN MOST OF THE MOURNING CAPES CAN TAKE MORE DAMAGE THAN A FUCKING ABRAMS, MAN.
IN SAN ANTONIO
THAT'S WHY YOU WANNA GO CHEMICAL AND GET YOUR CHLORINE OR PHOSGENE OR DIMETHYL METHYLPHOSPHONATE ON, KNOW WHAT I'M SAYIN'?
OR, F[redacted], A THERMOBARIC WEAPON'D BE PERFECT FOR AN ENCLOSED ENVIRONMENT LIKE THAT, WOULDN'T IT?

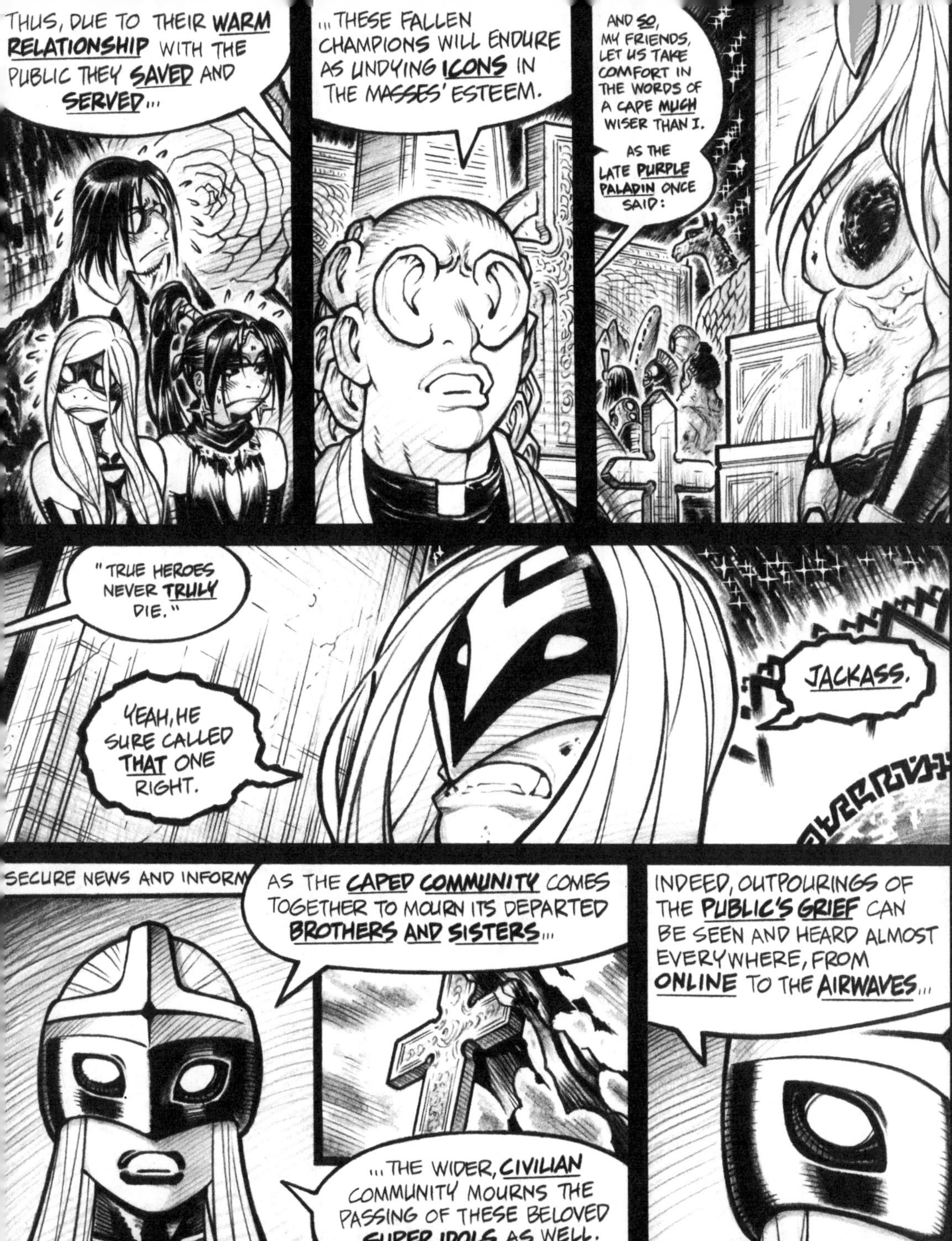
THUS, DUE TO THEIR WARM RELATIONSHIP WITH THE PUBLIC THEY SAVED AND SERVED...
...THESE FALLEN CHAMPIONS WILL ENDURE AS UNDYING ICONS IN THE MASSES' ESTEEM.
AND SO, MY FRIENDS, LET US TAKE COMFORT IN THE WORDS OF A CAPE MUCH WISER THAN I.
AS THE LATE PURPLE PALADIN ONCE SAID:
"TRUE HEROES NEVER TRULY DIE."
YEAH, HE SURE CALLED THAT ONE RIGHT.
JACKASS.
SECURE NEWS AND INFORM
AS THE CAPED COMMUNITY COMES TOGETHER TO MOURN ITS DEPARTED BROTHERS AND SISTERS...
...THE WIDER, CIVILIAN COMMUNITY MOURNS THE PASSING OF THESE BELOVED SUPER IDOLS AS WELL.
INDEED, OUTPOURINGS OF THE PUBLIC'S GRIEF CAN BE SEEN AND HEARD ALMOST EVERYWHERE, FROM ONLINE TO THE AIRWAVES...

LET'S GO TO **DENNIS**, ON LINE 3.

DENNIS?

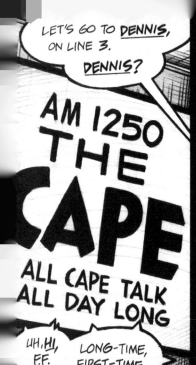

AM 1250 **THE** **CAPE**

ALL CAPE TALK ALL DAY LONG

UH, **HI**, F.F. LONG-TIME, FIRST-TIME.

WHOA. YOU SOUND **DOWN**, SIDEKICK. **SUPER** DOWN.

WELL, **YEAH**, F.F. HOW **ELSE** SHOULD I SOUND, AFTER A **TRAGEDY** LIKE THIS?

I MEAN, **DAMN**, THIS IS HORRENDOUS... THE WORST DISASTER SINCE **PURPLE PALADIN** DIED, AS FAR AS I'M CONCERNED.

AM 1250 THE

WELL, DENNIS, THE **REST** OF TODAY'S CALLERS SURE HAVE **AGREED** WITH YOU.

FEELS LIKE I'M RUNNING A **SUICIDE HOTLINE** TODAY, INSTEAD OF A **CAPE TALK** SHOW...

HEY, **I** SURE AM DEPRESSED, F.F. **BIG-TIME** DEPRESSED.

ROBOTOMY AND **EYE EYE SIR** GETTING KILLED WAS BAD ENOUGH... BUT LOSING **PHALLIK** AND **DIVANGELIC** ON THE SAME DAY?

AM 12

I'M **NEVER** GONNA WIN MY **FANTASY LEAGUE** NOW, WITH HALF MY ROSTER **BURNT TO A CAPED CRISP.**

THIS IS **JUST** LIKE THE YEAR I LOST OUT 'CAUSE THAT JACKASS **PURPLE PALADIN** BOUGHT IT.

TALK ABOUT A DAMN **TRAGEDY**...

MY **CONDOLENCES**, SIDEKICK.

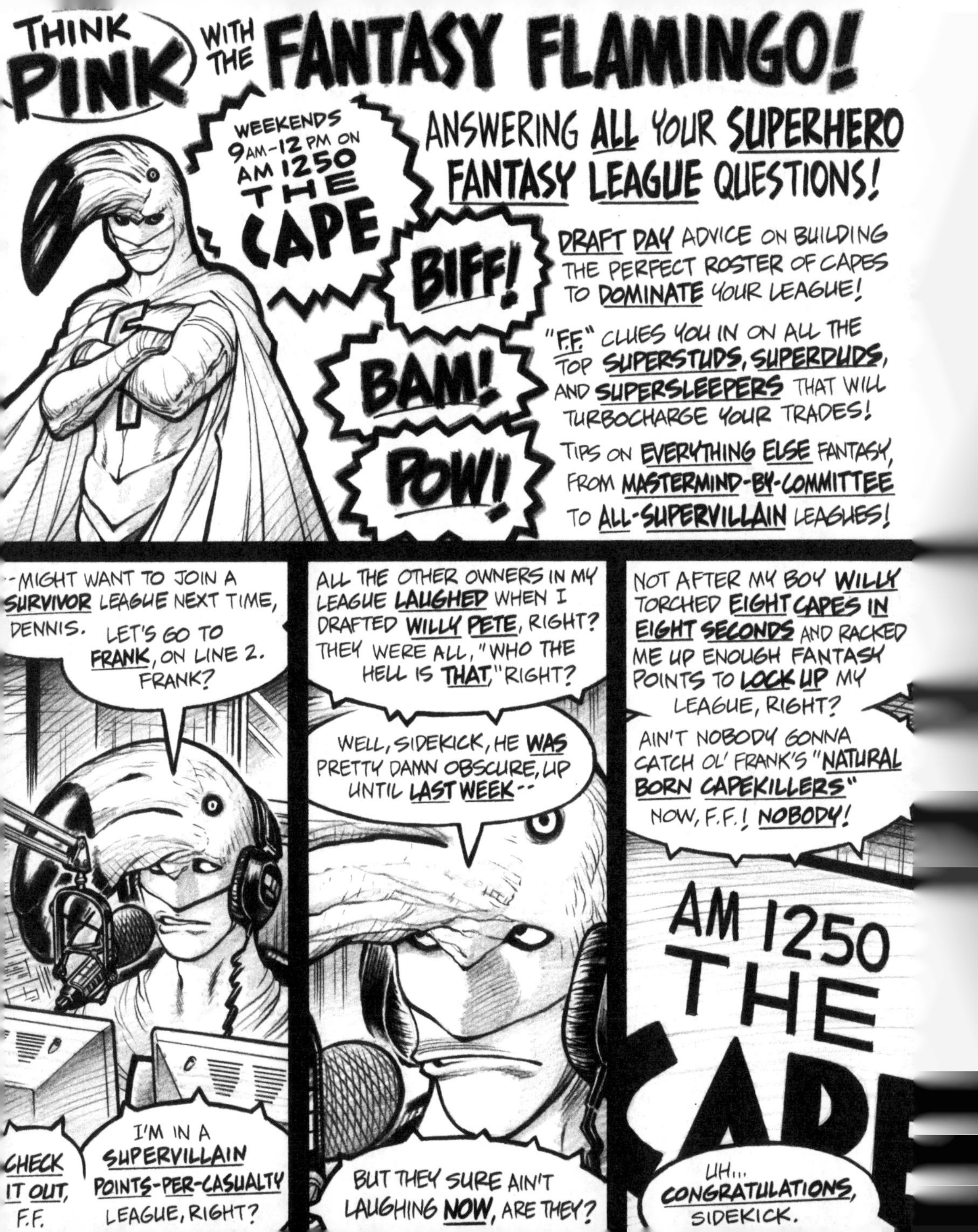

THINK PINK WITH THE FANTASY FLAMINGO!
WEEKENDS 9AM-12 PM ON AM 1250 THE CAPE
ANSWERING ALL YOUR SUPERHERO FANTASY LEAGUE QUESTIONS!
BIFF!
BAM!
POW!
DRAFT DAY ADVICE ON BUILDING THE PERFECT ROSTER OF CAPES TO DOMINATE YOUR LEAGUE!
"F.F." CLUES YOU IN ON ALL THE TOP SUPERSTUDS, SUPERDUDS, AND SUPERSLEEPERS THAT WILL TURBOCHARGE YOUR TRADES!
TIPS ON EVERYTHING ELSE FANTASY, FROM MASTERMIND-BY-COMMITTEE TO ALL-SUPERVILLAIN LEAGUES!
--MIGHT WANT TO JOIN A SURVIVOR LEAGUE NEXT TIME, DENNIS. LET'S GO TO FRANK, ON LINE 2. FRANK?
CHECK IT OUT, F.F.
I'M IN A SUPERVILLAIN POINTS-PER-CASUALTY LEAGUE, RIGHT?
ALL THE OTHER OWNERS IN MY LEAGUE LAUGHED WHEN I DRAFTED WILLY PETE, RIGHT? THEY WERE ALL, "WHO THE HELL IS THAT," RIGHT?
WELL, SIDEKICK, HE WAS PRETTY DAMN OBSCURE, UP UNTIL LAST WEEK--
BUT THEY SURE AIN'T LAUGHING NOW, ARE THEY?
NOT AFTER MY BOY WILLY TORCHED EIGHT CAPES IN EIGHT SECONDS AND RACKED ME UP ENOUGH FANTASY POINTS TO LOCK UP MY LEAGUE, RIGHT?
AIN'T NOBODY GONNA CATCH OL' FRANK'S "NATURAL BORN CAPEKILLERS" NOW, F.F.! NOBODY!
AM 1250 THE
UH... CONGRATULATIONS, SIDEKICK.

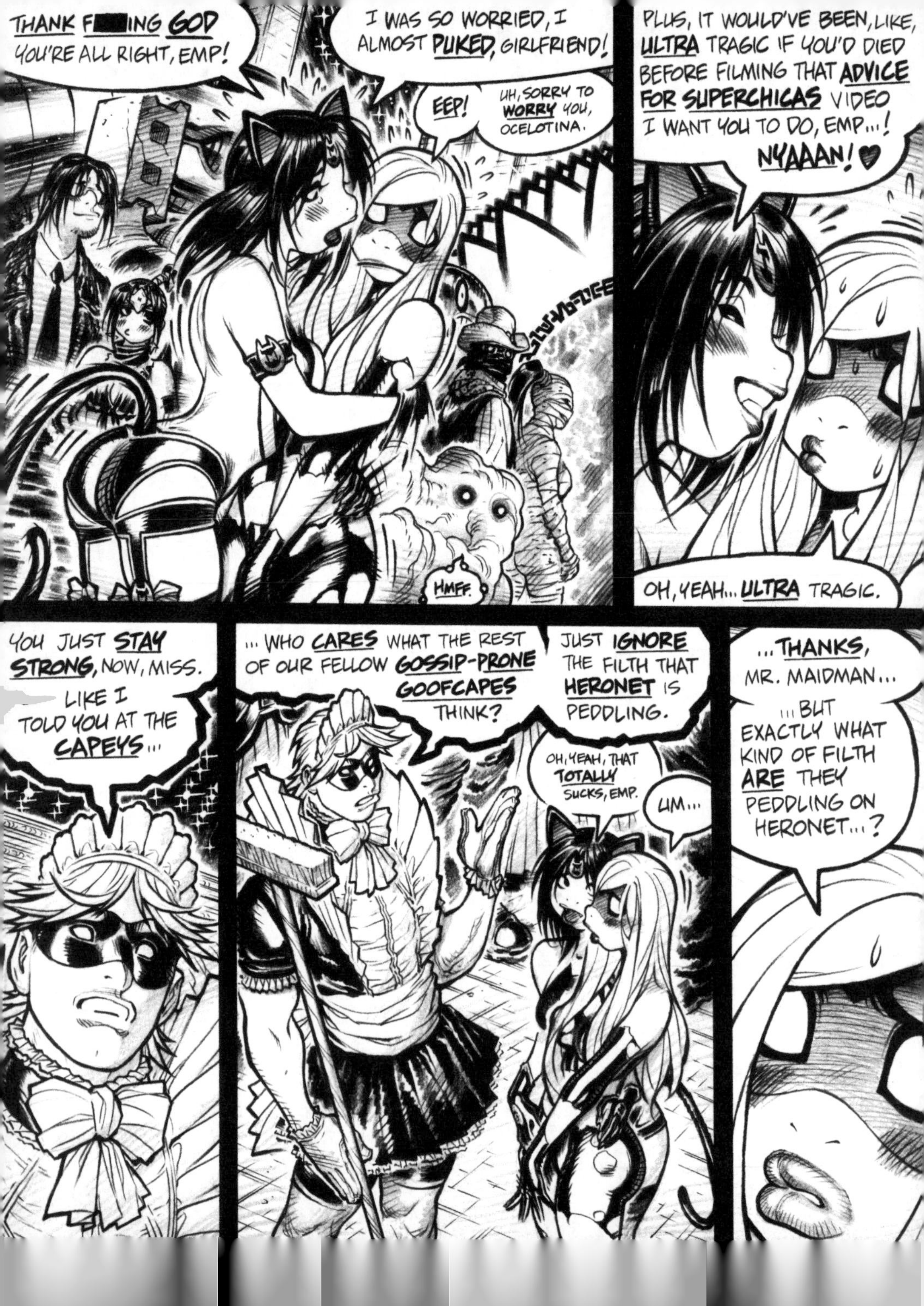

THANK F[redacted]ING GOD YOU'RE ALL RIGHT, EMP!
I WAS SO WORRIED, I ALMOST PUKED, GIRLFRIEND!
EEP!
UH, SORRY TO WORRY YOU, OCELOTINA.
HMFF.
PLUS, IT WOULD'VE BEEN, LIKE, ULTRA TRAGIC IF YOU'D DIED BEFORE FILMING THAT ADVICE FOR SUPERCHICAS VIDEO I WANT YOU TO DO, EMP...! NYAAAN! ♥
OH, YEAH... ULTRA TRAGIC.
YOU JUST STAY STRONG, NOW, MISS.
LIKE I TOLD YOU AT THE CAPEYS...
... WHO CARES WHAT THE REST OF OUR FELLOW GOSSIP-PRONE GOOFCAPES THINK?
JUST IGNORE THE FILTH THAT HERONET IS PEDDLING.
OH, YEAH, THAT TOTALLY SUCKS, EMP.
UM...
... THANKS, MR. MAIDMAN...
... BUT EXACTLY WHAT KIND OF FILTH ARE THEY PEDDLING ON HERONET...?

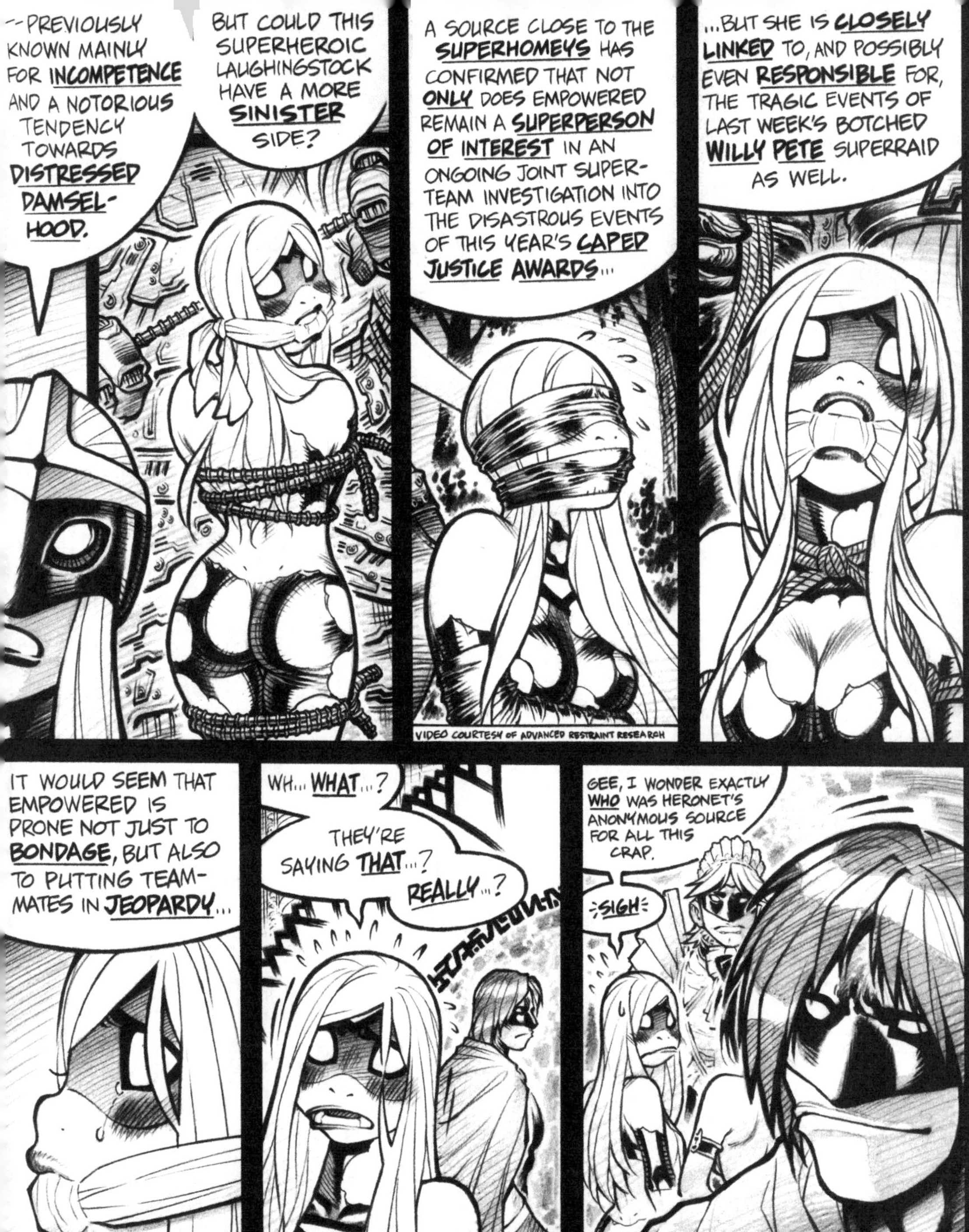
--PREVIOUSLY KNOWN MAINLY FOR INCOMPETENCE AND A NOTORIOUS TENDENCY TOWARDS DISTRESSED DAMSEL-HOOD.
BUT COULD THIS SUPERHEROIC LAUGHINGSTOCK HAVE A MORE SINISTER SIDE?
A SOURCE CLOSE TO THE SUPERHOMEYS HAS CONFIRMED THAT NOT ONLY DOES EMPOWERED REMAIN A SUPERPERSON OF INTEREST IN AN ONGOING JOINT SUPER-TEAM INVESTIGATION INTO THE DISASTROUS EVENTS OF THIS YEAR'S CAPED JUSTICE AWARDS...
VIDEO COURTESY OF ADVANCED RESTRAINT RESEARCH
...BUT SHE IS CLOSELY LINKED TO, AND POSSIBLY EVEN RESPONSIBLE FOR, THE TRAGIC EVENTS OF LAST WEEK'S BOTCHED WILLY PETE SUPERRAID AS WELL.
IT WOULD SEEM THAT EMPOWERED IS PRONE NOT JUST TO BONDAGE, BUT ALSO TO PUTTING TEAM-MATES IN JEOPARDY...
WH... WHAT...?
THEY'RE SAYING THAT...?
REALLY...?
GEE, I WONDER EXACTLY WHO WAS HERONET'S ANONYMOUS SOURCE FOR ALL THIS CRAP.
SIGH

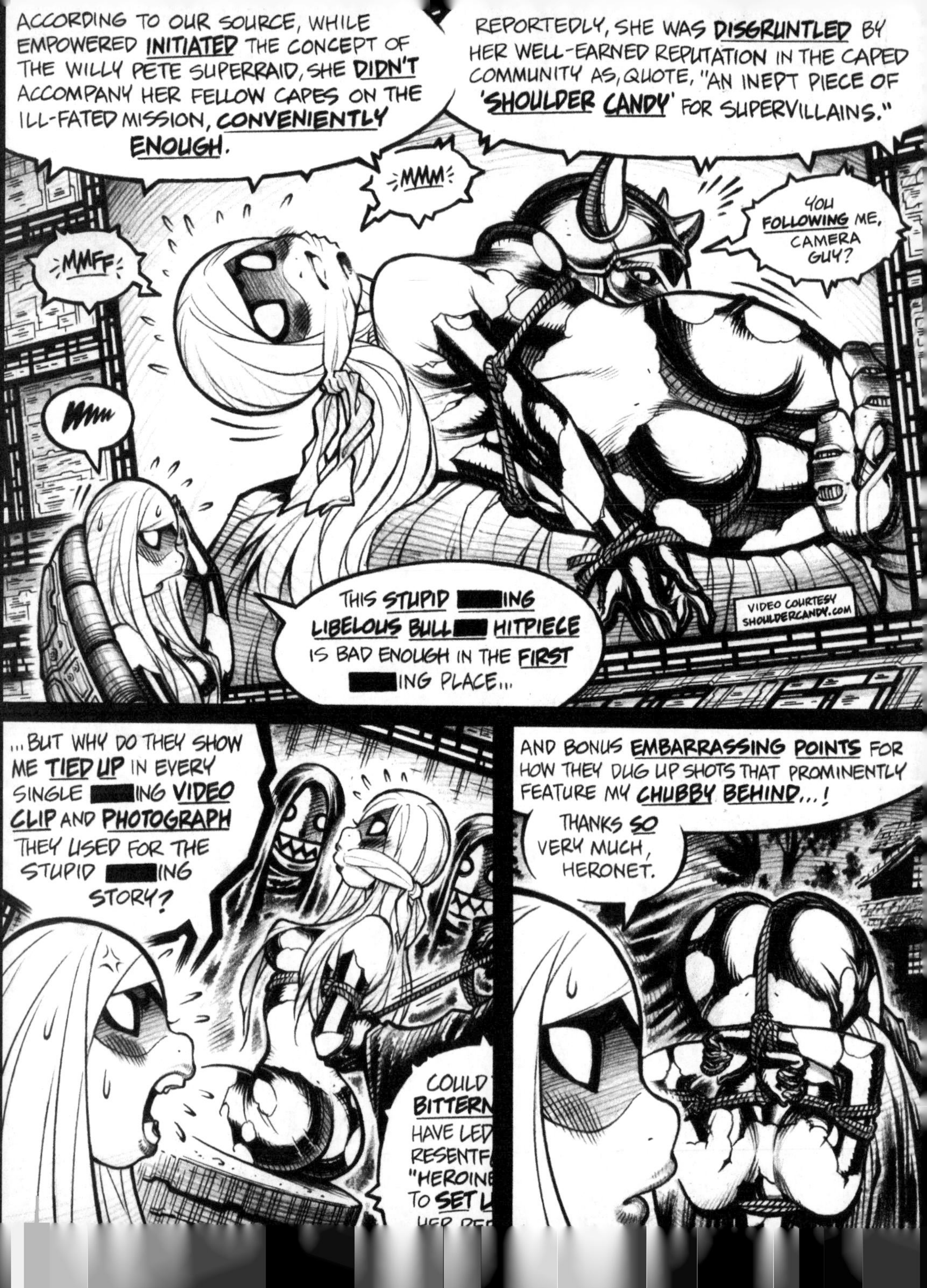
ACCORDING TO OUR SOURCE, WHILE EMPOWERED INITIATED THE CONCEPT OF THE WILLY PETE SUPERRAID, SHE DIDN'T ACCOMPANY HER FELLOW CAPES ON THE ILL-FATED MISSION, CONVENIENTLY ENOUGH.
REPORTEDLY, SHE WAS DISGRUNTLED BY HER WELL-EARNED REPUTATION IN THE CAPED COMMUNITY AS, QUOTE, "AN INEPT PIECE OF 'SHOULDER CANDY' FOR SUPERVILLAINS."
MMM
MMFF
YOU FOLLOWING ME, CAMERA GUY?
MMM
THIS STUPID [redacted]ING LIBELOUS BULL[redacted]HITPIECE IS BAD ENOUGH IN THE FIRST [redacted]ING PLACE...
VIDEO COURTESY SHOULDERCANDY.COM
...BUT WHY DO THEY SHOW ME TIED UP IN EVERY SINGLE [redacted]ING VIDEO CLIP AND PHOTOGRAPH THEY USED FOR THE STUPID [redacted]ING STORY?
COULD
BITTERN
HAVE LED
RESENTF
"HEROINE
TO SET
AND BONUS EMBARRASSING POINTS FOR HOW THEY DUG UP SHOTS THAT PROMINENTLY FEATURE MY CHUBBY BEHIND...!
THANKS SO VERY MUCH, HERONET.

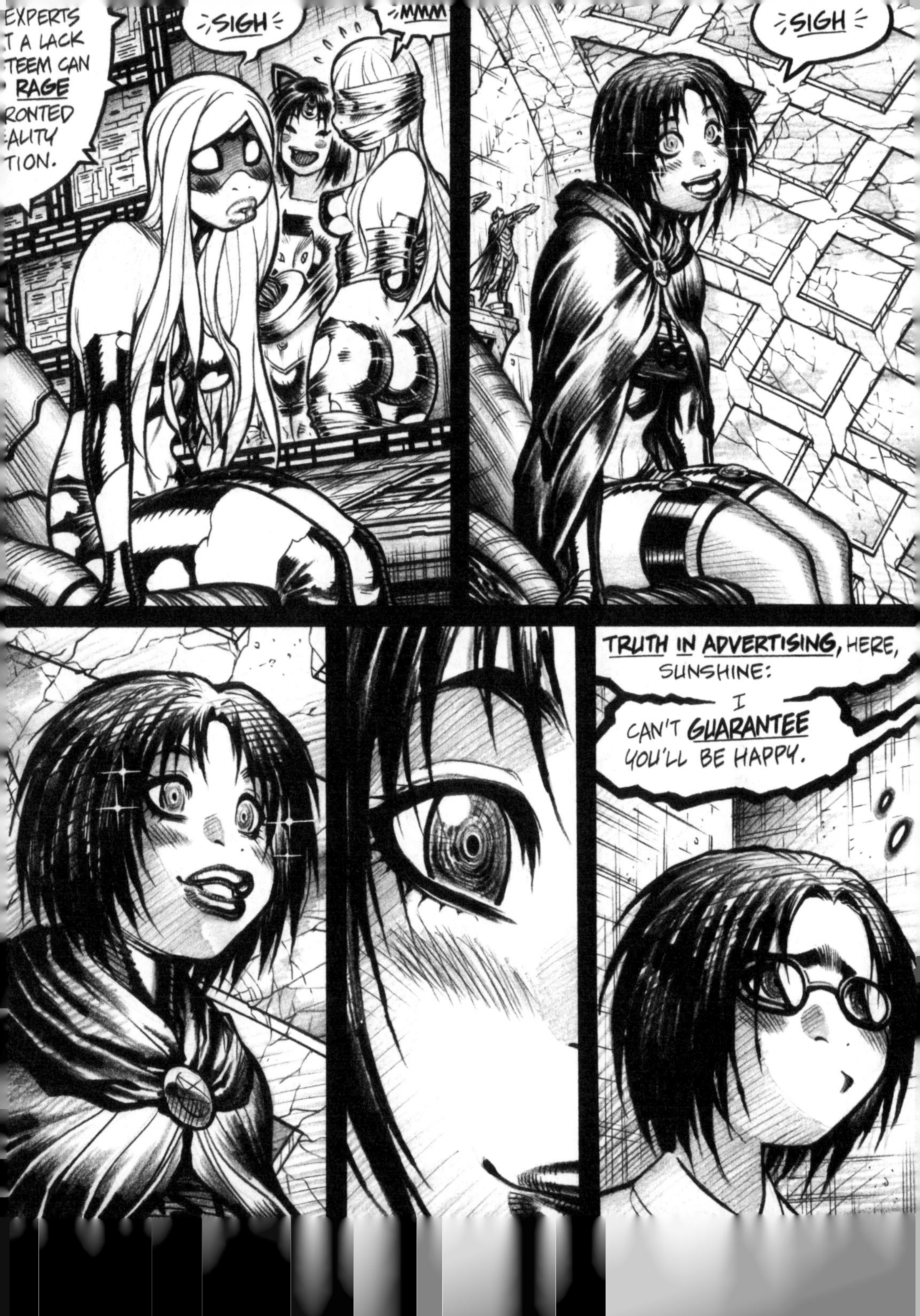
EXPERTS
T A LACK
TEEM CAN
RAGE
RONTED
ALITY
TION.
SIGH
MMM
SIGH
TRUTH IN ADVERTISING, HERE, SUNSHINE:
I CAN'T GUARANTEE YOU'LL BE HAPPY.

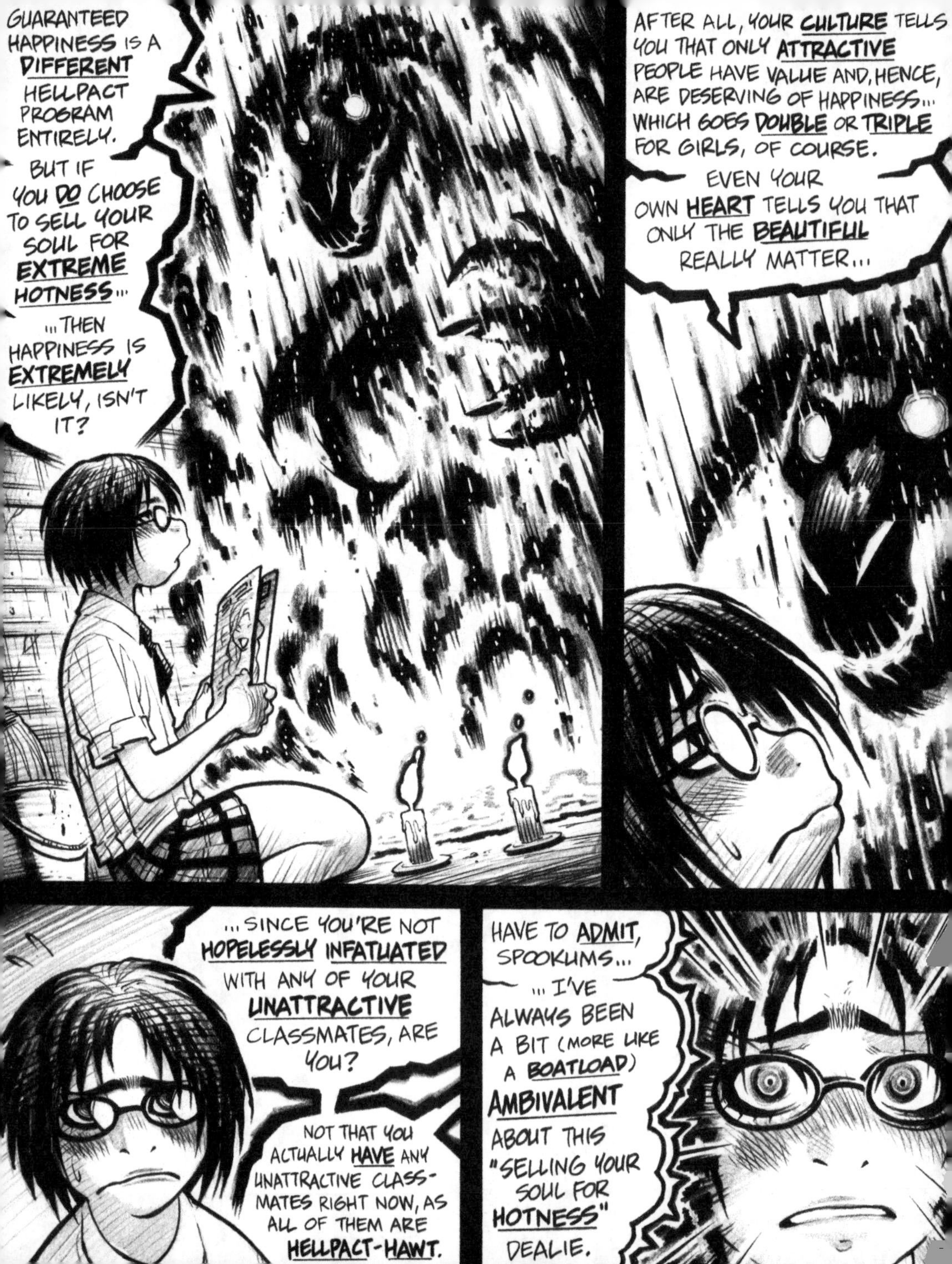
GUARANTEED HAPPINESS IS A DIFFERENT HELLPACT PROGRAM ENTIRELY.
BUT IF YOU DO CHOOSE TO SELL YOUR SOUL FOR EXTREME HOTNESS...
...THEN HAPPINESS IS EXTREMELY LIKELY, ISN'T IT?
AFTER ALL, YOUR CULTURE TELLS YOU THAT ONLY ATTRACTIVE PEOPLE HAVE VALUE AND, HENCE, ARE DESERVING OF HAPPINESS... WHICH GOES DOUBLE OR TRIPLE FOR GIRLS, OF COURSE.
EVEN YOUR OWN HEART TELLS YOU THAT ONLY THE BEAUTIFUL REALLY MATTER...
...SINCE YOU'RE NOT HOPELESSLY INFATUATED WITH ANY OF YOUR UNATTRACTIVE CLASSMATES, ARE YOU?
NOT THAT YOU ACTUALLY HAVE ANY UNATTRACTIVE CLASS-MATES RIGHT NOW, AS ALL OF THEM ARE HELLPACT-HAWT.
HAVE TO ADMIT, SPOOKUMS...
...I'VE ALWAYS BEEN A BIT (MORE LIKE A BOATLOAD) AMBIVALENT ABOUT THIS "SELLING YOUR SOUL FOR HOTNESS" DEALIE.

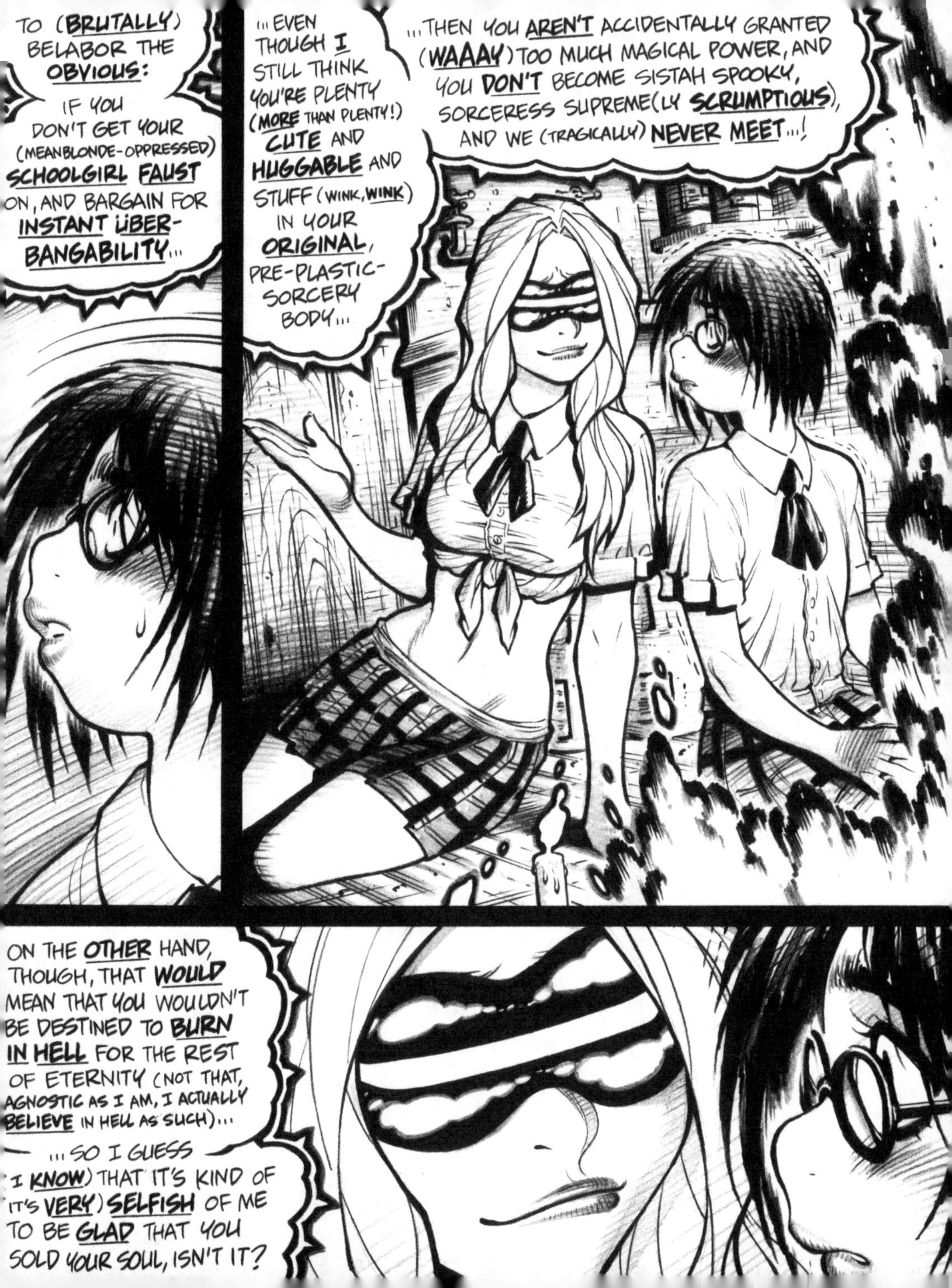

TO (BRUTALLY) BELABOR THE OBVIOUS: IF YOU DON'T GET YOUR (MEANBLONDE-OPPRESSED) SCHOOLGIRL FAUST ON, AND BARGAIN FOR INSTANT ÜBER-BANGABILITY...
...EVEN THOUGH I STILL THINK YOU'RE PLENTY (MORE THAN PLENTY!) CUTE AND HUGGABLE AND STUFF (WINK, WINK) IN YOUR ORIGINAL, PRE-PLASTIC-SORCERY BODY...
...THEN YOU AREN'T ACCIDENTALLY GRANTED (WAAAY) TOO MUCH MAGICAL POWER, AND YOU DON'T BECOME SISTAH SPOOKY, SORCERESS SUPREME(LY SCRUMPTIOUS), AND WE (TRAGICALLY) NEVER MEET...!
ON THE OTHER HAND, THOUGH, THAT WOULD MEAN THAT YOU WOULDN'T BE DESTINED TO BURN IN HELL FOR THE REST OF ETERNITY (NOT THAT, AGNOSTIC AS I AM, I ACTUALLY BELIEVE IN HELL AS SUCH)...
...SO I GUESS (I KNOW) THAT IT'S KIND OF (IT'S VERY) SELFISH OF ME TO BE GLAD THAT YOU SOLD YOUR SOUL, ISN'T IT?

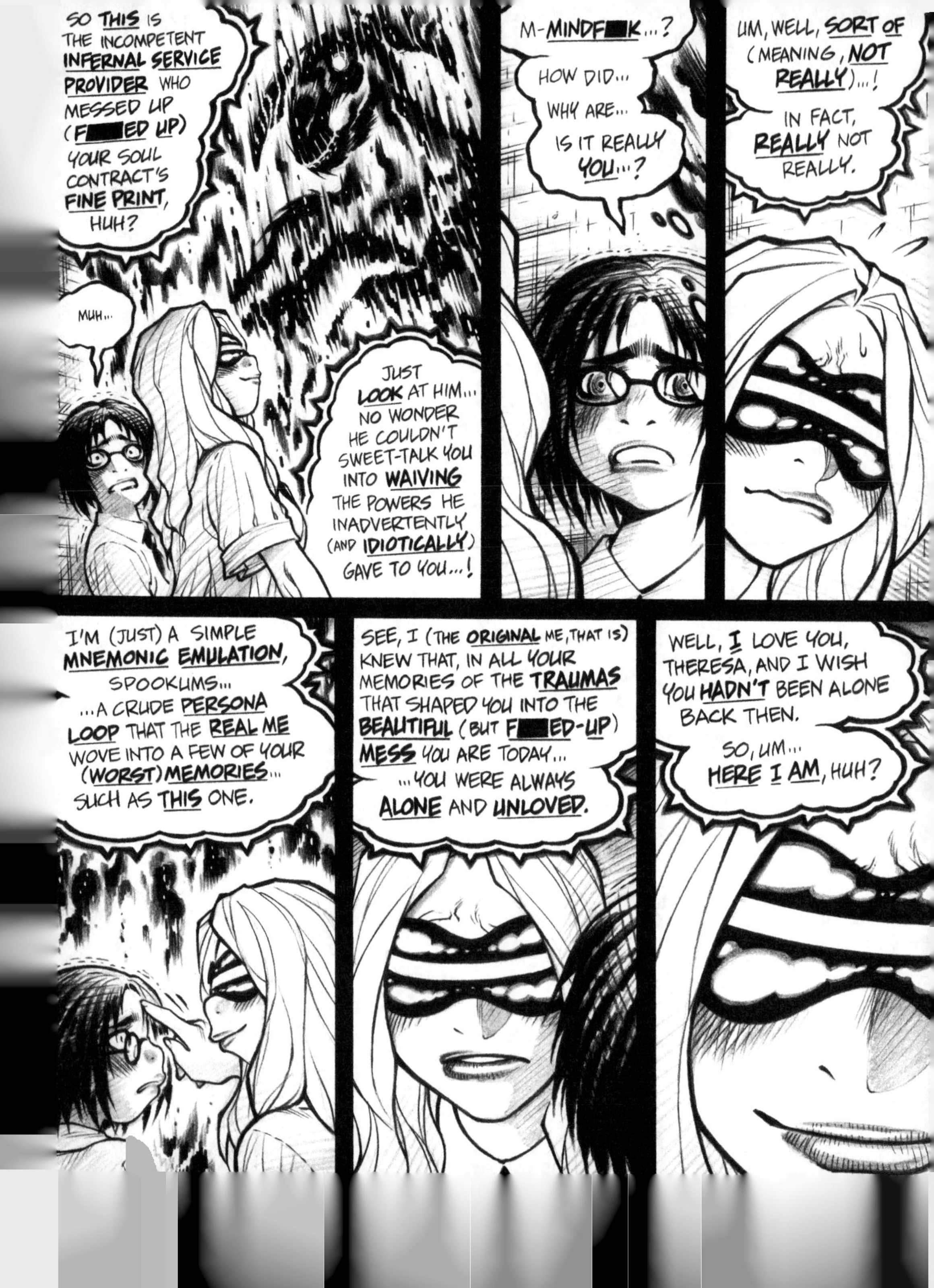
SO THIS IS THE INCOMPETENT INFERNAL SERVICE PROVIDER WHO MESSED UP (F[redacted]ED UP) YOUR SOUL CONTRACT'S FINE PRINT, HUH?
MUH...
JUST LOOK AT HIM... NO WONDER HE COULDN'T SWEET-TALK YOU INTO WAIVING THE POWERS HE INADVERTENTLY (AND IDIOTICALLY) GAVE TO YOU...!
M-MINDF[redacted]K...?
HOW DID... WHY ARE... IS IT REALLY YOU...?
UM, WELL, SORT OF (MEANING, NOT REALLY)...!
IN FACT, REALLY NOT REALLY.
I'M (JUST) A SIMPLE MNEMONIC EMULATION, SPOOKUMS...
...A CRUDE PERSONA LOOP THAT THE REAL ME WOVE INTO A FEW OF YOUR (WORST) MEMORIES... SUCH AS THIS ONE.
SEE, I (THE ORIGINAL ME, THAT IS) KNEW THAT, IN ALL YOUR MEMORIES OF THE TRAUMAS THAT SHAPED YOU INTO THE BEAUTIFUL (BUT F[redacted]ED-UP) MESS YOU ARE TODAY...
...YOU WERE ALWAYS ALONE AND UNLOVED.
WELL, I LOVE YOU, THERESA, AND I WISH YOU HADN'T BEEN ALONE BACK THEN.
SO, UM... HERE I AM, HUH?

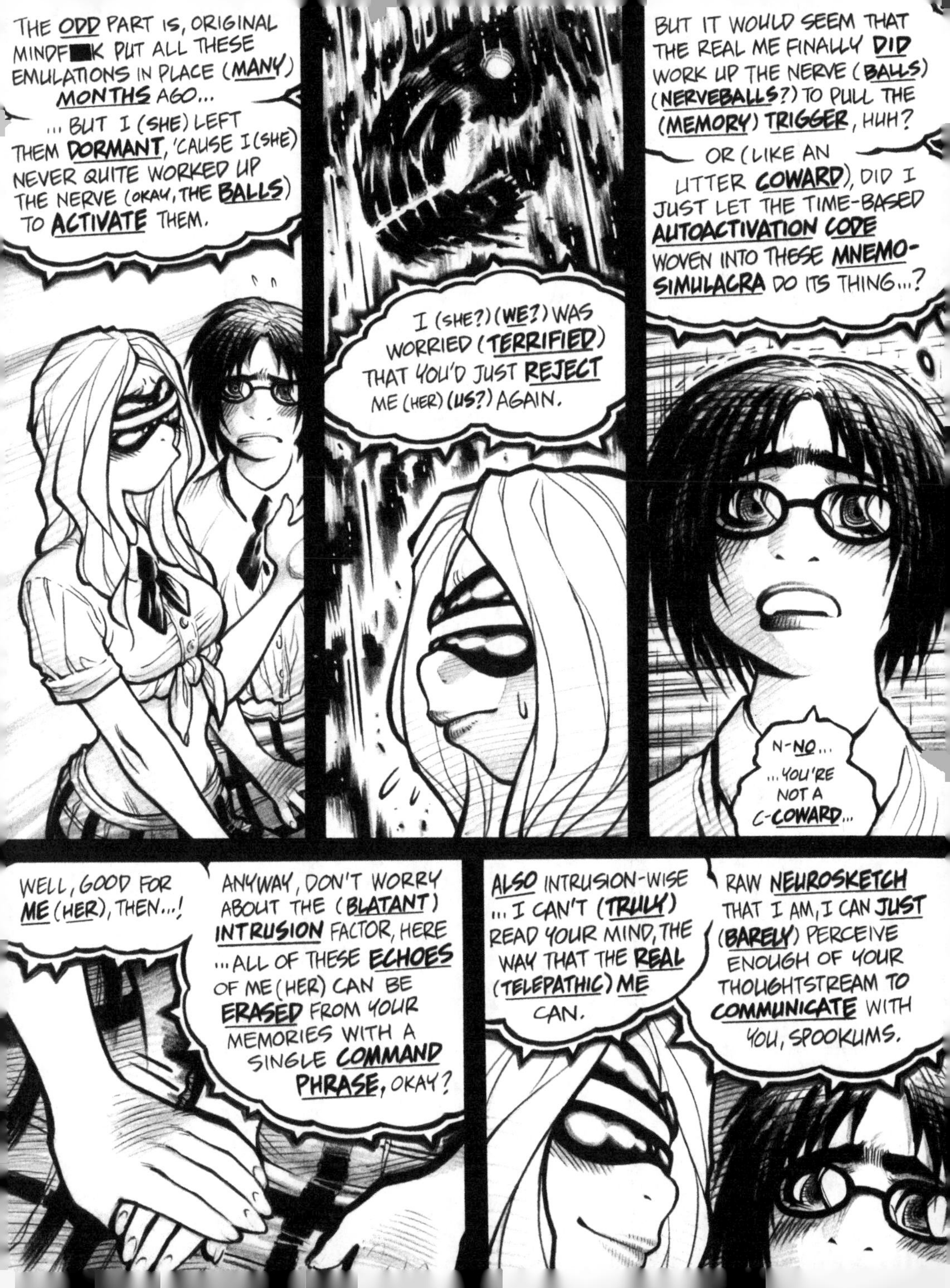
THE ODD PART IS, ORIGINAL MINDF[redacted]K PUT ALL THESE EMULATIONS IN PLACE (MANY) MONTHS AGO...
...BUT I (SHE) LEFT THEM DORMANT, 'CAUSE I (SHE) NEVER QUITE WORKED UP THE NERVE (OKAY, THE BALLS) TO ACTIVATE THEM.
I (SHE?) (WE?) WAS WORRIED (TERRIFIED) THAT YOU'D JUST REJECT ME (HER) (US?) AGAIN.
BUT IT WOULD SEEM THAT THE REAL ME FINALLY DID WORK UP THE NERVE (BALLS) (NERVEBALLS?) TO PULL THE (MEMORY) TRIGGER, HUH?
OR (LIKE AN UTTER COWARD), DID I JUST LET THE TIME-BASED AUTOACTIVATION CODE WOVEN INTO THESE MNEMO-SIMULACRA DO ITS THING...?
N-NO... ...YOU'RE NOT A C-COWARD...
WELL, GOOD FOR ME (HER), THEN...!
ANYWAY, DON'T WORRY ABOUT THE (BLATANT) INTRUSION FACTOR, HERE ...ALL OF THESE ECHOES OF ME (HER) CAN BE ERASED FROM YOUR MEMORIES WITH A SINGLE COMMAND PHRASE, OKAY?
ALSO INTRUSION-WISE ...I CAN'T (TRULY) READ YOUR MIND, THE WAY THAT THE REAL (TELEPATHIC) ME CAN.
RAW NEUROSKETCH THAT I AM, I CAN JUST (BARELY) PERCEIVE ENOUGH OF YOUR THOUGHTSTREAM TO COMMUNICATE WITH YOU, SPOOKUMS.

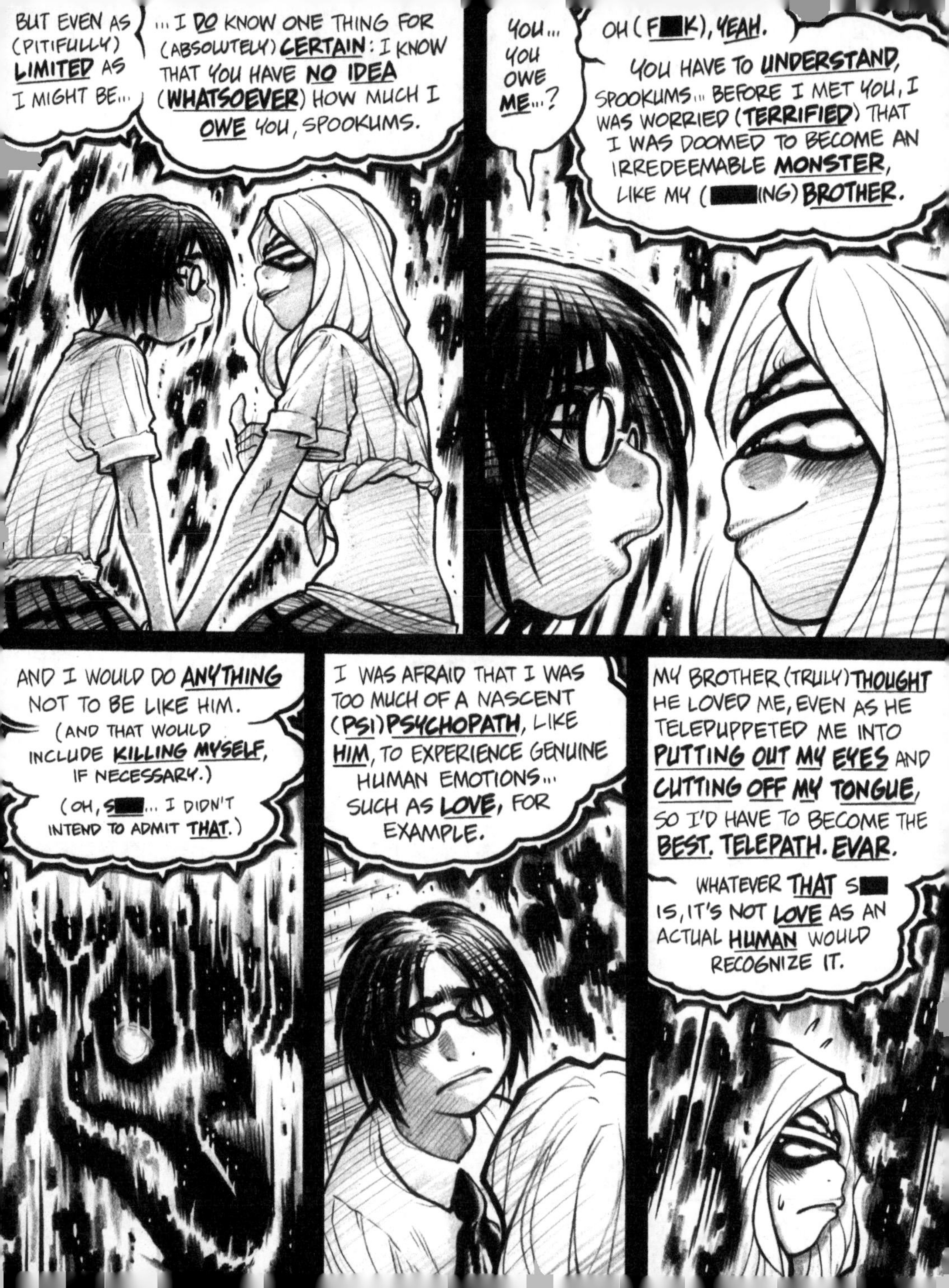
BUT EVEN AS (PITIFULLY) LIMITED AS I MIGHT BE...
...I DO KNOW ONE THING FOR (ABSOLUTELY) CERTAIN: I KNOW THAT YOU HAVE NO IDEA (WHATSOEVER) HOW MUCH I OWE YOU, SPOOKUMS.
YOU... YOU OWE ME...?
OH (F[redacted]K), YEAH.
YOU HAVE TO UNDERSTAND, SPOOKUMS... BEFORE I MET YOU, I WAS WORRIED (TERRIFIED) THAT I WAS DOOMED TO BECOME AN IRREDEEMABLE MONSTER, LIKE MY ([redacted]ING) BROTHER.
AND I WOULD DO ANYTHING NOT TO BE LIKE HIM.
(AND THAT WOULD INCLUDE KILLING MYSELF, IF NECESSARY.)
(OH, S[redacted]... I DIDN'T INTEND TO ADMIT THAT.)
I WAS AFRAID THAT I WAS TOO MUCH OF A NASCENT (PSI)PSYCHOPATH, LIKE HIM, TO EXPERIENCE GENUINE HUMAN EMOTIONS... SUCH AS LOVE, FOR EXAMPLE.
MY BROTHER (TRULY) THOUGHT HE LOVED ME, EVEN AS HE TELEPUPPETED ME INTO PUTTING OUT MY EYES AND CUTTING OFF MY TONGUE, SO I'D HAVE TO BECOME THE BEST. TELEPATH. EVAR.
WHATEVER THAT S[redacted] IS, IT'S NOT LOVE AS AN ACTUAL HUMAN WOULD RECOGNIZE IT.

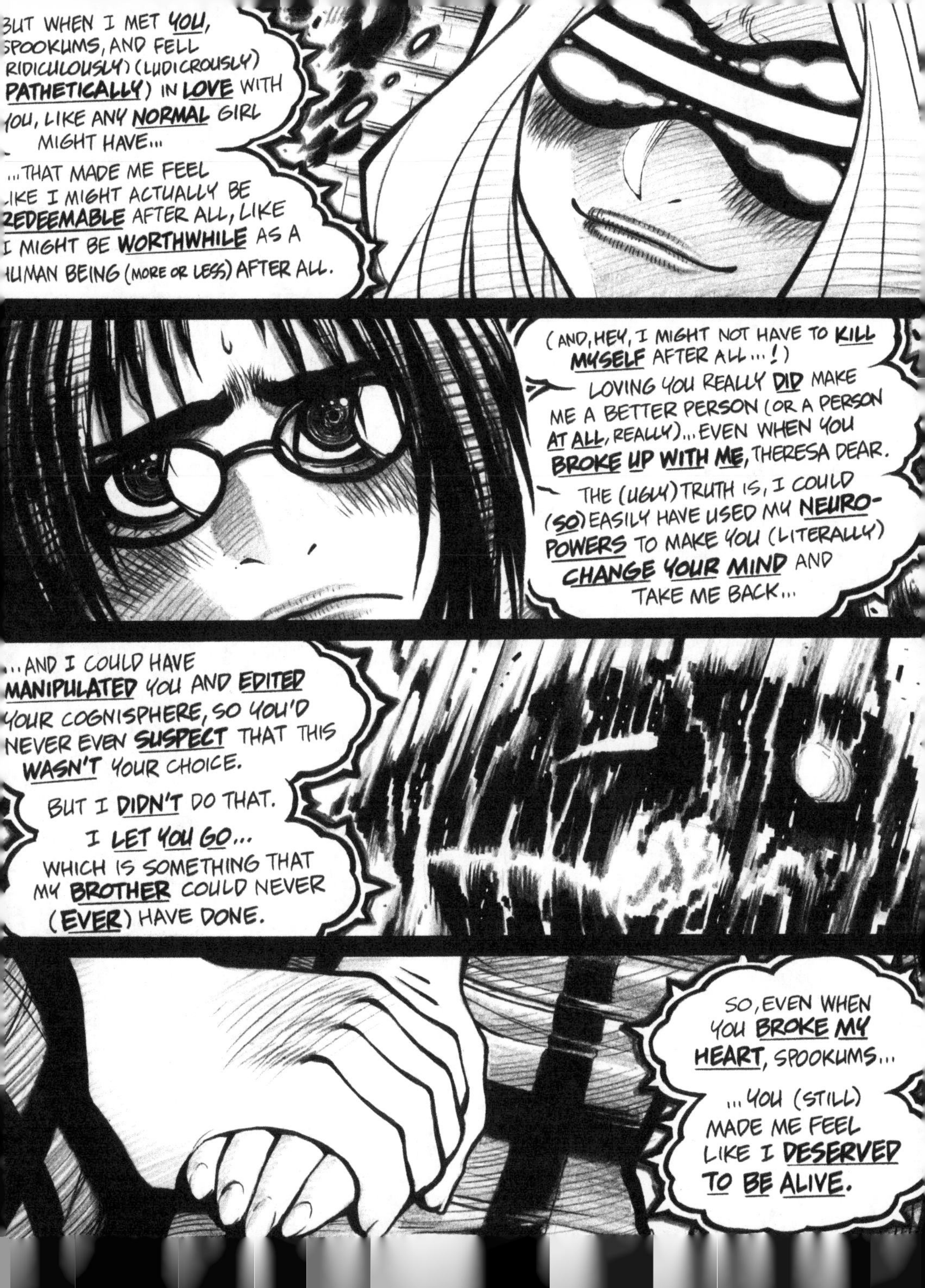
BUT WHEN I MET YOU, SPOOKUMS, AND FELL RIDICULOUSLY) (LUDICROUSLY) PATHETICALLY) IN LOVE WITH YOU, LIKE ANY NORMAL GIRL MIGHT HAVE...
...THAT MADE ME FEEL LIKE I MIGHT ACTUALLY BE REDEEMABLE AFTER ALL, LIKE I MIGHT BE WORTHWHILE AS A HUMAN BEING (MORE OR LESS) AFTER ALL.
(AND, HEY, I MIGHT NOT HAVE TO KILL MYSELF AFTER ALL...!)
LOVING YOU REALLY DID MAKE ME A BETTER PERSON (OR A PERSON AT ALL, REALLY)... EVEN WHEN YOU BROKE UP WITH ME, THERESA DEAR.
THE (UGLY) TRUTH IS, I COULD (SO) EASILY HAVE USED MY NEURO-POWERS TO MAKE YOU (LITERALLY) CHANGE YOUR MIND AND TAKE ME BACK...
...AND I COULD HAVE MANIPULATED YOU AND EDITED YOUR COGNISPHERE, SO YOU'D NEVER EVEN SUSPECT THAT THIS WASN'T YOUR CHOICE.
BUT I DIDN'T DO THAT.
I LET YOU GO... WHICH IS SOMETHING THAT MY BROTHER COULD NEVER (EVER) HAVE DONE.
SO, EVEN WHEN YOU BROKE MY HEART, SPOOKUMS...
...YOU (STILL) MADE ME FEEL LIKE I DESERVED TO BE ALIVE.

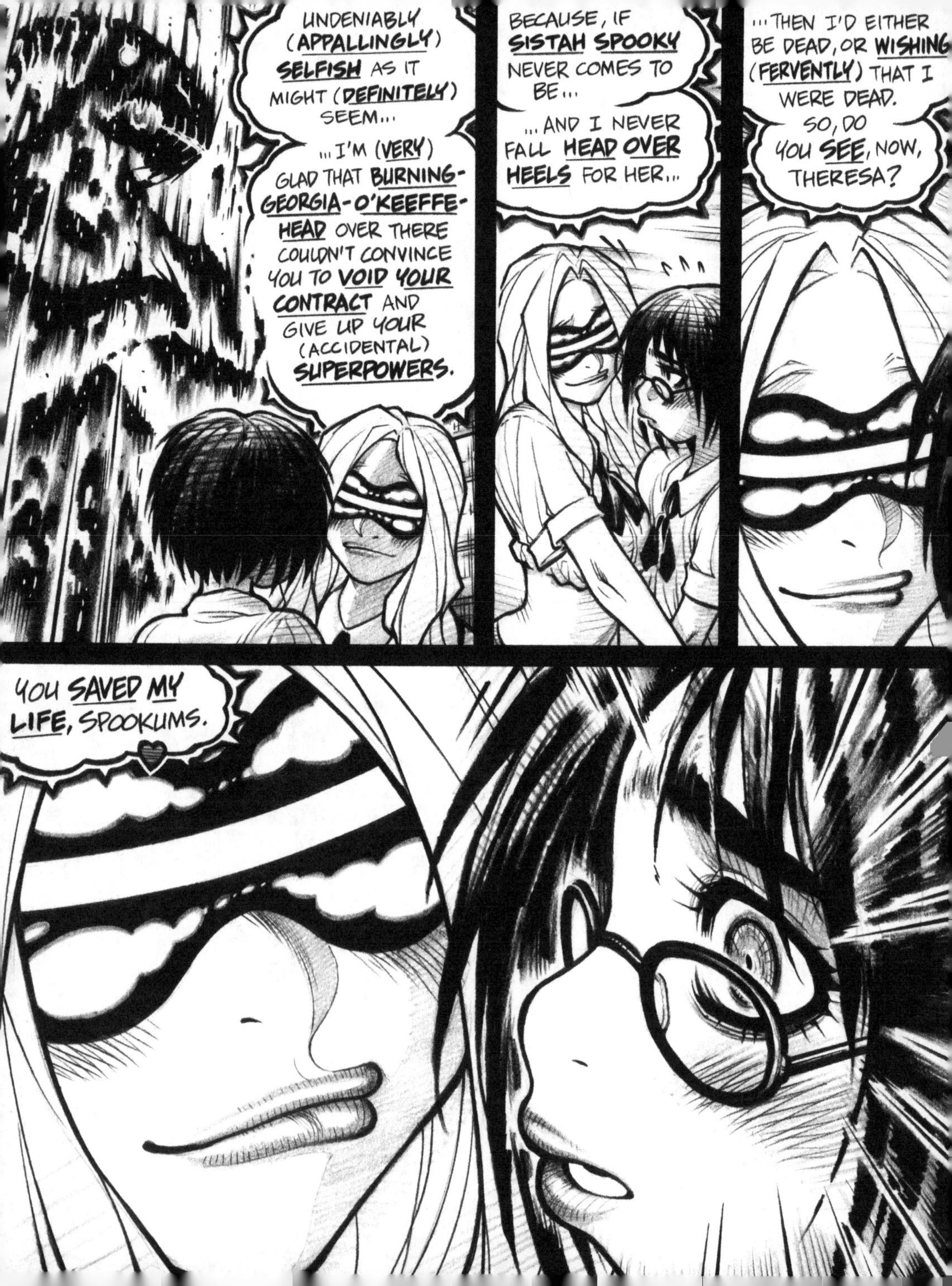
UNDENIABLY (APPALLINGLY) SELFISH AS IT MIGHT (DEFINITELY) SEEM...
...I'M (VERY) GLAD THAT BURNING-GEORGIA-O'KEEFFE-HEAD OVER THERE COULDN'T CONVINCE YOU TO VOID YOUR CONTRACT AND GIVE UP YOUR (ACCIDENTAL) SUPERPOWERS.
BECAUSE, IF SISTAH SPOOKY NEVER COMES TO BE...
...AND I NEVER FALL HEAD OVER HEELS FOR HER...
...THEN I'D EITHER BE DEAD, OR WISHING (FERVENTLY) THAT I WERE DEAD.
SO, DO YOU SEE, NOW, THERESA?
YOU SAVED MY LIFE, SPOOKUMS.

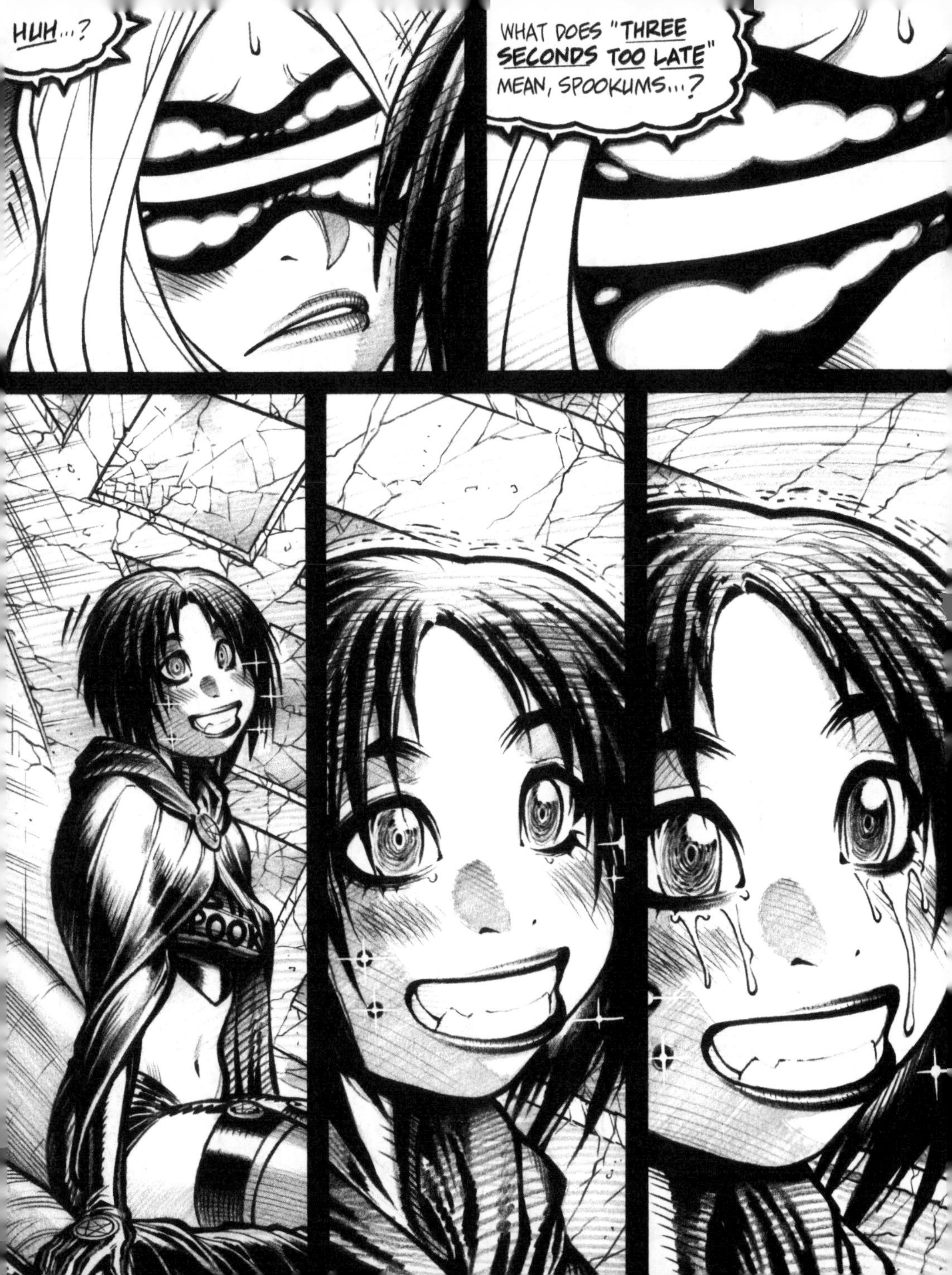
HUH...?
WHAT DOES "THREE SECONDS TOO LATE" MEAN, SPOOKUMS...?
SPOOK

Empowered™

Don't Let Them Bury Me; I'm Not (Quite) Dead

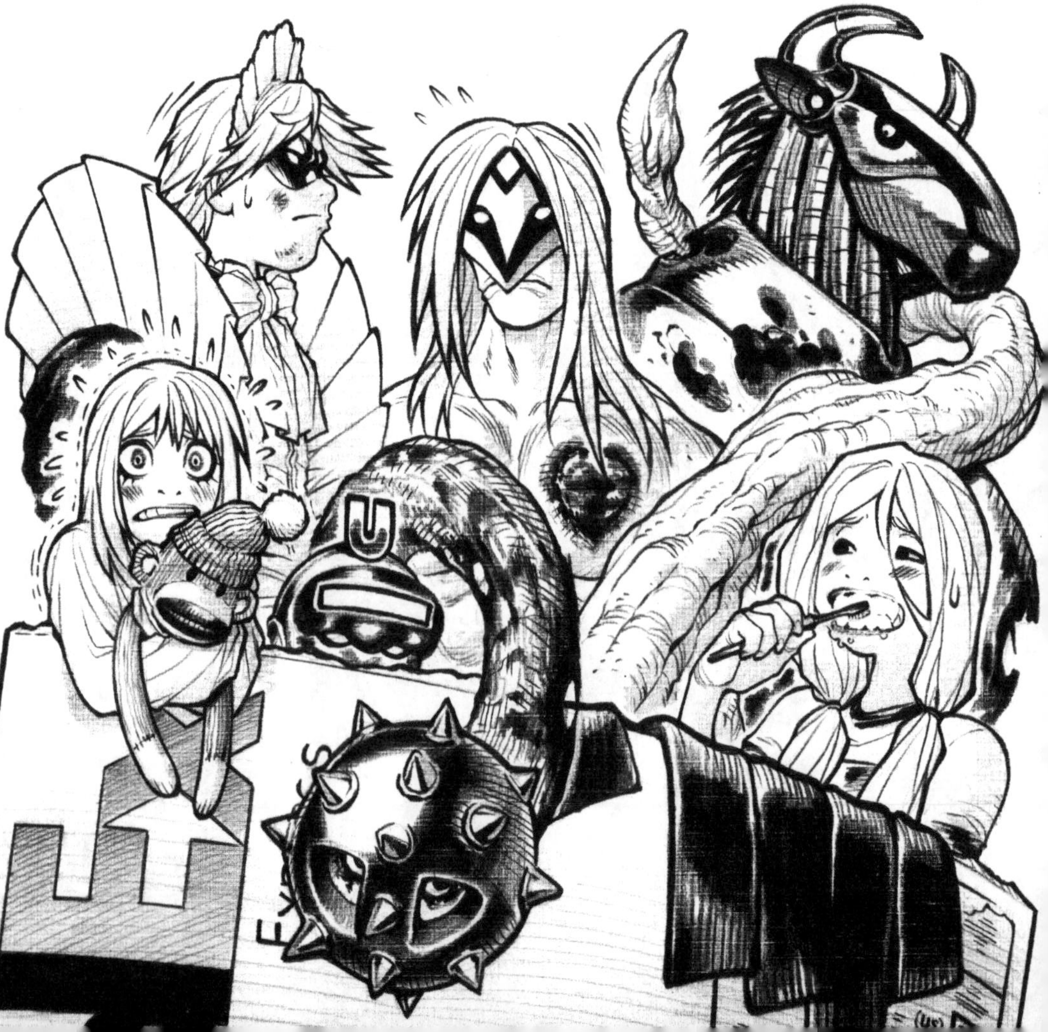

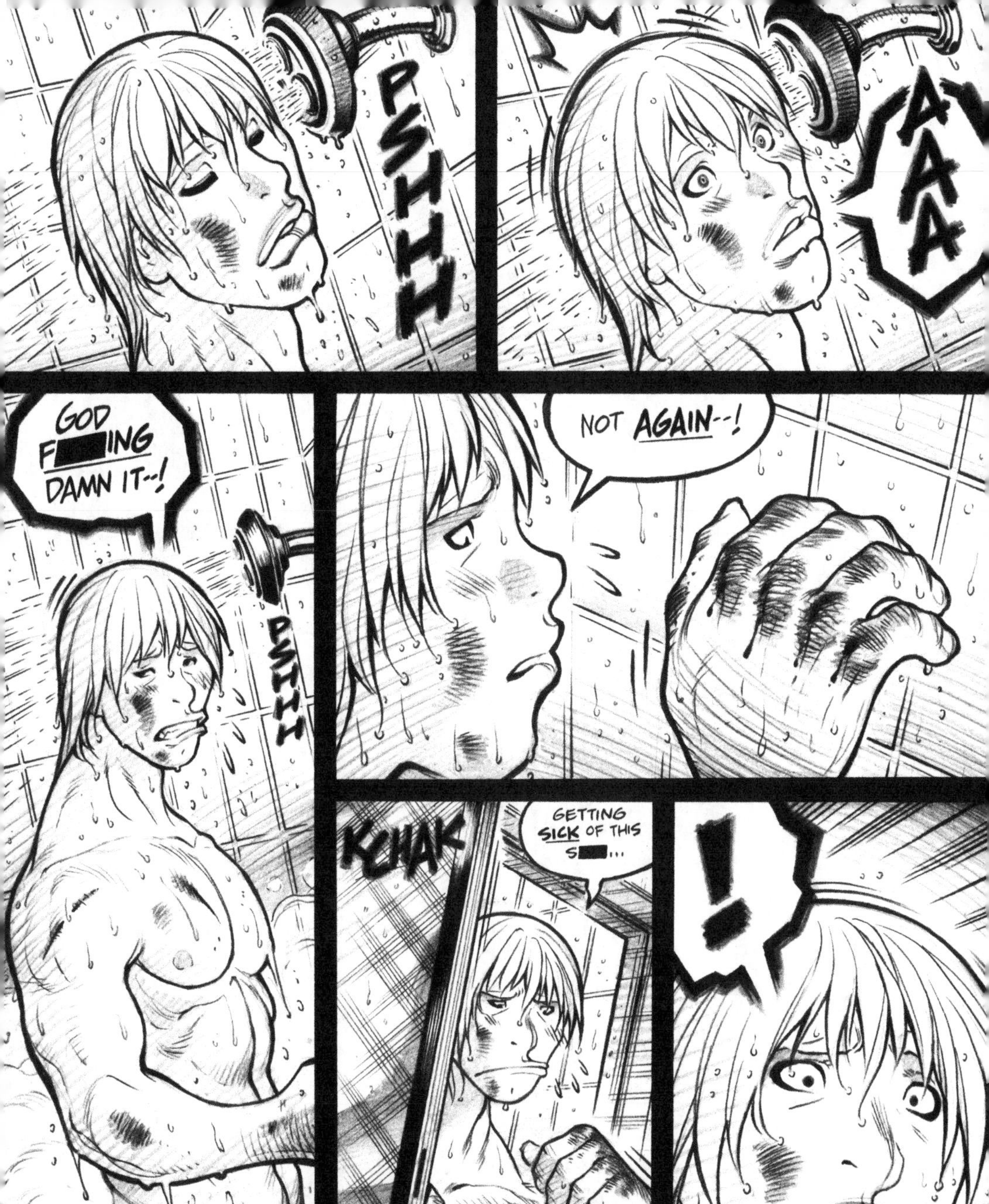
PSHHH
AAA
GOD F[redacted]ING DAMN IT--!
PSHHH
NOT AGAIN--!
KCHAK
GETTING SICK OF THIS S[redacted]...
!

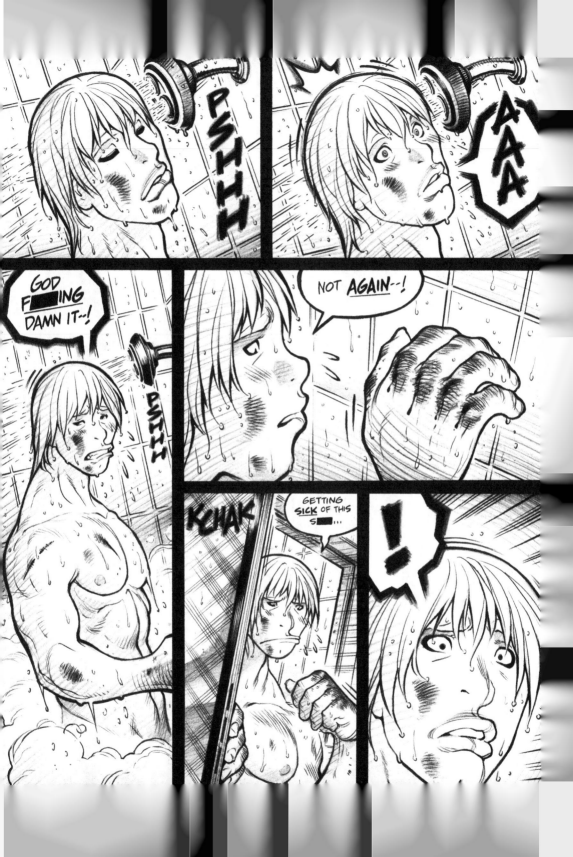

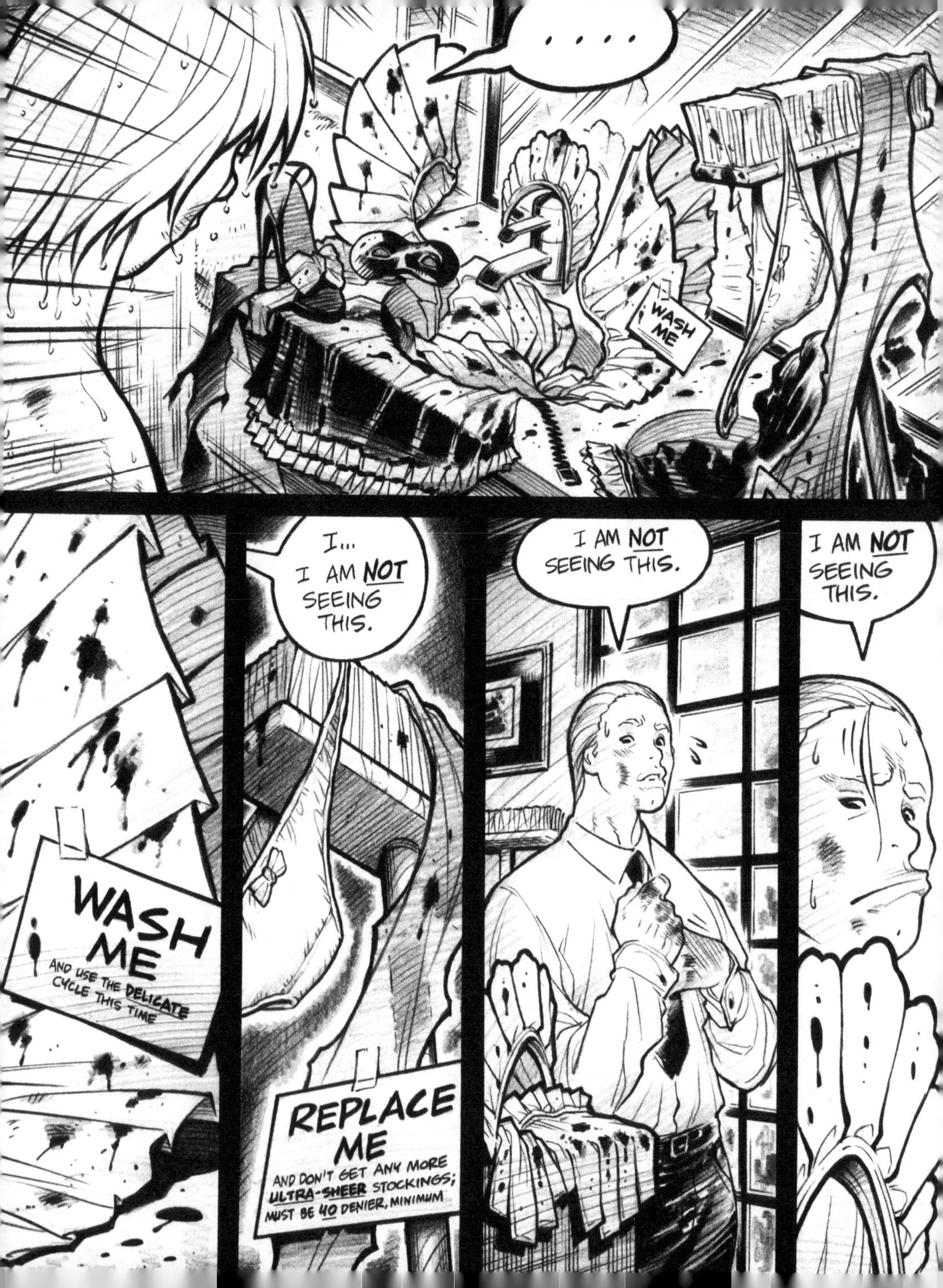
. . . . .
WASH ME
WASH ME
AND USE THE DELICATE CYCLE THIS TIME
I... I AM NOT SEEING THIS.
REPLACE ME
AND DON'T GET ANY MORE ULTRA-SHEER STOCKINGS; MUST BE 40 DENIER, MINIMUM
I AM NOT SEEING THIS.
I AM NOT SEEING THIS.

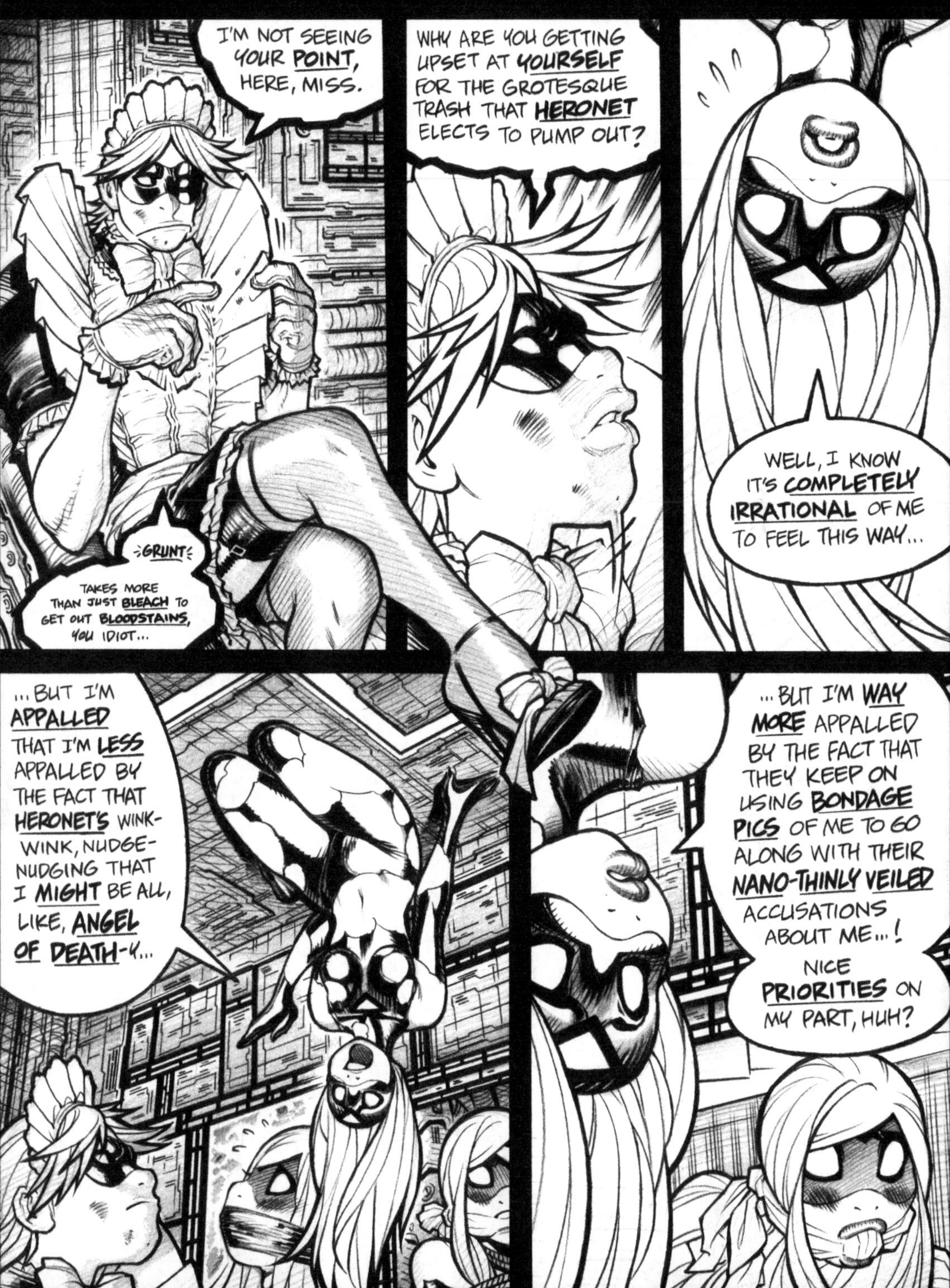
I'M NOT SEEING YOUR POINT, HERE, MISS.
WHY ARE YOU GETTING UPSET AT YOURSELF FOR THE GROTESQUE TRASH THAT HERONET ELECTS TO PUMP OUT?
GRUNT
TAKES MORE THAN JUST BLEACH TO GET OUT BLOODSTAINS, YOU IDIOT...
WELL, I KNOW IT'S COMPLETELY IRRATIONAL OF ME TO FEEL THIS WAY...
...BUT I'M APPALLED THAT I'M LESS APPALLED BY THE FACT THAT HERONET'S WINK-WINK, NUDGE-NUDGING THAT I MIGHT BE ALL, LIKE, ANGEL OF DEATH-Y...
...BUT I'M WAY MORE APPALLED BY THE FACT THAT THEY KEEP ON USING BONDAGE PICS OF ME TO GO ALONG WITH THEIR NANO-THINLY VEILED ACCUSATIONS ABOUT ME...!
NICE PRIORITIES ON MY PART, HUH?

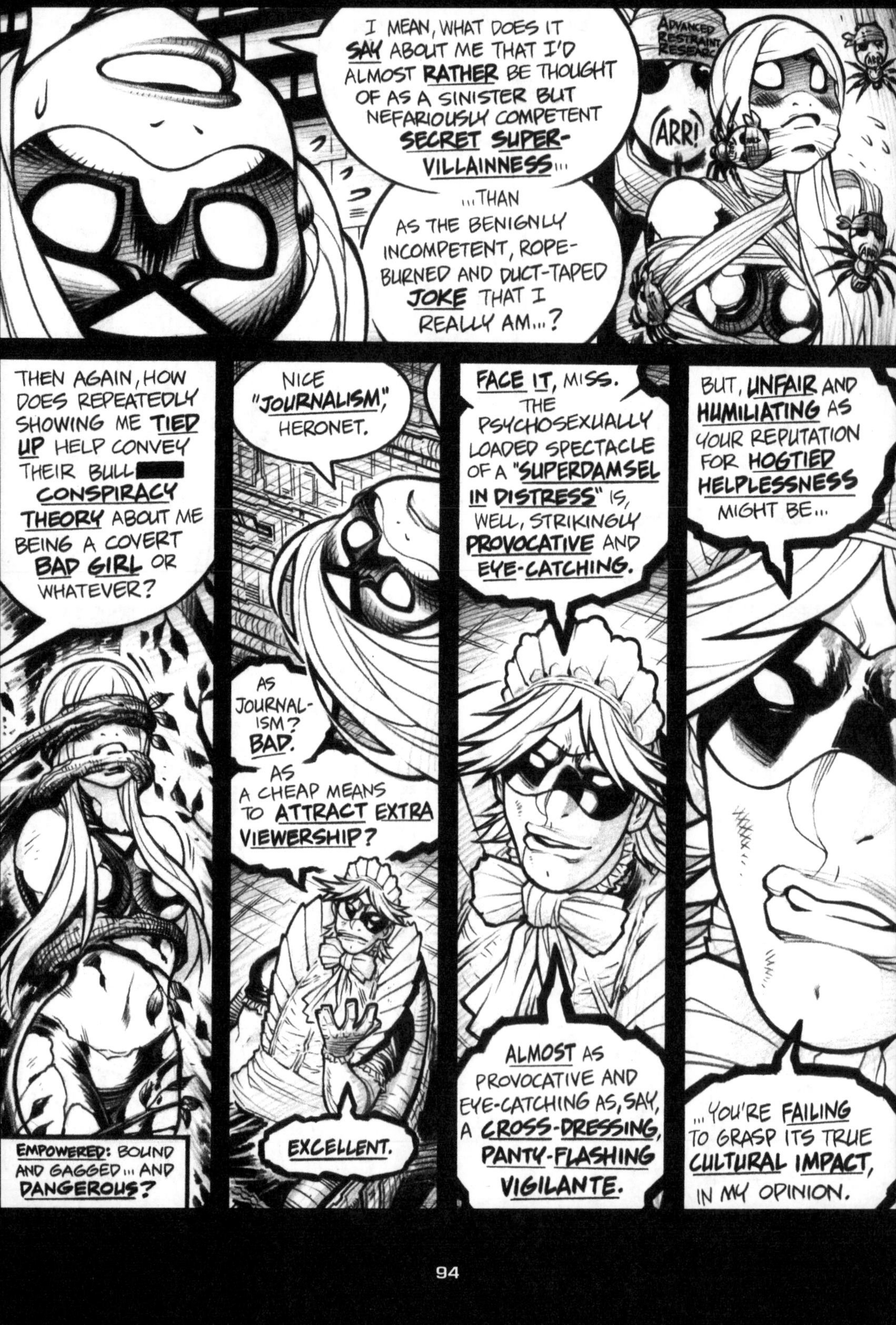

I MEAN, WHAT DOES IT SAY ABOUT ME THAT I'D ALMOST RATHER BE THOUGHT OF AS A SINISTER BUT NEFARIOUSLY COMPETENT SECRET SUPER-VILLAINNESS...
...THAN AS THE BENIGNLY INCOMPETENT, ROPE-BURNED AND DUCT-TAPED JOKE THAT I REALLY AM...?
ADVANCED RESTRAINT RESEARC
ARR!
THEN AGAIN, HOW DOES REPEATEDLY SHOWING ME TIED UP HELP CONVEY THEIR BULL[redacted] CONSPIRACY THEORY ABOUT ME BEING A COVERT BAD GIRL OR WHATEVER?
EMPOWERED: BOUND AND GAGGED... AND DANGEROUS?
NICE "JOURNALISM," HERONET.
AS JOURNALISM? BAD.
AS A CHEAP MEANS TO ATTRACT EXTRA VIEWERSHIP?
EXCELLENT.
FACE IT, MISS. THE PSYCHOSEXUALLY LOADED SPECTACLE OF A "SUPERDAMSEL IN DISTRESS" IS, WELL, STRIKINGLY PROVOCATIVE AND EYE-CATCHING.
ALMOST AS PROVOCATIVE AND EYE-CATCHING AS, SAY, A CROSS-DRESSING, PANTY-FLASHING VIGILANTE.
BUT, UNFAIR AND HUMILIATING AS YOUR REPUTATION FOR HOGTIED HELPLESSNESS MIGHT BE...
...YOU'RE FAILING TO GRASP ITS TRUE CULTURAL IMPACT, IN MY OPINION.

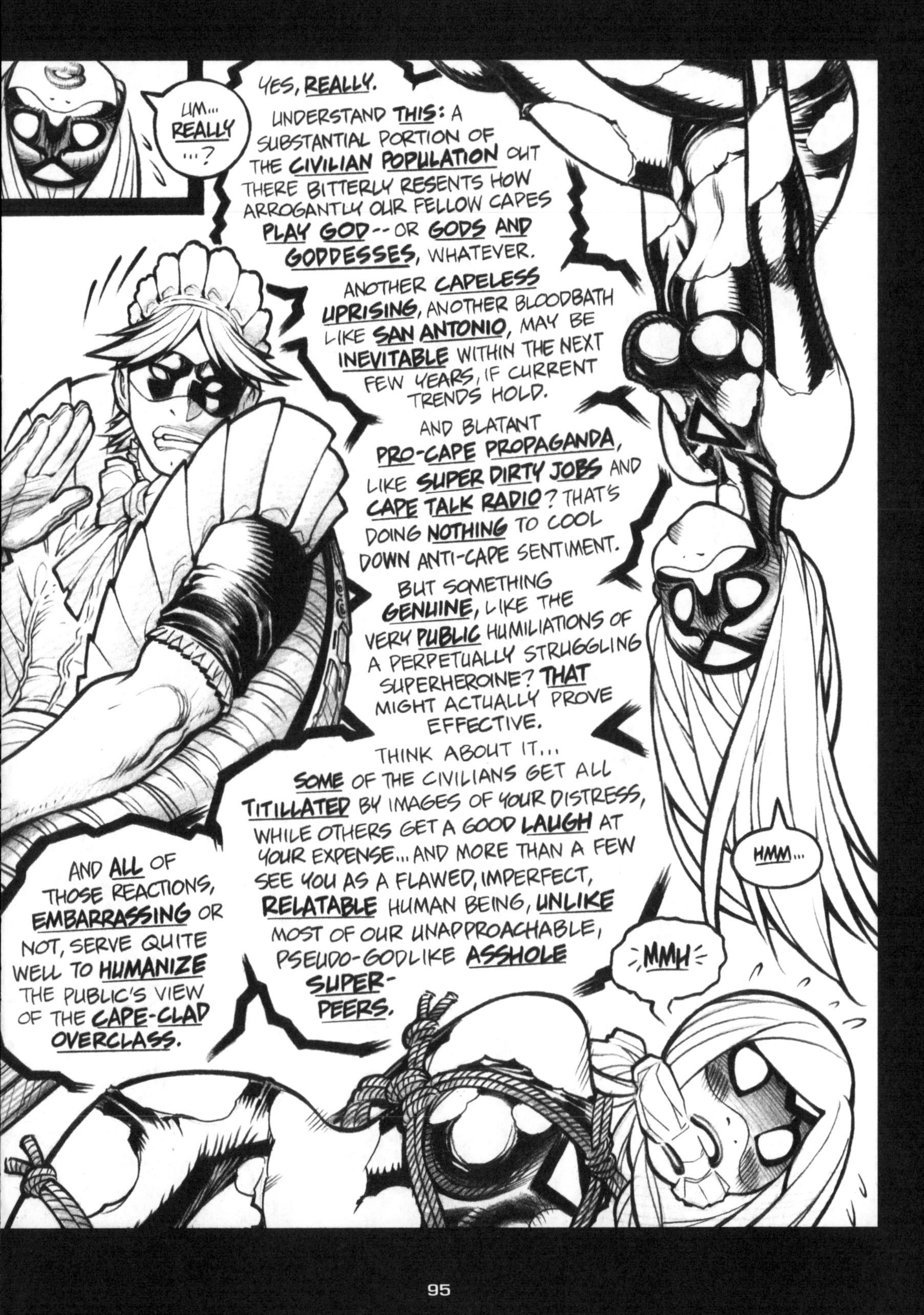
UM... REALLY ...?
YES, REALLY.
UNDERSTAND THIS: A SUBSTANTIAL PORTION OF THE CIVILIAN POPULATION OUT THERE BITTERLY RESENTS HOW ARROGANTLY OUR FELLOW CAPES PLAY GOD--OR GODS AND GODDESSES, WHATEVER.
ANOTHER CAPELESS UPRISING, ANOTHER BLOODBATH LIKE SAN ANTONIO, MAY BE INEVITABLE WITHIN THE NEXT FEW YEARS, IF CURRENT TRENDS HOLD.
AND BLATANT PRO-CAPE PROPAGANDA, LIKE SUPER DIRTY JOBS AND CAPE TALK RADIO? THAT'S DOING NOTHING TO COOL DOWN ANTI-CAPE SENTIMENT.
BUT SOMETHING GENUINE, LIKE THE VERY PUBLIC HUMILIATIONS OF A PERPETUALLY STRUGGLING SUPERHEROINE? THAT MIGHT ACTUALLY PROVE EFFECTIVE.
THINK ABOUT IT...
SOME OF THE CIVILIANS GET ALL TITILLATED BY IMAGES OF YOUR DISTRESS, WHILE OTHERS GET A GOOD LAUGH AT YOUR EXPENSE... AND MORE THAN A FEW SEE YOU AS A FLAWED, IMPERFECT, RELATABLE HUMAN BEING, UNLIKE MOST OF OUR UNAPPROACHABLE, PSEUDO-GODLIKE ASSHOLE SUPER-PEERS.
HMM...
MMH
AND ALL OF THOSE REACTIONS, EMBARRASSING OR NOT, SERVE QUITE WELL TO HUMANIZE THE PUBLIC'S VIEW OF THE CAPE-CLAD OVERCLASS.

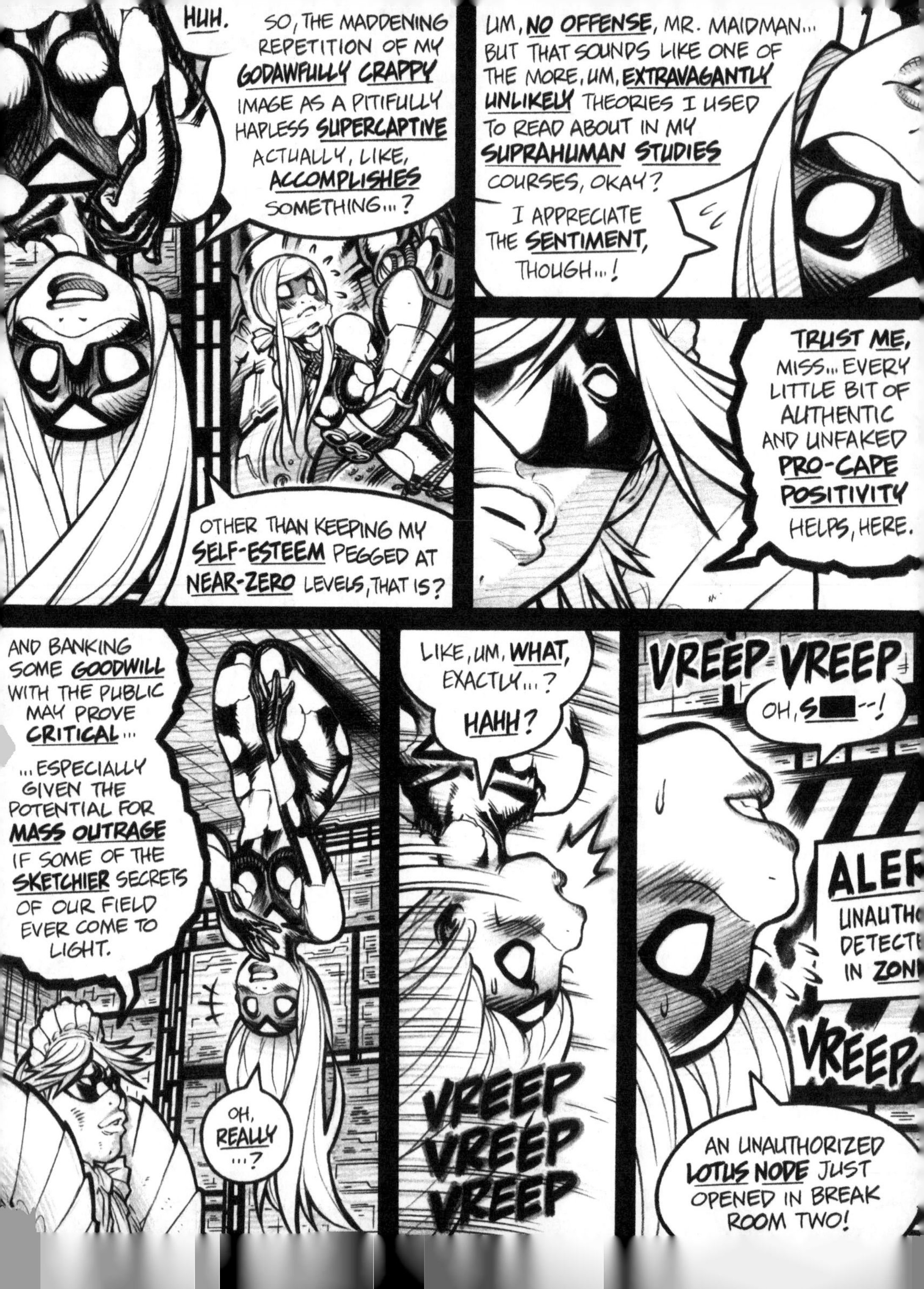
HUH.
SO, THE MADDENING REPETITION OF MY GODAWFULLY CRAPPY IMAGE AS A PITIFULLY HAPLESS SUPERCAPTIVE ACTUALLY, LIKE, ACCOMPLISHES SOMETHING...?
OTHER THAN KEEPING MY SELF-ESTEEM PEGGED AT NEAR-ZERO LEVELS, THAT IS?
UM, NO OFFENSE, MR. MAIDMAN... BUT THAT SOUNDS LIKE ONE OF THE MORE, UM, EXTRAVAGANTLY UNLIKELY THEORIES I USED TO READ ABOUT IN MY SUPRAHUMAN STUDIES COURSES, OKAY?
I APPRECIATE THE SENTIMENT, THOUGH...!
TRUST ME, MISS... EVERY LITTLE BIT OF AUTHENTIC AND UNFAKED PRO-CAPE POSITIVITY HELPS, HERE.
AND BANKING SOME GOODWILL WITH THE PUBLIC MAY PROVE CRITICAL...
...ESPECIALLY GIVEN THE POTENTIAL FOR MASS OUTRAGE IF SOME OF THE SKETCHIER SECRETS OF OUR FIELD EVER COME TO LIGHT.
OH, REALLY...?
LIKE, UM, WHAT, EXACTLY...?
HAHH?
VREEP VREEP VREEP
VREEP VREEP
OH, S[redacted]--!
VREEP
AN UNAUTHORIZED LOTUS NODE JUST OPENED IN BREAK ROOM TWO!

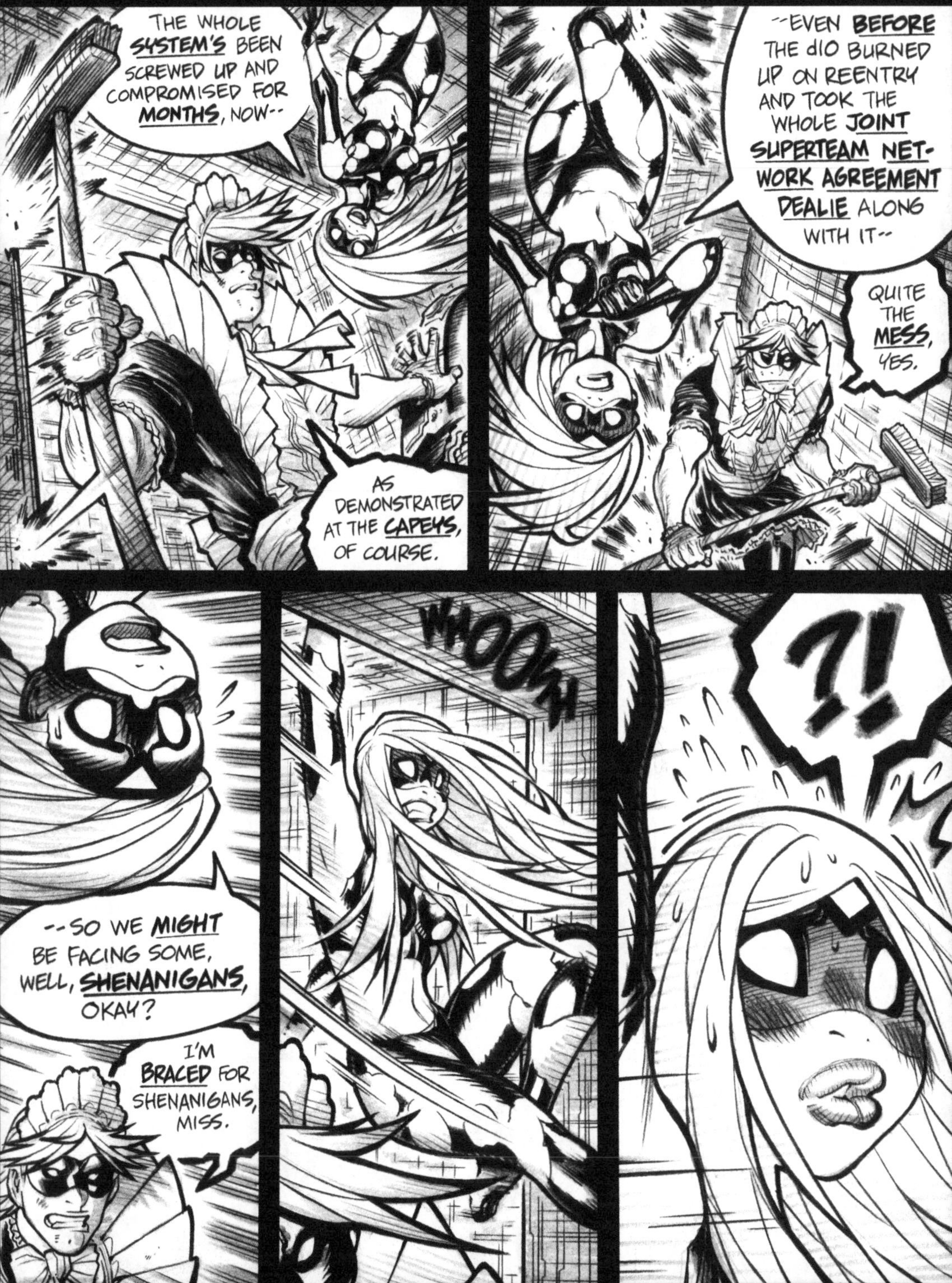
THE WHOLE SYSTEM'S BEEN SCREWED UP AND COMPROMISED FOR MONTHS, NOW--
AS DEMONSTRATED AT THE CAPEYS, OF COURSE.
--EVEN BEFORE THE dIO BURNED UP ON REENTRY AND TOOK THE WHOLE JOINT SUPERTEAM NET-WORK AGREEMENT DEALIE ALONG WITH IT--
QUITE THE MESS, YES.
--SO WE MIGHT BE FACING SOME, WELL, SHENANIGANS, OKAY?
I'M BRACED FOR SHENANIGANS, MISS.
WHOOM
?!

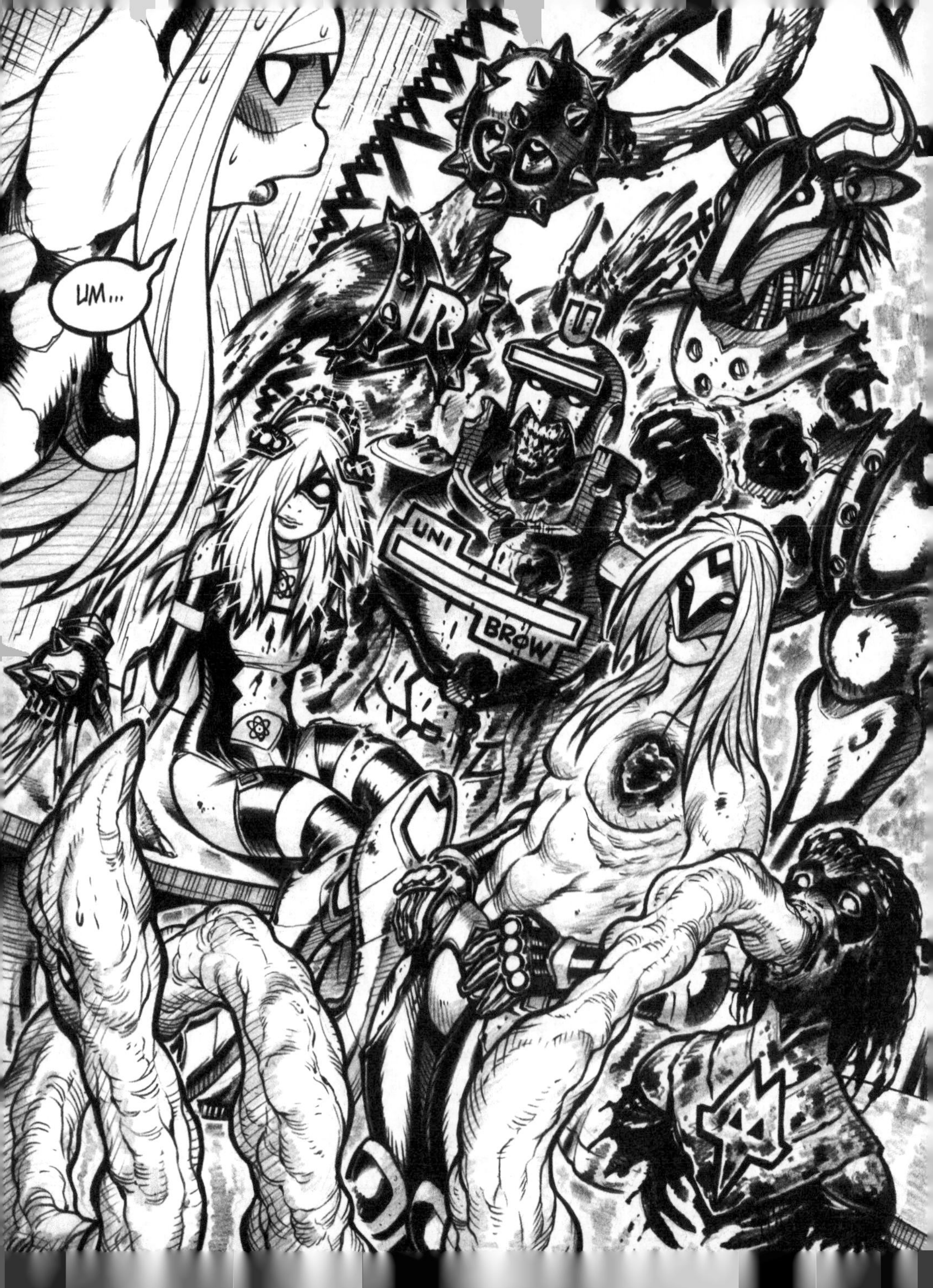
UM...
UNI
BROW

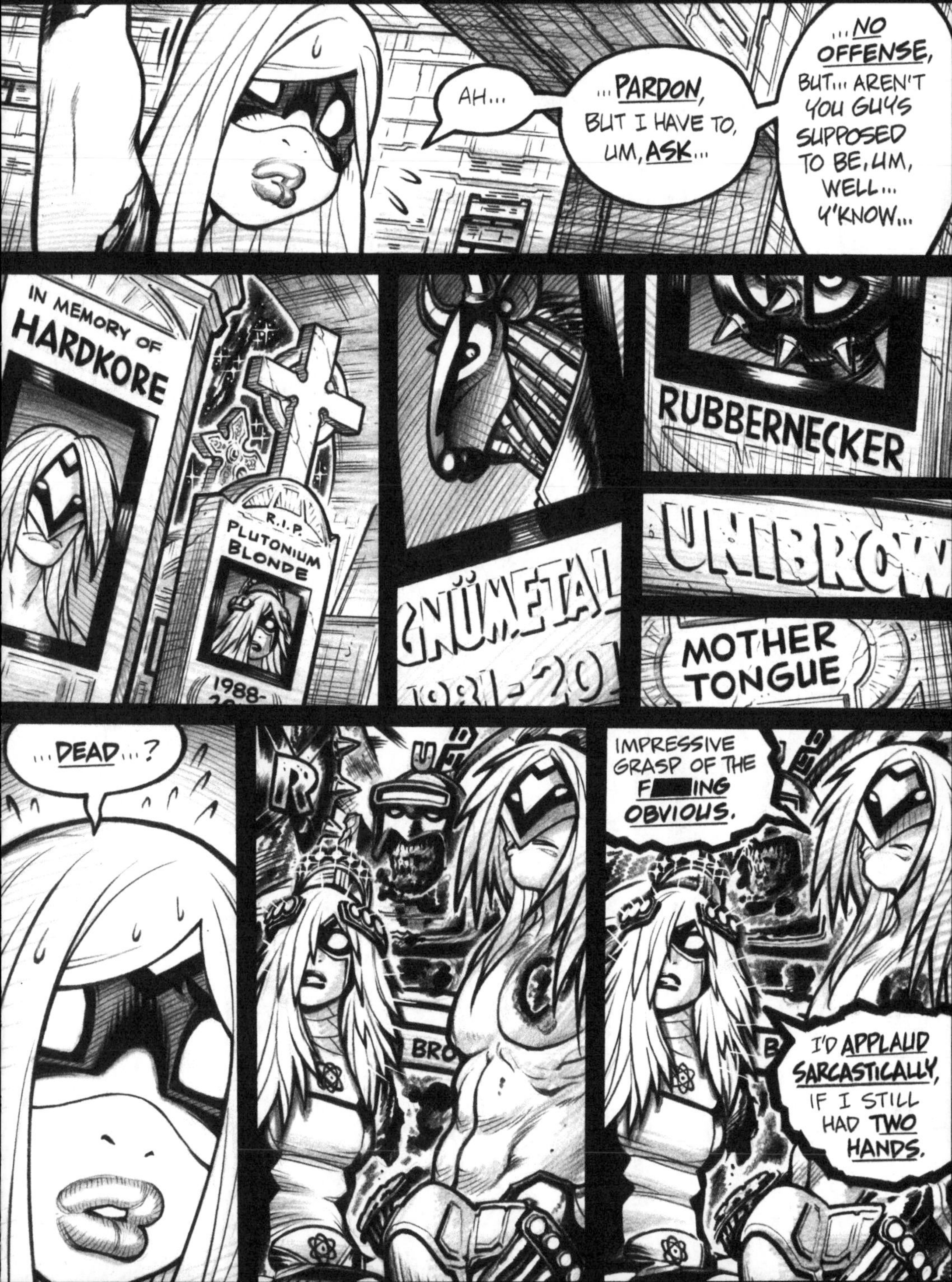
AH...
...PARDON, BUT I HAVE TO, UM, ASK...
...NO OFFENSE, BUT... AREN'T YOU GUYS SUPPOSED TO BE, UM, WELL... Y'KNOW...
IN MEMORY OF HARDKORE
R.I.P. PLUTONIUM BLONDE
1988-
RUBBERNECKER
UNIBRO
GNÜMETAL
MOTHER TONGUE
...DEAD...?
IMPRESSIVE GRASP OF THE F[redacted]ING OBVIOUS.
I'D APPLAUD SARCASTICALLY, IF I STILL HAD TWO HANDS.

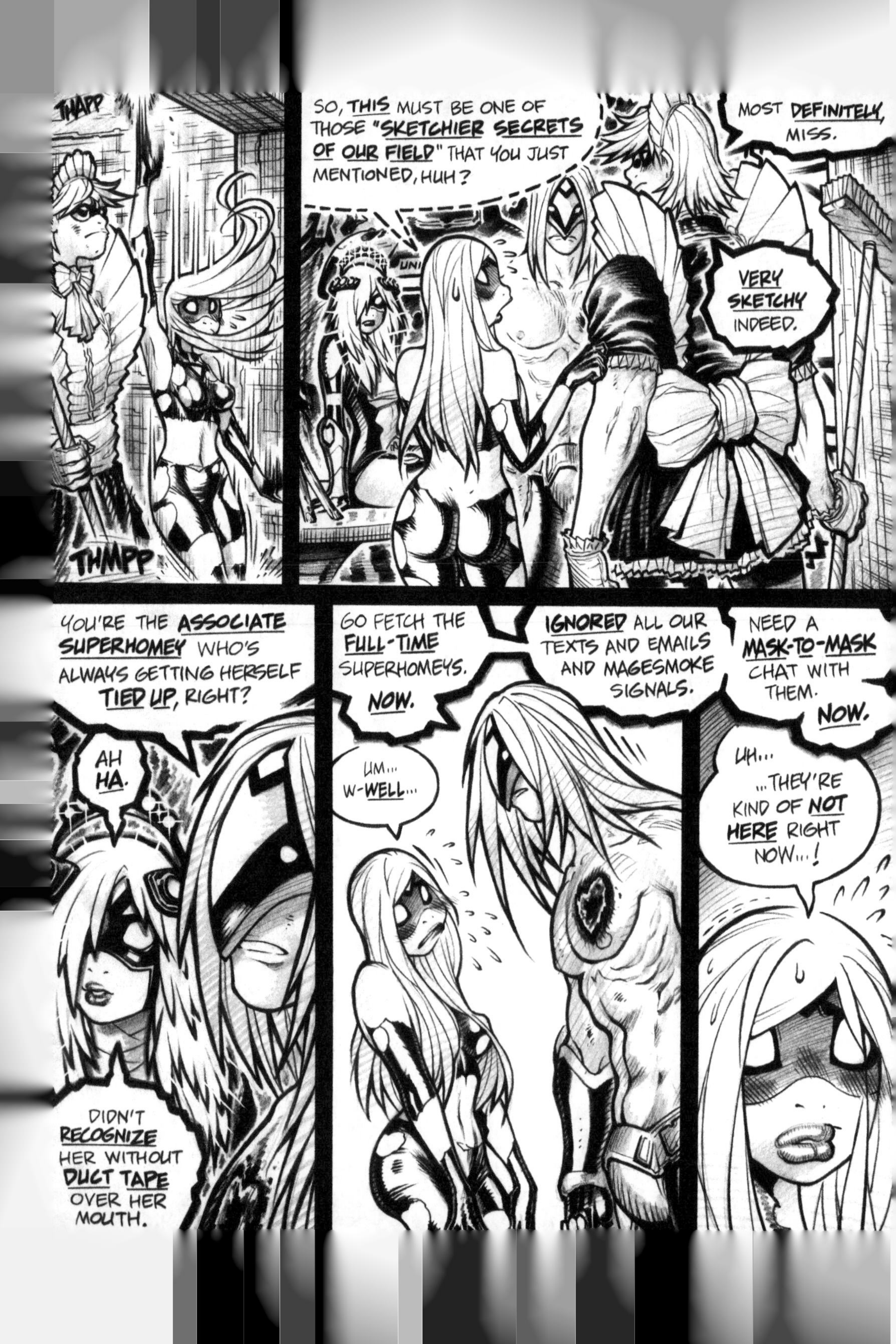
THAPP
THMPP
SO, THIS MUST BE ONE OF THOSE "SKETCHIER SECRETS OF OUR FIELD" THAT YOU JUST MENTIONED, HUH?
MOST DEFINITELY, MISS.
VERY SKETCHY INDEED.
YOU'RE THE ASSOCIATE SUPERHOMEY WHO'S ALWAYS GETTING HERSELF TIED UP, RIGHT?
AH HA.
DIDN'T RECOGNIZE HER WITHOUT DUCT TAPE OVER HER MOUTH.
GO FETCH THE FULL-TIME SUPERHOMEYS. NOW.
IGNORED ALL OUR TEXTS AND EMAILS AND MAGESMOKE SIGNALS.
UM... W-WELL...
NEED A MASK-TO-MASK CHAT WITH THEM. NOW.
UH... ...THEY'RE KIND OF NOT HERE RIGHT NOW...!

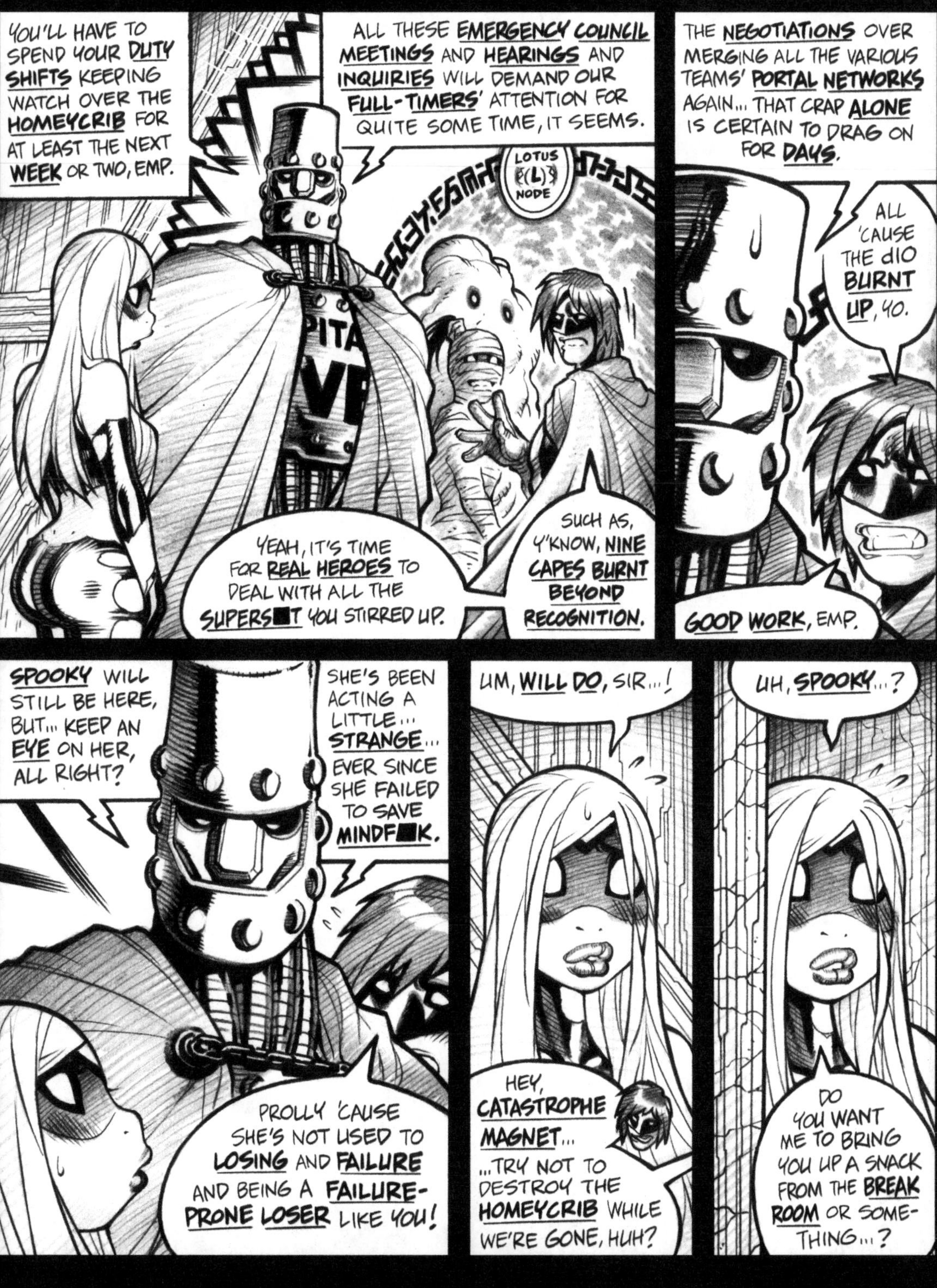
YOU'LL HAVE TO SPEND YOUR DUTY SHIFTS KEEPING WATCH OVER THE HOMEYCRIB FOR AT LEAST THE NEXT WEEK OR TWO, EMP.
ALL THESE EMERGENCY COUNCIL MEETINGS AND HEARINGS AND INQUIRIES WILL DEMAND OUR FULL-TIMERS' ATTENTION FOR QUITE SOME TIME, IT SEEMS.
LOTUS (L) NODE
PITA
VE
YEAH, IT'S TIME FOR REAL HEROES TO DEAL WITH ALL THE SUPERS[redacted]T YOU STIRRED UP.
SUCH AS, Y'KNOW, NINE CAPES BURNT BEYOND RECOGNITION.
THE NEGOTIATIONS OVER MERGING ALL THE VARIOUS TEAMS' PORTAL NETWORKS AGAIN... THAT CRAP ALONE IS CERTAIN TO DRAG ON FOR DAYS.
ALL 'CAUSE THE dIO BURNT UP, YO.
GOOD WORK, EMP.
SPOOKY WILL STILL BE HERE, BUT... KEEP AN EYE ON HER, ALL RIGHT?
SHE'S BEEN ACTING A LITTLE... STRANGE... EVER SINCE SHE FAILED TO SAVE MINDF[redacted]K.
PROLLY 'CAUSE SHE'S NOT USED TO LOSING AND FAILURE AND BEING A FAILURE-PRONE LOSER LIKE YOU!
UM, WILL DO, SIR...!
HEY, CATASTROPHE MAGNET...
...TRY NOT TO DESTROY THE HOMEYCRIB WHILE WE'RE GONE, HUH?
UH, SPOOKY...?
DO YOU WANT ME TO BRING YOU UP A SNACK FROM THE BREAK ROOM OR SOME-THING...?

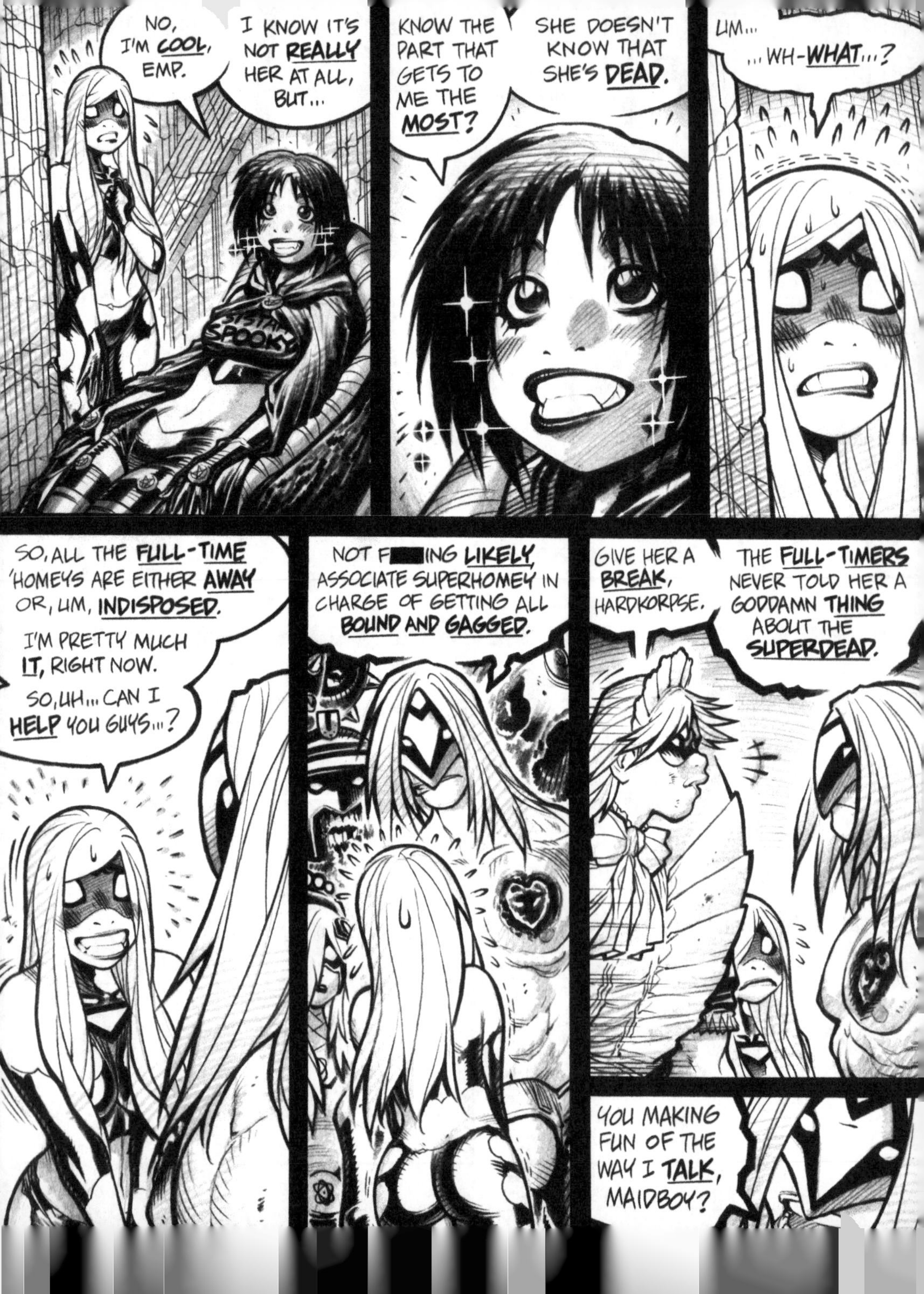
NO, I'M COOL, EMP.
I KNOW IT'S NOT REALLY HER AT ALL, BUT...
SPOOKY
KNOW THE PART THAT GETS TO ME THE MOST?
SHE DOESN'T KNOW THAT SHE'S DEAD.
UM...
...WH-WHAT...?
SO, ALL THE FULL-TIME 'HOMEYS ARE EITHER AWAY OR, UM, INDISPOSED.
I'M PRETTY MUCH IT, RIGHT NOW.
SO, UH... CAN I HELP YOU GUYS...?
NOT F[redacted]ING LIKELY, ASSOCIATE SUPERHOMEY IN CHARGE OF GETTING ALL BOUND AND GAGGED.
GIVE HER A BREAK, HARDKORPSE.
THE FULL-TIMERS NEVER TOLD HER A GODDAMN THING ABOUT THE SUPERDEAD.
YOU MAKING FUN OF THE WAY I TALK, MAIDBOY?

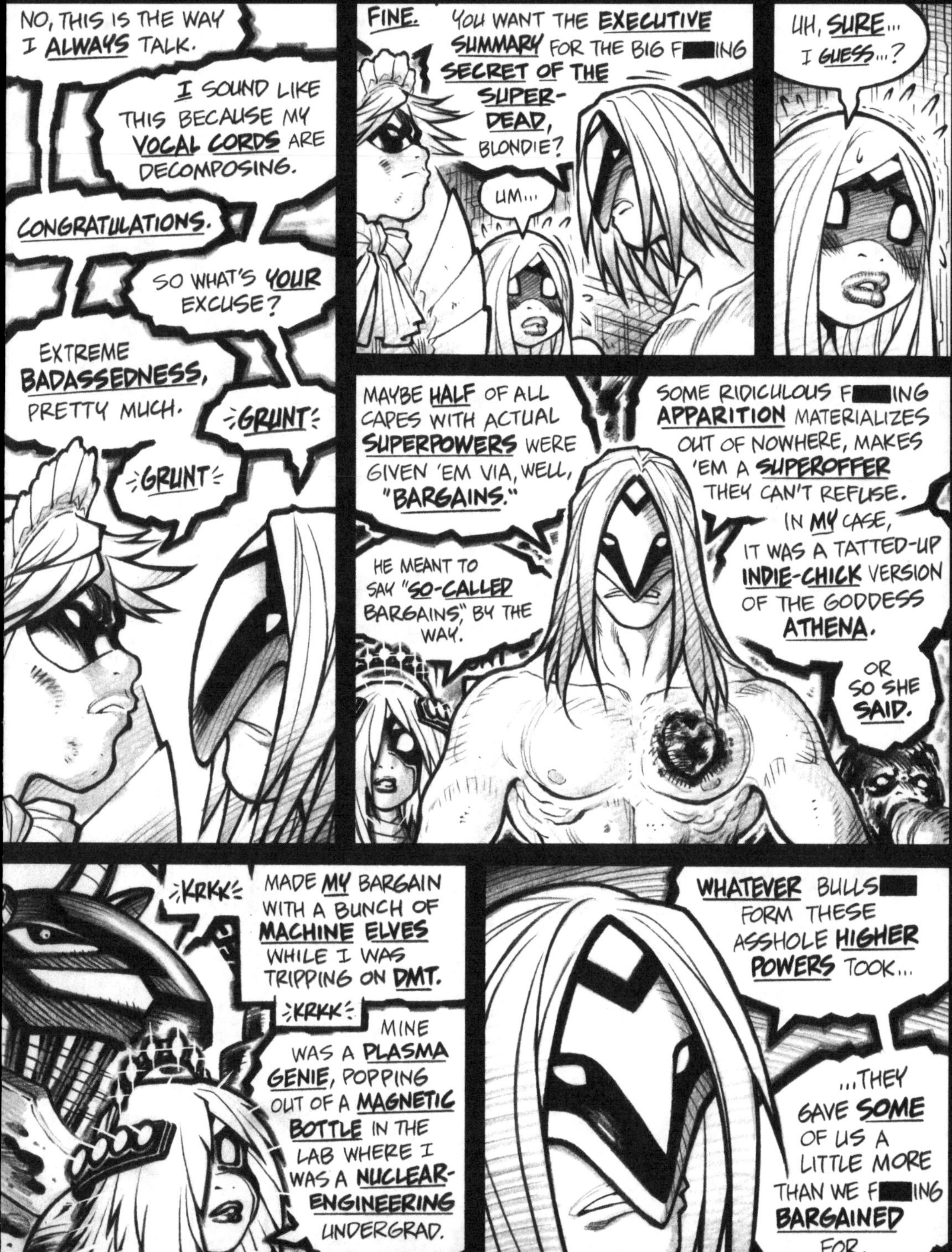
NO, THIS IS THE WAY I ALWAYS TALK.
I SOUND LIKE THIS BECAUSE MY VOCAL CORDS ARE DECOMPOSING.
CONGRATULATIONS.
SO WHAT'S YOUR EXCUSE?
EXTREME BADASSEDNESS, PRETTY MUCH.
GRUNT
GRUNT
FINE.
YOU WANT THE EXECUTIVE SUMMARY FOR THE BIG F[redacted]ING SECRET OF THE SUPER-DEAD, BLONDIE?
UM...
UH, SURE... I GUESS...?
MAYBE HALF OF ALL CAPES WITH ACTUAL SUPERPOWERS WERE GIVEN 'EM VIA, WELL, "BARGAINS."
HE MEANT TO SAY "SO-CALLED BARGAINS," BY THE WAY.
SOME RIDICULOUS F[redacted]ING APPARITION MATERIALIZES OUT OF NOWHERE, MAKES 'EM A SUPEROFFER THEY CAN'T REFUSE.
IN MY CASE, IT WAS A TATTED-UP INDIE-CHICK VERSION OF THE GODDESS ATHENA.
OR SO SHE SAID.
KRKK
MADE MY BARGAIN WITH A BUNCH OF MACHINE ELVES WHILE I WAS TRIPPING ON DMT.
KRKK
MINE WAS A PLASMA GENIE, POPPING OUT OF A MAGNETIC BOTTLE IN THE LAB WHERE I WAS A NUCLEAR-ENGINEERING UNDERGRAD.
WHATEVER BULLS[redacted] FORM THESE ASSHOLE HIGHER POWERS TOOK...
...THEY GAVE SOME OF US A LITTLE MORE THAN WE F[redacted]ING BARGAINED FOR.

TURNS OUT, FOR AN OH-SO-LUCKY FEW OF US... ...OUR **BODIES** ARE STILL MORTAL...

...B-BUT OUR S-SUPERPOWERS **AREN'T.**

WE GET **KILLED IN** ACTION.

DIE **GLORIOUSLY,** DIE **PATHETICALLY,** WHATEVER.

BUT OUR F▓▓ING **POWERS** LEAVE US STILL **CONSCIOUS,** STILL **AWARE**...

IF WE HAVE ANY **GRAY MATTER** LEFT, THAT IS.

SLRPP

SHLUPP

SHLUPP

...EVEN AS OUR BODIES **DECOMPOSE** AND **ROT** TO F�▓▓ING **PIECES.**

N-NOT P-**PRETTY.** ALSO, N-NOT **FUN.**

E-ESPECIALLY IF TH-THEY **AUTOPSY** YOU WHILE Y-YOU'RE STILL IN D-**DEATHSHOCK,** Y'KNOW...?

VOLUNTARY MUSCLE CONTROL TAKES A LONG TIME TO COME BACK AFTER YOUR INITIAL DEATH.

HOURS, EVEN **DAYS** MIGHT PASS BEFORE YOU CAN MAKE YOUR CORPSE EVEN **TWITCH.**

WHICH IS H-HOW THE FIRST W-WAVE OF **SUPERDEAD** WOUND UP G-GETTING **BURIED** S-**SEMI-ALIVE,** Y'KNOW?

GAKK --!

POOR **TOMMY TOKAMAK** FREAKED OUT AND BLEW UP **SUPRAHUMAN MAUSOLEUM #1** WHILE TRYING TO BLAST HIMSELF OUT OF HIS OWN GRAVE...

B-**BURIED ALIVE**...? **SEMI-ALIVE**...?

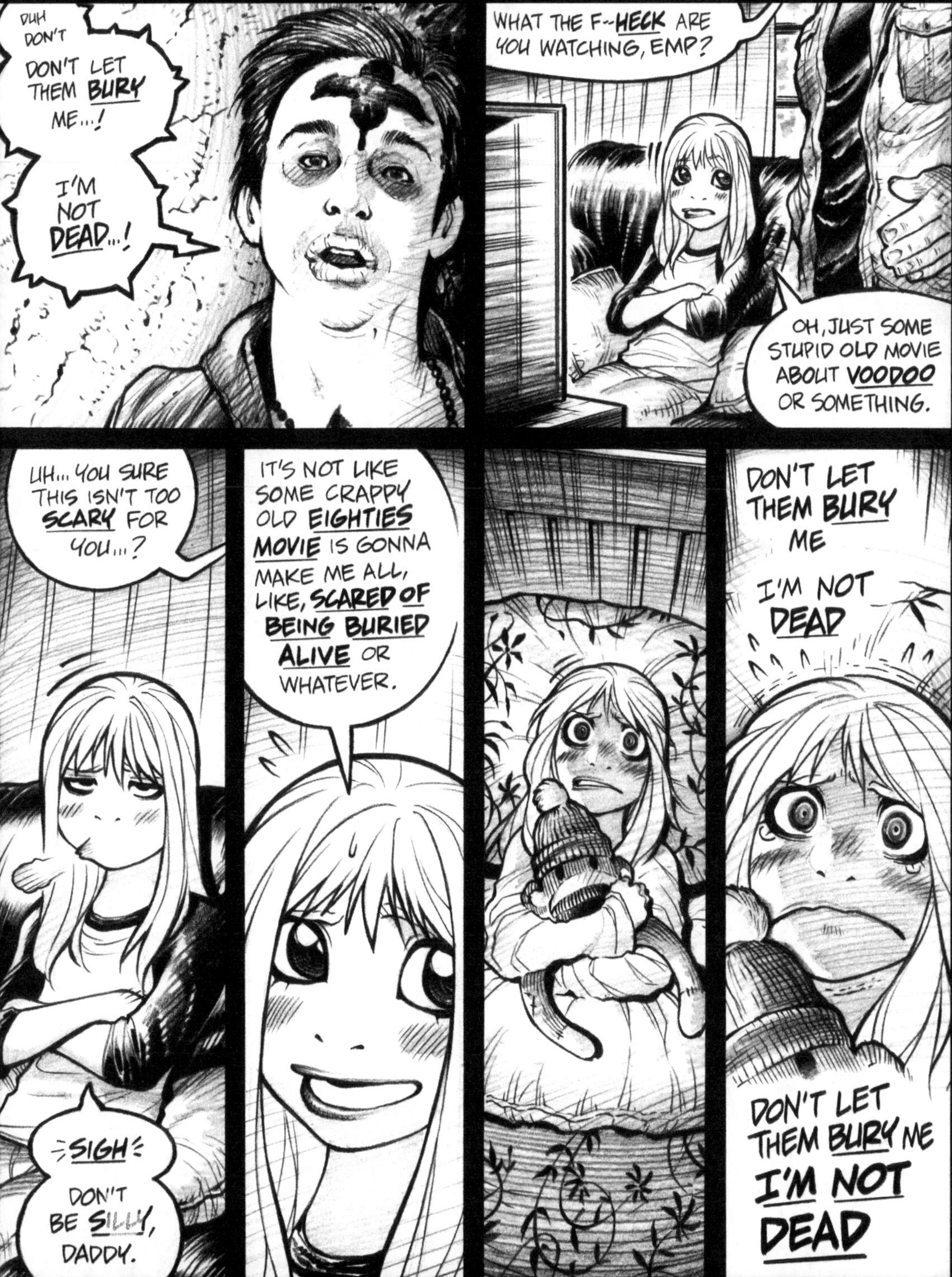
DUH DON'T
DON'T LET THEM BURY ME...!
I'M NOT DEAD...!
WHAT THE F--HECK ARE YOU WATCHING, EMP?
OH, JUST SOME STUPID OLD MOVIE ABOUT VOODOO OR SOMETHING.
UH... YOU SURE THIS ISN'T TOO SCARY FOR YOU...?
SIGH
DON'T BE SILLY, DADDY.
IT'S NOT LIKE SOME CRAPPY OLD EIGHTIES MOVIE IS GONNA MAKE ME ALL, LIKE, SCARED OF BEING BURIED ALIVE OR WHATEVER.
DON'T LET THEM BURY ME
I'M NOT DEAD
DON'T LET THEM BURY ME I'M NOT DEAD

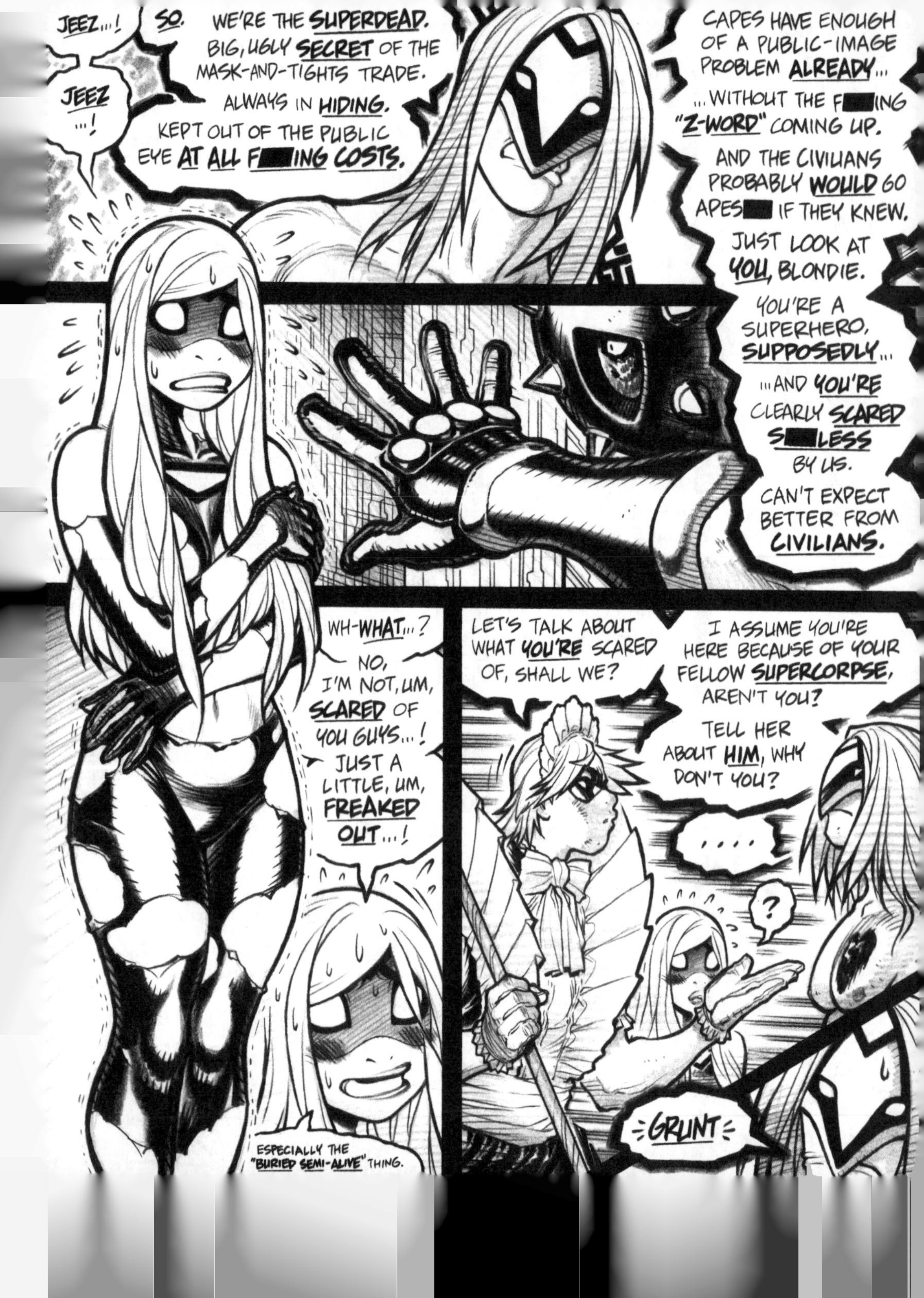

JEEZ...!
JEEZ...!
SO. WE'RE THE SUPERDEAD. BIG, UGLY SECRET OF THE MASK-AND-TIGHTS TRADE.
ALWAYS IN HIDING. KEPT OUT OF THE PUBLIC EYE AT ALL F[redacted]ING COSTS.
CAPES HAVE ENOUGH OF A PUBLIC-IMAGE PROBLEM ALREADY...
...WITHOUT THE F[redacted]ING "Z-WORD" COMING UP.
AND THE CIVILIANS PROBABLY WOULD GO APES[redacted] IF THEY KNEW.
JUST LOOK AT YOU, BLONDIE.
YOU'RE A SUPERHERO, SUPPOSEDLY...
...AND YOU'RE CLEARLY SCARED S[redacted]LESS BY US.
CAN'T EXPECT BETTER FROM CIVILIANS.
WH-WHAT...?
NO, I'M NOT, UM, SCARED OF YOU GUYS...! JUST A LITTLE, UM, FREAKED OUT...!
ESPECIALLY THE "BURIED SEMI-ALIVE" THING.
LET'S TALK ABOUT WHAT YOU'RE SCARED OF, SHALL WE?
I ASSUME YOU'RE HERE BECAUSE OF YOUR FELLOW SUPERCORPSE, AREN'T YOU?
TELL HER ABOUT HIM, WHY DON'T YOU?
....
?
GRUNT

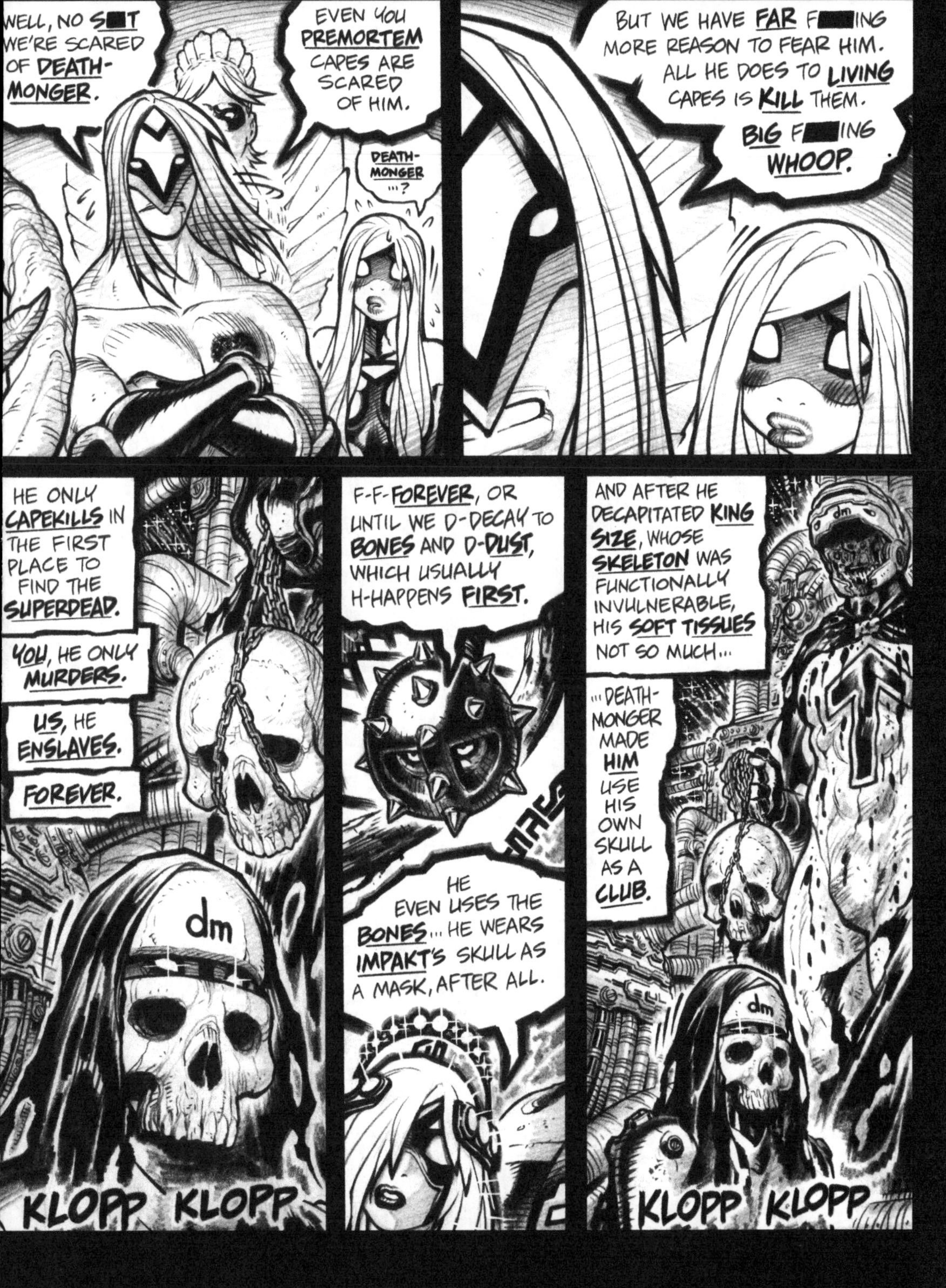
WELL, NO S[redacted]T WE'RE SCARED OF DEATH-MONGER.
EVEN YOU PREMORTEM CAPES ARE SCARED OF HIM.
DEATH-MONGER ...?
BUT WE HAVE FAR F[redacted]ING MORE REASON TO FEAR HIM. ALL HE DOES TO LIVING CAPES IS KILL THEM.
BIG F[redacted]ING WHOOP.
HE ONLY CAPEKILLS IN THE FIRST PLACE TO FIND THE SUPERDEAD.
YOU, HE ONLY MURDERS.
US, HE ENSLAVES.
FOREVER.
KLOPP KLOPP
F-F-FOREVER, OR UNTIL WE D-DECAY TO BONES AND D-DUST, WHICH USUALLY H-HAPPENS FIRST.
HE EVEN USES THE BONES... HE WEARS IMPAKT'S SKULL AS A MASK, AFTER ALL.
AND AFTER HE DECAPITATED KING SIZE, WHOSE SKELETON WAS FUNCTIONALLY INVULNERABLE, HIS SOFT TISSUES NOT SO MUCH...
...DEATH-MONGER MADE HIM USE HIS OWN SKULL AS A CLUB.
KLOPP KLOPP

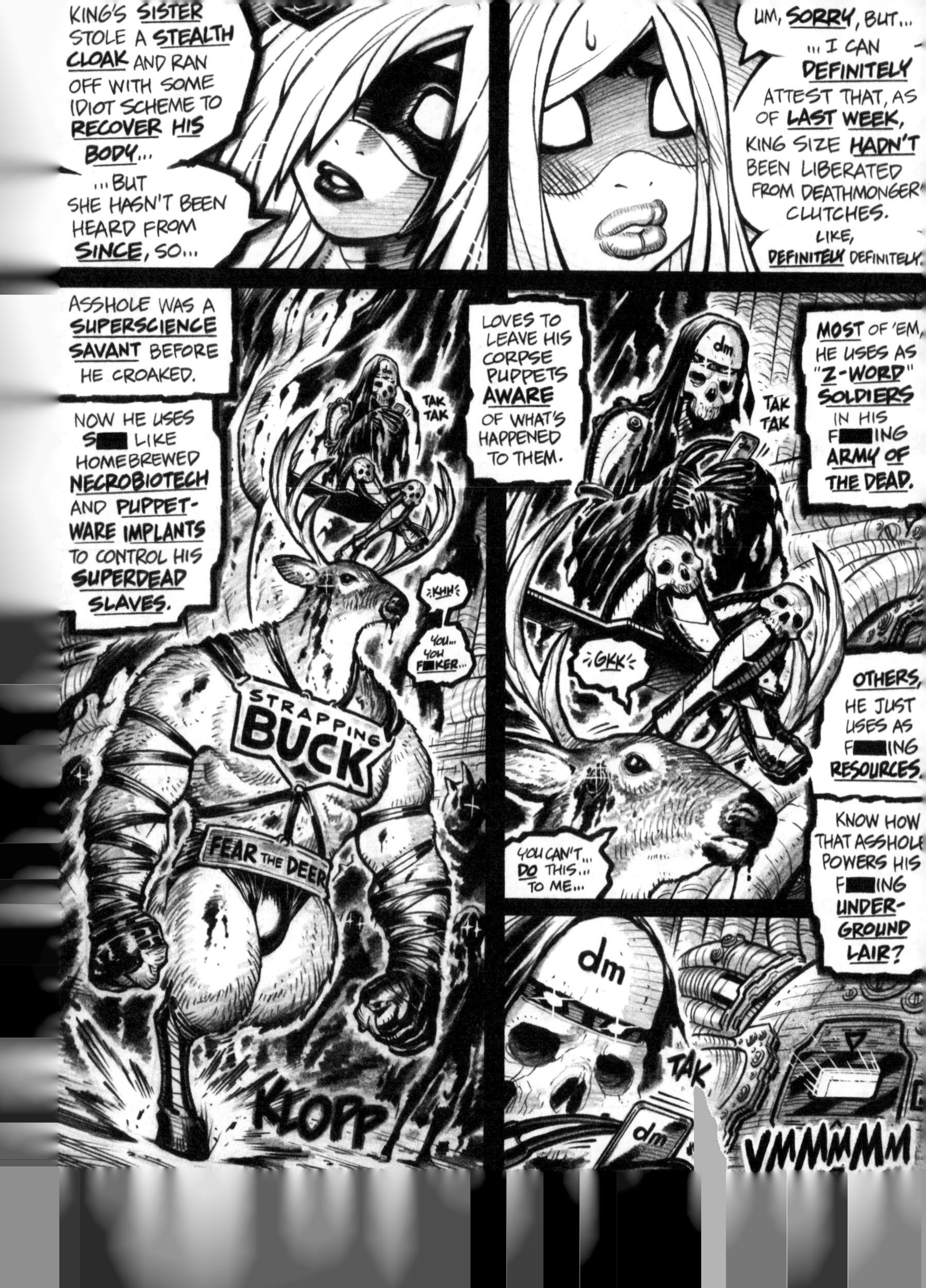
KING'S SISTER STOLE A STEALTH CLOAK AND RAN OFF WITH SOME IDIOT SCHEME TO RECOVER HIS BODY...
...BUT SHE HASN'T BEEN HEARD FROM SINCE, SO...
UM, SORRY, BUT...
...I CAN DEFINITELY ATTEST THAT, AS OF LAST WEEK, KING SIZE HADN'T BEEN LIBERATED FROM DEATHMONGER' CLUTCHES.
LIKE, DEFINITELY DEFINITELY.
ASSHOLE WAS A SUPERSCIENCE SAVANT BEFORE HE CROAKED.
NOW HE USES S[redacted] LIKE HOMEBREWED NECROBIOTECH AND PUPPET-WARE IMPLANTS TO CONTROL HIS SUPERDEAD SLAVES.
TAK TAK
KHH
YOU... YOU F[redacted]KER...
STRAPPING BUCK
FEAR THE DEER
KLOPP
LOVES TO LEAVE HIS CORPSE PUPPETS AWARE OF WHAT'S HAPPENED TO THEM.
dm
TAK TAK
MOST OF 'EM, HE USES AS "Z-WORD" SOLDIERS IN HIS F[redacted]ING ARMY OF THE DEAD.
GKK
OTHERS, HE JUST USES AS F[redacted]ING RESOURCES.
YOU CAN'T... DO THIS... TO ME...
KNOW HOW THAT ASSHOLE POWERS HIS F[redacted]ING UNDER-GROUND LAIR?
dm
TAK
dm
VMMMMM

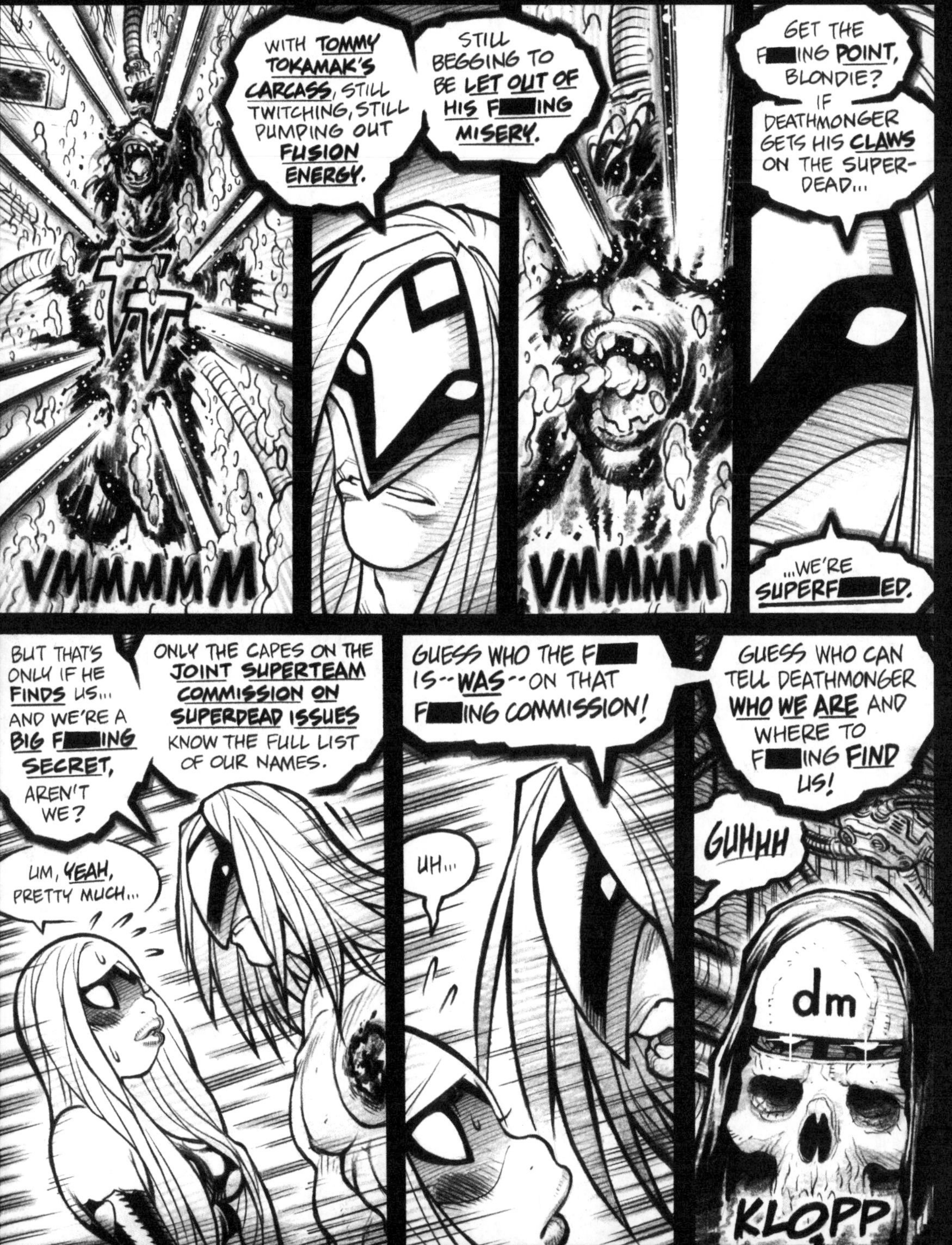
WITH TOMMY TOKAMAK'S CARCASS, STILL TWITCHING, STILL PUMPING OUT FUSION ENERGY.
VMMMMM
STILL BEGGING TO BE LET OUT OF HIS F[redacted]ING MISERY.
VMMMM
GET THE F[redacted]ING POINT, BLONDIE? IF DEATHMONGER GETS HIS CLAWS ON THE SUPER-DEAD...
...WE'RE SUPERF[redacted]ED.
BUT THAT'S ONLY IF HE FINDS US... AND WE'RE A BIG F[redacted]ING SECRET, AREN'T WE?
ONLY THE CAPES ON THE JOINT SUPERTEAM COMMISSION ON SUPERDEAD ISSUES KNOW THE FULL LIST OF OUR NAMES.
UM, YEAH, PRETTY MUCH...
GUESS WHO THE F[redacted] IS--WAS--ON THAT F[redacted]ING COMMISSION!
UH...
GUESS WHO CAN TELL DEATHMONGER WHO WE ARE AND WHERE TO F[redacted]ING FIND US!
GUHHH
dm
KLOPP

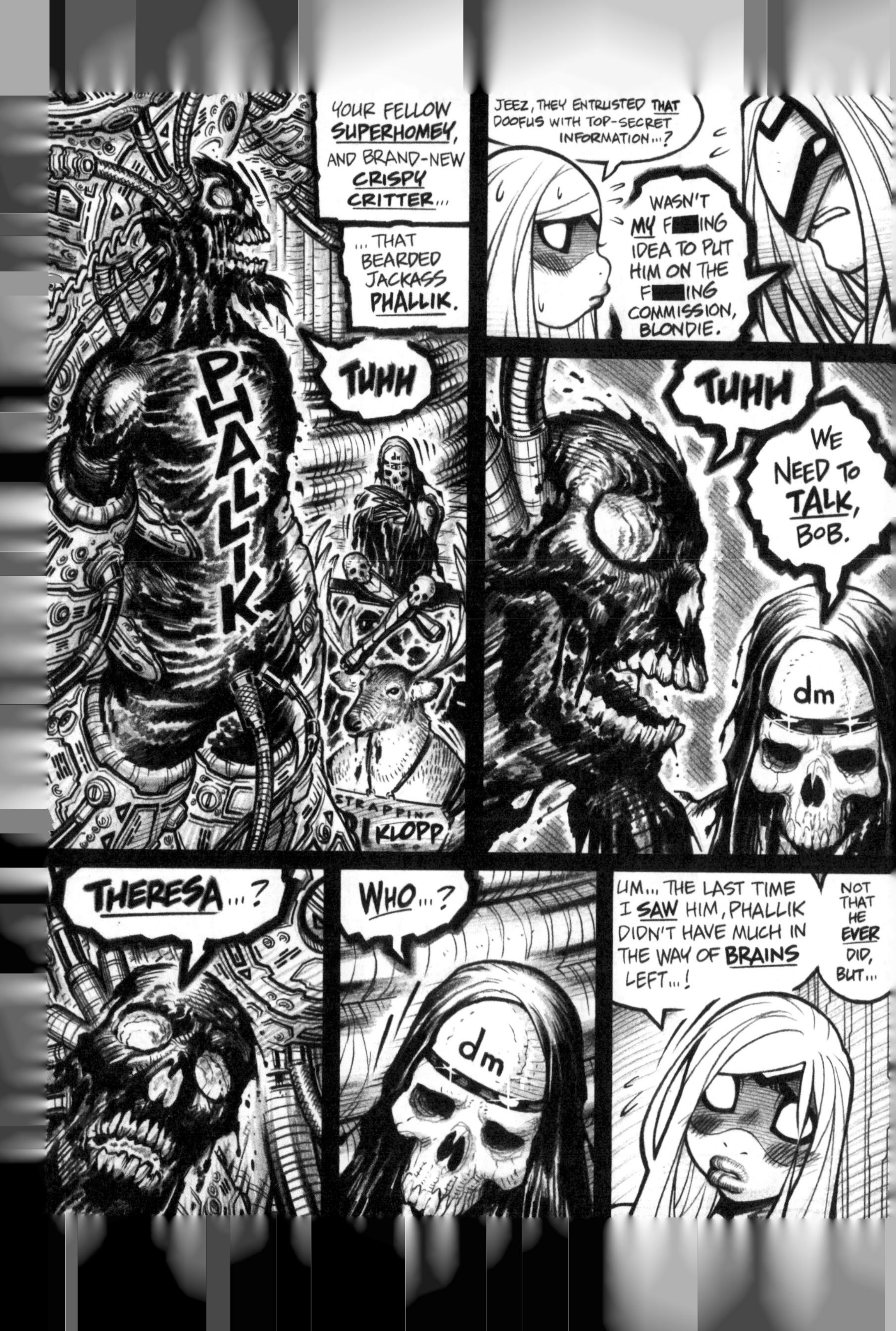
YOUR FELLOW SUPERHOMEY, AND BRAND-NEW CRISPY CRITTER...
...THAT BEARDED JACKASS PHALLIK.
JEEZ, THEY ENTRUSTED THAT DOOFUS WITH TOP-SECRET INFORMATION...?
WASN'T MY F[redacted]ING IDEA TO PUT HIM ON THE F[redacted]ING COMMISSION, BLONDIE.
TUHH
PHALLIK
TUHH
WE NEED TO TALK, BOB.
dm
THERESA...?
WHO...?
dm
UM... THE LAST TIME I SAW HIM, PHALLIK DIDN'T HAVE MUCH IN THE WAY OF BRAINS LEFT...!
NOT THAT HE EVER DID, BUT...

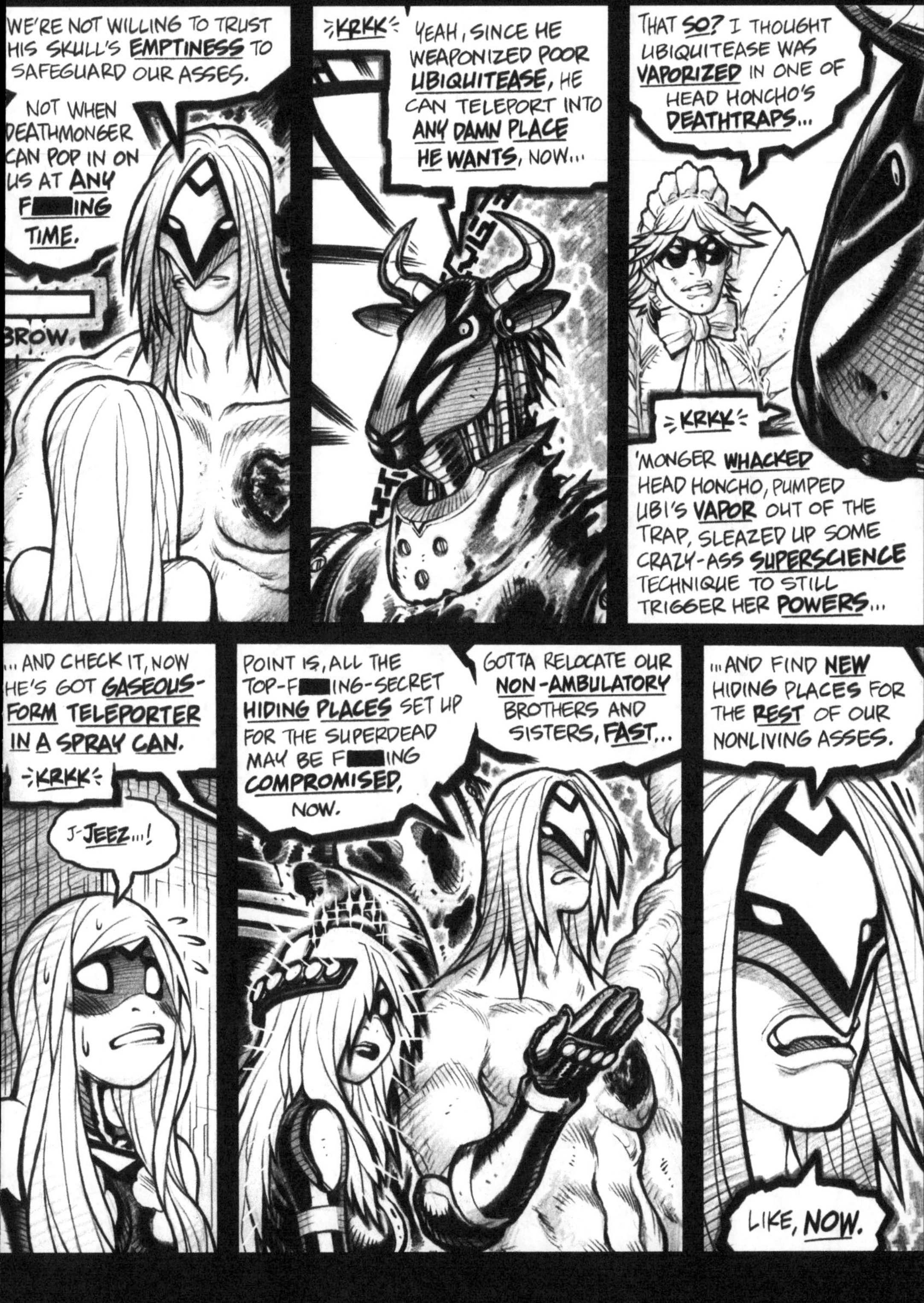
WE'RE NOT WILLING TO TRUST HIS SKULL'S EMPTINESS TO SAFEGUARD OUR ASSES.
NOT WHEN DEATHMONGER CAN POP IN ON US AT ANY F[redacted]ING TIME.
BROW
KRKK
YEAH, SINCE HE WEAPONIZED POOR UBIQUITEASE, HE CAN TELEPORT INTO ANY DAMN PLACE HE WANTS, NOW...
THAT SO? I THOUGHT UBIQUITEASE WAS VAPORIZED IN ONE OF HEAD HONCHO'S DEATHTRAPS...
KRKK
'MONGER WHACKED HEAD HONCHO, PUMPED UBI'S VAPOR OUT OF THE TRAP, SLEAZED UP SOME CRAZY-ASS SUPERSCIENCE TECHNIQUE TO STILL TRIGGER HER POWERS...
...AND CHECK IT, NOW HE'S GOT GASEOUS-FORM TELEPORTER IN A SPRAY CAN.
KRKK
J-JEEZ...!
POINT IS, ALL THE TOP-F[redacted]ING-SECRET HIDING PLACES SET UP FOR THE SUPERDEAD MAY BE F[redacted]ING COMPROMISED, NOW.
GOTTA RELOCATE OUR NON-AMBULATORY BROTHERS AND SISTERS, FAST...
...AND FIND NEW HIDING PLACES FOR THE REST OF OUR NONLIVING ASSES.
LIKE, NOW.

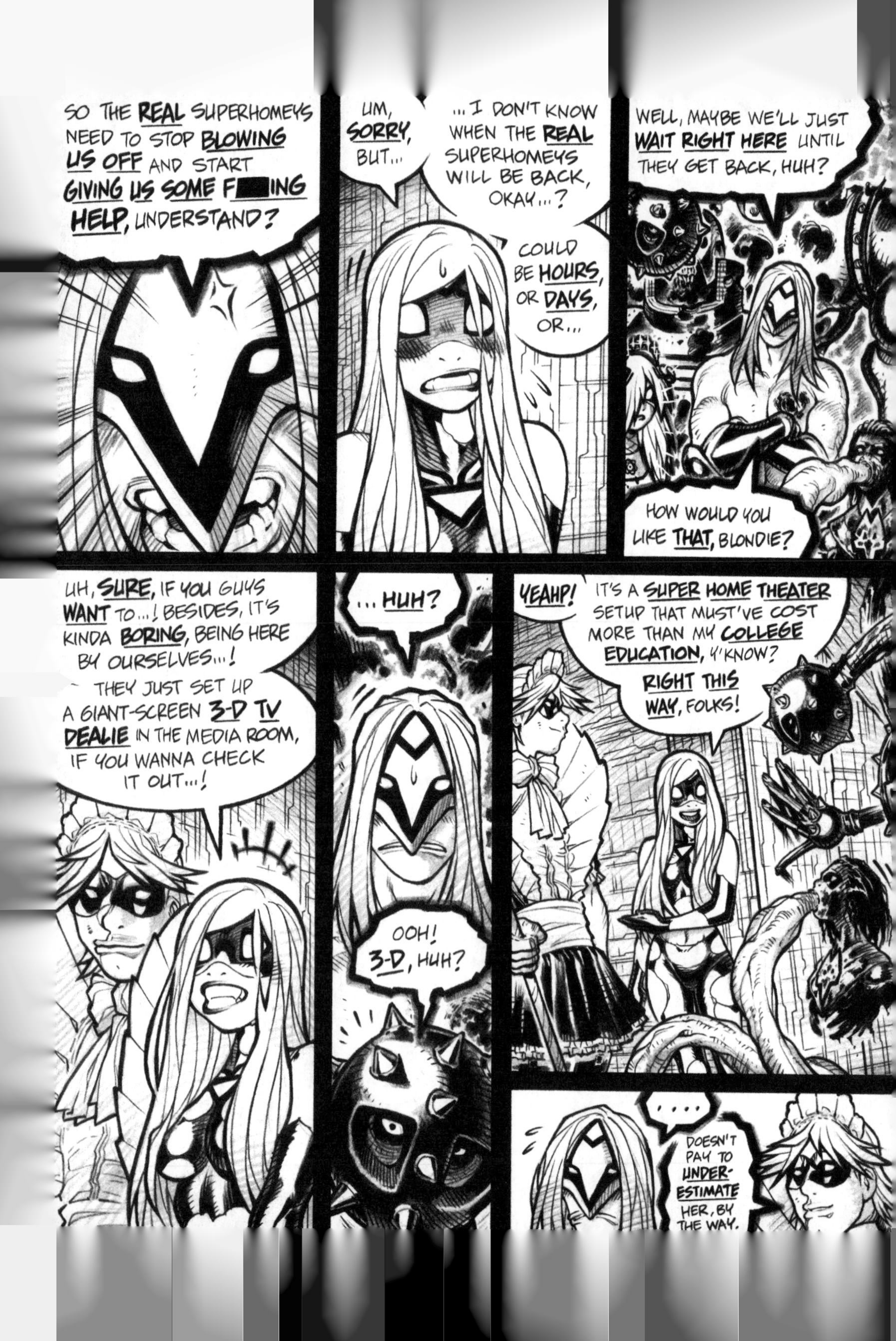
SO THE REAL SUPERHOMEYS NEED TO STOP BLOWING US OFF AND START GIVING US SOME F[redacted]ING HELP, UNDERSTAND?
UM, SORRY, BUT...
...I DON'T KNOW WHEN THE REAL SUPERHOMEYS WILL BE BACK, OKAY...?
COULD BE HOURS, OR DAYS, OR...
WELL, MAYBE WE'LL JUST WAIT RIGHT HERE UNTIL THEY GET BACK, HUH?
HOW WOULD YOU LIKE THAT, BLONDIE?
UH, SURE, IF YOU GUYS WANT TO...! BESIDES, IT'S KINDA BORING, BEING HERE BY OURSELVES...!
THEY JUST SET UP A GIANT-SCREEN 3-D TV DEALIE IN THE MEDIA ROOM, IF YOU WANNA CHECK IT OUT...!
...HUH?
OOH! 3-D, HUH?
YEAHP!
IT'S A SUPER HOME THEATER SETUP THAT MUST'VE COST MORE THAN MY COLLEGE EDUCATION, Y'KNOW?
RIGHT THIS WAY, FOLKS!
....
DOESN'T PAY TO UNDER-ESTIMATE HER, BY THE WAY.

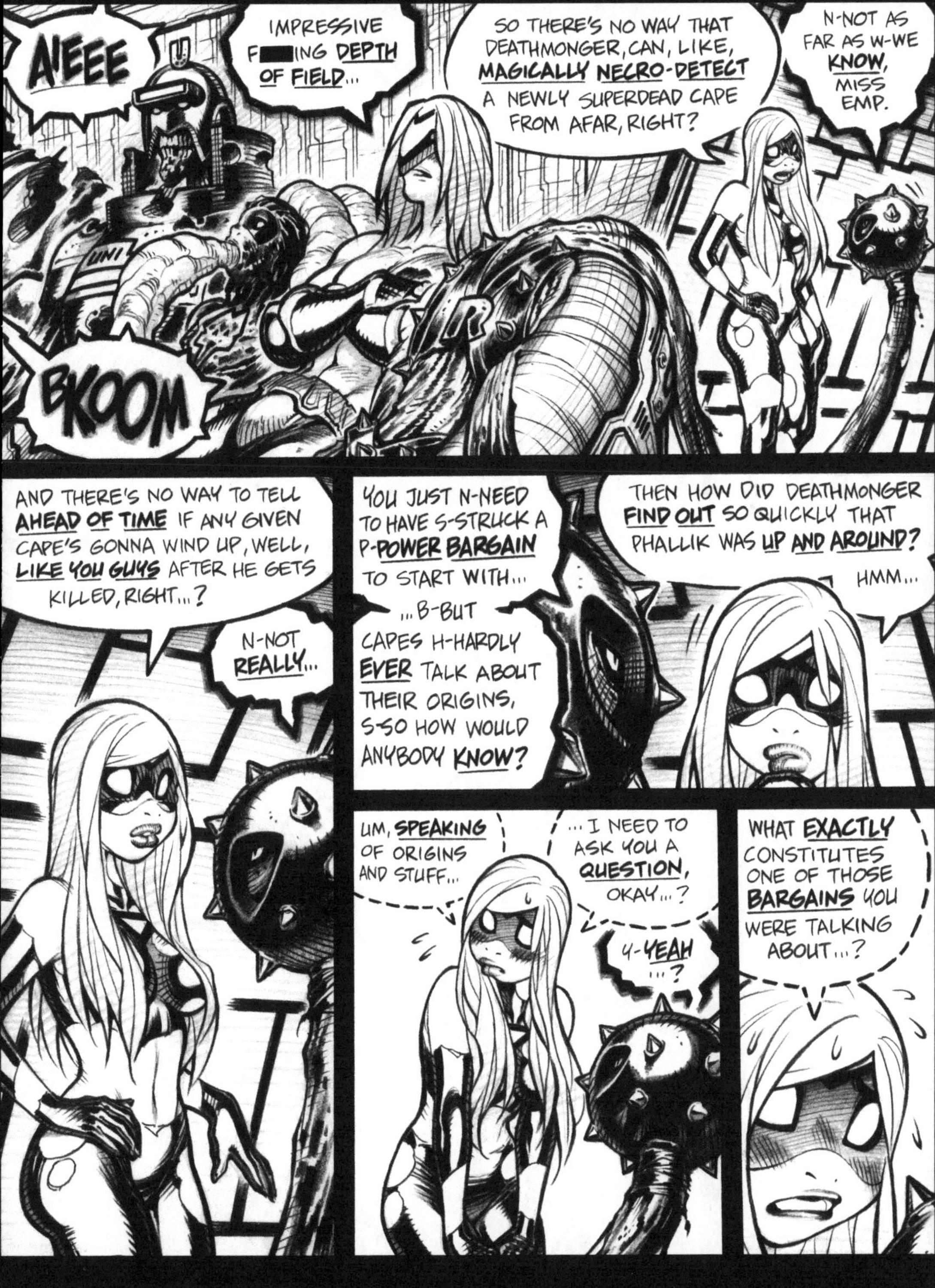
AIEEE
IMPRESSIVE F[redacted]ING DEPTH OF FIELD...
SO THERE'S NO WAY THAT DEATHMONGER, CAN, LIKE, MAGICALLY NECRO-DETECT A NEWLY SUPERDEAD CAPE FROM AFAR, RIGHT?
N-NOT AS FAR AS W-WE KNOW, MISS EMP.
UNI
BKOOM
AND THERE'S NO WAY TO TELL AHEAD OF TIME IF ANY GIVEN CAPE'S GONNA WIND UP, WELL, LIKE YOU GUYS AFTER HE GETS KILLED, RIGHT...?
N-NOT REALLY...
YOU JUST N-NEED TO HAVE S-STRUCK A P-POWER BARGAIN TO START WITH...
...B-BUT CAPES H-HARDLY EVER TALK ABOUT THEIR ORIGINS, S-SO HOW WOULD ANYBODY KNOW?
THEN HOW DID DEATHMONGER FIND OUT SO QUICKLY THAT PHALLIK WAS UP AND AROUND?
HMM...
UM, SPEAKING OF ORIGINS AND STUFF...
...I NEED TO ASK YOU A QUESTION, OKAY...?
Y-YEAH...?
WHAT EXACTLY CONSTITUTES ONE OF THOSE BARGAINS YOU WERE TALKING ABOUT...?

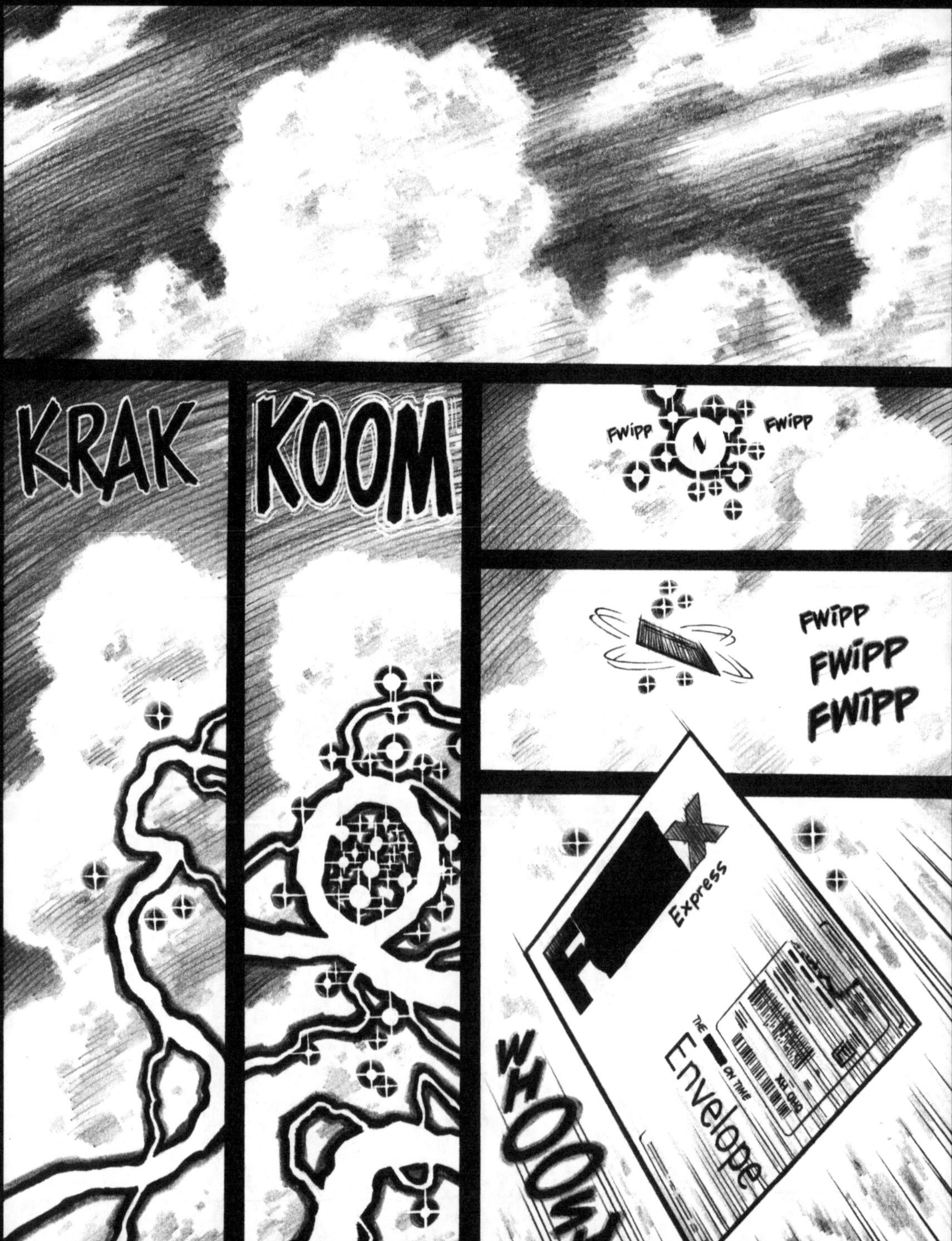
KRAK
KOOM
FWIPP
FWIPP
FWIPP
FWIPP
FWIPP
Express
THE [redacted] ON TIME
Envelope
WHOOM

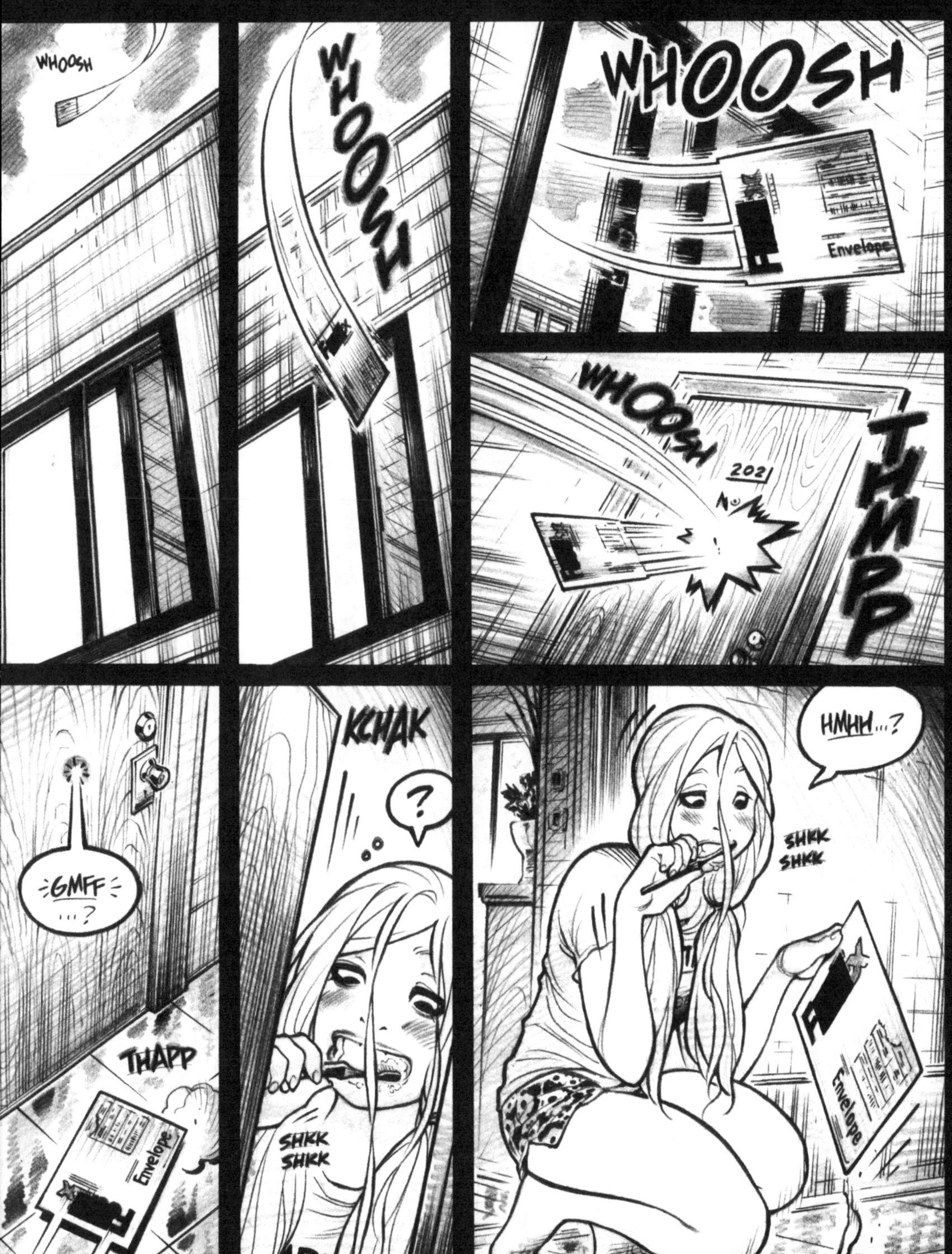
WHOOSH
WHOOSH
WHOOSH
Envelope
WHOOSH
THMPP
GMFF
...?
THAPP
Envelope
KCHAK
?
SHKK
SHKK
API
HMHH...?
SHKK
SHKK
Envelope

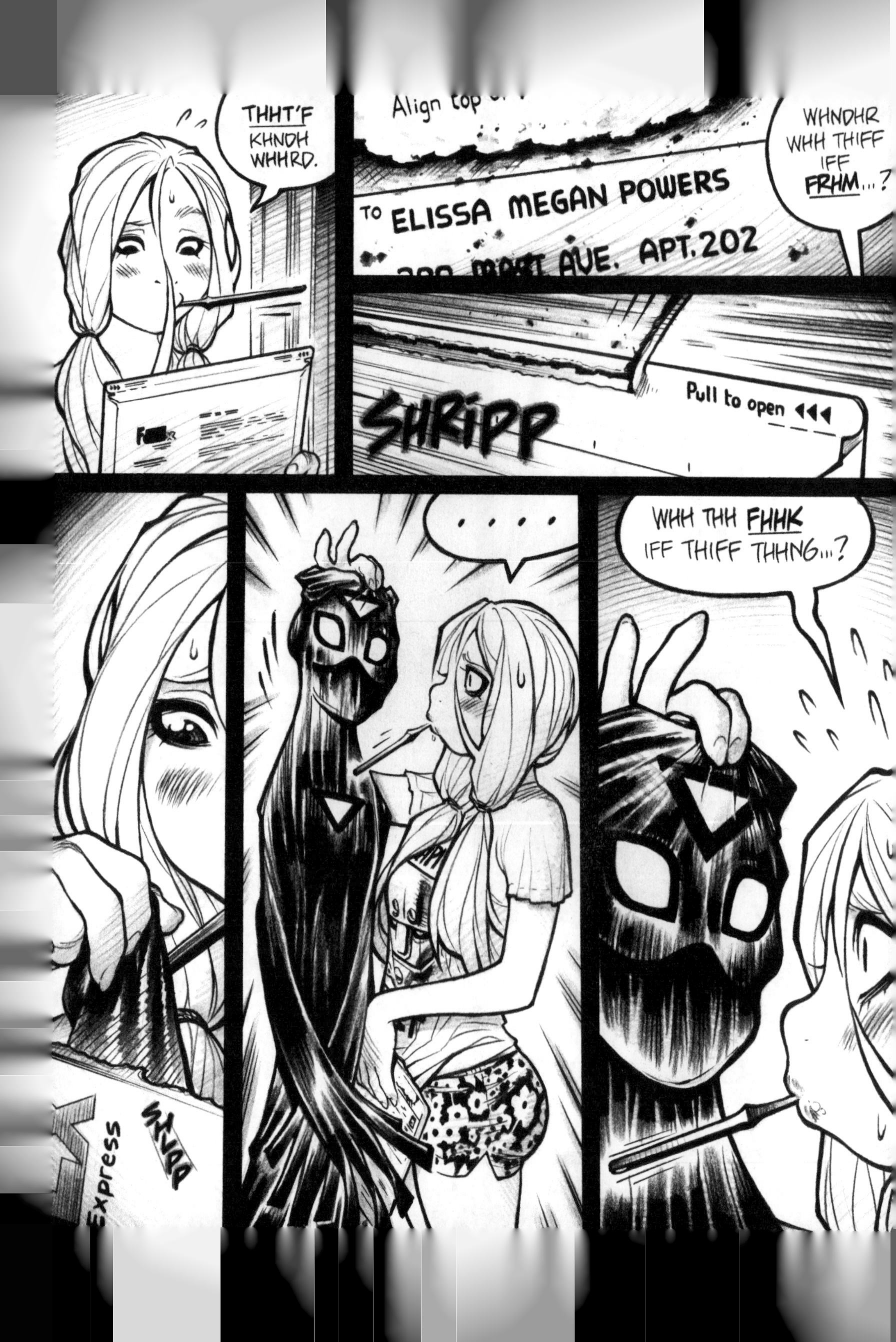
THHT'F KHNDH WHHRD.
Align top o
TO ELISSA MEGAN POWERS
AVE. APT. 202
WHNDHR WHH THIFF IFF FRHM...?
Pull to open
SHRIPP
....
WHH THH FHHK IFF THIFF THHNG...?
Express

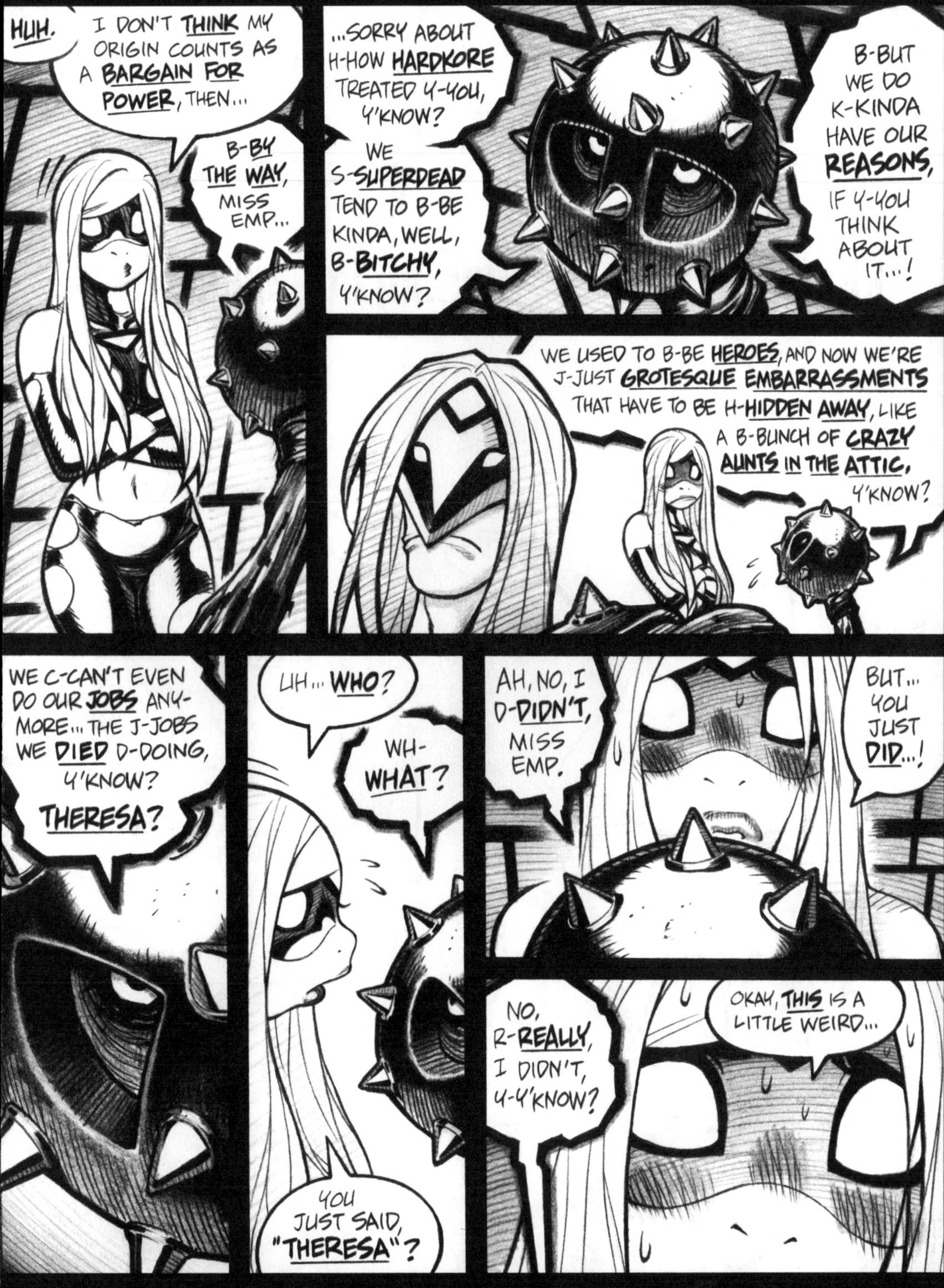
HUH.
I DON'T THINK MY ORIGIN COUNTS AS A BARGAIN FOR POWER, THEN...
B-BY THE WAY, MISS EMP...
...SORRY ABOUT H-HOW HARDKORE TREATED Y-YOU, Y'KNOW?
WE S-SUPERDEAD TEND TO B-BE KINDA, WELL, B-BITCHY, Y'KNOW?
B-BUT WE DO K-KINDA HAVE OUR REASONS, IF Y-YOU THINK ABOUT IT...!
WE USED TO B-BE HEROES, AND NOW WE'RE J-JUST GROTESQUE EMBARRASSMENTS THAT HAVE TO BE H-HIDDEN AWAY, LIKE A B-BUNCH OF CRAZY AUNTS IN THE ATTIC, Y'KNOW?
WE C-CAN'T EVEN DO OUR JOBS ANY-MORE... THE J-JOBS WE DIED D-DOING, Y'KNOW?
THERESA?
UH... WHO?
WH-WHAT?
YOU JUST SAID, "THERESA"?
AH, NO, I D-DIDN'T, MISS EMP.
BUT... YOU JUST DID...!
NO, R-REALLY, I DIDN'T, Y-Y'KNOW?
OKAY, THIS IS A LITTLE WEIRD...

Empowered™

My Advice for Struggling Superheroines

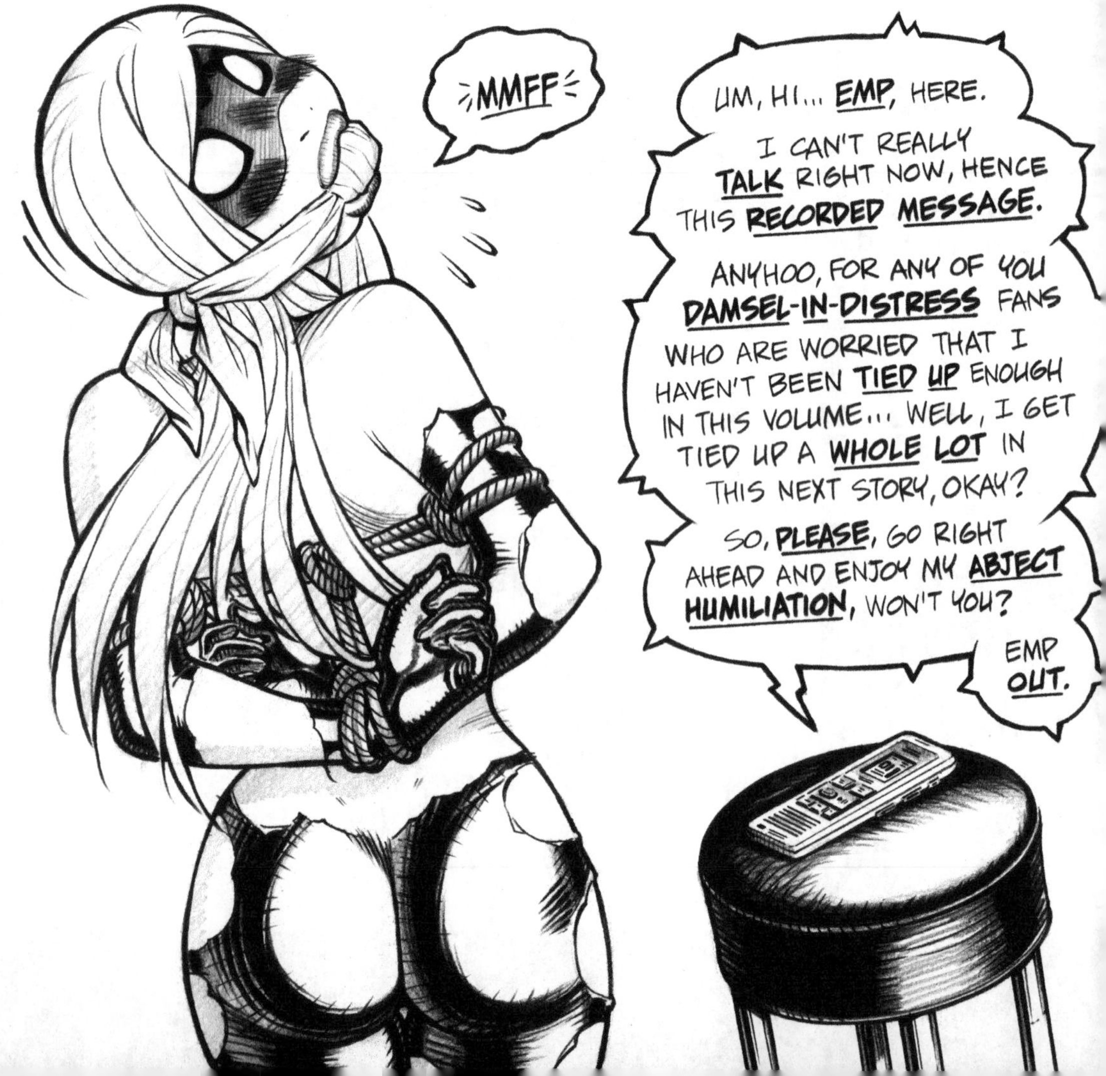
MMFF
UM, HI... EMP, HERE.
I CAN'T REALLY TALK RIGHT NOW, HENCE THIS RECORDED MESSAGE.
ANYHOO, FOR ANY OF YOU DAMSEL-IN-DISTRESS FANS WHO ARE WORRIED THAT I HAVEN'T BEEN TIED UP ENOUGH IN THIS VOLUME... WELL, I GET TIED UP A WHOLE LOT IN THIS NEXT STORY, OKAY?
SO, PLEASE, GO RIGHT AHEAD AND ENJOY MY ABJECT HUMILIATION, WON'T YOU?
EMP OUT.

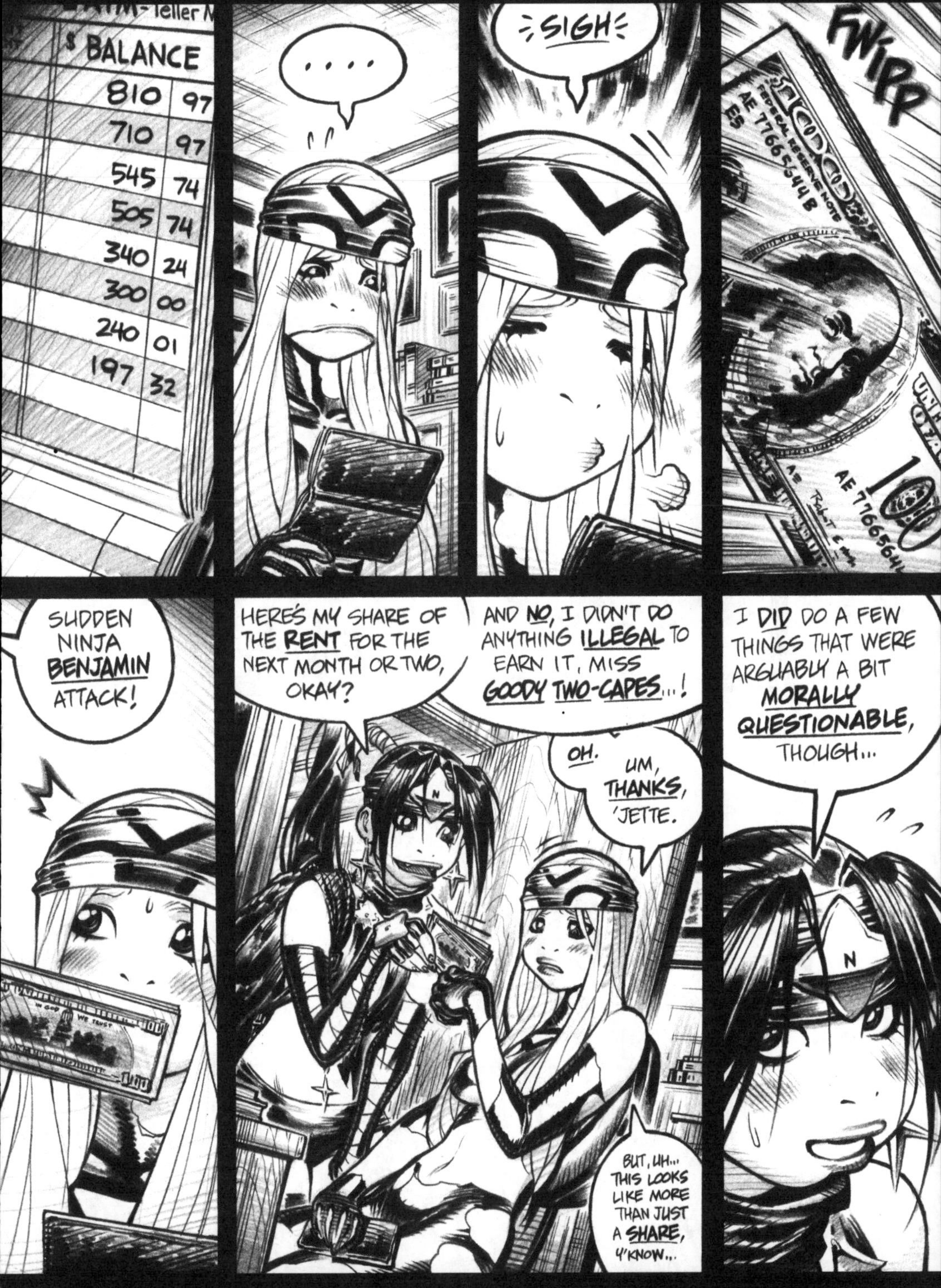
ATM-Teller M
$ BALANCE
810 97
710 97
545 74
505 74
340 24
300 00
240 01
197 32
....
SIGH
FWIPP
FEDERAL RESERVE NOTE
AE 77665448 B
SUDDEN NINJA BENJAMIN ATTACK!
HERE'S MY SHARE OF THE RENT FOR THE NEXT MONTH OR TWO, OKAY?
AND NO, I DIDN'T DO ANYTHING ILLEGAL TO EARN IT, MISS GOODY TWO-CAPES...!
OH.
UM, THANKS, 'JETTE.
BUT, UH... THIS LOOKS LIKE MORE THAN JUST A SHARE, Y'KNOW...
I DID DO A FEW THINGS THAT WERE ARGUABLY A BIT MORALLY QUESTIONABLE, THOUGH...

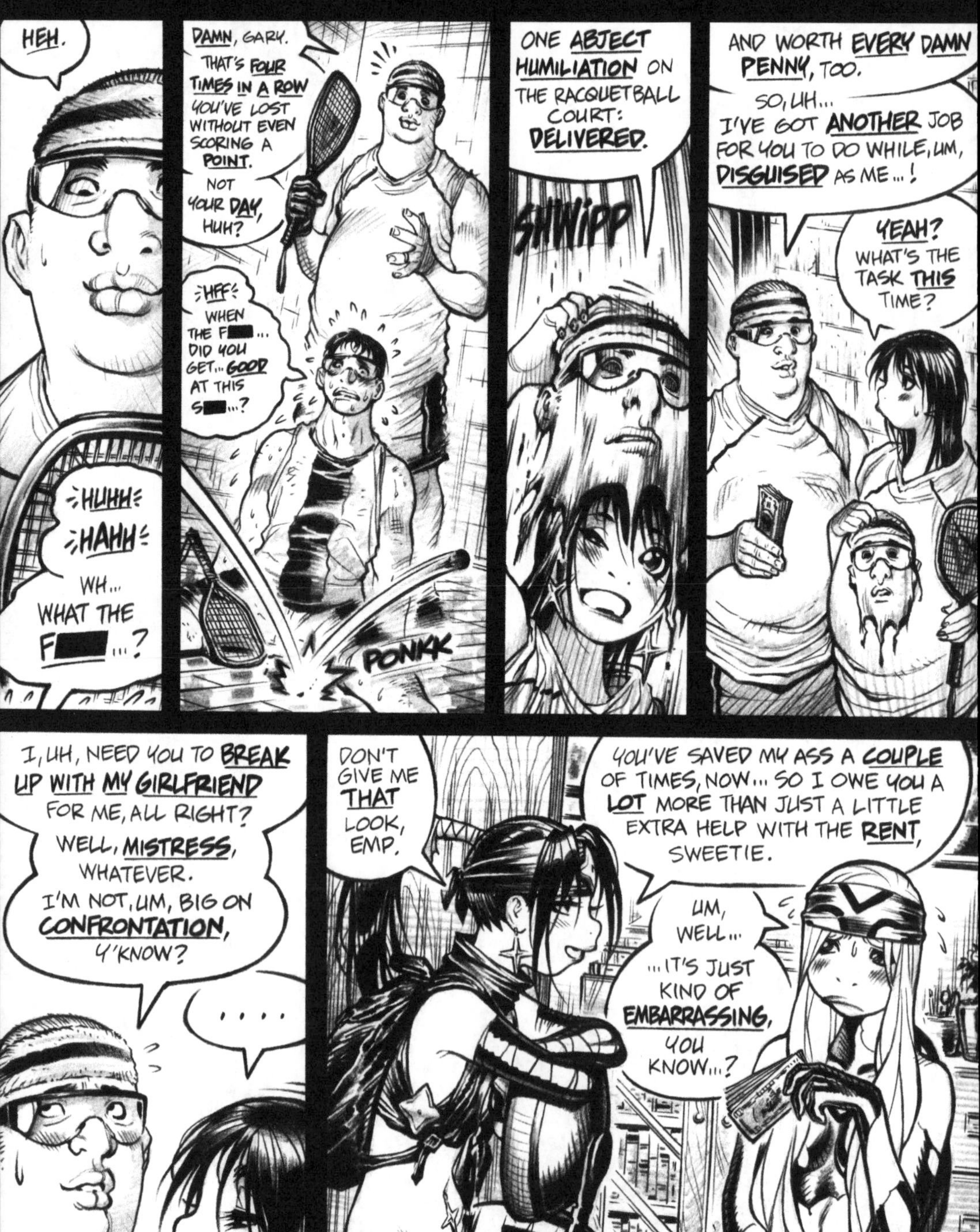
HEH.
DAMN, GARY.
THAT'S FOUR TIMES IN A ROW YOU'VE LOST WITHOUT EVEN SCORING A POINT.
NOT YOUR DAY, HUH?
HFF
WHEN THE F[redacted]... DID YOU GET... GOOD AT THIS S[redacted]...?
HUHH
HAHH
WH... WHAT THE F[redacted]...?
PONKK
ONE ABJECT HUMILIATION ON THE RACQUETBALL COURT: DELIVERED.
SHWIPP
AND WORTH EVERY DAMN PENNY, TOO.
SO, UH... I'VE GOT ANOTHER JOB FOR YOU TO DO WHILE, UM, DISGUISED AS ME...!
YEAH? WHAT'S THE TASK THIS TIME?
I, UH, NEED YOU TO BREAK UP WITH MY GIRLFRIEND FOR ME, ALL RIGHT?
WELL, MISTRESS, WHATEVER.
I'M NOT, UM, BIG ON CONFRONTATION, Y'KNOW?
....
DON'T GIVE ME THAT LOOK, EMP.
YOU'VE SAVED MY ASS A COUPLE OF TIMES, NOW... SO I OWE YOU A LOT MORE THAN JUST A LITTLE EXTRA HELP WITH THE RENT, SWEETIE.
UM, WELL...
...IT'S JUST KIND OF EMBARRASSING, YOU KNOW...?

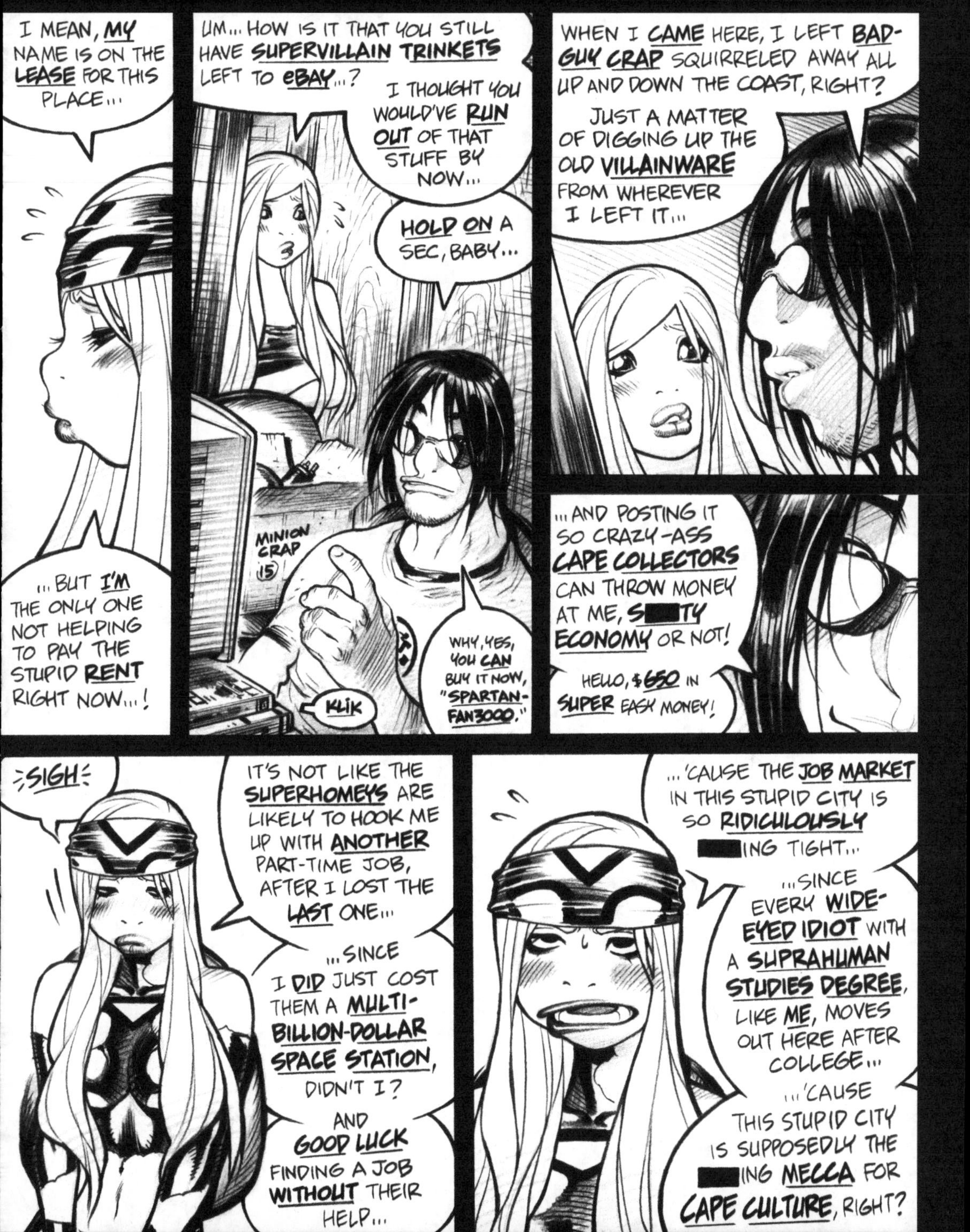

I MEAN, MY NAME IS ON THE LEASE FOR THIS PLACE...
...BUT I'M THE ONLY ONE NOT HELPING TO PAY THE STUPID RENT RIGHT NOW...!
UM... HOW IS IT THAT YOU STILL HAVE SUPERVILLAIN TRINKETS LEFT TO eBAY...?
I THOUGHT YOU WOULD'VE RUN OUT OF THAT STUFF BY NOW...
HOLD ON A SEC, BABY...
MINION CRAP 15
KLIK
WHY, YES, YOU CAN BUY IT NOW, "SPARTAN-FAN3000."
WHEN I CAME HERE, I LEFT BAD-GUY CRAP SQUIRRELED AWAY ALL UP AND DOWN THE COAST, RIGHT?
JUST A MATTER OF DIGGING UP THE OLD VILLAINWARE FROM WHEREVER I LEFT IT...
...AND POSTING IT SO CRAZY-ASS CAPE COLLECTORS CAN THROW MONEY AT ME, S[redacted]TY ECONOMY OR NOT!
HELLO, $650 IN SUPER EASY MONEY!
SIGH
IT'S NOT LIKE THE SUPERHOMEYS ARE LIKELY TO HOOK ME UP WITH ANOTHER PART-TIME JOB, AFTER I LOST THE LAST ONE...
...SINCE I DID JUST COST THEM A MULTI-BILLION-DOLLAR SPACE STATION, DIDN'T I?
AND GOOD LUCK FINDING A JOB WITHOUT THEIR HELP...
...'CAUSE THE JOB MARKET IN THIS STUPID CITY IS SO RIDICULOUSLY [redacted]ING TIGHT...
...SINCE EVERY WIDE-EYED IDIOT WITH A SUPRAHUMAN STUDIES DEGREE, LIKE ME, MOVES OUT HERE AFTER COLLEGE...
...'CAUSE THIS STUPID CITY IS SUPPOSEDLY THE [redacted]ING MECCA FOR CAPE CULTURE, RIGHT?

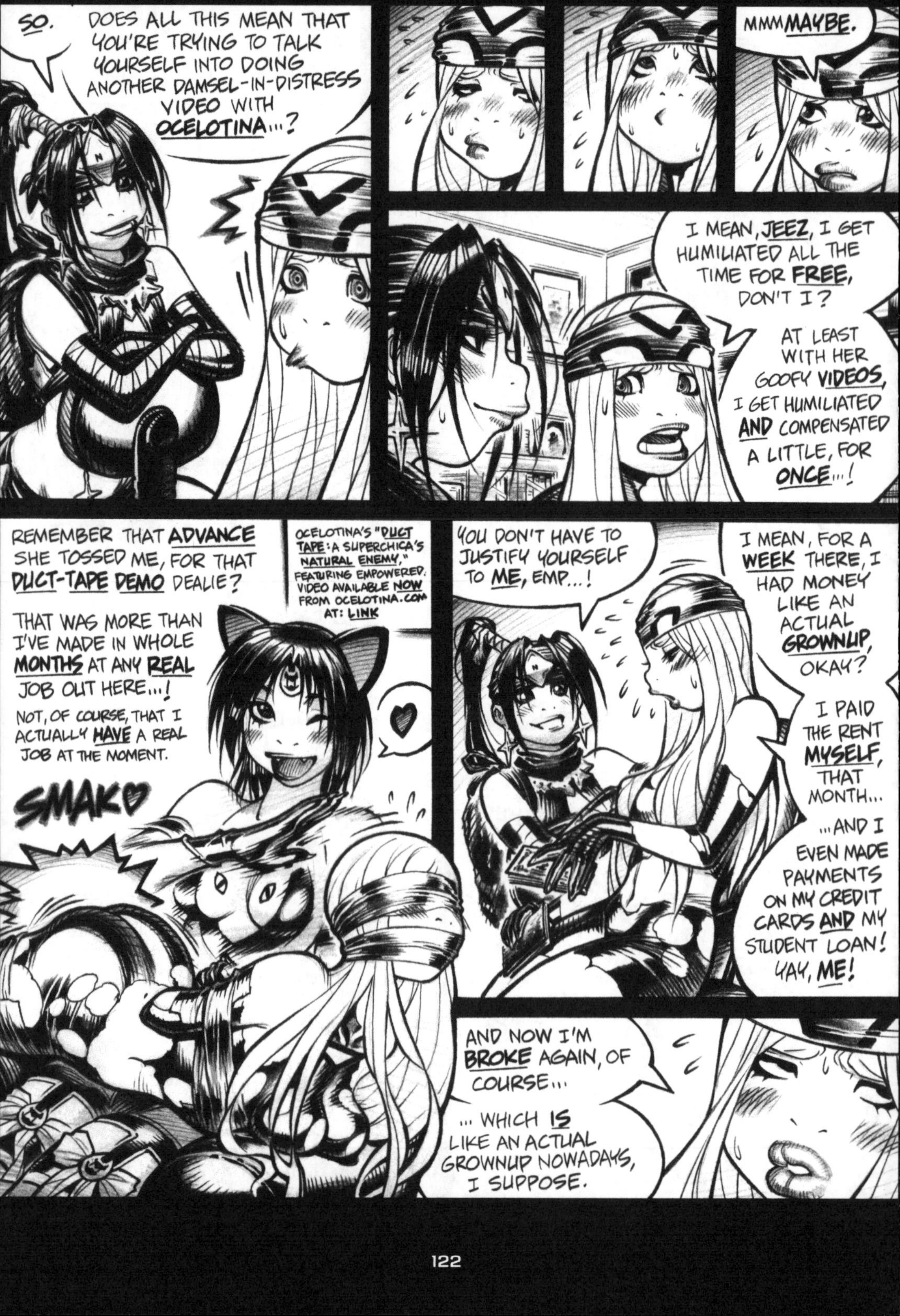
SO.
DOES ALL THIS MEAN THAT YOU'RE TRYING TO TALK YOURSELF INTO DOING ANOTHER DAMSEL-IN-DISTRESS VIDEO WITH OCELOTINA...?
MMMMAYBE.
I MEAN, JEEZ, I GET HUMILIATED ALL THE TIME FOR FREE, DON'T I?
AT LEAST WITH HER GOOFY VIDEOS, I GET HUMILIATED AND COMPENSATED A LITTLE, FOR ONCE...!
REMEMBER THAT ADVANCE SHE TOSSED ME, FOR THAT DUCT-TAPE DEMO DEALIE?
OCELOTINA'S "DUCT TAPE: A SUPERCHICA'S NATURAL ENEMY," FEATURING EMPOWERED. VIDEO AVAILABLE NOW FROM OCELOTINA.COM AT: LINK
THAT WAS MORE THAN I'VE MADE IN WHOLE MONTHS AT ANY REAL JOB OUT HERE...!
NOT, OF COURSE, THAT I ACTUALLY HAVE A REAL JOB AT THE MOMENT.
SMAK♡
YOU DON'T HAVE TO JUSTIFY YOURSELF TO ME, EMP...!
I MEAN, FOR A WEEK THERE, I HAD MONEY LIKE AN ACTUAL GROWNUP, OKAY?
I PAID THE RENT MYSELF, THAT MONTH...
...AND I EVEN MADE PAYMENTS ON MY CREDIT CARDS AND MY STUDENT LOAN! YAY, ME!
AND NOW I'M BROKE AGAIN, OF COURSE...
... WHICH IS LIKE AN ACTUAL GROWNUP NOWADAYS, I SUPPOSE.

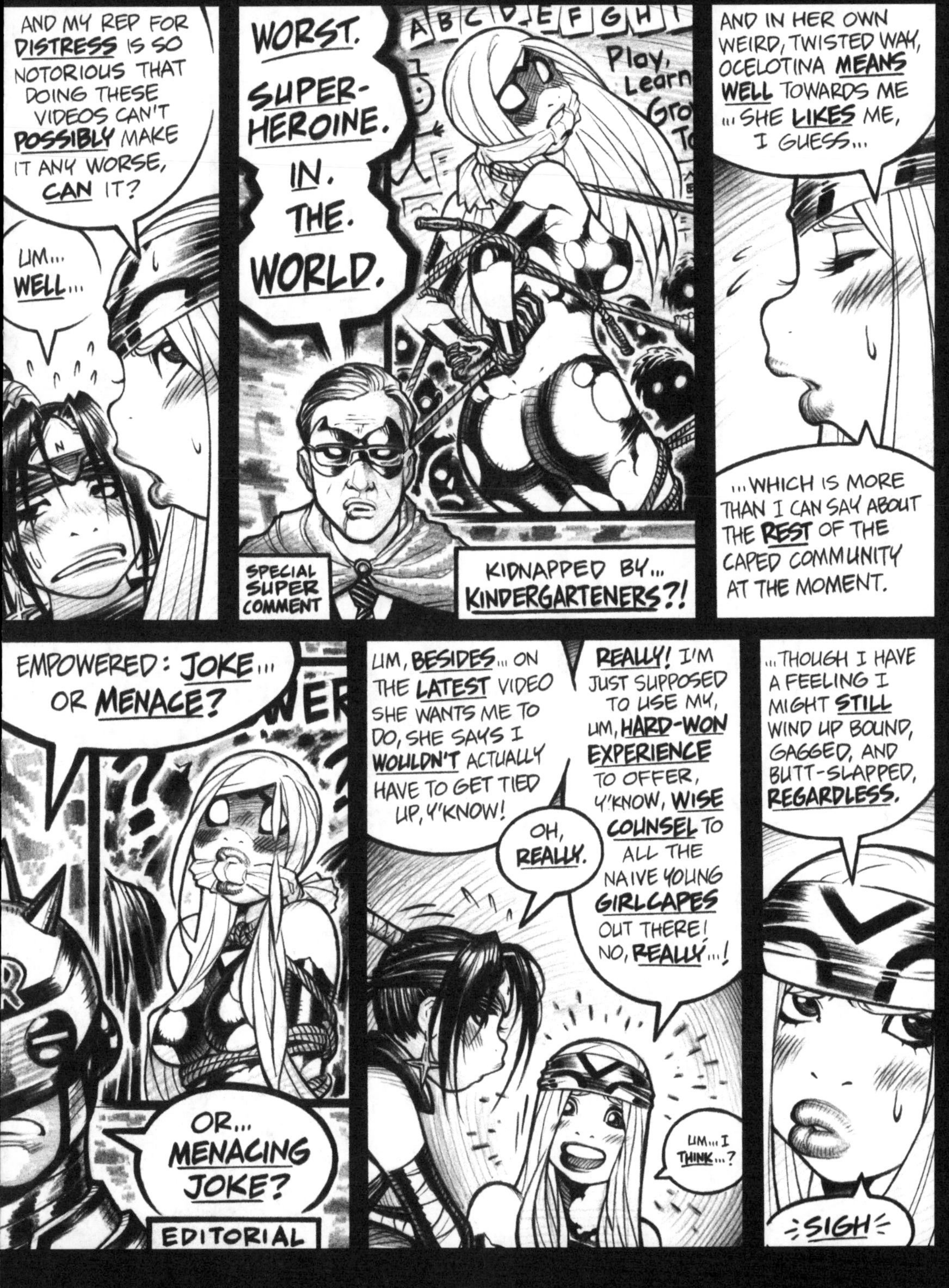
AND MY REP FOR DISTRESS IS SO NOTORIOUS THAT DOING THESE VIDEOS CAN'T POSSIBLY MAKE IT ANY WORSE, CAN IT?
UM... WELL...
WORST. SUPER-HEROINE. IN. THE. WORLD.
SPECIAL SUPER COMMENT
KIDNAPPED BY... KINDERGARTENERS?!
AND IN HER OWN WEIRD, TWISTED WAY, OCELOTINA MEANS WELL TOWARDS ME ...SHE LIKES ME, I GUESS...
...WHICH IS MORE THAN I CAN SAY ABOUT THE REST OF THE CAPED COMMUNITY AT THE MOMENT.
EMPOWERED: JOKE... OR MENACE?
OR... MENACING JOKE?
EDITORIAL
UM, BESIDES... ON THE LATEST VIDEO SHE WANTS ME TO DO, SHE SAYS I WOULDN'T ACTUALLY HAVE TO GET TIED UP, Y'KNOW!
OH, REALLY.
REALLY! I'M JUST SUPPOSED TO USE MY, UM, HARD-WON EXPERIENCE TO OFFER, Y'KNOW, WISE COUNSEL TO ALL THE NAIVE YOUNG GIRLCAPES OUT THERE! NO, REALLY...!
UM... I THINK...?
...THOUGH I HAVE A FEELING I MIGHT STILL WIND UP BOUND, GAGGED, AND BUTT-SLAPPED, REGARDLESS.
SIGH

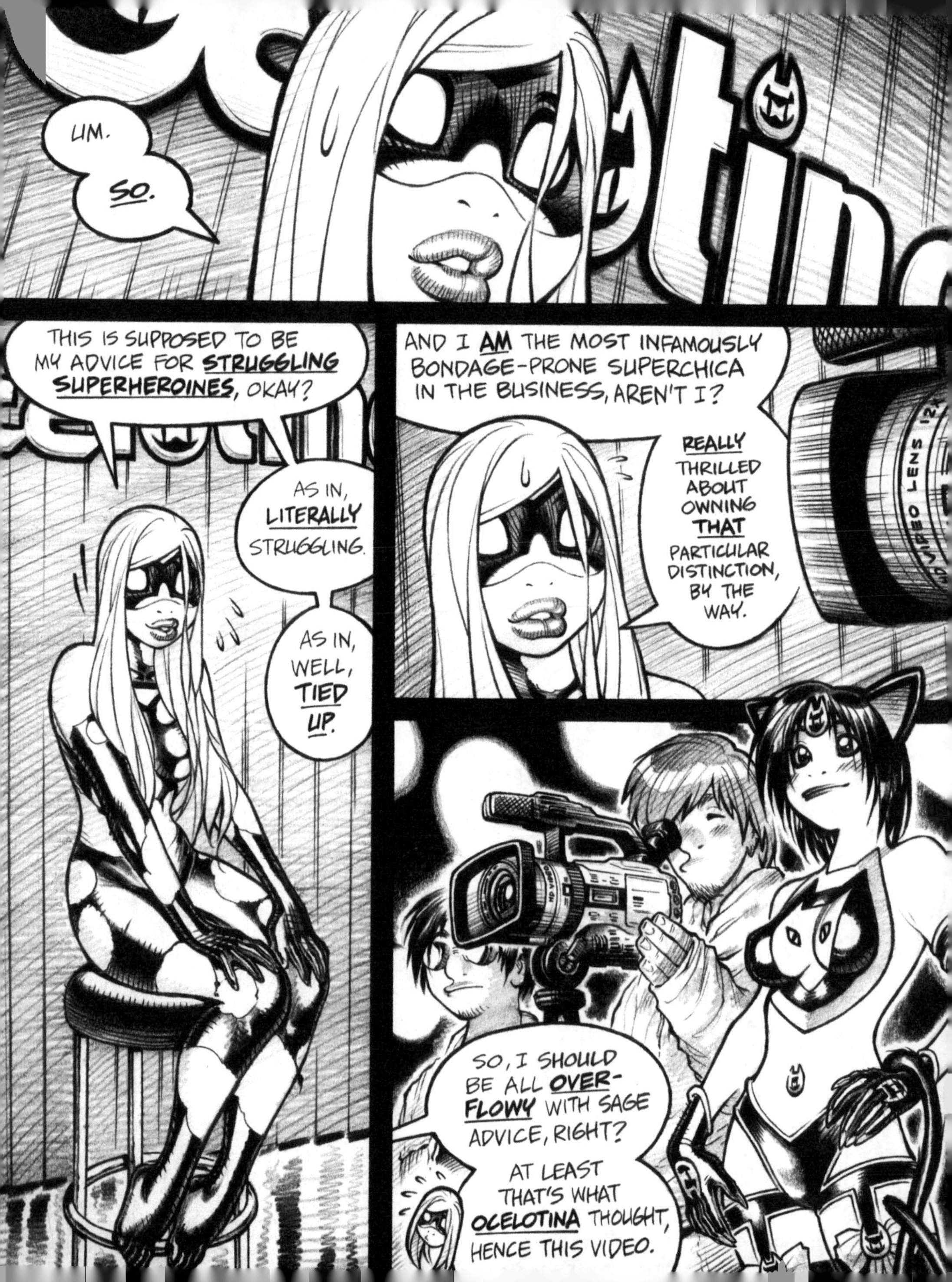
UM.
SO.
THIS IS SUPPOSED TO BE MY ADVICE FOR STRUGGLING SUPERHEROINES, OKAY?
AS IN, LITERALLY STRUGGLING.
AS IN, WELL, TIED UP.
AND I AM THE MOST INFAMOUSLY BONDAGE-PRONE SUPERCHICA IN THE BUSINESS, AREN'T I?
REALLY THRILLED ABOUT OWNING THAT PARTICULAR DISTINCTION, BY THE WAY.
VIDEO LENS 12X
SO, I SHOULD BE ALL OVER-FLOWY WITH SAGE ADVICE, RIGHT?
AT LEAST THAT'S WHAT OCELOTINA THOUGHT, HENCE THIS VIDEO.

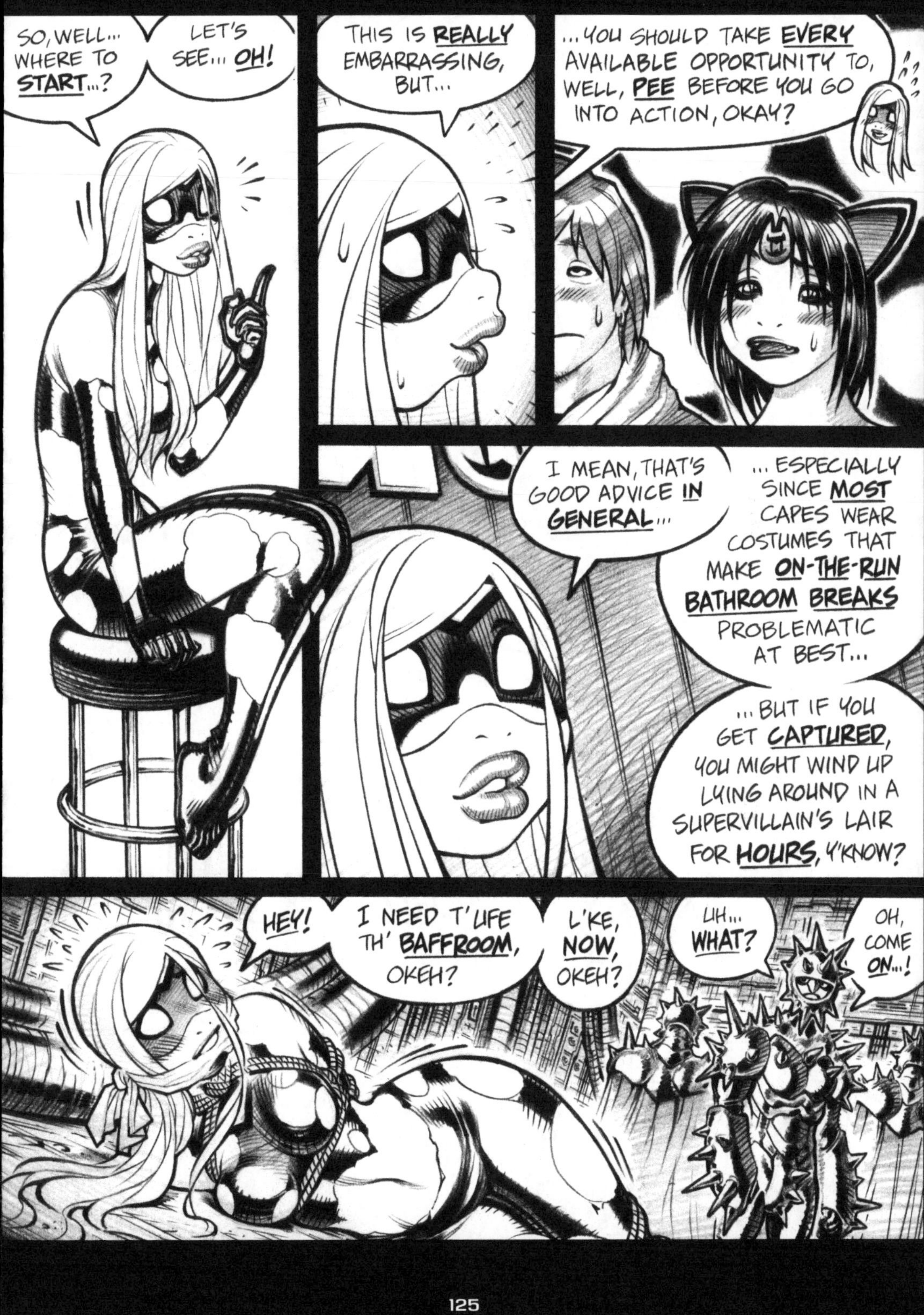
SO, WELL... WHERE TO **START**...?
LET'S SEE... **OH**!
THIS IS **REALLY** EMBARRASSING, BUT...
...YOU SHOULD TAKE **EVERY** AVAILABLE OPPORTUNITY TO, WELL, **PEE** BEFORE YOU GO INTO ACTION, OKAY?
I MEAN, THAT'S GOOD ADVICE **IN GENERAL**...
...ESPECIALLY SINCE **MOST** CAPES WEAR COSTUMES THAT MAKE **ON-THE-RUN BATHROOM BREAKS** PROBLEMATIC AT BEST...
...BUT IF YOU GET **CAPTURED**, YOU MIGHT WIND UP LYING AROUND IN A SUPERVILLAIN'S LAIR FOR **HOURS**, Y'KNOW?
HEY!
I NEED T'UFE TH' **BAFFROOM**, OKEH?
L'KE, **NOW**, OKEH?
UH... **WHAT**?
OH, COME **ON**...!

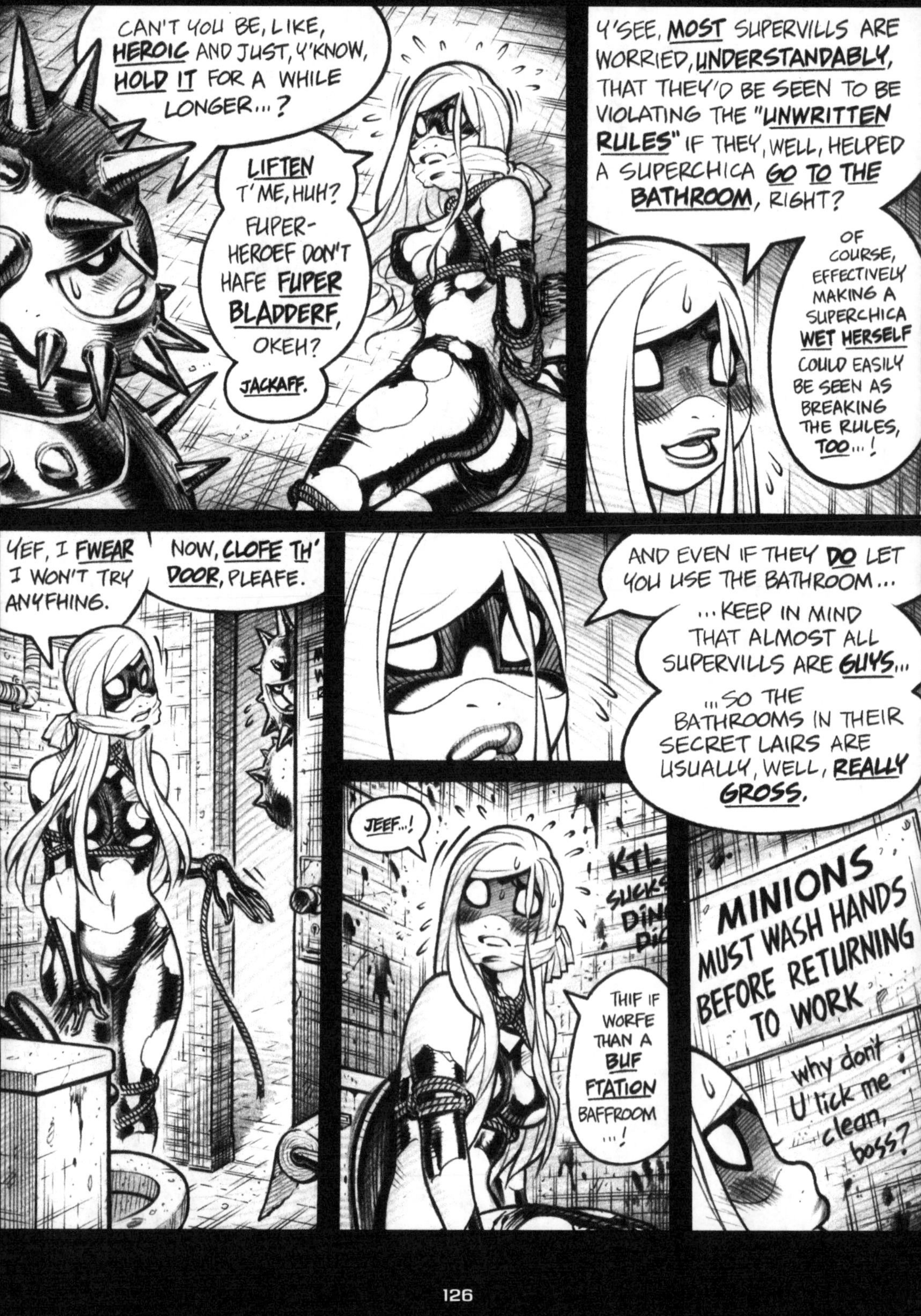
CAN'T YOU BE, LIKE, HEROIC AND JUST, Y'KNOW, HOLD IT FOR A WHILE LONGER...?
LIFTEN T'ME, HUH? FUPER-HEROEF DON'T HAFE FUPER BLADDERF, OKEH?
JACKAFF.
Y'SEE, MOST SUPERVILLS ARE WORRIED, UNDERSTANDABLY, THAT THEY'D BE SEEN TO BE VIOLATING THE "UNWRITTEN RULES" IF THEY, WELL, HELPED A SUPERCHICA GO TO THE BATHROOM, RIGHT?
OF COURSE, EFFECTIVELY MAKING A SUPERCHICA WET HERSELF COULD EASILY BE SEEN AS BREAKING THE RULES, TOO...!
YEF, I FWEAR I WON'T TRY ANYFHING.
NOW, CLOFE TH' DOOR, PLEAFE.
AND EVEN IF THEY DO LET YOU USE THE BATHROOM...
...KEEP IN MIND THAT ALMOST ALL SUPERVILLS ARE GUYS...
...SO THE BATHROOMS IN THEIR SECRET LAIRS ARE USUALLY, WELL, REALLY GROSS.
JEEF...!
THIF IF WORFE THAN A BUF FTATION BAFFROOM...!
MINIONS MUST WASH HANDS BEFORE RETURNING TO WORK
why don't U lick me clean, boss?

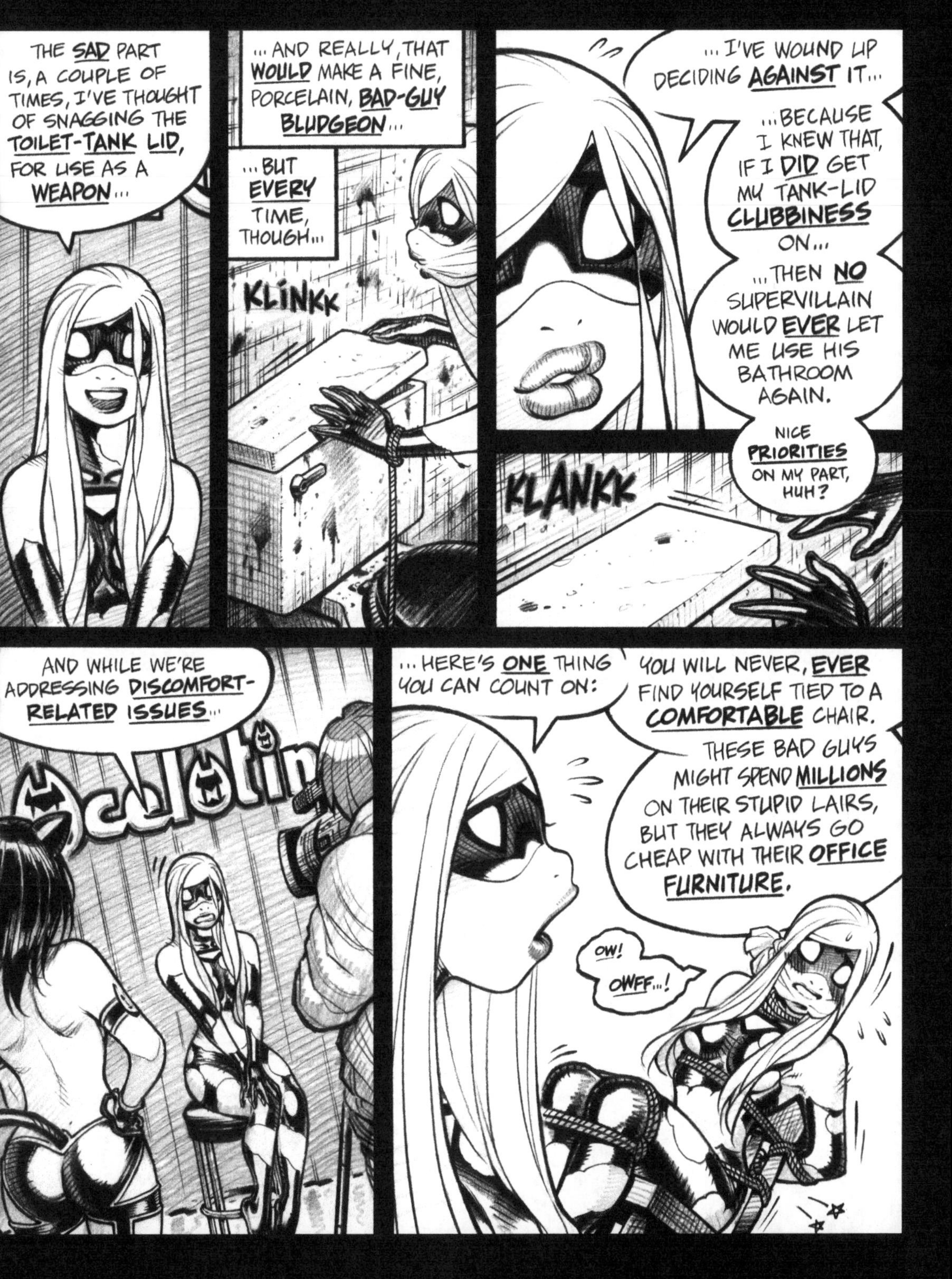
THE SAD PART IS, A COUPLE OF TIMES, I'VE THOUGHT OF SNAGGING THE TOILET-TANK LID, FOR USE AS A WEAPON...
...AND REALLY, THAT WOULD MAKE A FINE, PORCELAIN, BAD-GUY BLUDGEON...
...BUT EVERY TIME, THOUGH...
KLINKK
...I'VE WOUND UP DECIDING AGAINST IT...
...BECAUSE I KNEW THAT, IF I DID GET MY TANK-LID CLUBBINESS ON...
...THEN NO SUPERVILLAIN WOULD EVER LET ME USE HIS BATHROOM AGAIN.
NICE PRIORITIES ON MY PART, HUH?
KLANKK
AND WHILE WE'RE ADDRESSING DISCOMFORT-RELATED ISSUES...
...HERE'S ONE THING YOU CAN COUNT ON:
YOU WILL NEVER, EVER FIND YOURSELF TIED TO A COMFORTABLE CHAIR.
THESE BAD GUYS MIGHT SPEND MILLIONS ON THEIR STUPID LAIRS, BUT THEY ALWAYS GO CHEAP WITH THEIR OFFICE FURNITURE.
OW!
OWFF...!

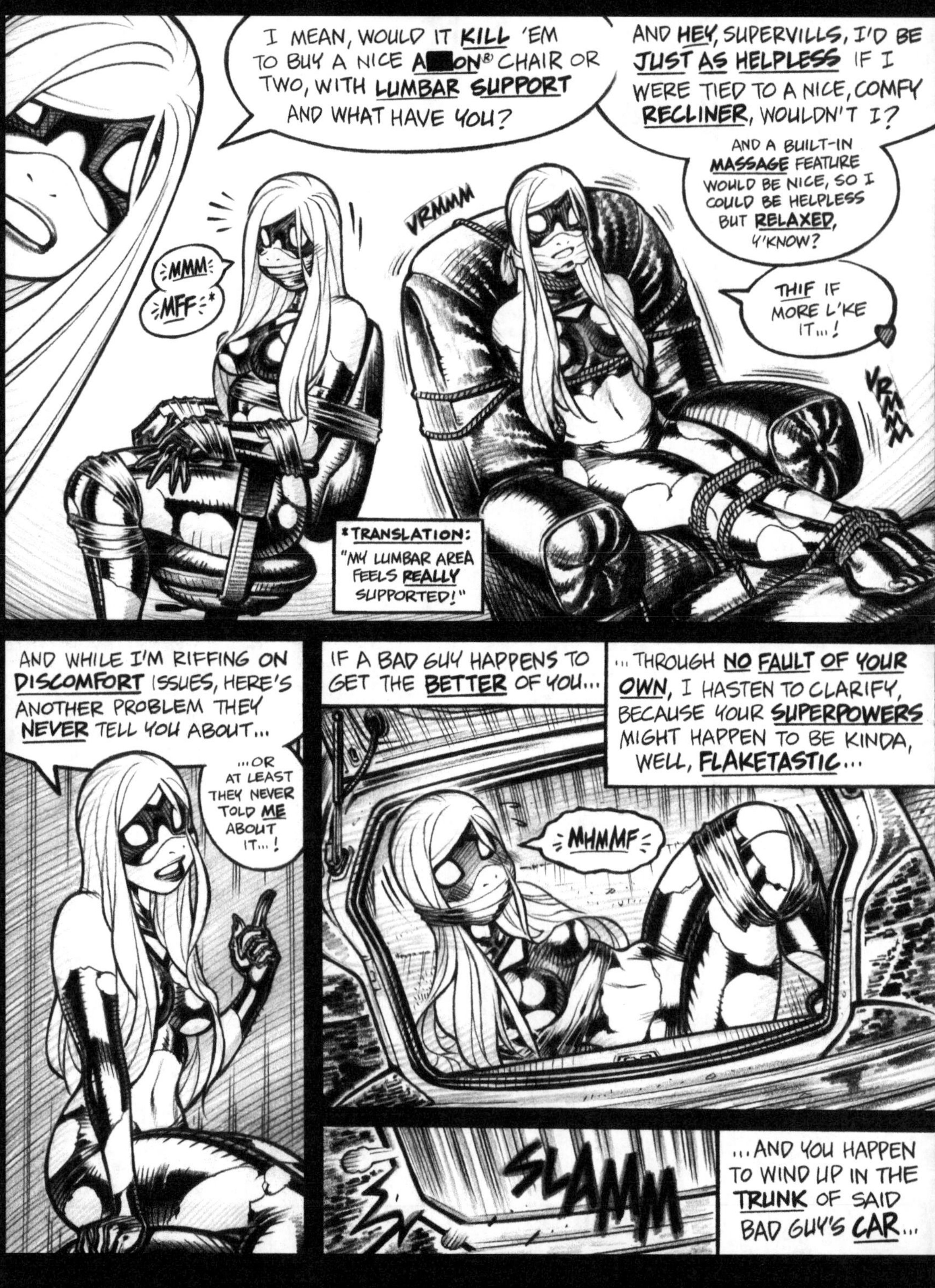

I MEAN, WOULD IT KILL 'EM TO BUY A NICE A[redacted]ON® CHAIR OR TWO, WITH LUMBAR SUPPORT AND WHAT HAVE YOU?
AND HEY, SUPERVILLS, I'D BE JUST AS HELPLESS IF I WERE TIED TO A NICE, COMFY RECLINER, WOULDN'T I?
AND A BUILT-IN MASSAGE FEATURE WOULD BE NICE, SO I COULD BE HELPLESS BUT RELAXED, Y'KNOW?
MMM
MFF*
VRMMM
THIF IF MORE L'KE IT...!
VRMMM
*TRANSLATION: "MY LUMBAR AREA FEELS REALLY SUPPORTED!"
AND WHILE I'M RIFFING ON DISCOMFORT ISSUES, HERE'S ANOTHER PROBLEM THEY NEVER TELL YOU ABOUT...
...OR AT LEAST THEY NEVER TOLD ME ABOUT IT...!
IF A BAD GUY HAPPENS TO GET THE BETTER OF YOU...
...THROUGH NO FAULT OF YOUR OWN, I HASTEN TO CLARIFY, BECAUSE YOUR SUPERPOWERS MIGHT HAPPEN TO BE KINDA, WELL, FLAKETASTIC...
MHMMF
SLAMM
...AND YOU HAPPEN TO WIND UP IN THE TRUNK OF SAID BAD GUY'S CAR...

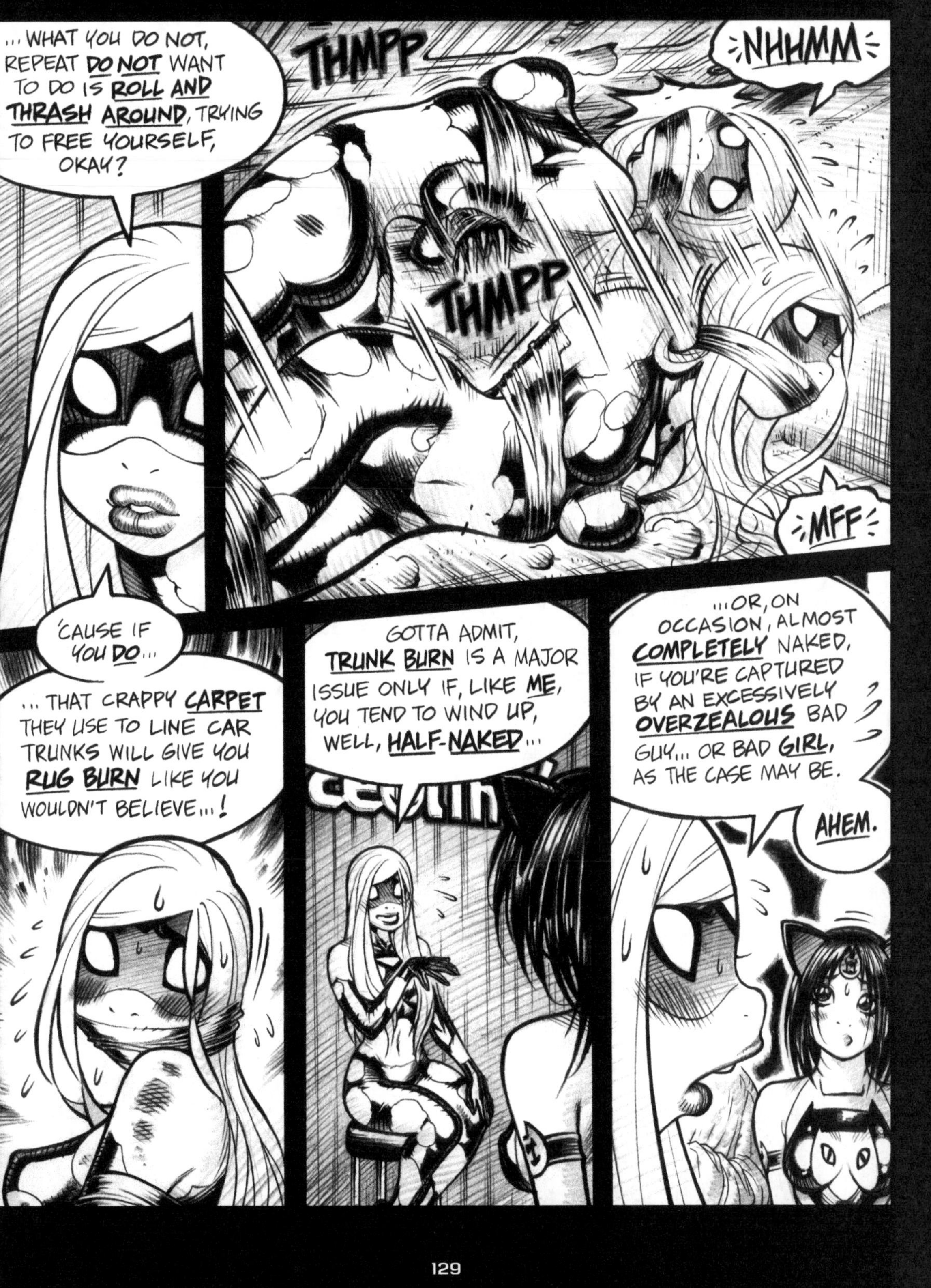
...WHAT YOU DO NOT, REPEAT DO NOT WANT TO DO IS ROLL AND THRASH AROUND, TRYING TO FREE YOURSELF, OKAY?
THMPP
NHHMM
THMPP
MFF
'CAUSE IF YOU DO...
...THAT CRAPPY CARPET THEY USE TO LINE CAR TRUNKS WILL GIVE YOU RUG BURN LIKE YOU WOULDN'T BELIEVE...!
GOTTA ADMIT, TRUNK BURN IS A MAJOR ISSUE ONLY IF, LIKE ME, YOU TEND TO WIND UP, WELL, HALF-NAKED...
...OR, ON OCCASION, ALMOST COMPLETELY NAKED, IF YOU'RE CAPTURED BY AN EXCESSIVELY OVERZEALOUS BAD GUY... OR BAD GIRL, AS THE CASE MAY BE.
AHEM.

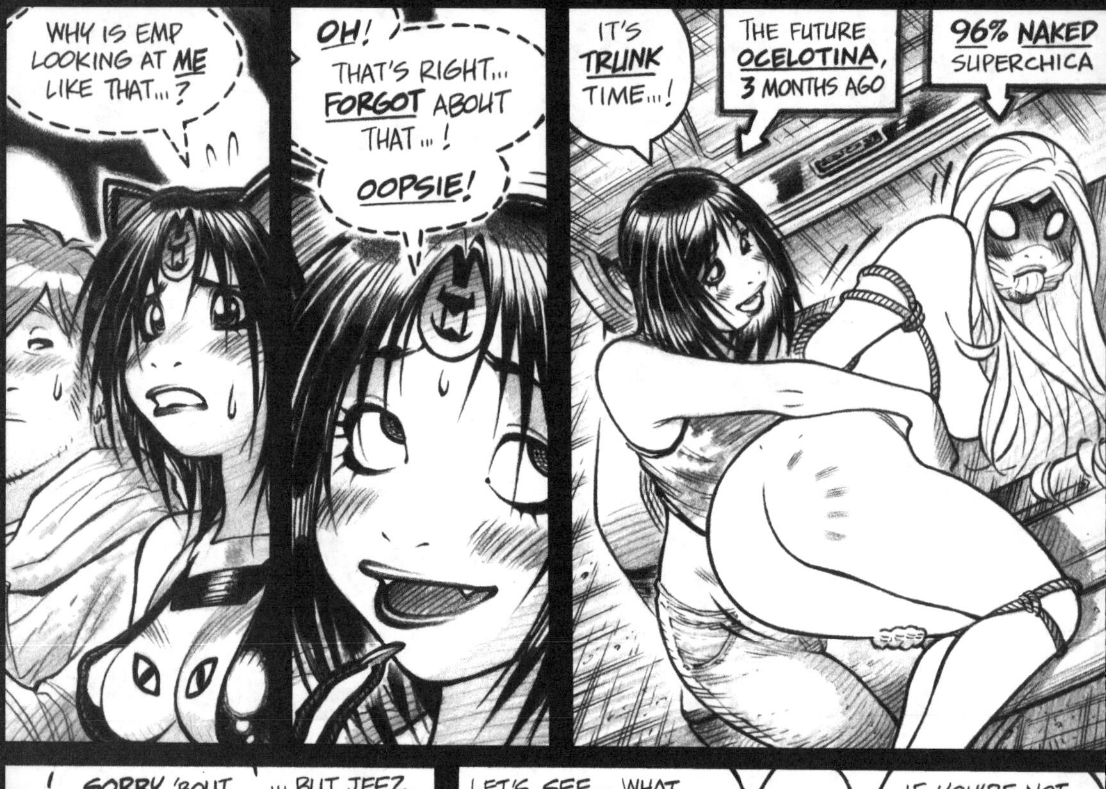

WHY IS EMP LOOKING AT ME LIKE THAT...?
OH! THAT'S RIGHT... FORGOT ABOUT THAT...! OOPSIE!
IT'S TRUNK TIME...!
THE FUTURE OCELOTINA, 3 MONTHS AGO
96% NAKED SUPERCHICA
SORRY 'BOUT THAT...
...BUT JEEZ, YOU'RE SO ADORABLY KIDNAPPABLE, EMP...! NYAAAN!
HMFF.
ANY-HOO.
LET'S SEE... WHAT ELSE SHOULD I TELL YOU ABOUT...
OH!
IF YOU'RE NOT ALREADY DOING YOGA, THEN YOU SHOULD SERIOUSLY LOOK INTO IT, Y'KNOW?
COMES IN WAY HANDY, BELIEVE IT OR NOT!
HNNH
HATHA YOGA "BOW" POSE (DHANURĀSANA) धनुरासन

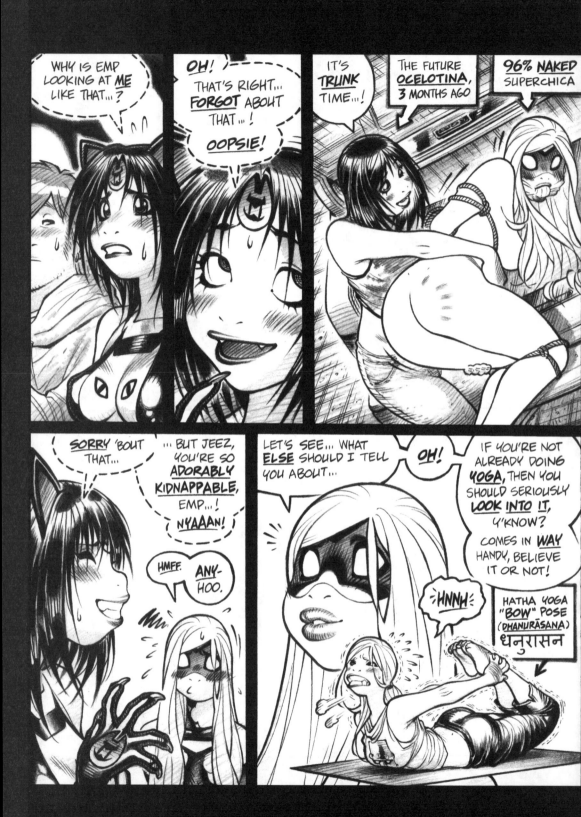

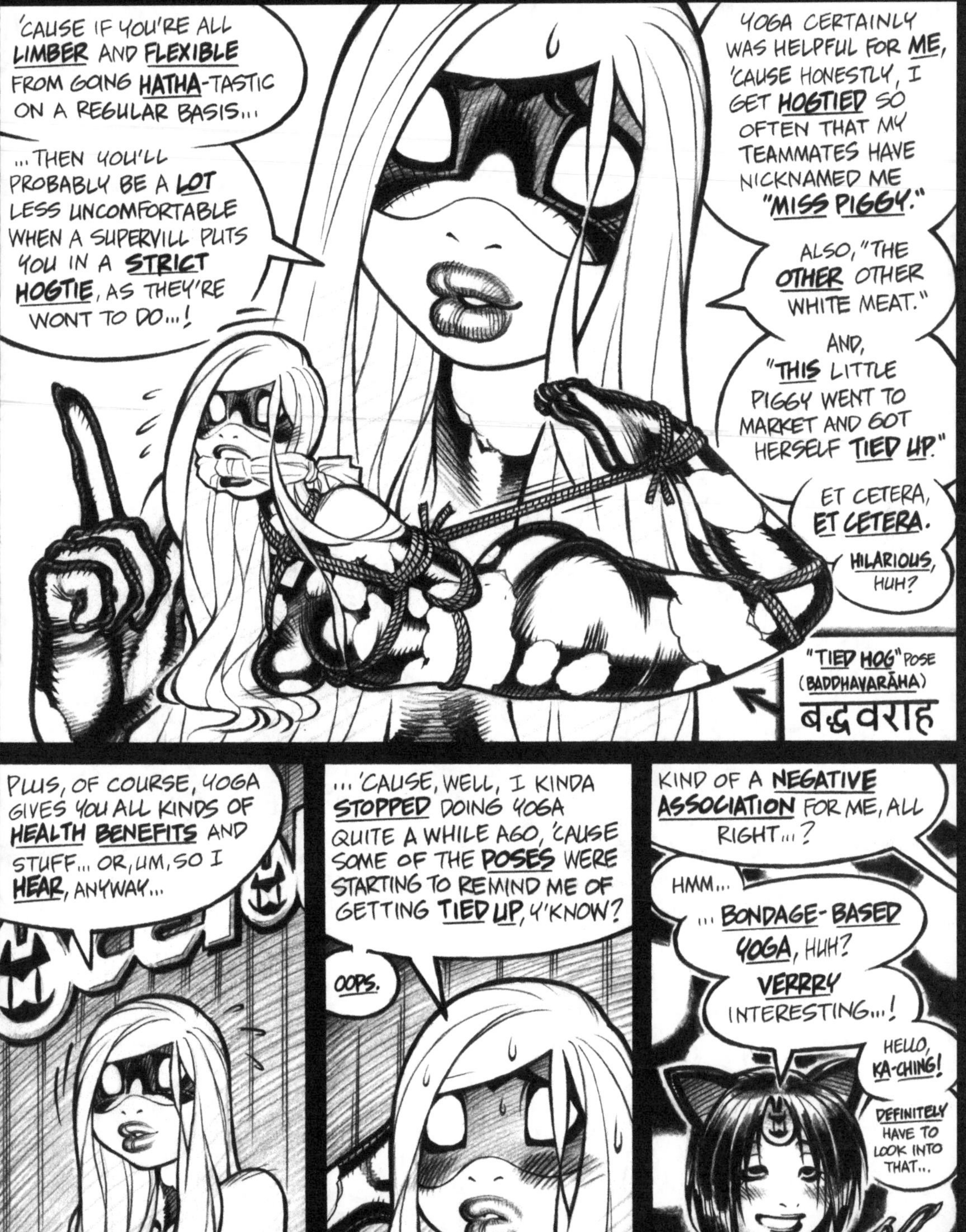
'CAUSE IF YOU'RE ALL LIMBER AND FLEXIBLE FROM GOING HATHA-TASTIC ON A REGULAR BASIS...
...THEN YOU'LL PROBABLY BE A LOT LESS UNCOMFORTABLE WHEN A SUPERVILL PUTS YOU IN A STRICT HOGTIE, AS THEY'RE WONT TO DO...!
YOGA CERTAINLY WAS HELPFUL FOR ME, 'CAUSE HONESTLY, I GET HOGTIED SO OFTEN THAT MY TEAMMATES HAVE NICKNAMED ME "MISS PIGGY."
ALSO, "THE OTHER OTHER WHITE MEAT."
AND, "THIS LITTLE PIGGY WENT TO MARKET AND GOT HERSELF TIED UP."
ET CETERA, ET CETERA.
HILARIOUS, HUH?
"TIED HOG" POSE (BADDHAVARĀHA)
बद्धवराह
PLUS, OF COURSE, YOGA GIVES YOU ALL KINDS OF HEALTH BENEFITS AND STUFF... OR, UM, SO I HEAR, ANYWAY...
...'CAUSE, WELL, I KINDA STOPPED DOING YOGA QUITE A WHILE AGO, 'CAUSE SOME OF THE POSES WERE STARTING TO REMIND ME OF GETTING TIED UP, Y'KNOW?
OOPS.
KIND OF A NEGATIVE ASSOCIATION FOR ME, ALL RIGHT...?
HMM...
...BONDAGE-BASED YOGA, HUH? VERRRY INTERESTING...!
HELLO, KA-CHING!
DEFINITELY HAVE TO LOOK INTO THAT...

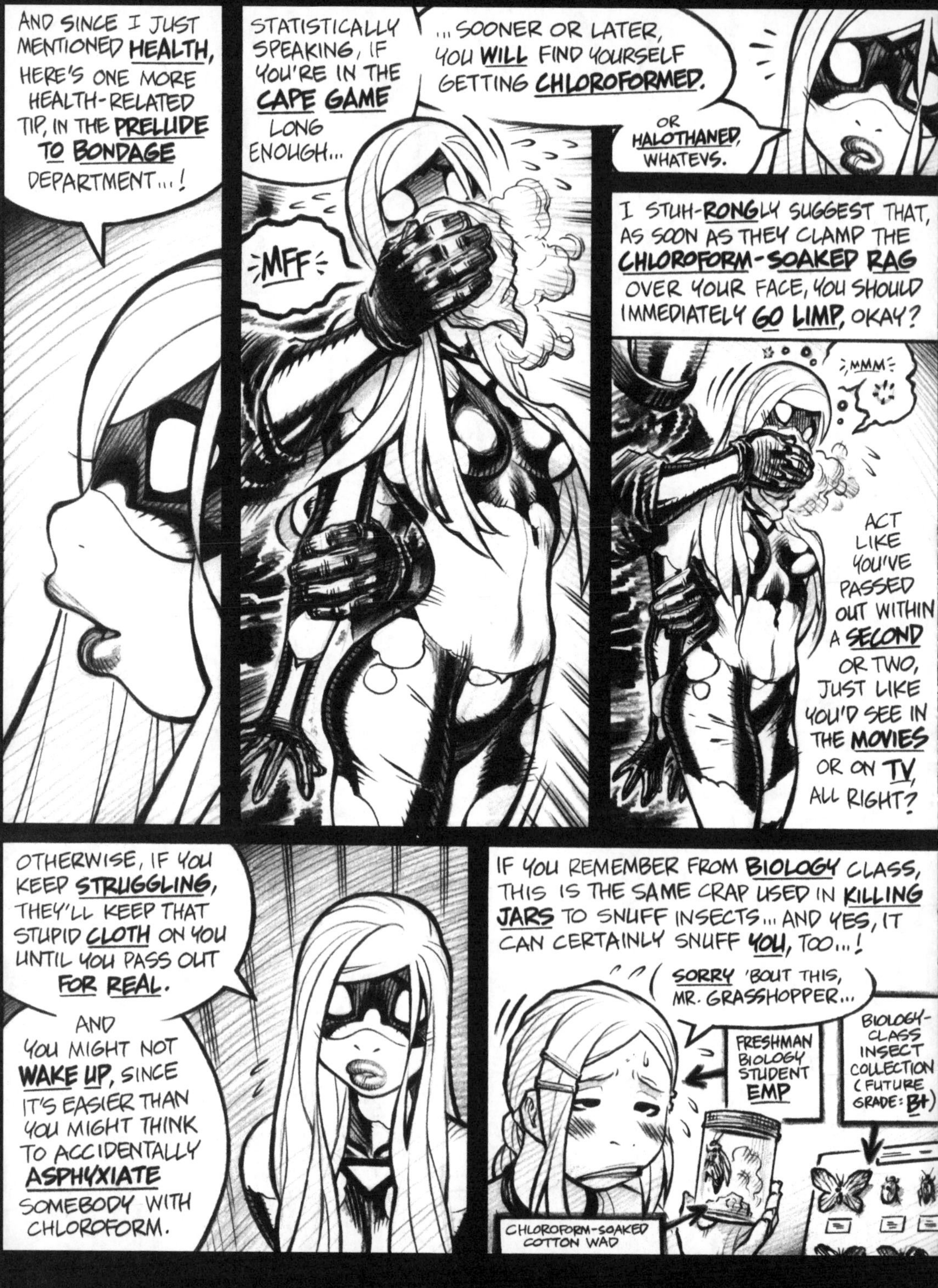

AND SINCE I JUST MENTIONED HEALTH, HERE'S ONE MORE HEALTH-RELATED TIP, IN THE PRELUDE TO BONDAGE DEPARTMENT...!
STATISTICALLY SPEAKING, IF YOU'RE IN THE CAPE GAME LONG ENOUGH...
...SOONER OR LATER, YOU WILL FIND YOURSELF GETTING CHLOROFORMED.
OR HALOTHANED, WHATEVS.
MFF
I STUH-RONGLY SUGGEST THAT, AS SOON AS THEY CLAMP THE CHLOROFORM-SOAKED RAG OVER YOUR FACE, YOU SHOULD IMMEDIATELY GO LIMP, OKAY?
MMM
ACT LIKE YOU'VE PASSED OUT WITHIN A SECOND OR TWO, JUST LIKE YOU'D SEE IN THE MOVIES OR ON TV, ALL RIGHT?
OTHERWISE, IF YOU KEEP STRUGGLING, THEY'LL KEEP THAT STUPID CLOTH ON YOU UNTIL YOU PASS OUT FOR REAL.
AND YOU MIGHT NOT WAKE UP, SINCE IT'S EASIER THAN YOU MIGHT THINK TO ACCIDENTALLY ASPHYXIATE SOMEBODY WITH CHLOROFORM.
IF YOU REMEMBER FROM BIOLOGY CLASS, THIS IS THE SAME CRAP USED IN KILLING JARS TO SNUFF INSECTS... AND YES, IT CAN CERTAINLY SNUFF YOU, TOO...!
SORRY 'BOUT THIS, MR. GRASSHOPPER...
FRESHMAN BIOLOGY STUDENT EMP
BIOLOGY-CLASS INSECT COLLECTION (FUTURE GRADE: B+)
CHLOROFORM-SOAKED COTTON WAD

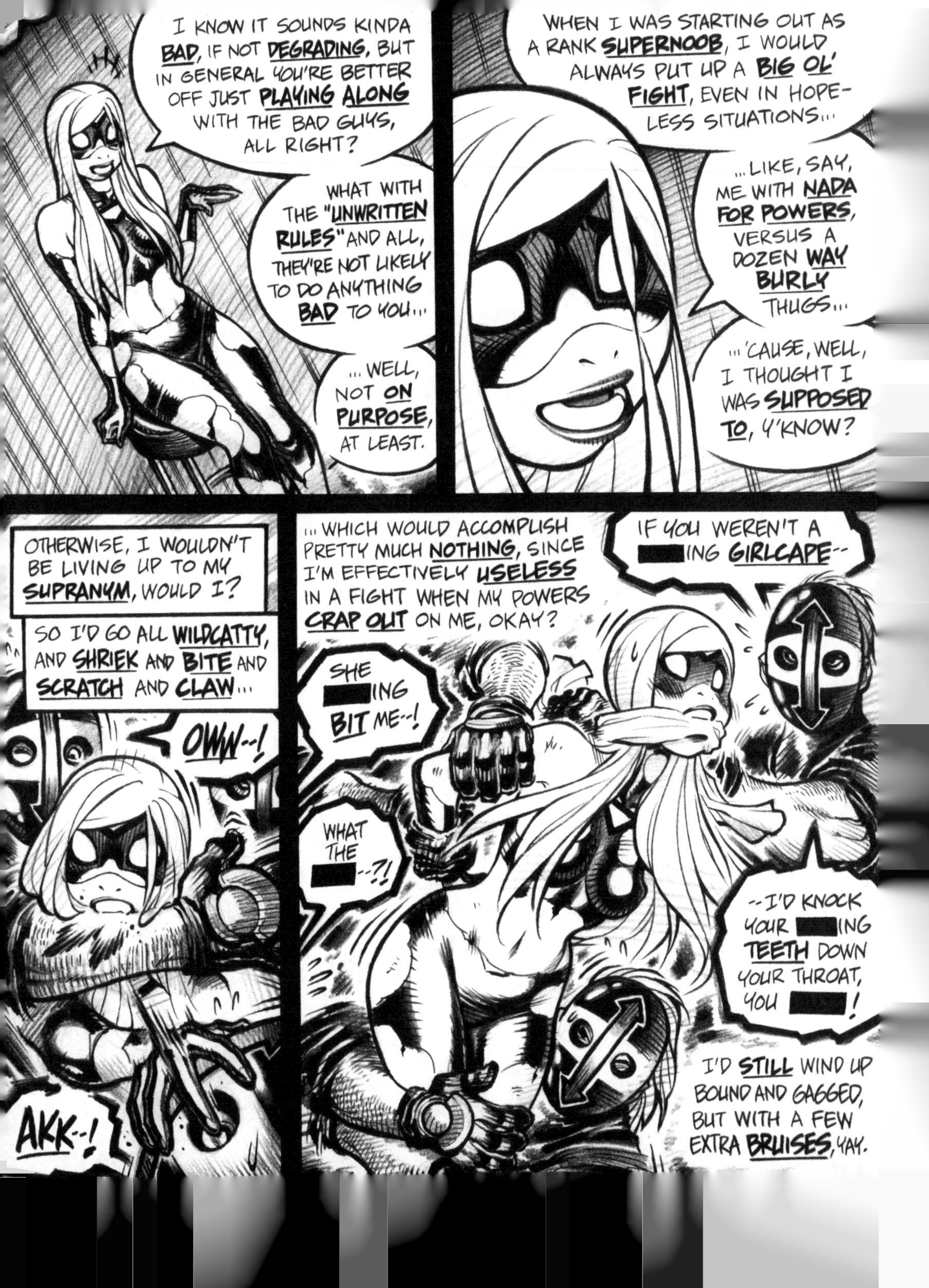
I KNOW IT SOUNDS KINDA BAD, IF NOT DEGRADING, BUT IN GENERAL YOU'RE BETTER OFF JUST PLAYING ALONG WITH THE BAD GUYS, ALL RIGHT?
WHAT WITH THE "UNWRITTEN RULES" AND ALL, THEY'RE NOT LIKELY TO DO ANYTHING BAD TO YOU...
...WELL, NOT ON PURPOSE, AT LEAST.
WHEN I WAS STARTING OUT AS A RANK SUPERNOOB, I WOULD ALWAYS PUT UP A BIG OL' FIGHT, EVEN IN HOPE-LESS SITUATIONS...
...LIKE, SAY, ME WITH NADA FOR POWERS, VERSUS A DOZEN WAY BURLY THUGS...
...'CAUSE, WELL, I THOUGHT I WAS SUPPOSED TO, Y'KNOW?
OTHERWISE, I WOULDN'T BE LIVING UP TO MY SUPRANYM, WOULD I?
SO I'D GO ALL WILDCATTY, AND SHRIEK AND BITE AND SCRATCH AND CLAW...
OWW--!
AKK--!
...WHICH WOULD ACCOMPLISH PRETTY MUCH NOTHING, SINCE I'M EFFECTIVELY USELESS IN A FIGHT WHEN MY POWERS CRAP OUT ON ME, OKAY?
SHE [redacted]ING BIT ME--!
WHAT THE [redacted]--?!
IF YOU WEREN'T A [redacted]ING GIRLCAPE--
--I'D KNOCK YOUR [redacted]ING TEETH DOWN YOUR THROAT, YOU [redacted]!
I'D STILL WIND UP BOUND AND GAGGED, BUT WITH A FEW EXTRA BRUISES, YAY.

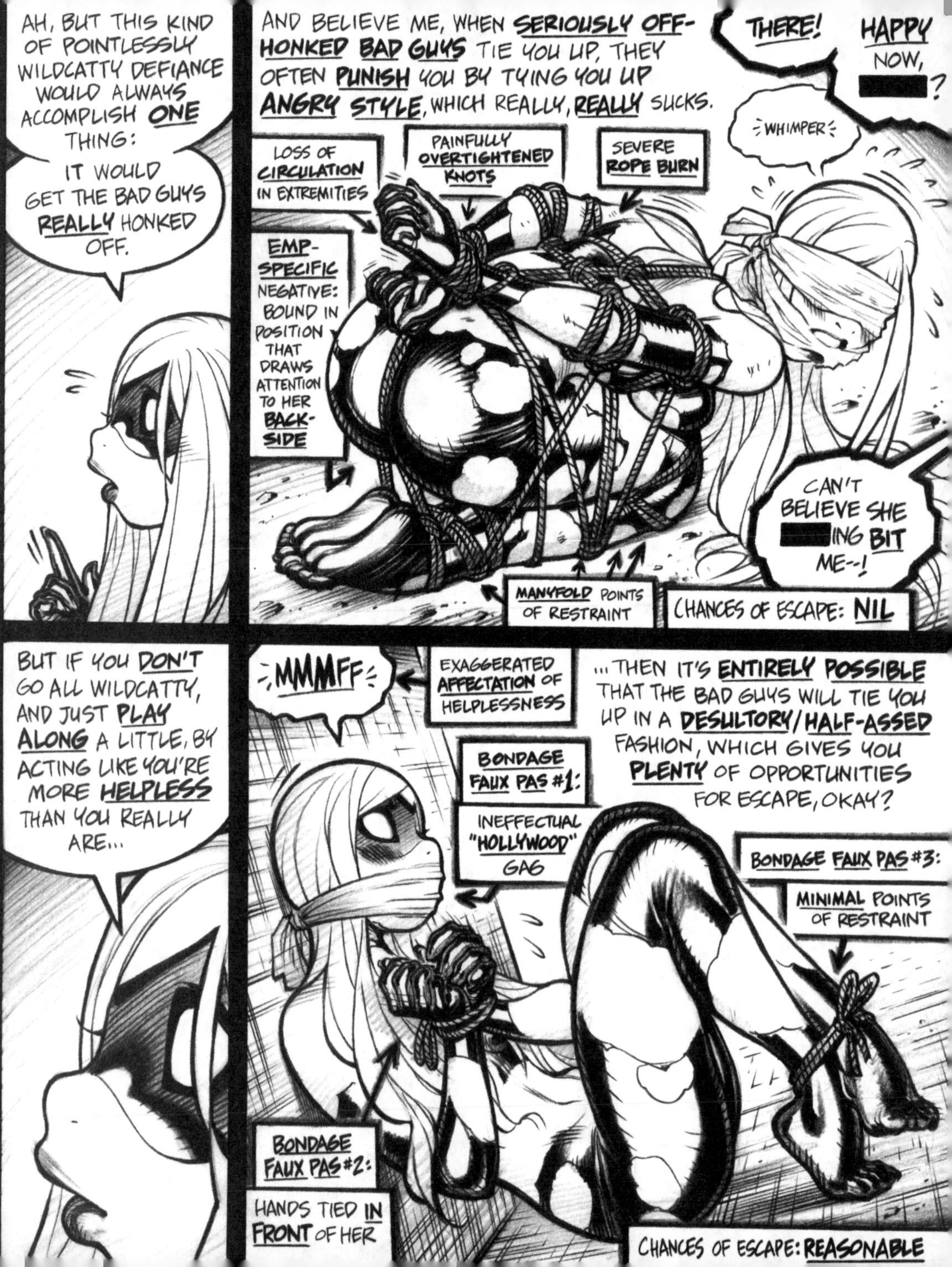
AH, BUT THIS KIND OF POINTLESSLY WILDCATTY DEFIANCE WOULD ALWAYS ACCOMPLISH ONE THING:
IT WOULD GET THE BAD GUYS REALLY HONKED OFF.
AND BELIEVE ME, WHEN SERIOUSLY OFF-HONKED BAD GUYS TIE YOU UP, THEY OFTEN PUNISH YOU BY TYING YOU UP ANGRY STYLE, WHICH REALLY, REALLY SUCKS.
THERE!
HAPPY NOW, [redacted]?
WHIMPER
LOSS OF CIRCULATION IN EXTREMITIES
PAINFULLY OVERTIGHTENED KNOTS
SEVERE ROPE BURN
EMP-SPECIFIC NEGATIVE: BOUND IN POSITION THAT DRAWS ATTENTION TO HER BACK-SIDE
CAN'T BELIEVE SHE [redacted]ING BIT ME--!
MANYFOLD POINTS OF RESTRAINT
CHANCES OF ESCAPE: NIL
BUT IF YOU DON'T GO ALL WILDCATTY, AND JUST PLAY ALONG A LITTLE, BY ACTING LIKE YOU'RE MORE HELPLESS THAN YOU REALLY ARE...
MMMFF
EXAGGERATED AFFECTATION OF HELPLESSNESS
...THEN IT'S ENTIRELY POSSIBLE THAT THE BAD GUYS WILL TIE YOU UP IN A DESULTORY/HALF-ASSED FASHION, WHICH GIVES YOU PLENTY OF OPPORTUNITIES FOR ESCAPE, OKAY?
BONDAGE FAUX PAS #1:
INEFFECTUAL "HOLLYWOOD" GAG
BONDAGE FAUX PAS #3:
MINIMAL POINTS OF RESTRAINT
BONDAGE FAUX PAS #2:
HANDS TIED IN FRONT OF HER
CHANCES OF ESCAPE: REASONABLE

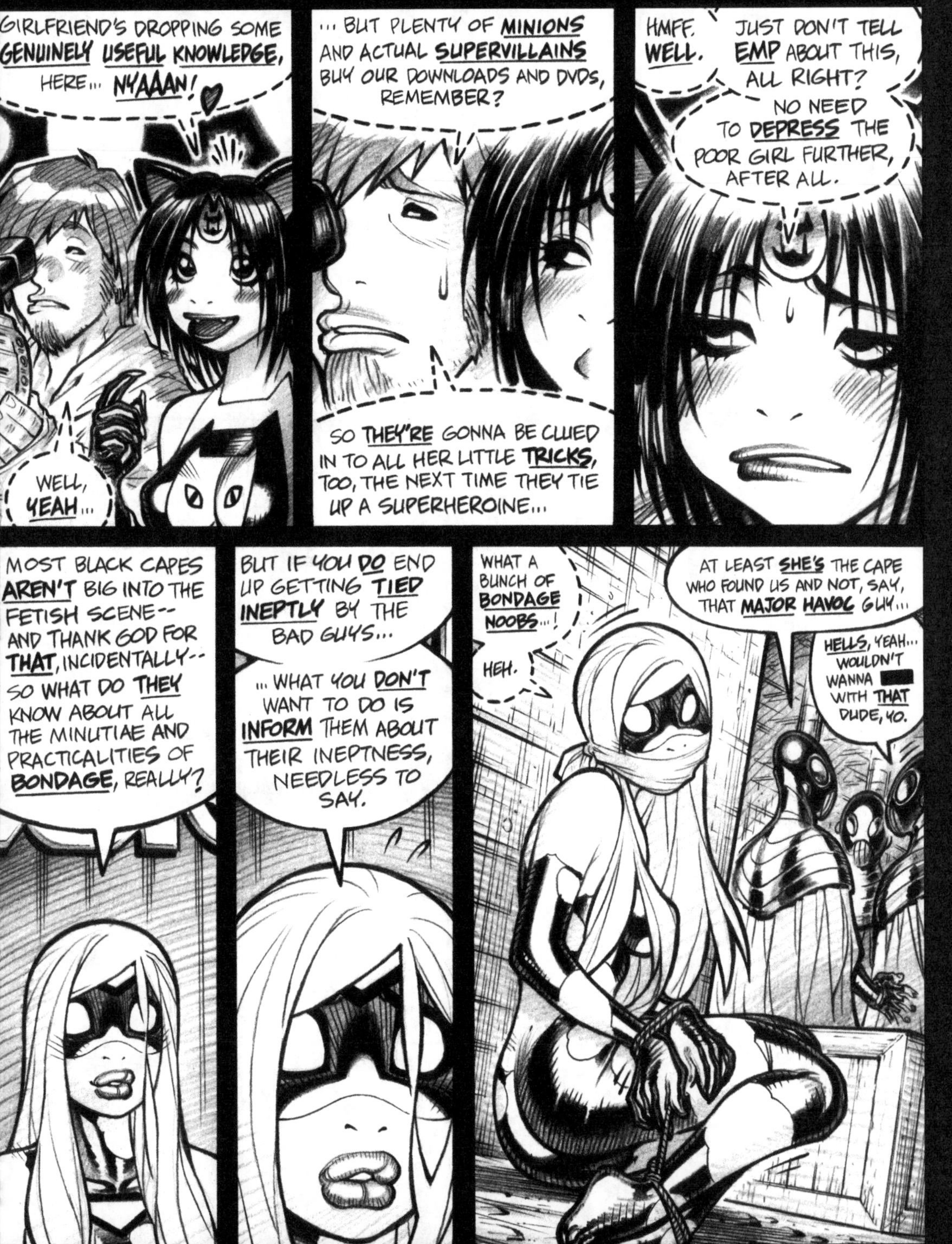
GIRLFRIEND'S DROPPING SOME GENUINELY USEFUL KNOWLEDGE, HERE... NYAAAN!
WELL, YEAH...
...BUT PLENTY OF MINIONS AND ACTUAL SUPERVILLAINS BUY OUR DOWNLOADS AND DVDS, REMEMBER?
SO THEY'RE GONNA BE CLUED IN TO ALL HER LITTLE TRICKS, TOO, THE NEXT TIME THEY TIE UP A SUPERHEROINE...
HMFF. WELL.
JUST DON'T TELL EMP ABOUT THIS, ALL RIGHT?
NO NEED TO DEPRESS THE POOR GIRL FURTHER, AFTER ALL.
MOST BLACK CAPES AREN'T BIG INTO THE FETISH SCENE-- AND THANK GOD FOR THAT, INCIDENTALLY-- SO WHAT DO THEY KNOW ABOUT ALL THE MINUTIAE AND PRACTICALITIES OF BONDAGE, REALLY?
BUT IF YOU DO END UP GETTING TIED INEPTLY BY THE BAD GUYS...
...WHAT YOU DON'T WANT TO DO IS INFORM THEM ABOUT THEIR INEPTNESS, NEEDLESS TO SAY.
WHAT A BUNCH OF BONDAGE NOOBS...!
HEH.
AT LEAST SHE'S THE CAPE WHO FOUND US AND NOT, SAY, THAT MAJOR HAVOC GUY...
HELLS, YEAH... WOULDN'T WANNA [redacted] WITH THAT DUDE, YO.

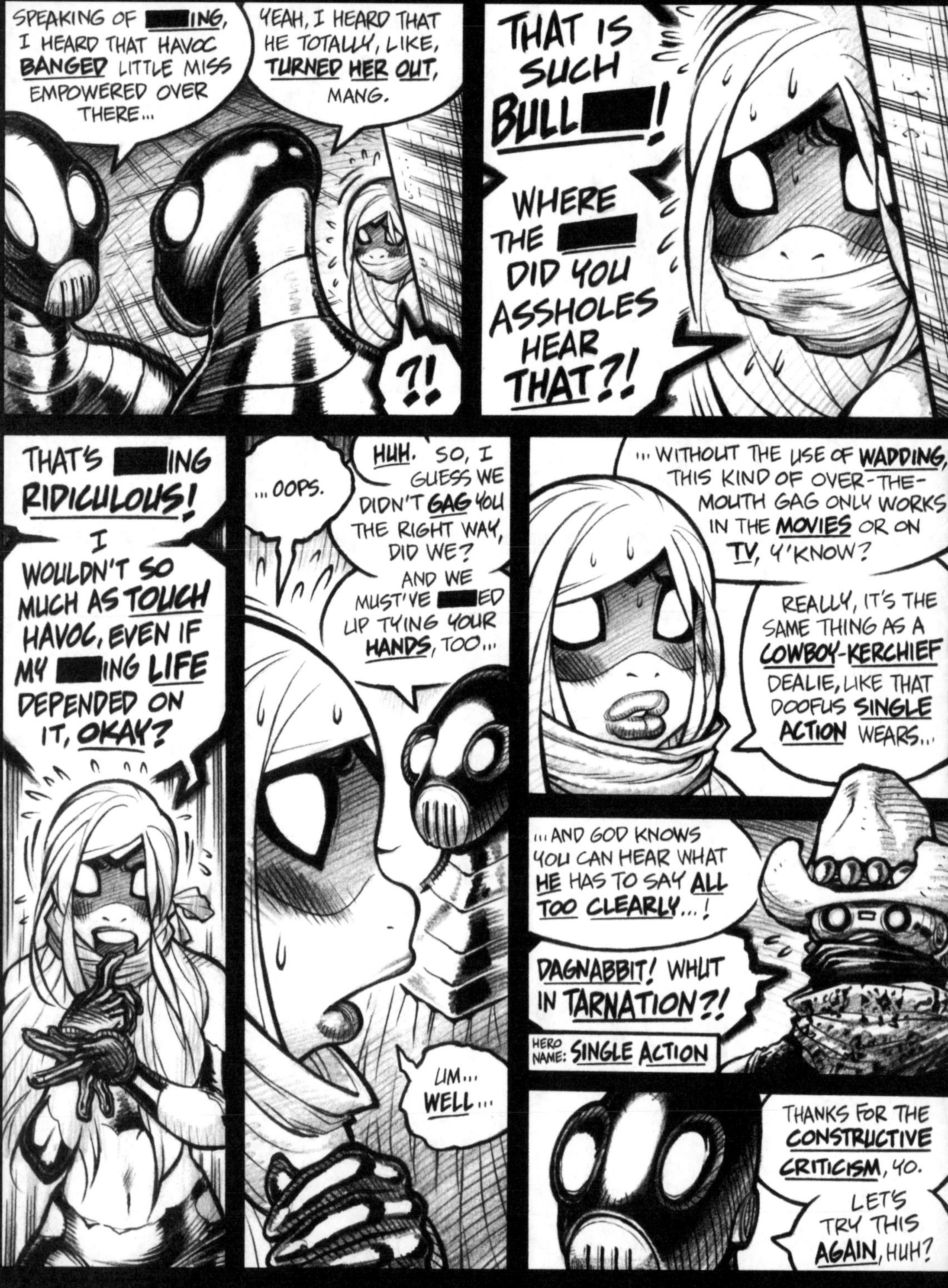

SPEAKING OF [redacted]ING, I HEARD THAT HAVOC BANGED LITTLE MISS EMPOWERED OVER THERE...
YEAH, I HEARD THAT HE TOTALLY, LIKE, TURNED HER OUT, MANG.
?!
THAT IS SUCH BULL[redacted]!
WHERE THE [redacted] DID YOU ASSHOLES HEAR THAT?!
THAT'S [redacted]ING RIDICULOUS!
I WOULDN'T SO MUCH AS TOUCH HAVOC, EVEN IF MY [redacted]ING LIFE DEPENDED ON IT, OKAY?
...OOPS.
HUH. SO, I GUESS WE DIDN'T GAG YOU THE RIGHT WAY, DID WE?
AND WE MUST'VE [redacted]ED UP TYING YOUR HANDS, TOO...
UM... WELL...
...WITHOUT THE USE OF WADDING, THIS KIND OF OVER-THE-MOUTH GAG ONLY WORKS IN THE MOVIES OR ON TV, Y'KNOW?
REALLY, IT'S THE SAME THING AS A COWBOY-KERCHIEF DEALIE, LIKE THAT DOOFUS SINGLE ACTION WEARS...
...AND GOD KNOWS YOU CAN HEAR WHAT HE HAS TO SAY ALL TOO CLEARLY...!
DAGNABBIT! WHUT IN TARNATION?!
HERO NAME: SINGLE ACTION
THANKS FOR THE CONSTRUCTIVE CRITICISM, YO.
LET'S TRY THIS AGAIN, HUH?

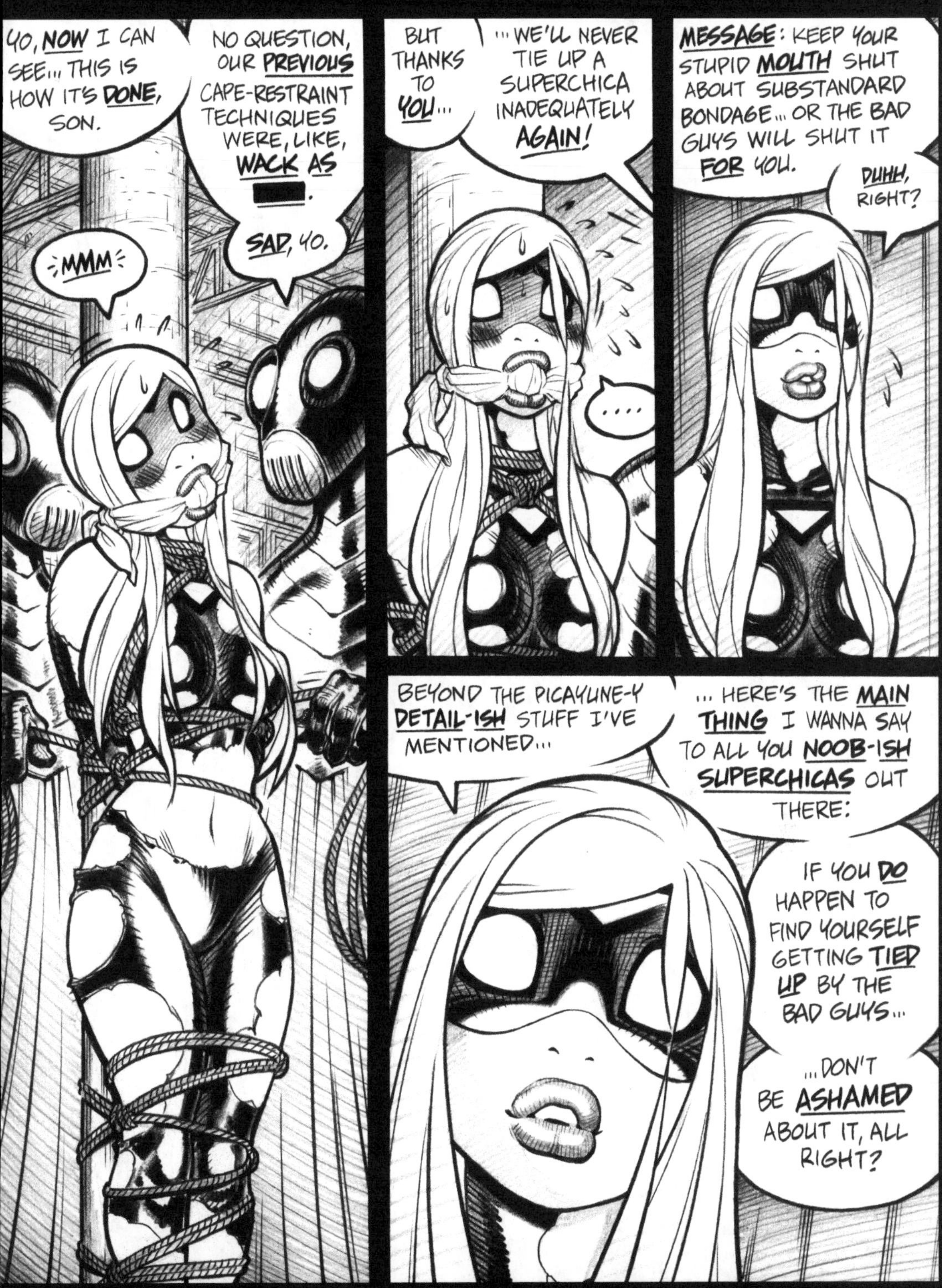
YO, NOW I CAN SEE... THIS IS HOW IT'S DONE, SON.
NO QUESTION, OUR PREVIOUS CAPE-RESTRAINT TECHNIQUES WERE, LIKE, WACK AS [redacted].
SAD, YO.
MMM
BUT THANKS TO YOU...
...WE'LL NEVER TIE UP A SUPERCHICA INADEQUATELY AGAIN!
....
MESSAGE: KEEP YOUR STUPID MOUTH SHUT ABOUT SUBSTANDARD BONDAGE... OR THE BAD GUYS WILL SHUT IT FOR YOU.
DUHH, RIGHT?
BEYOND THE PICAYUNE-Y DETAIL-ISH STUFF I'VE MENTIONED...
... HERE'S THE MAIN THING I WANNA SAY TO ALL YOU NOOB-ISH SUPERCHICAS OUT THERE:
IF YOU DO HAPPEN TO FIND YOURSELF GETTING TIED UP BY THE BAD GUYS...
...DON'T BE ASHAMED ABOUT IT, ALL RIGHT?

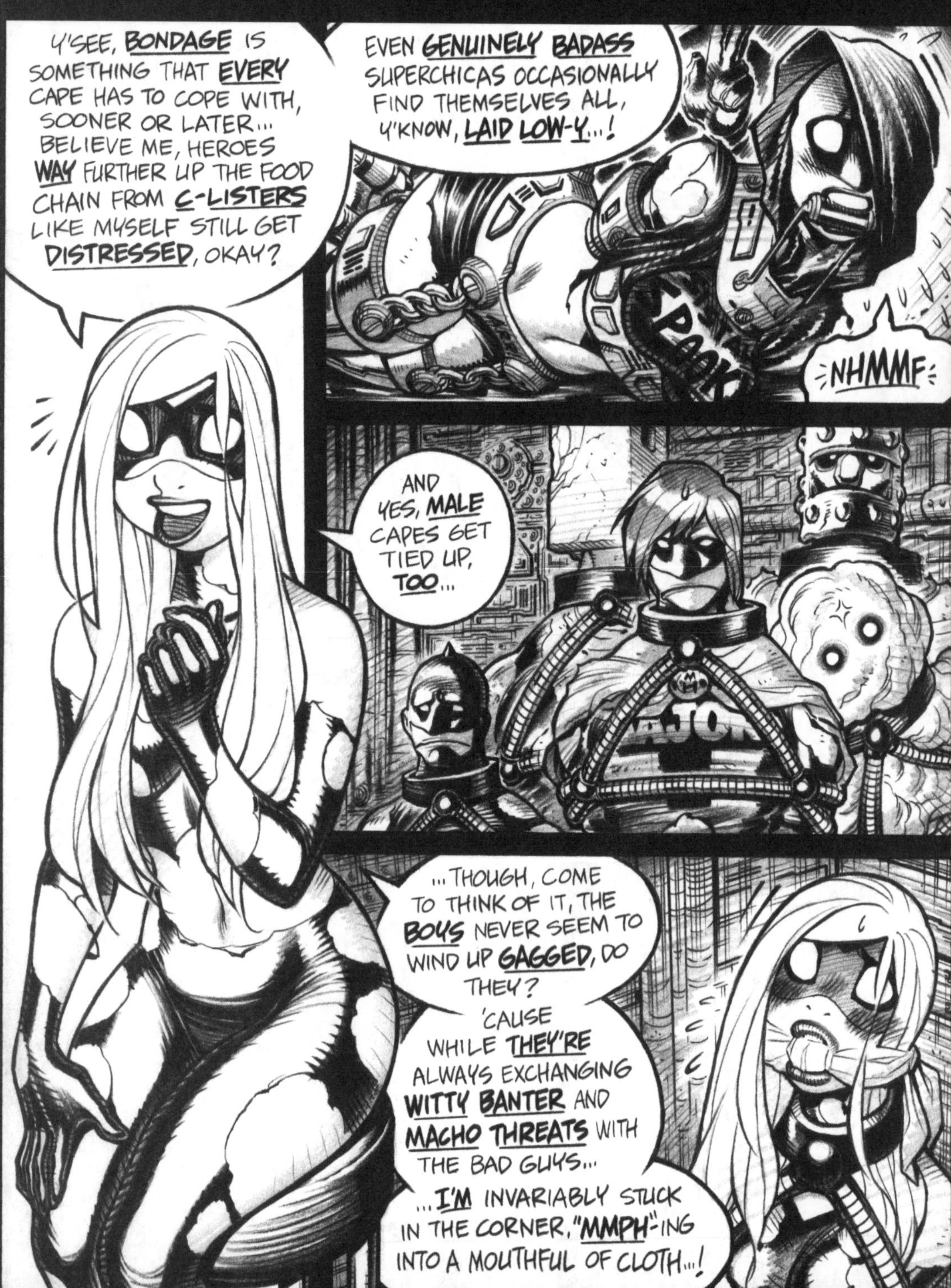

Y'SEE, BONDAGE IS SOMETHING THAT EVERY CAPE HAS TO COPE WITH, SOONER OR LATER... BELIEVE ME, HEROES WAY FURTHER UP THE FOOD CHAIN FROM C-LISTERS LIKE MYSELF STILL GET DISTRESSED, OKAY?
EVEN GENUINELY BADASS SUPERCHICAS OCCASIONALLY FIND THEMSELVES ALL, Y'KNOW, LAID LOW-Y...!
NHMMF
AND YES, MALE CAPES GET TIED UP, TOO...
...THOUGH, COME TO THINK OF IT, THE BOYS NEVER SEEM TO WIND UP GAGGED, DO THEY?
'CAUSE WHILE THEY'RE ALWAYS EXCHANGING WITTY BANTER AND MACHO THREATS WITH THE BAD GUYS...
...I'M INVARIABLY STUCK IN THE CORNER, "MMPH"-ING INTO A MOUTHFUL OF CLOTH...!

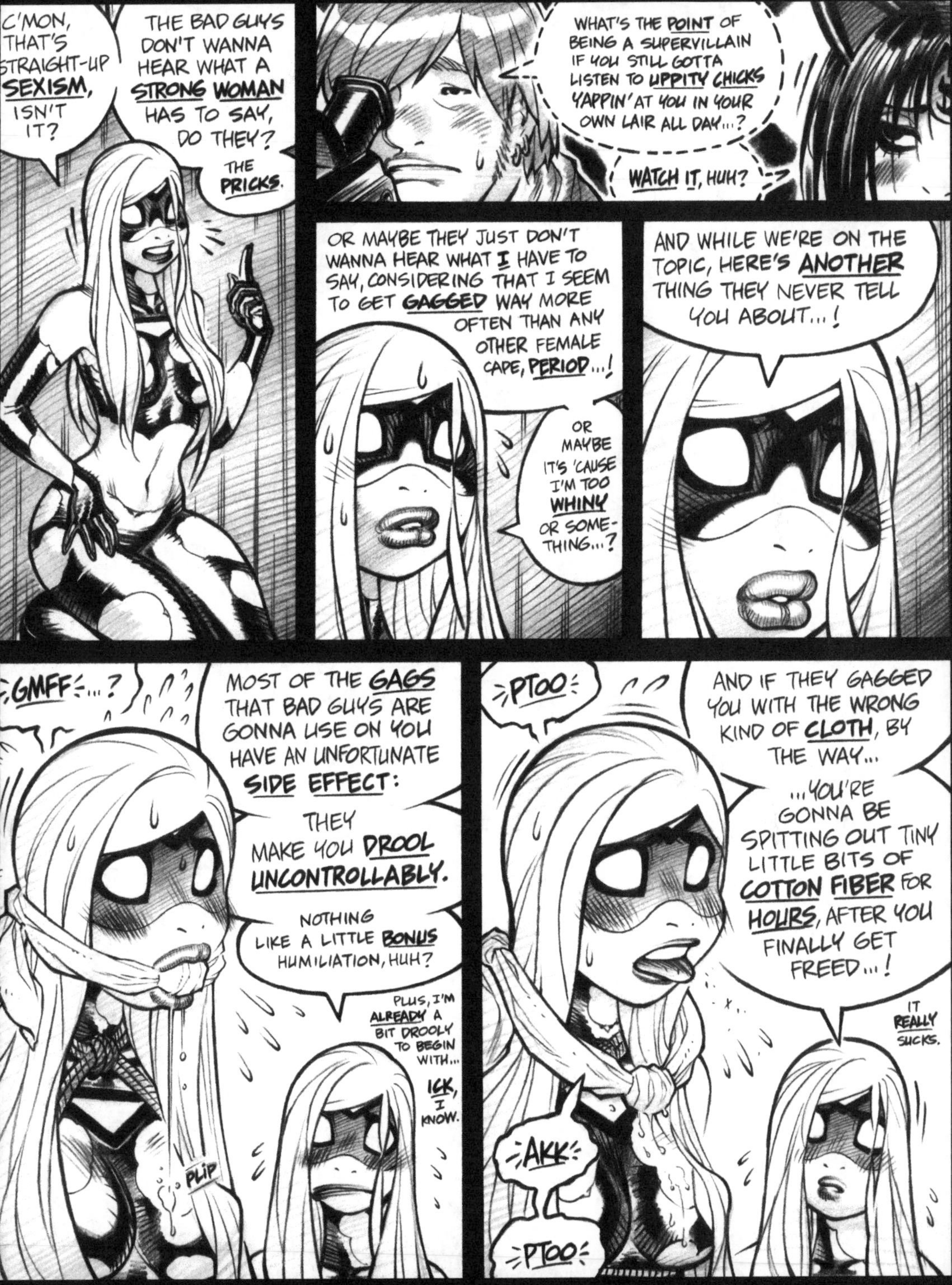
C'MON, THAT'S STRAIGHT-UP SEXISM, ISN'T IT?
THE BAD GUYS DON'T WANNA HEAR WHAT A STRONG WOMAN HAS TO SAY, DO THEY?
THE PRICKS.
WHAT'S THE POINT OF BEING A SUPERVILLAIN IF YOU STILL GOTTA LISTEN TO UPPITY CHICKS YAPPIN' AT YOU IN YOUR OWN LAIR ALL DAY...?
WATCH IT, HUH?
OR MAYBE THEY JUST DON'T WANNA HEAR WHAT I HAVE TO SAY, CONSIDERING THAT I SEEM TO GET GAGGED WAY MORE OFTEN THAN ANY OTHER FEMALE CAPE, PERIOD...!
OR MAYBE IT'S 'CAUSE I'M TOO WHINY OR SOMETHING...?
AND WHILE WE'RE ON THE TOPIC, HERE'S ANOTHER THING THEY NEVER TELL YOU ABOUT...!
GMFF...?
MOST OF THE GAGS THAT BAD GUYS ARE GONNA USE ON YOU HAVE AN UNFORTUNATE SIDE EFFECT:
THEY MAKE YOU DROOL UNCONTROLLABLY.
NOTHING LIKE A LITTLE BONUS HUMILIATION, HUH?
PLUS, I'M ALREADY A BIT DROOLY TO BEGIN WITH...
ICK, I KNOW.
PLIP
PTOO
AND IF THEY GAGGED YOU WITH THE WRONG KIND OF CLOTH, BY THE WAY...
...YOU'RE GONNA BE SPITTING OUT TINY LITTLE BITS OF COTTON FIBER FOR HOURS, AFTER YOU FINALLY GET FREED...!
IT REALLY SUCKS.
AKK
PTOO

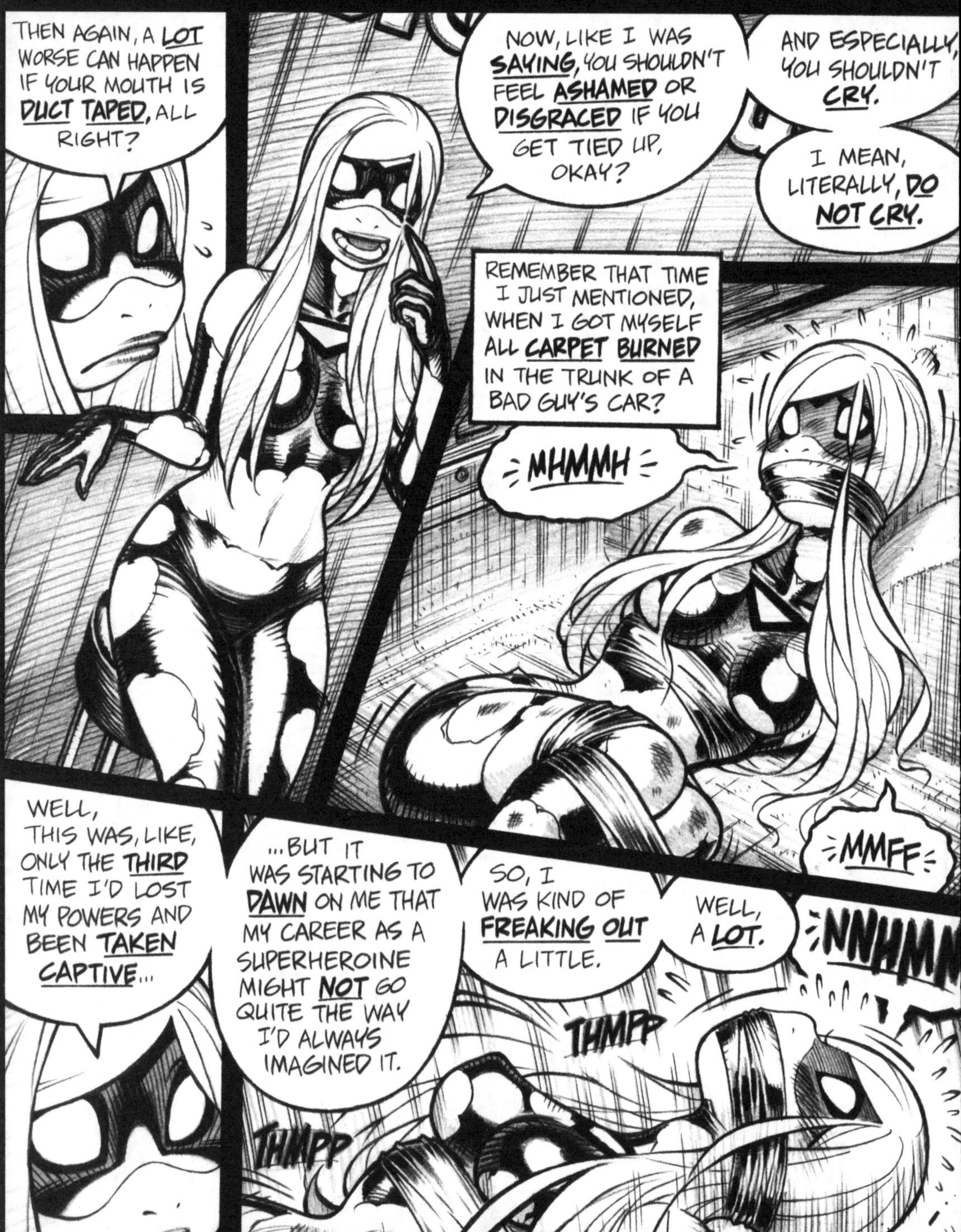
THEN AGAIN, A LOT WORSE CAN HAPPEN IF YOUR MOUTH IS DUCT TAPED, ALL RIGHT?
NOW, LIKE I WAS SAYING, YOU SHOULDN'T FEEL ASHAMED OR DISGRACED IF YOU GET TIED UP, OKAY?
AND ESPECIALLY, YOU SHOULDN'T CRY.
I MEAN, LITERALLY, DO NOT CRY.
REMEMBER THAT TIME I JUST MENTIONED, WHEN I GOT MYSELF ALL CARPET BURNED IN THE TRUNK OF A BAD GUY'S CAR?
MHMMH
MMFF
WELL, THIS WAS, LIKE, ONLY THE THIRD TIME I'D LOST MY POWERS AND BEEN TAKEN CAPTIVE...
...BUT IT WAS STARTING TO DAWN ON ME THAT MY CAREER AS A SUPERHEROINE MIGHT NOT GO QUITE THE WAY I'D ALWAYS IMAGINED IT.
SO, I WAS KIND OF FREAKING OUT A LITTLE.
WELL, A LOT.
NNHMM
THMPP
THMPP

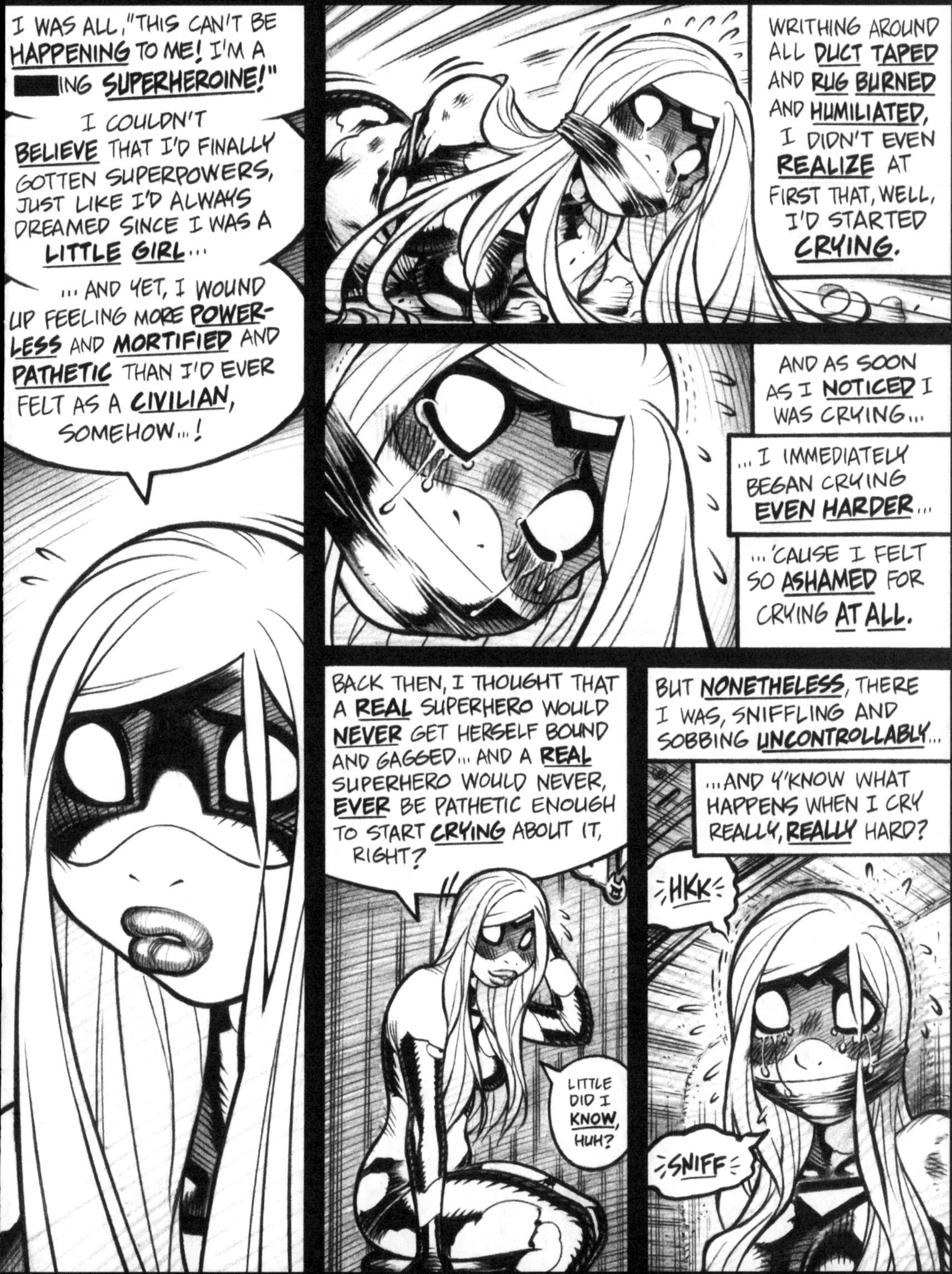

I WAS ALL, "THIS CAN'T BE HAPPENING TO ME! I'M A [redacted]ING SUPERHEROINE!"
I COULDN'T BELIEVE THAT I'D FINALLY GOTTEN SUPERPOWERS, JUST LIKE I'D ALWAYS DREAMED SINCE I WAS A LITTLE GIRL...
... AND YET, I WOUND UP FEELING MORE POWERLESS AND MORTIFIED AND PATHETIC THAN I'D EVER FELT AS A CIVILIAN, SOMEHOW...!
WRITHING AROUND ALL DUCT TAPED AND RUG BURNED AND HUMILIATED, I DIDN'T EVEN REALIZE AT FIRST THAT, WELL, I'D STARTED CRYING.
AND AS SOON AS I NOTICED I WAS CRYING...
...I IMMEDIATELY BEGAN CRYING EVEN HARDER...
...'CAUSE I FELT SO ASHAMED FOR CRYING AT ALL.
BACK THEN, I THOUGHT THAT A REAL SUPERHERO WOULD NEVER GET HERSELF BOUND AND GAGGED... AND A REAL SUPERHERO WOULD NEVER, EVER BE PATHETIC ENOUGH TO START CRYING ABOUT IT, RIGHT?
LITTLE DID I KNOW, HUH?
BUT NONETHELESS, THERE I WAS, SNIFFLING AND SOBBING UNCONTROLLABLY...
...AND Y'KNOW WHAT HAPPENS WHEN I CRY REALLY, REALLY HARD?
HKK
SNIFF

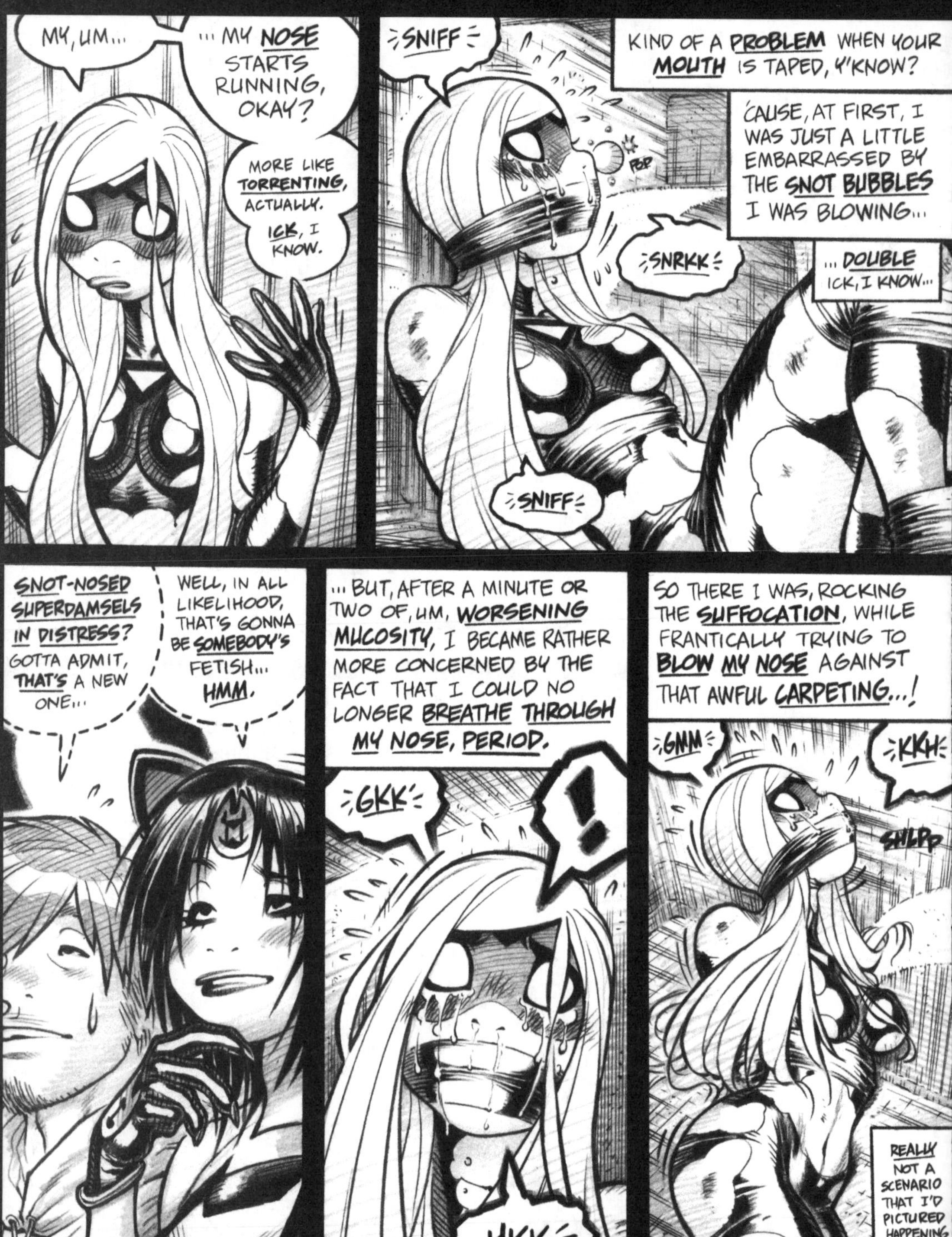
MY, UM...
...MY NOSE STARTS RUNNING, OKAY?
MORE LIKE TORRENTING, ACTUALLY. ICK, I KNOW.
SNIFF
KIND OF A PROBLEM WHEN YOUR MOUTH IS TAPED, Y'KNOW?
'CAUSE, AT FIRST, I WAS JUST A LITTLE EMBARRASSED BY THE SNOT BUBBLES I WAS BLOWING...
POP
SNRKK
...DOUBLE ICK, I KNOW...
SNIFF
SNOT-NOSED SUPERDAMSELS IN DISTRESS? GOTTA ADMIT, THAT'S A NEW ONE...
WELL, IN ALL LIKELIHOOD, THAT'S GONNA BE SOMEBODY'S FETISH... HMM.
...BUT, AFTER A MINUTE OR TWO OF, UM, WORSENING MUCOSITY, I BECAME RATHER MORE CONCERNED BY THE FACT THAT I COULD NO LONGER BREATHE THROUGH MY NOSE, PERIOD.
GKK
!
HKK
SO THERE I WAS, ROCKING THE SUFFOCATION, WHILE FRANTICALLY TRYING TO BLOW MY NOSE AGAINST THAT AWFUL CARPETING...!
GMM
KKH
REALLY NOT A SCENARIO THAT I'D PICTURED HAPPENING TO ME, BY THE WAY.

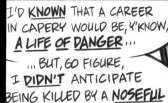

I'D **KNOWN** THAT A CAREER IN CAPERY WOULD BE, Y'KNOW, **A LIFE OF DANGER**...

...BUT, GO FIGURE, I **DIDN'T** ANTICIPATE BEING KILLED BY A **NOSEFUL OF MUCUS**, HUH?

I MEAN, A NOSE**FUL** OF MY **OWN** MUCUS, AS OPPOSED TO, SAY, **MUCUS MASTER'S** POWER SET.

SNOT-NOSED, **SUFFOCATING** SUPERDAMSELS IN DISTRESS?

IF YOU'RE INTO **BREATHPLAY**, YOU MIGHT FIND THIS **HAWT**, I GUESS...

INAPPROPRIATE, OKAY? I'M NOT **COOL** WITH EXPLOITING BREATHPLAY, DUMBASS.

ALSO IN THE "**LITTLE DID I KNOW**" DEPARTMENT: THIS WOULD TURN OUT TO BE ONLY THE FIRST OF **MULTIPLE** TIMES I'D END UP THINKING, "PLEASE, PLEASE, **PLEASE** DON'T LET ME **DIE** LIKE THIS!"

≶PHBTT≶   ≶MFF≶

TALK ABOUT A **SERIOUSLY** IGNOMINIOUS DEMISE, HUH?

YOU WANNA KNOW THE MOST **DEGRADING** THING ABOUT THE WHOLE MISERABLE EXPERIENCE?

THE **WORST** PART WAS KNOWING THAT I WAS GONNA **DIE** BECAUSE I'M SUCH A PATHETIC LITTLE **CRYBABY**...!

I MEAN, MY **AUTOPSY** WAS GONNA READ, "DEATH BY **SNIVELING**," RIGHT?

SNUFFED BY A **SNOOTFUL OF SNOT** ...PRETTY **SAD**, DON'T YOU THINK?

JEEZ, EMP...!

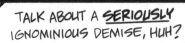

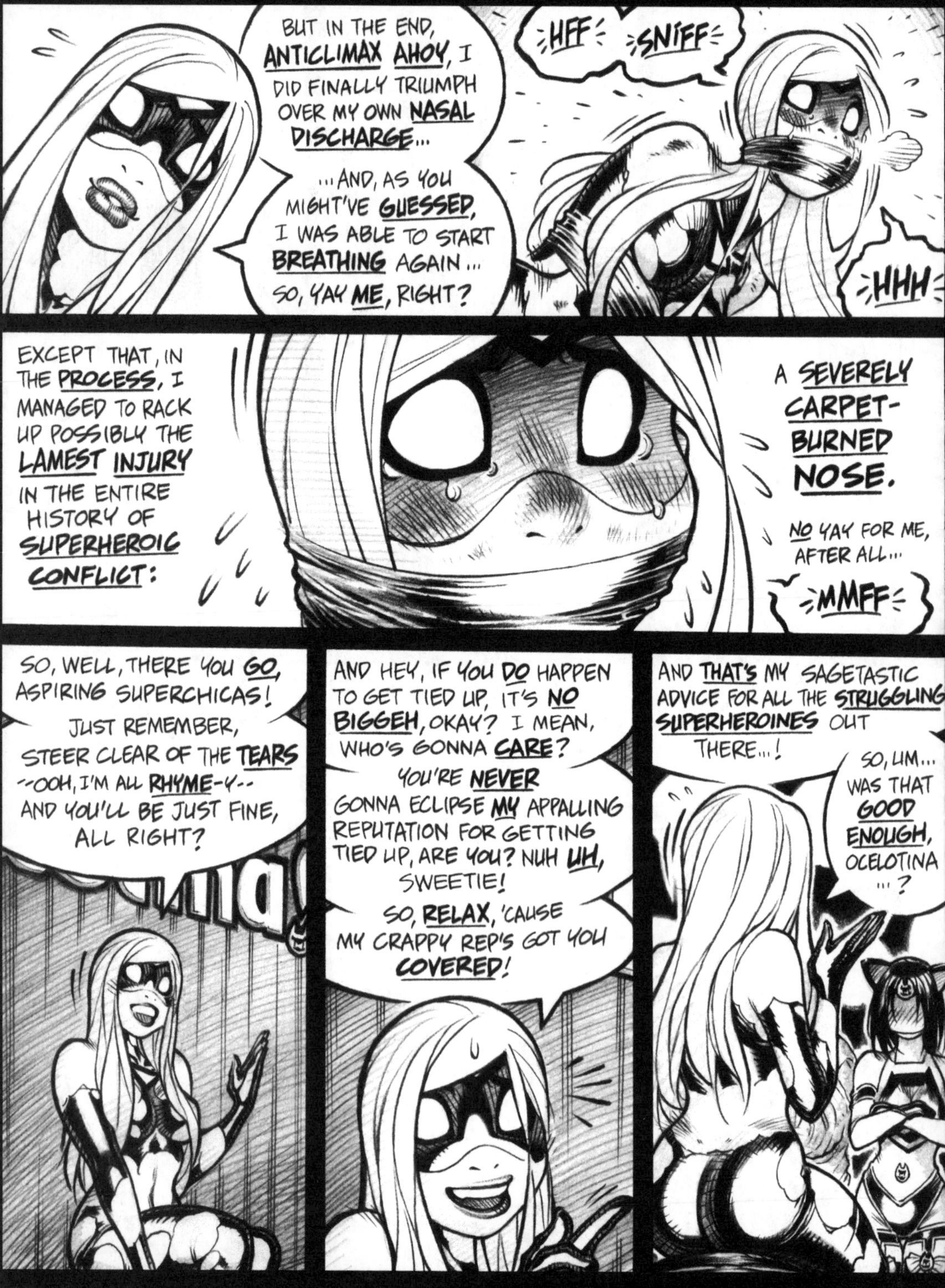
BUT IN THE END, ANTICLIMAX AHOY, I DID FINALLY TRIUMPH OVER MY OWN NASAL DISCHARGE...
...AND, AS YOU MIGHT'VE GUESSED, I WAS ABLE TO START BREATHING AGAIN... SO, YAY ME, RIGHT?
HFF
SNIFF
HHH
EXCEPT THAT, IN THE PROCESS, I MANAGED TO RACK UP POSSIBLY THE LAMEST INJURY IN THE ENTIRE HISTORY OF SUPERHEROIC CONFLICT:
A SEVERELY CARPET-BURNED NOSE.
NO YAY FOR ME, AFTER ALL...
MMFF
SO, WELL, THERE YOU GO, ASPIRING SUPERCHICAS!
JUST REMEMBER, STEER CLEAR OF THE TEARS --OOH, I'M ALL RHYME-Y-- AND YOU'LL BE JUST FINE, ALL RIGHT?
AND HEY, IF YOU DO HAPPEN TO GET TIED UP, IT'S NO BIGGEH, OKAY? I MEAN, WHO'S GONNA CARE?
YOU'RE NEVER GONNA ECLIPSE MY APPALLING REPUTATION FOR GETTING TIED UP, ARE YOU? NUH UH, SWEETIE!
SO, RELAX, 'CAUSE MY CRAPPY REP'S GOT YOU COVERED!
AND THAT'S MY SAGETASTIC ADVICE FOR ALL THE STRUGGLING SUPERHEROINES OUT THERE...!
SO, UM... WAS THAT GOOD ENOUGH, OCELOTINA ...?

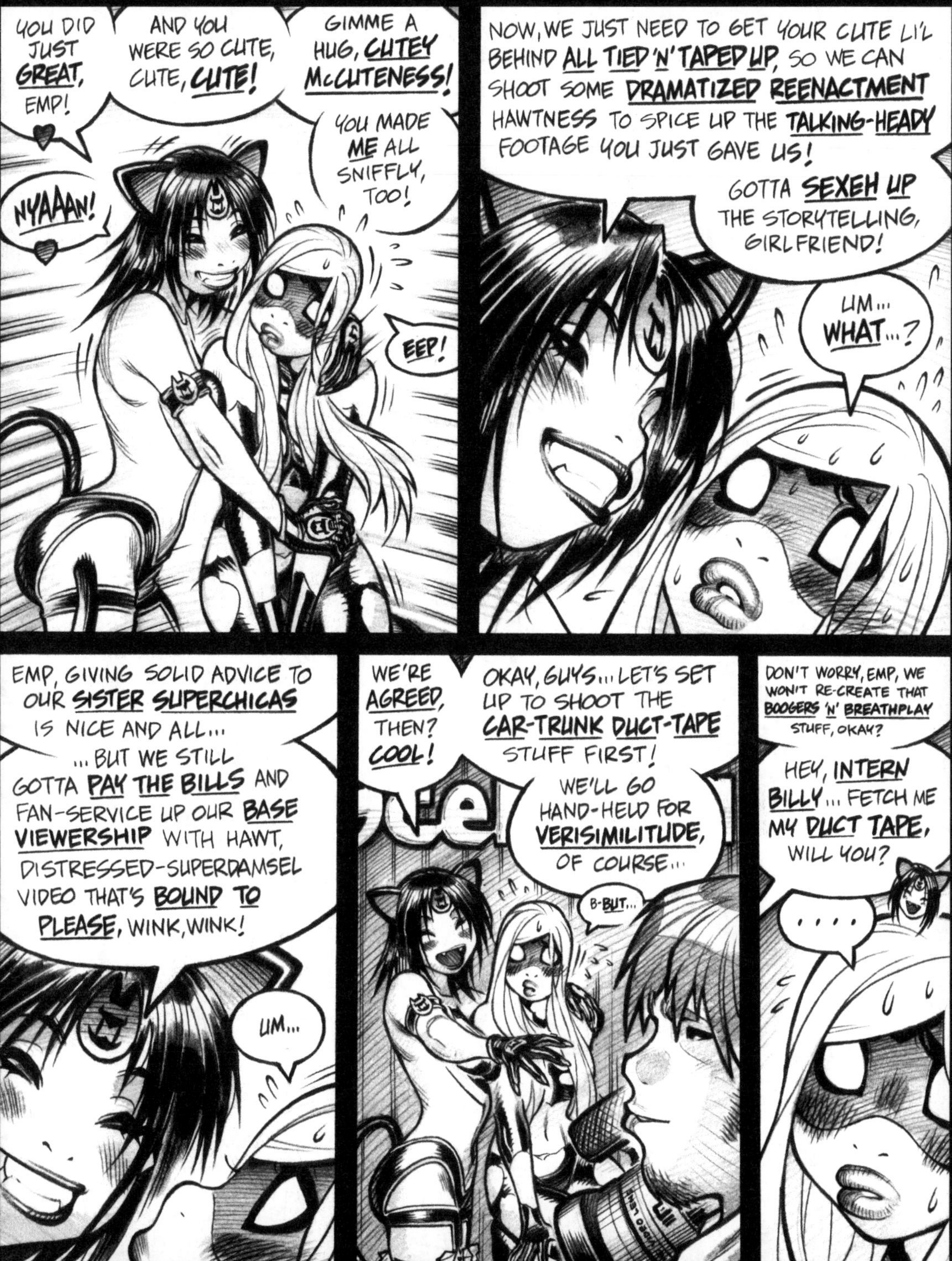

YOU DID JUST GREAT, EMP!
AND YOU WERE SO CUTE, CUTE, CUTE!
GIMME A HUG, CUTEY McCUTENESS!
YOU MADE ME ALL SNIFFLY, TOO!
NYAAAN!
EEP!
NOW, WE JUST NEED TO GET YOUR CUTE LI'L BEHIND ALL TIED 'N' TAPED UP, SO WE CAN SHOOT SOME DRAMATIZED REENACTMENT HAWTNESS TO SPICE UP THE TALKING-HEADY FOOTAGE YOU JUST GAVE US!
GOTTA SEXEH UP THE STORYTELLING, GIRLFRIEND!
UM... WHAT...?
EMP, GIVING SOLID ADVICE TO OUR SISTER SUPERCHICAS IS NICE AND ALL...
...BUT WE STILL GOTTA PAY THE BILLS AND FAN-SERVICE UP OUR BASE VIEWERSHIP WITH HAWT, DISTRESSED-SUPERDAMSEL VIDEO THAT'S BOUND TO PLEASE, WINK, WINK!
UM...
WE'RE AGREED, THEN? COOL!
OKAY, GUYS... LET'S SET UP TO SHOOT THE CAR-TRUNK DUCT-TAPE STUFF FIRST!
WE'LL GO HAND-HELD FOR VERISIMILITUDE, OF COURSE...
B-BUT...
DON'T WORRY, EMP, WE WON'T RE-CREATE THAT BOOGERS 'N' BREATHPLAY STUFF, OKAY?
HEY, INTERN BILLY... FETCH ME MY DUCT TAPE, WILL YOU?
....

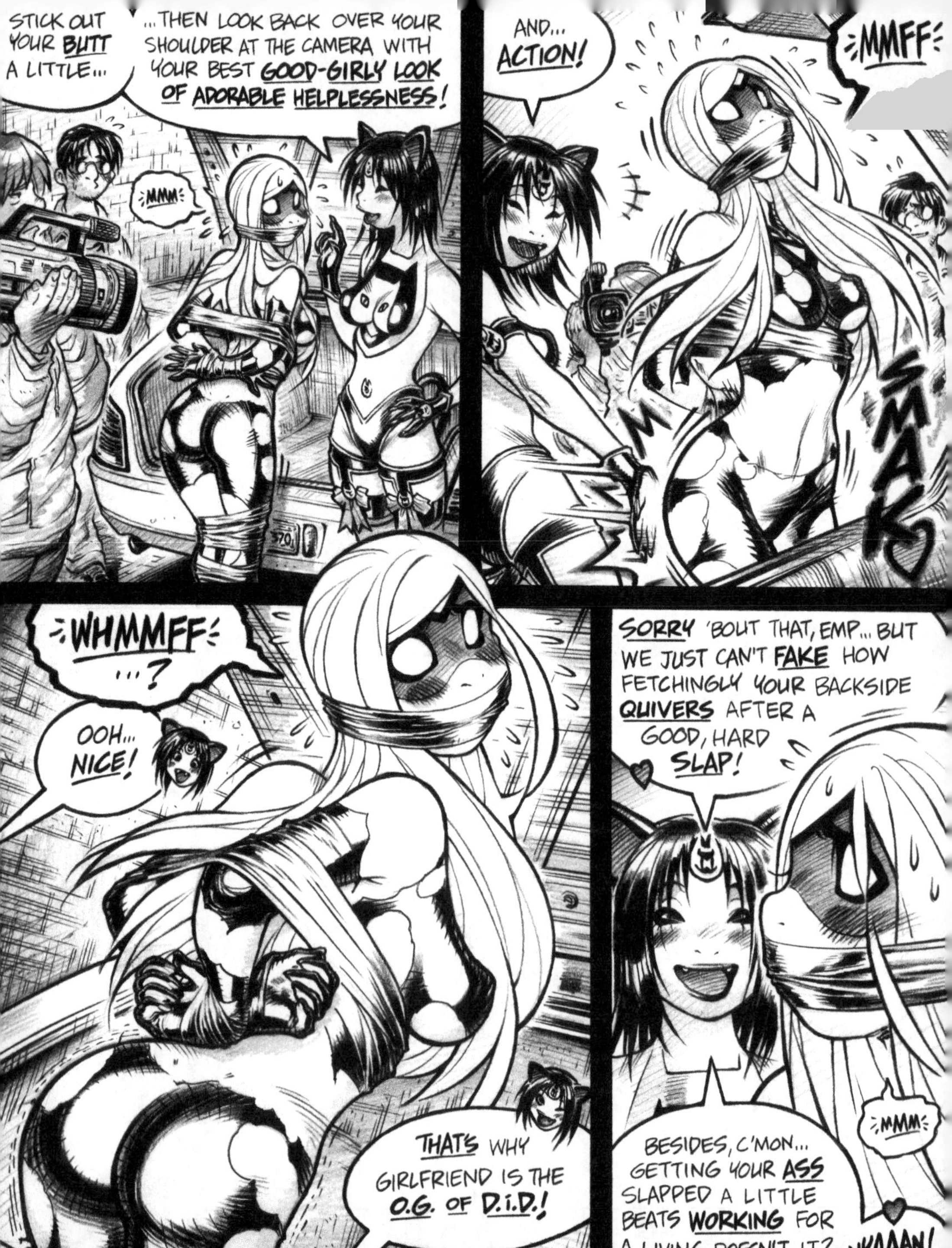
STICK OUT YOUR BUTT A LITTLE...
...THEN LOOK BACK OVER YOUR SHOULDER AT THE CAMERA WITH YOUR BEST GOOD-GIRLY LOOK OF ADORABLE HELPLESSNESS!
MMM
AND... ACTION!
MMFF
SMAK
WHMMFF ...?
OOH... NICE!
THAT'S WHY GIRLFRIEND IS THE O.G. OF D.i.D.!
SORRY 'BOUT THAT, EMP... BUT WE JUST CAN'T FAKE HOW FETCHINGLY YOUR BACKSIDE QUIVERS AFTER A GOOD, HARD SLAP!
BESIDES, C'MON... GETTING YOUR ASS SLAPPED A LITTLE BEATS WORKING FOR A LIVING, DOESN'T IT?
MMM
NYAAAN!

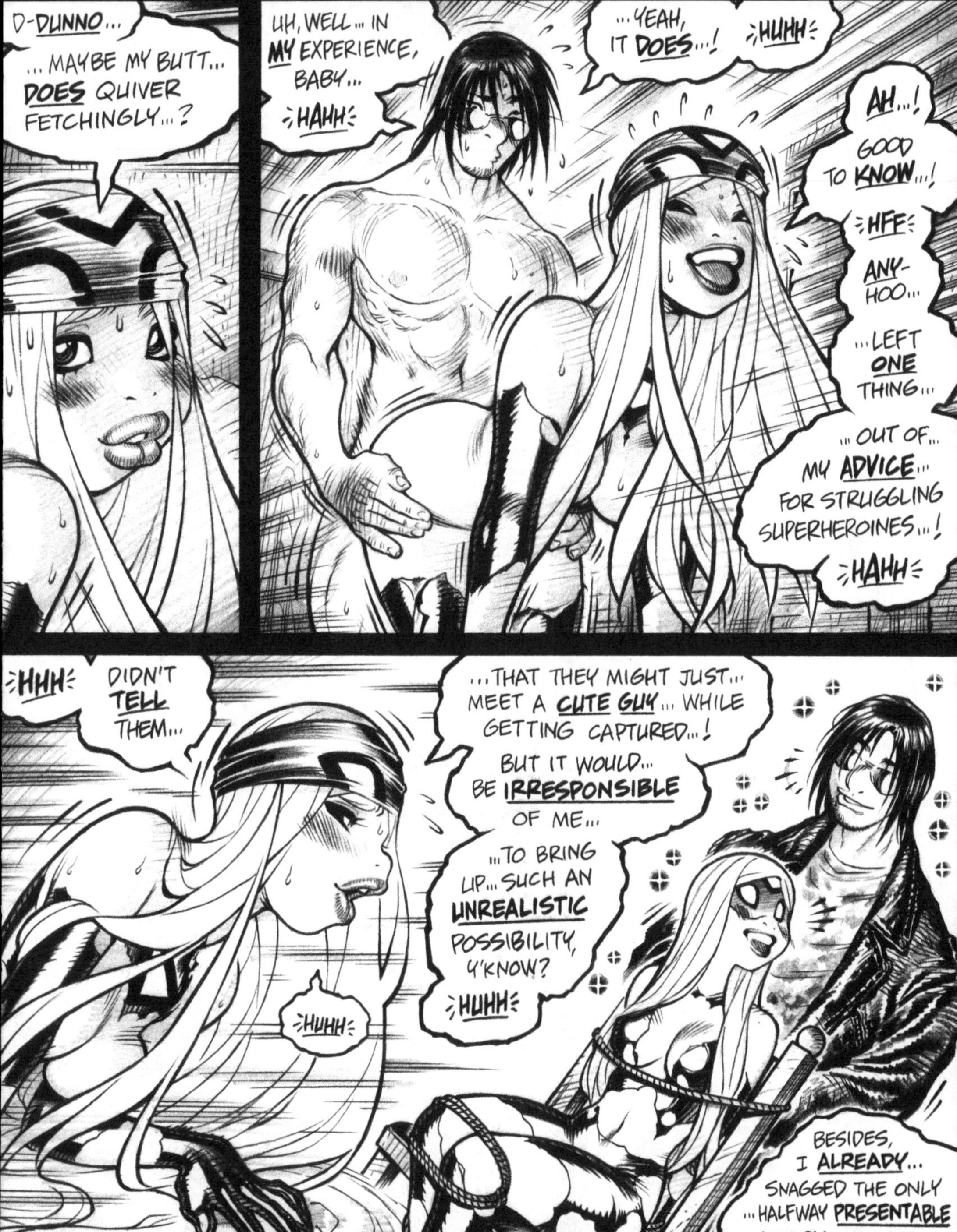
D-DUNNO...
...MAYBE MY BUTT... DOES QUIVER FETCHINGLY...?
UH, WELL... IN MY EXPERIENCE, BABY...
HAHH
...YEAH, IT DOES...!
HUHH
AH...!
GOOD TO KNOW...!
HFF
ANY-HOO...
...LEFT ONE THING...
...OUT OF... MY ADVICE... FOR STRUGGLING SUPERHEROINES...!
HAHH
HHH
DIDN'T TELL THEM...
...THAT THEY MIGHT JUST... MEET A CUTE GUY... WHILE GETTING CAPTURED...!
BUT IT WOULD... BE IRRESPONSIBLE OF ME...
...TO BRING UP... SUCH AN UNREALISTIC POSSIBILITY, Y'KNOW?
HUHH
HUHH
BESIDES, I ALREADY... SNAGGED THE ONLY ...HALFWAY PRESENTABLE MINION... IN THE BUSINESS...!

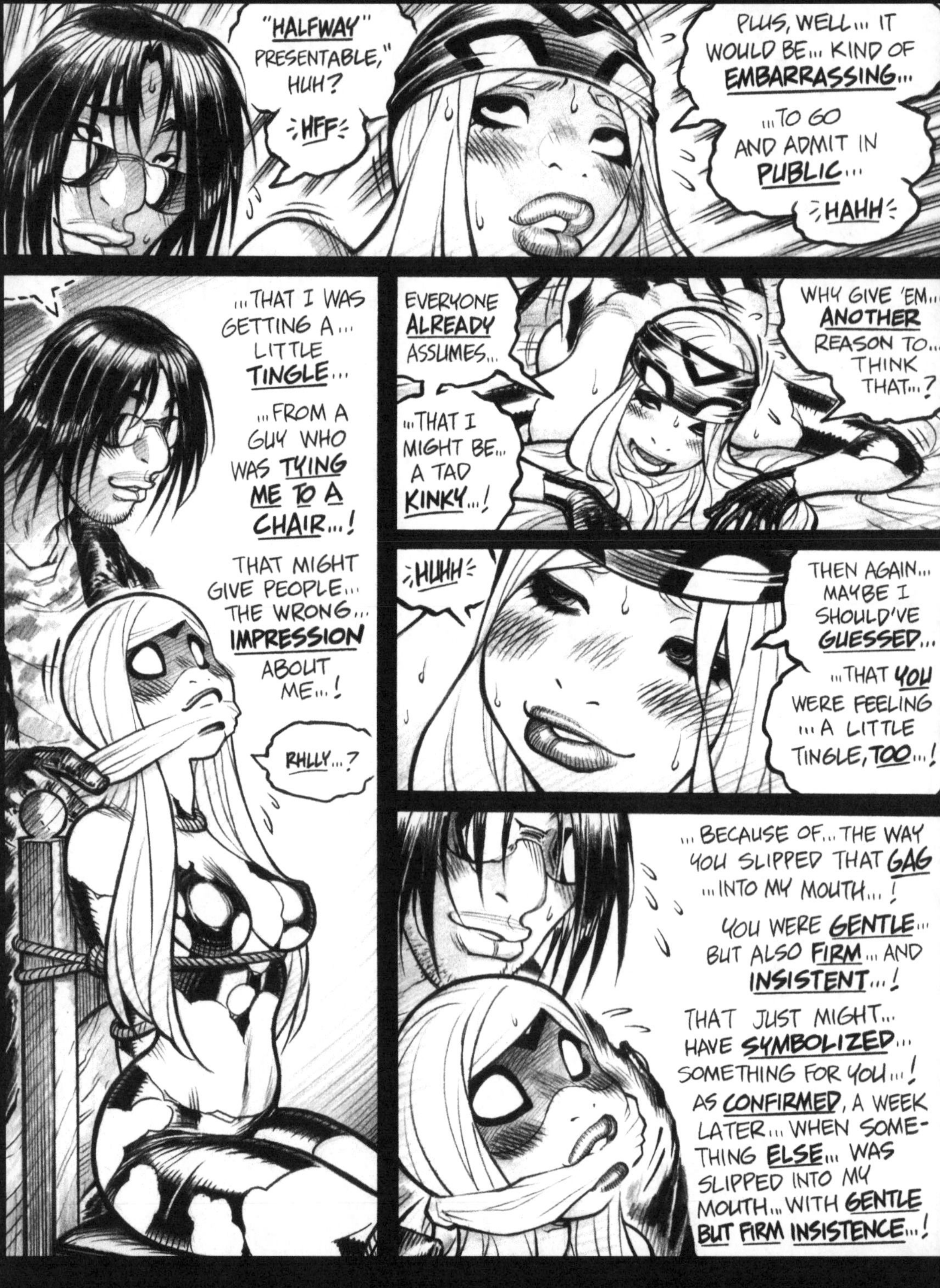
"HALFWAY" PRESENTABLE," HUH?
HFF
PLUS, WELL... IT WOULD BE... KIND OF EMBARRASSING...
...TO GO AND ADMIT IN PUBLIC...
HAHH
...THAT I WAS GETTING A... LITTLE TINGLE...
...FROM A GUY WHO WAS TYING ME TO A CHAIR...!
THAT MIGHT GIVE PEOPLE... THE WRONG... IMPRESSION ABOUT ME...!
RHLLY...?
EVERYONE ALREADY ASSUMES...
...THAT I MIGHT BE... A TAD KINKY...!
WHY GIVE 'EM... ANOTHER REASON TO... THINK THAT...?
HUHH
THEN AGAIN... MAYBE I SHOULD'VE GUESSED...
...THAT YOU WERE FEELING ...A LITTLE TINGLE, TOO...!
...BECAUSE OF... THE WAY YOU SLIPPED THAT GAG ...INTO MY MOUTH...!
YOU WERE GENTLE... BUT ALSO FIRM... AND INSISTENT...!
THAT JUST MIGHT... HAVE SYMBOLIZED... SOMETHING FOR YOU...!
AS CONFIRMED, A WEEK LATER... WHEN SOME-THING ELSE... WAS SLIPPED INTO MY MOUTH... WITH GENTLE BUT FIRM INSISTENCE...!

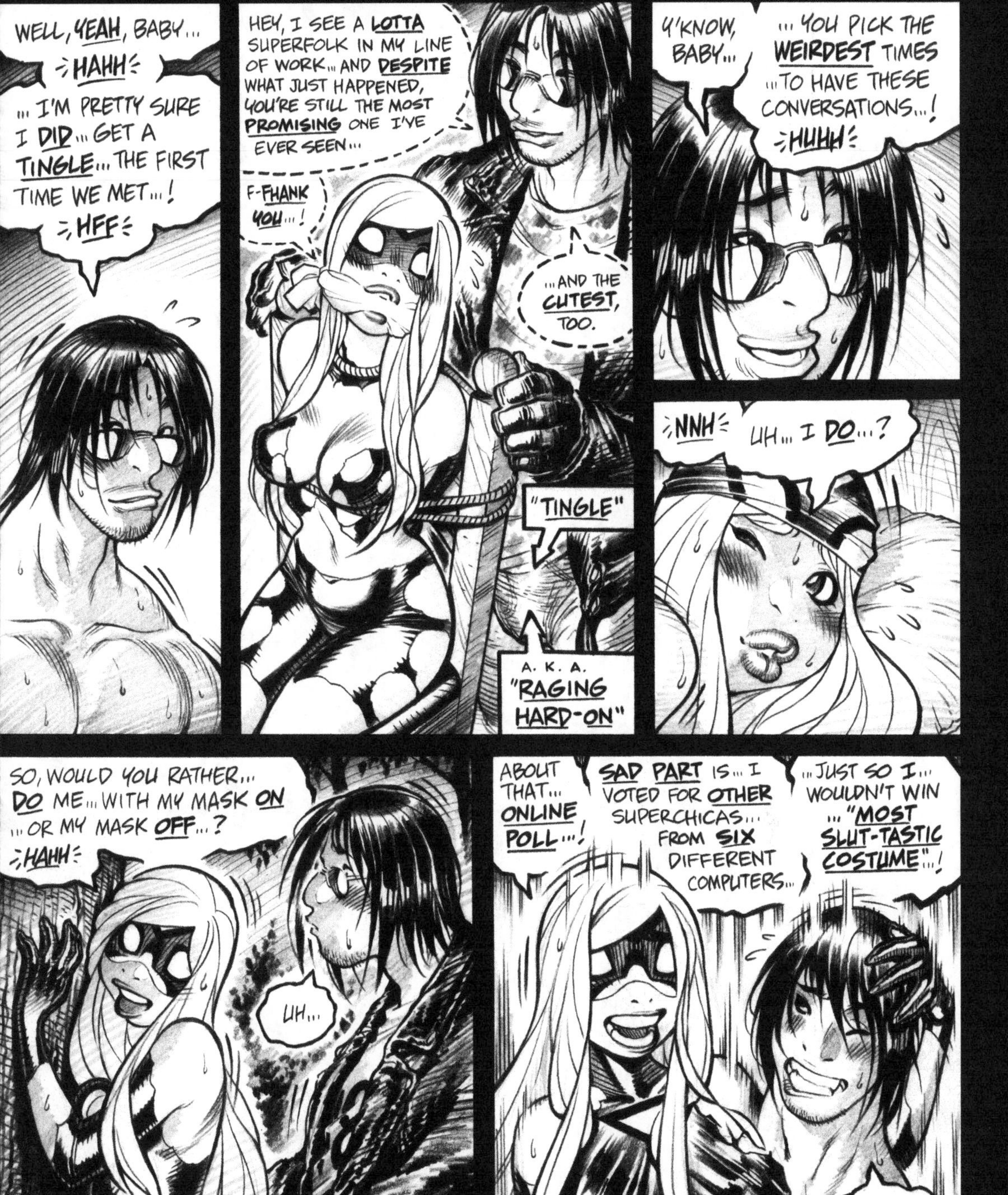
WELL, YEAH, BABY... HAHH ... I'M PRETTY SURE I DID... GET A TINGLE... THE FIRST TIME WE MET...! HFF
HEY, I SEE A LOTTA SUPERFOLK IN MY LINE OF WORK... AND DESPITE WHAT JUST HAPPENED, YOU'RE STILL THE MOST PROMISING ONE I'VE EVER SEEN...
F-FHANK YOU...!
...AND THE CUTEST, TOO.
"TINGLE"
A. K. A. "RAGING HARD-ON"
Y'KNOW, BABY...
...YOU PICK THE WEIRDEST TIMES ...TO HAVE THESE CONVERSATIONS...! HUHH
NNH
UH... I DO...?
SO, WOULD YOU RATHER... DO ME... WITH MY MASK ON ...OR MY MASK OFF...? HAHH
UH...
ABOUT THAT... ONLINE POLL...!
SAD PART IS... I VOTED FOR OTHER SUPERCHICAS... FROM SIX DIFFERENT COMPUTERS...
...JUST SO I... WOULDN'T WIN ..."MOST SLUT-TASTIC COSTUME"...!
REALLY.

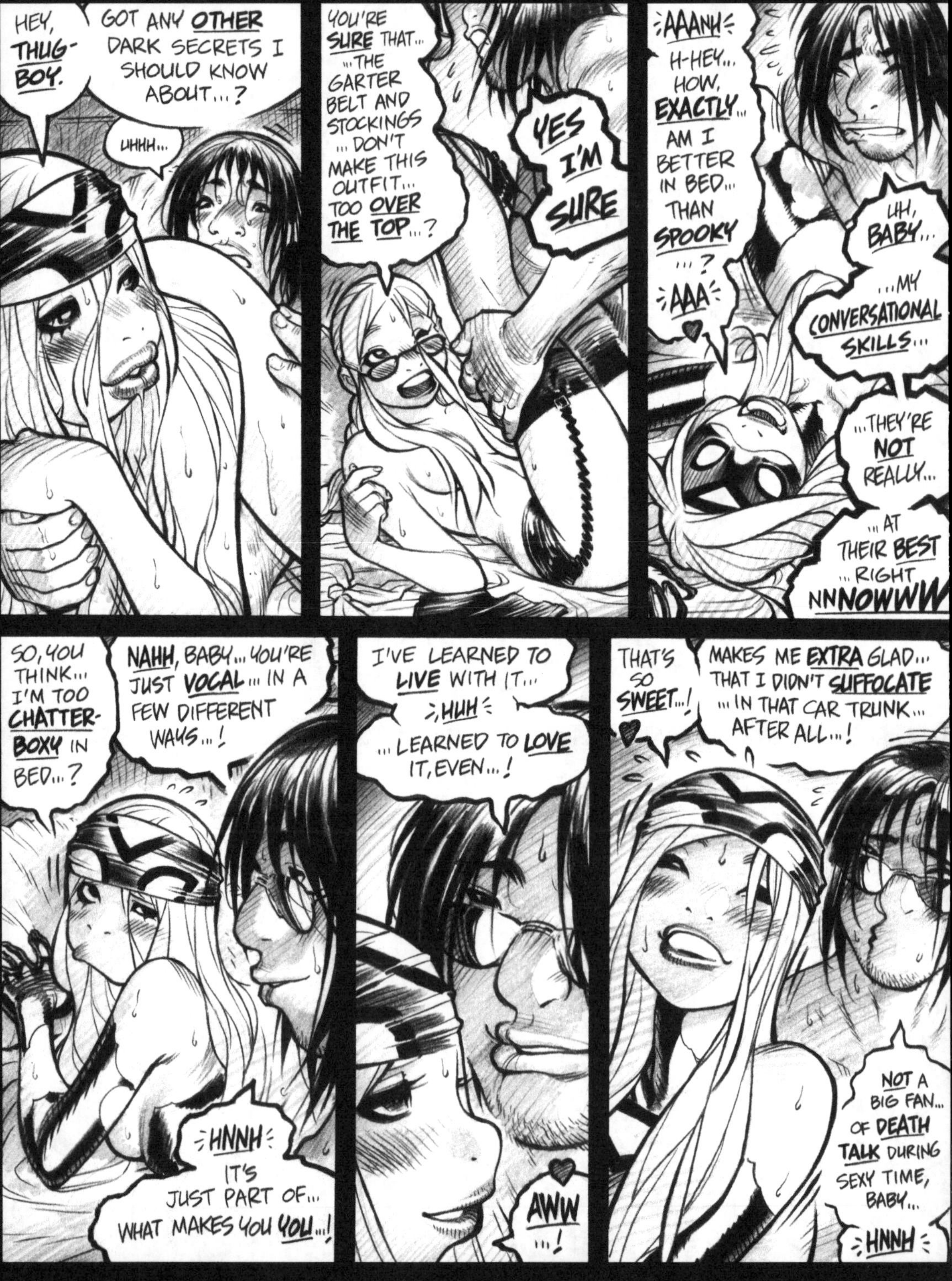
HEY, THUG-BOY.
GOT ANY OTHER DARK SECRETS I SHOULD KNOW ABOUT...?
UHHH...
YOU'RE SURE THAT... ...THE GARTER BELT AND STOCKINGS ...DON'T MAKE THIS OUTFIT... TOO OVER THE TOP...?
YES I'M SURE
AAANH
H-HEY... HOW, EXACTLY... AM I BETTER IN BED... THAN SPOOKY ...?
AAA
UH, BABY... ...MY CONVERSATIONAL SKILLS...
...THEY'RE NOT REALLY...
...AT THEIR BEST ...RIGHT NNNOWWW
SO, YOU THINK... I'M TOO CHATTER-BOXY IN BED...?
NAHH, BABY... YOU'RE JUST VOCAL... IN A FEW DIFFERENT WAYS...!
HNNH
IT'S JUST PART OF... WHAT MAKES YOU YOU...!
I'VE LEARNED TO LIVE WITH IT...
HUH
...LEARNED TO LOVE IT, EVEN...!
AWW ...!
THAT'S SO SWEET...!
MAKES ME EXTRA GLAD... THAT I DIDN'T SUFFOCATE ...IN THAT CAR TRUNK... AFTER ALL...!
NOT A BIG FAN... OF DEATH TALK DURING SEXY TIME, BABY...
HNNH

Empowered™

A Very Long and Very Uncomfortable Eternity

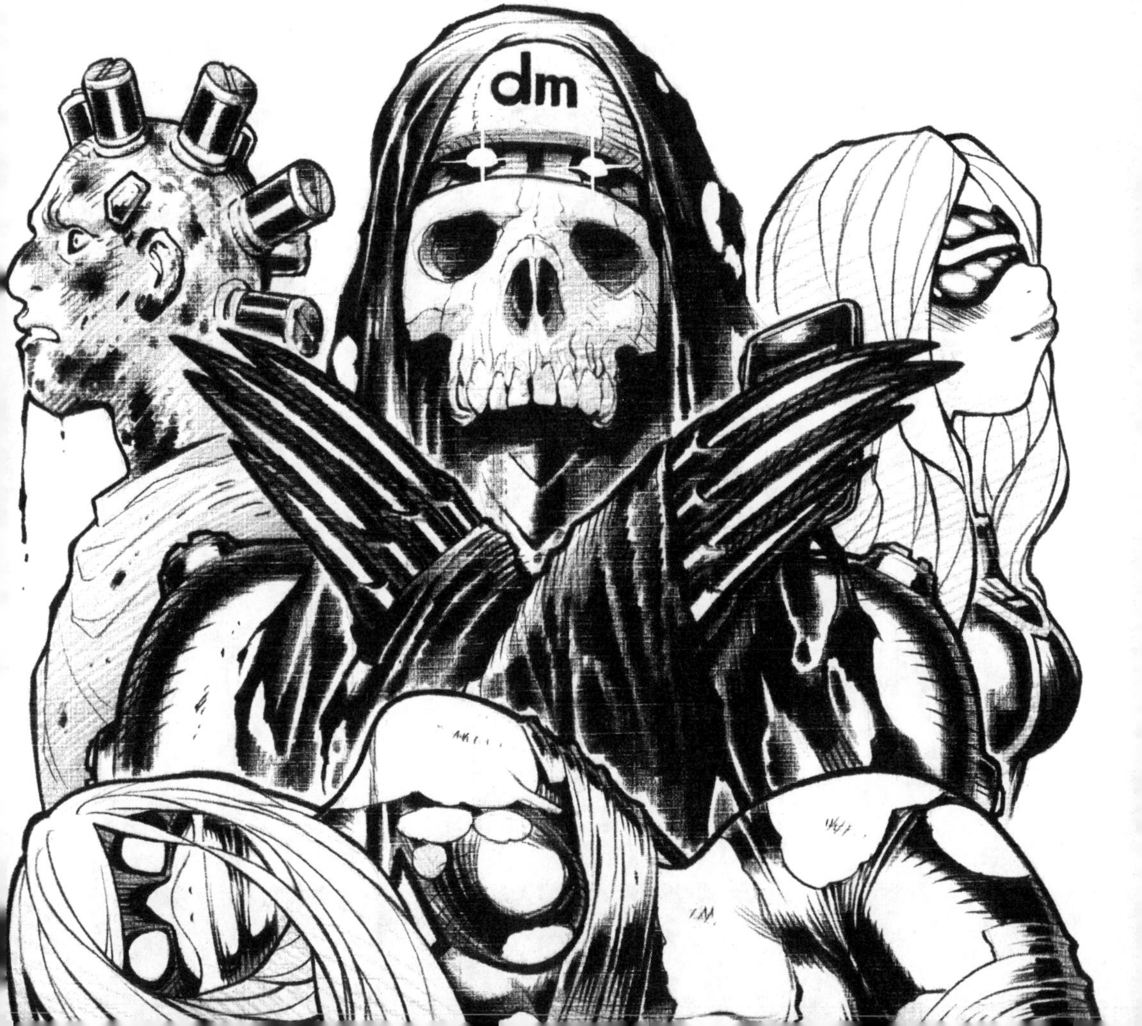
dm

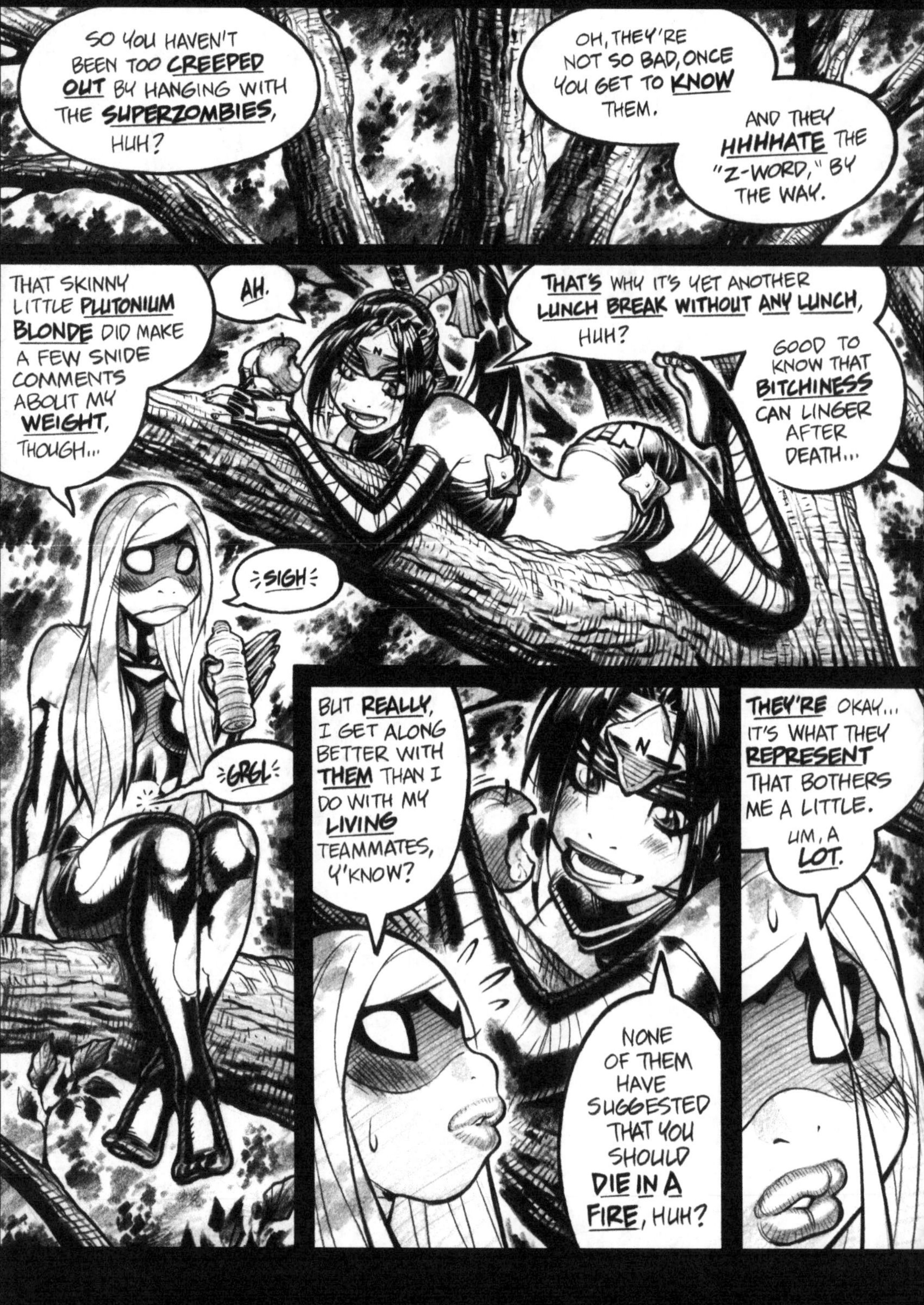
SO YOU HAVEN'T BEEN TOO CREEPED OUT BY HANGING WITH THE SUPERZOMBIES, HUH?
OH, THEY'RE NOT SO BAD, ONCE YOU GET TO KNOW THEM.
AND THEY HHHHATE THE "Z-WORD," BY THE WAY.
AH.
THAT'S WHY IT'S YET ANOTHER LUNCH BREAK WITHOUT ANY LUNCH, HUH?
THAT SKINNY LITTLE PLUTONIUM BLONDE DID MAKE A FEW SNIDE COMMENTS ABOUT MY WEIGHT, THOUGH...
GOOD TO KNOW THAT BITCHINESS CAN LINGER AFTER DEATH...
SIGH
GRGL
BUT REALLY, I GET ALONG BETTER WITH THEM THAN I DO WITH MY LIVING TEAMMATES, Y'KNOW?
NONE OF THEM HAVE SUGGESTED THAT YOU SHOULD DIE IN A FIRE, HUH?
THEY'RE OKAY... IT'S WHAT THEY REPRESENT THAT BOTHERS ME A LITTLE.
UM, A LOT.

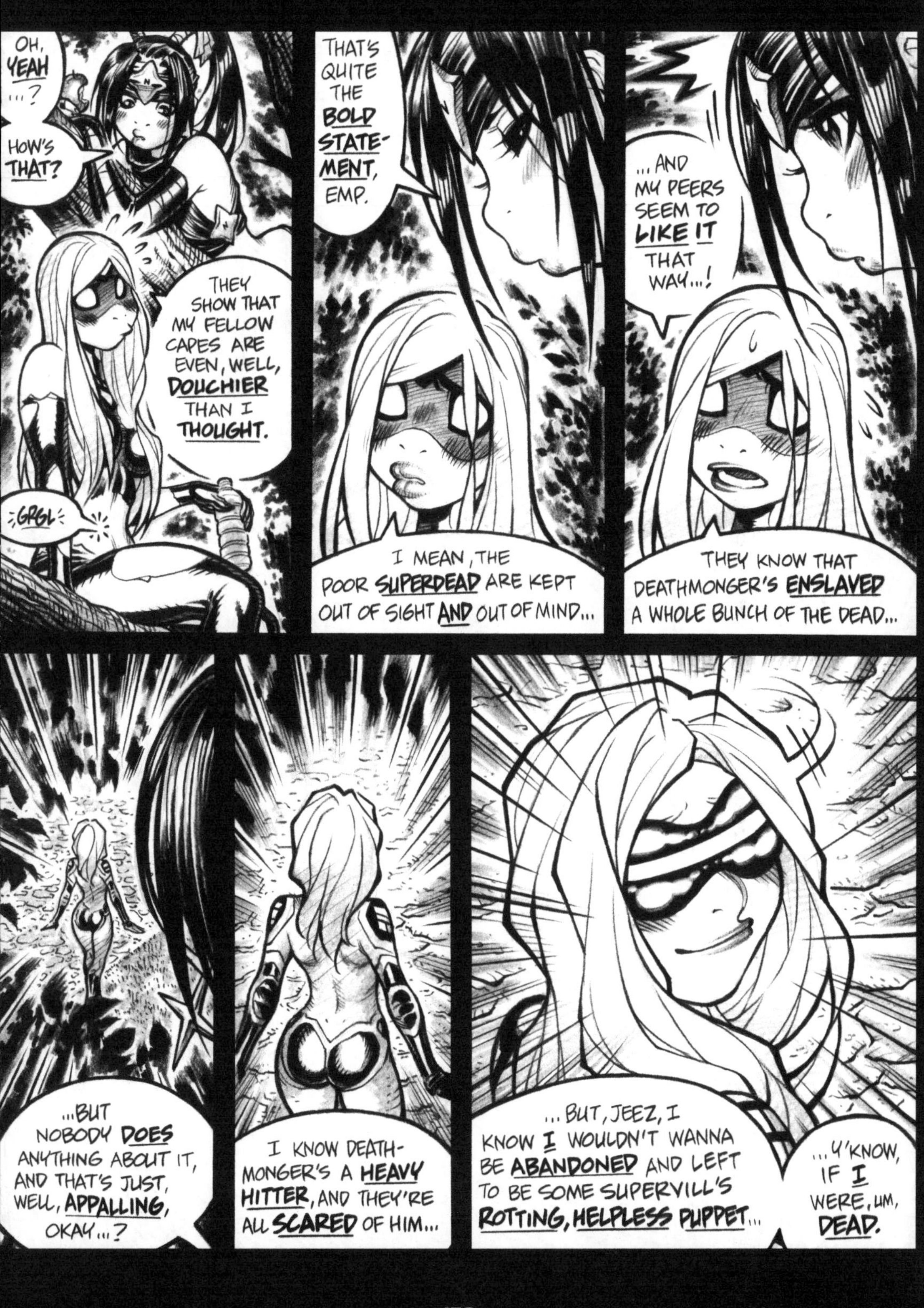
OH, YEAH ...?
HOW'S THAT?
THEY SHOW THAT MY FELLOW CAPES ARE EVEN, WELL, DOUCHIER THAN I THOUGHT.
GRGL
THAT'S QUITE THE BOLD STATEMENT, EMP.
I MEAN, THE POOR SUPERDEAD ARE KEPT OUT OF SIGHT AND OUT OF MIND...
...AND MY PEERS SEEM TO LIKE IT THAT WAY...!
THEY KNOW THAT DEATHMONGER'S ENSLAVED A WHOLE BUNCH OF THE DEAD...
...BUT NOBODY DOES ANYTHING ABOUT IT, AND THAT'S JUST, WELL, APPALLING, OKAY...?
I KNOW DEATH-MONGER'S A HEAVY HITTER, AND THEY'RE ALL SCARED OF HIM...
...BUT, JEEZ, I KNOW I WOULDN'T WANNA BE ABANDONED AND LEFT TO BE SOME SUPERVILL'S ROTTING, HELPLESS PUPPET...
...Y'KNOW, IF I WERE, UM, DEAD.

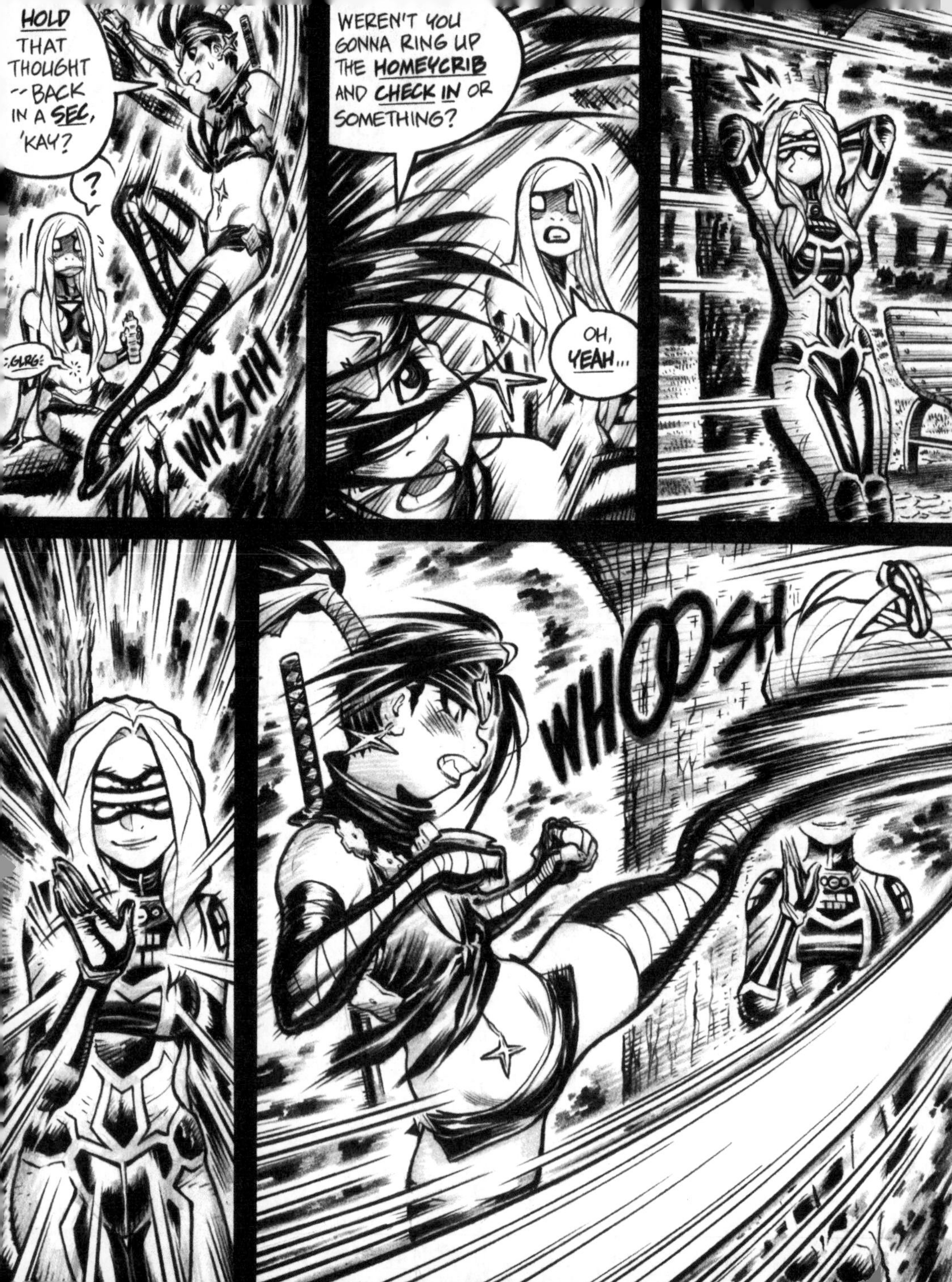
HOLD THAT THOUGHT --BACK IN A SEC, 'KAY?
?
GLRG
WHSHH
WEREN'T YOU GONNA RING UP THE HOMEYCRIB AND CHECK IN OR SOMETHING?
OH, YEAH...
WHOOSH

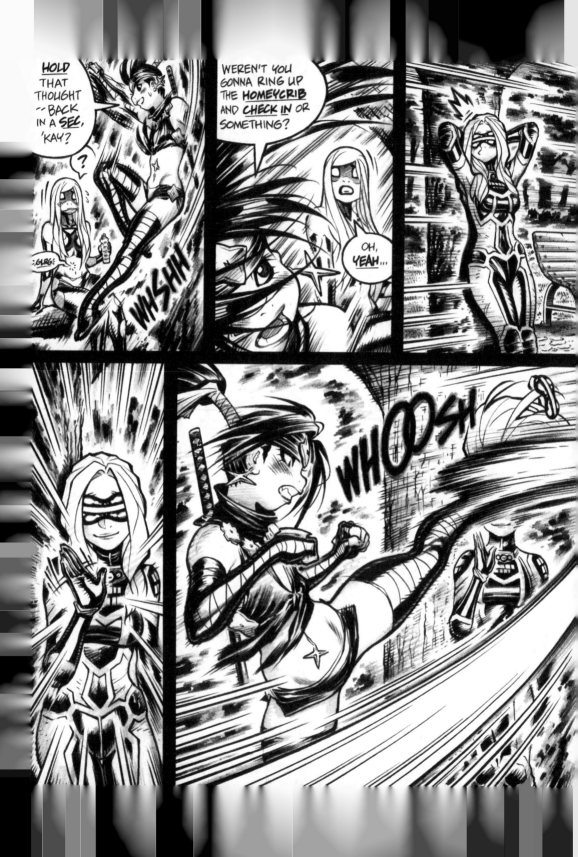

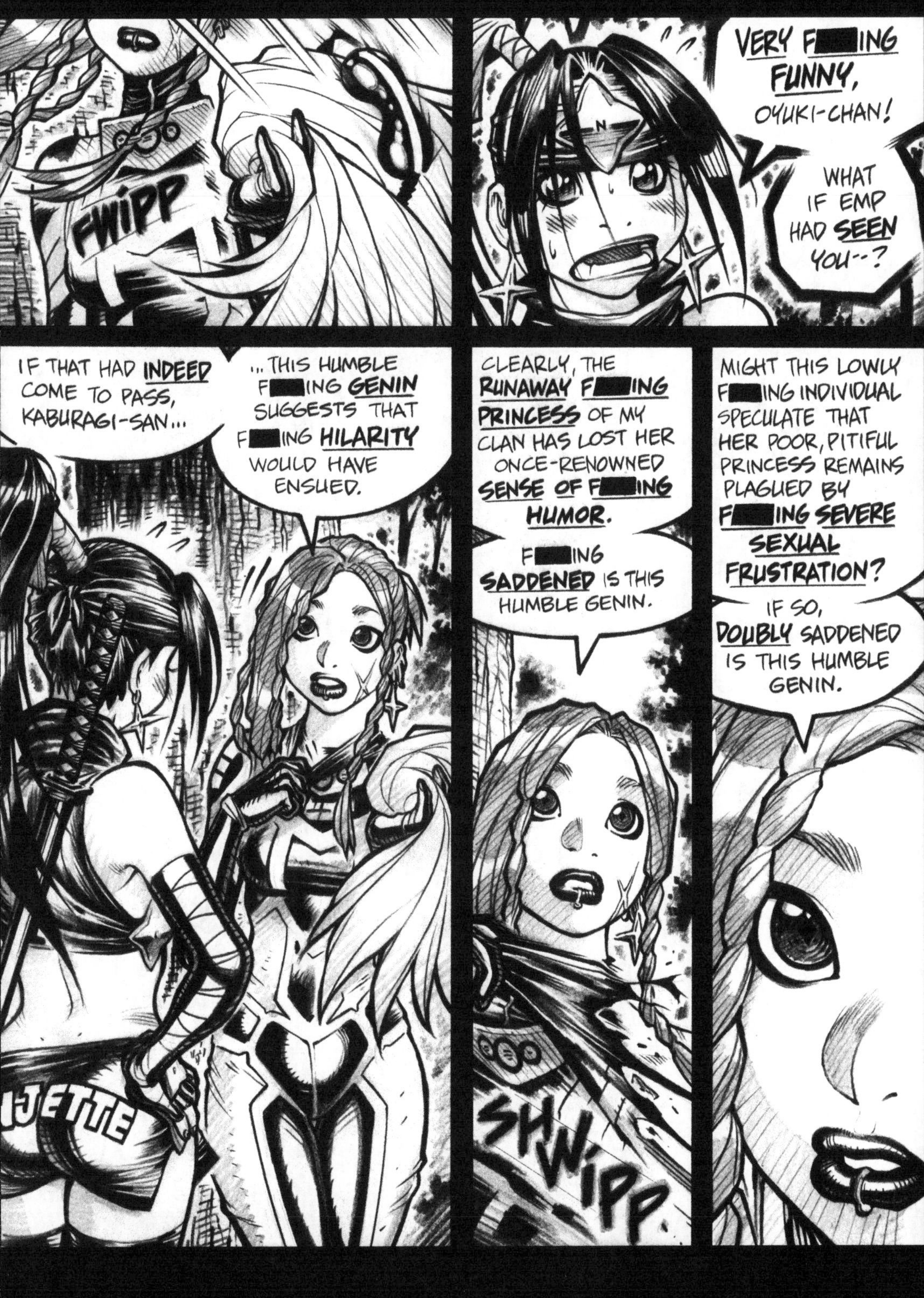
FWIPP
VERY F[redacted]ING FUNNY, OYUKI-CHAN!
WHAT IF EMP HAD SEEN YOU--?
IF THAT HAD INDEED COME TO PASS, KABURAGI-SAN...
...THIS HUMBLE F[redacted]ING GENIN SUGGESTS THAT F[redacted]ING HILARITY WOULD HAVE ENSUED.
IJETTE
CLEARLY, THE RUNAWAY F[redacted]ING PRINCESS OF MY CLAN HAS LOST HER ONCE-RENOWNED SENSE OF F[redacted]ING HUMOR.
F[redacted]ING SADDENED IS THIS HUMBLE GENIN.
SHWIPP
MIGHT THIS LOWLY F[redacted]ING INDIVIDUAL SPECULATE THAT HER POOR, PITIFUL PRINCESS REMAINS PLAGUED BY F[redacted]ING SEVERE SEXUAL FRUSTRATION?
IF SO, DOUBLY SADDENED IS THIS HUMBLE GENIN.

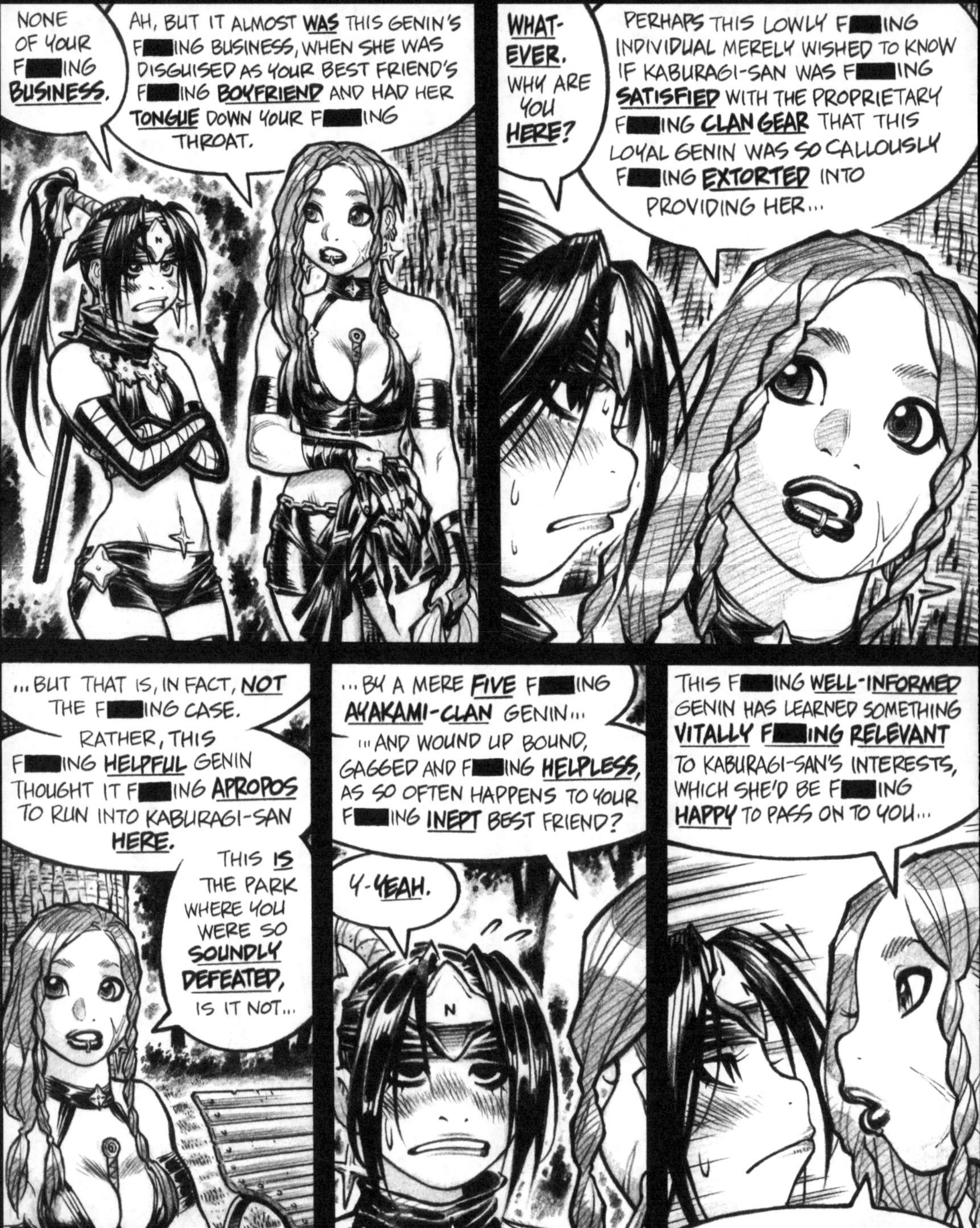

NONE OF YOUR F[redacted]ING BUSINESS.
AH, BUT IT ALMOST WAS THIS GENIN'S F[redacted]ING BUSINESS, WHEN SHE WAS DISGUISED AS YOUR BEST FRIEND'S F[redacted]ING BOYFRIEND AND HAD HER TONGUE DOWN YOUR F[redacted]ING THROAT.
WHAT-EVER. WHY ARE YOU HERE?
PERHAPS THIS LOWLY F[redacted]ING INDIVIDUAL MERELY WISHED TO KNOW IF KABURAGI-SAN WAS F[redacted]ING SATISFIED WITH THE PROPRIETARY F[redacted]ING CLAN GEAR THAT THIS LOYAL GENIN WAS SO CALLOUSLY F[redacted]ING EXTORTED INTO PROVIDING HER...
...BUT THAT IS, IN FACT, NOT THE F[redacted]ING CASE.
RATHER, THIS F[redacted]ING HELPFUL GENIN THOUGHT IT F[redacted]ING APROPOS TO RUN INTO KABURAGI-SAN HERE.
THIS IS THE PARK WHERE YOU WERE SO SOUNDLY DEFEATED, IS IT NOT...
...BY A MERE FIVE F[redacted]ING AYAKAMI-CLAN GENIN...
...AND WOUND UP BOUND, GAGGED AND F[redacted]ING HELPLESS, AS SO OFTEN HAPPENS TO YOUR F[redacted]ING INEPT BEST FRIEND?
Y-YEAH.
WHAT'S YOUR POINT?
THIS F[redacted]ING WELL-INFORMED GENIN HAS LEARNED SOMETHING VITALLY F[redacted]ING RELEVANT TO KABURAGI-SAN'S INTERESTS, WHICH SHE'D BE F[redacted]ING HAPPY TO PASS ON TO YOU...
...IF, THAT IS, YOU WERE TO ASK HER F[redacted]ING NICELY.

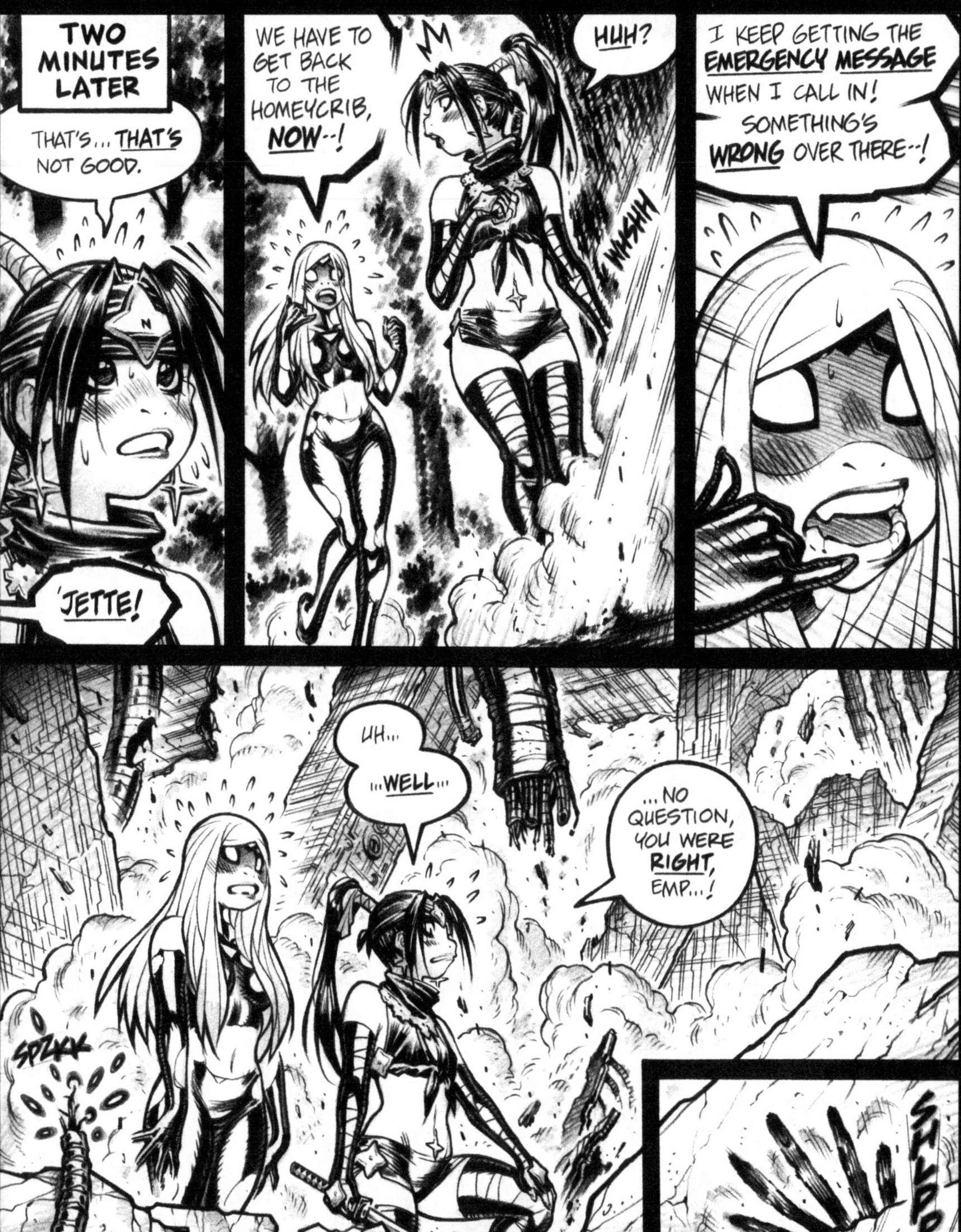

TWO MINUTES LATER
THAT'S... THAT'S NOT GOOD.
'JETTE!
WE HAVE TO GET BACK TO THE HOMEYCRIB, NOW--!
HUH?
WHSHH
I KEEP GETTING THE EMERGENCY MESSAGE WHEN I CALL IN! SOMETHING'S WRONG OVER THERE--!
UH...
...WELL...
...NO QUESTION, YOU WERE RIGHT, EMP...!
SPZKK
SHLPP

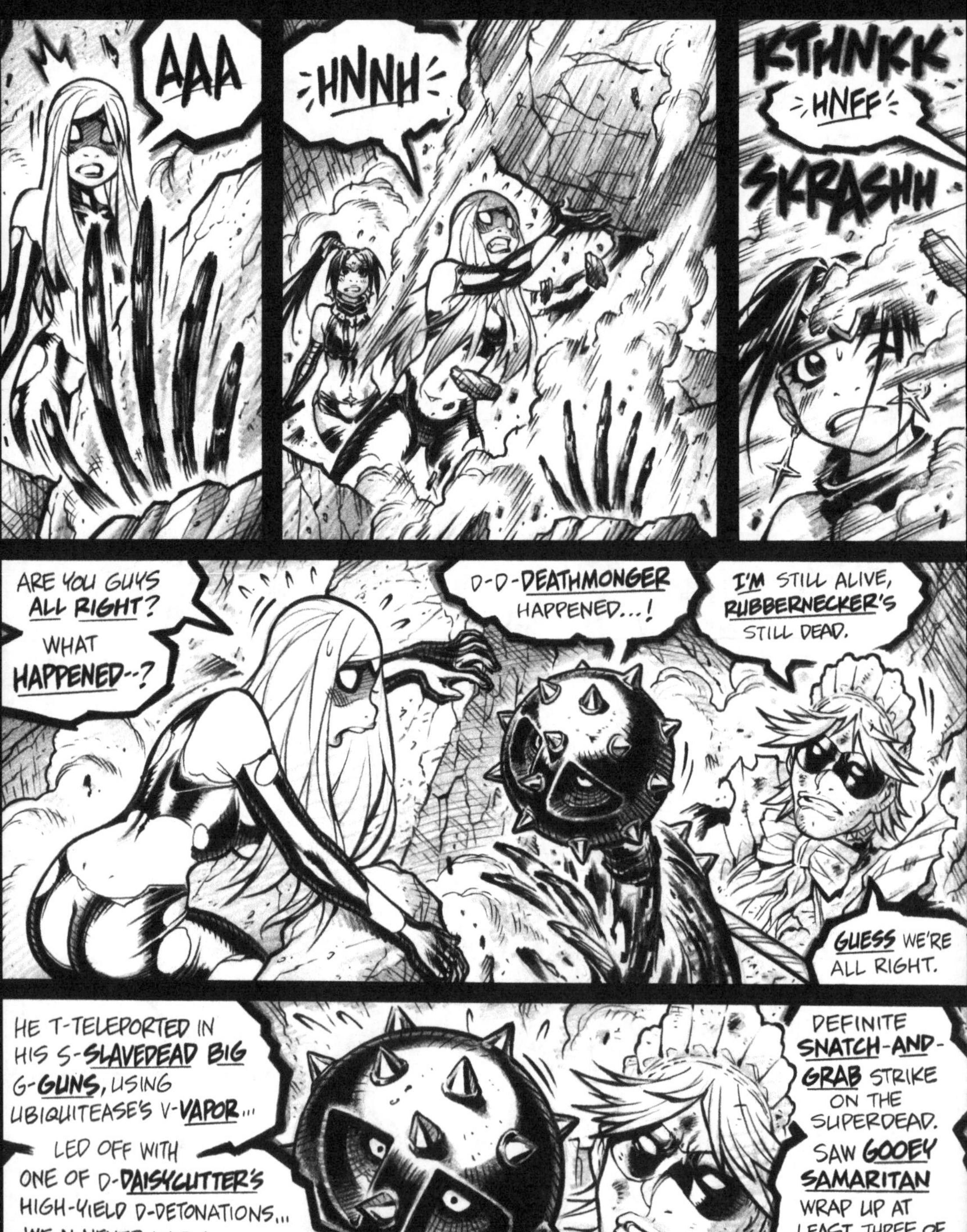
AAA
HNNH
KTHNKK
HNFF
SKRASHH
ARE YOU GUYS ALL RIGHT? WHAT HAPPENED--?
D-D-DEATHMONGER HAPPENED...!
I'M STILL ALIVE, RUBBERNECKER'S STILL DEAD.
GUESS WE'RE ALL RIGHT.
HE T-TELEPORTED IN HIS S-SLAVEDEAD BIG G-GUNS, USING UBIQUITEASE'S V-VAPOR...
LED OFF WITH ONE OF D-DAISYCUTTER'S HIGH-YIELD D-DETONATIONS... WE N-NEVER HAD A F-F[redacted]ING CHANCE...!
DEFINITE SNATCH-AND-GRAB STRIKE ON THE SUPERDEAD.
SAW GOOEY SAMARITAN WRAP UP AT LEAST THREE OF 'EM, BEFORE THE WALLS FELL ON ME.

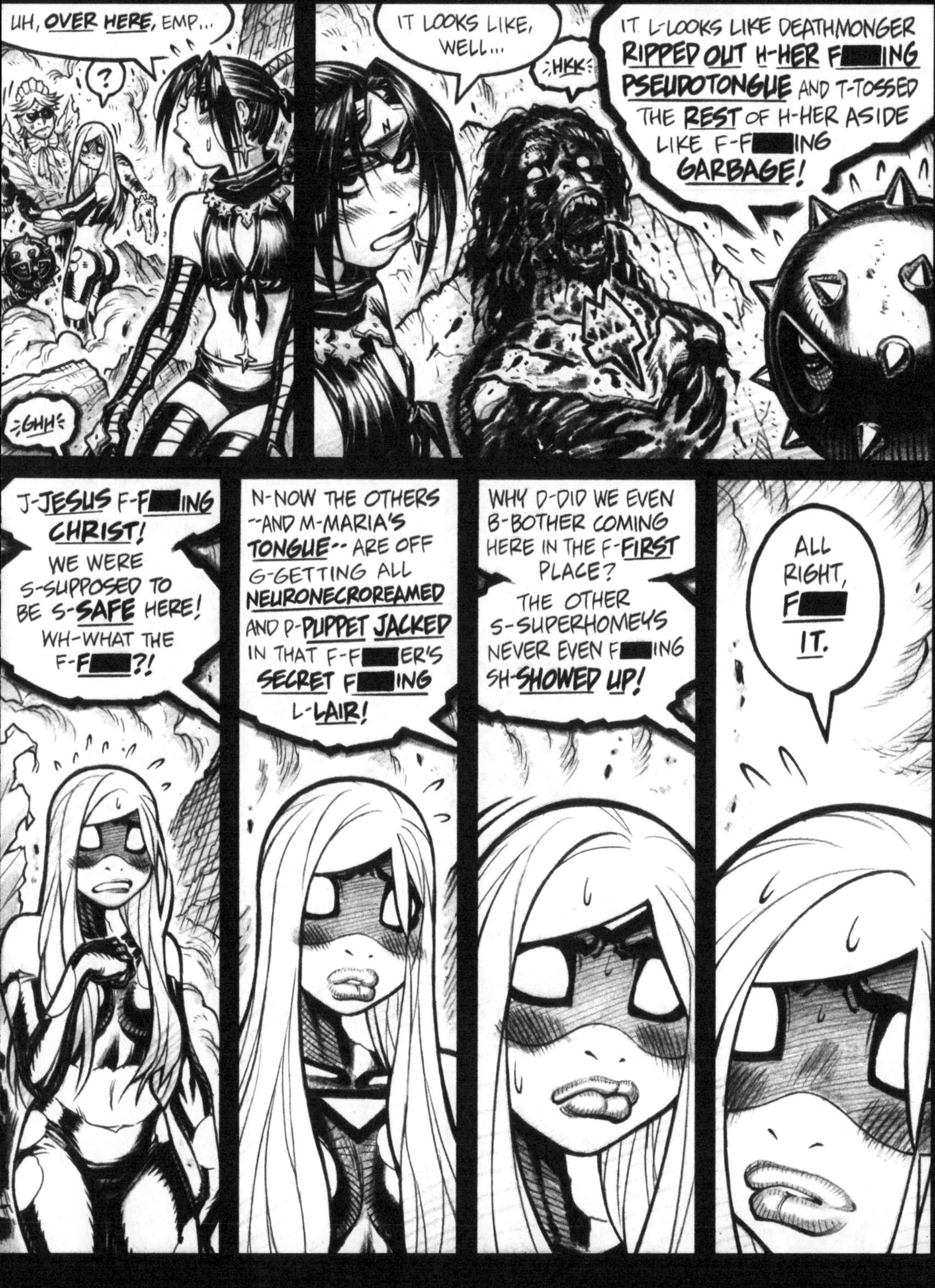
UH, OVER HERE, EMP...
?
GHH
IT LOOKS LIKE, WELL...
HKK
IT. L-LOOKS LIKE DEATHMONGER RIPPED OUT H-HER F[redacted]ING PSEUDOTONGUE AND T-TOSSED THE REST OF H-HER ASIDE LIKE F-F[redacted]ING GARBAGE!
J-JESUS F-F[redacted]ING CHRIST! WE WERE S-SUPPOSED TO BE S-SAFE HERE! WH-WHAT THE F-F[redacted]?!
N-NOW THE OTHERS --AND M-MARIA'S TONGUE-- ARE OFF G-GETTING ALL NEURONECROREAMED AND P-PUPPET JACKED IN THAT F-F[redacted]ER'S SECRET F[redacted]ING L-LAIR!
WHY D-DID WE EVEN B-BOTHER COMING HERE IN THE F-FIRST PLACE? THE OTHER S-SUPERHOMEYS NEVER EVEN F[redacted]ING SH-SHOWED UP!
ALL RIGHT, F[redacted] IT.

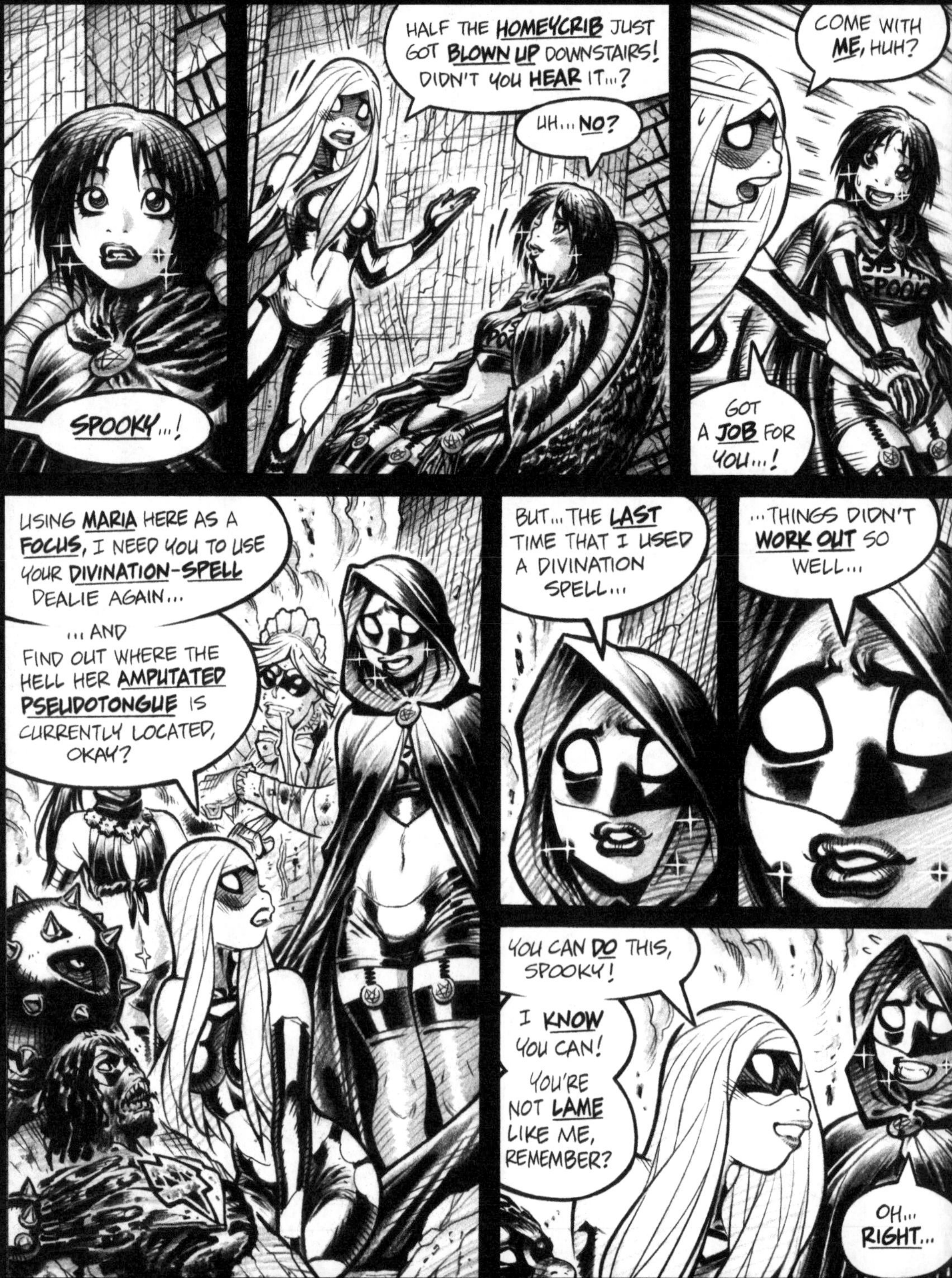
SPOOKY...!
HALF THE HOMEYCRIB JUST GOT BLOWN UP DOWNSTAIRS! DIDN'T YOU HEAR IT...?
UH... NO?
COME WITH ME, HUH?
GOT A JOB FOR YOU...!
USING MARIA HERE AS A FOCUS, I NEED YOU TO USE YOUR DIVINATION-SPELL DEALIE AGAIN...
...AND FIND OUT WHERE THE HELL HER AMPUTATED PSEUDOTONGUE IS CURRENTLY LOCATED, OKAY?
BUT... THE LAST TIME THAT I USED A DIVINATION SPELL...
...THINGS DIDN'T WORK OUT SO WELL...
YOU CAN DO THIS, SPOOKY!
I KNOW YOU CAN!
YOU'RE NOT LAME LIKE ME, REMEMBER?
OH... RIGHT...

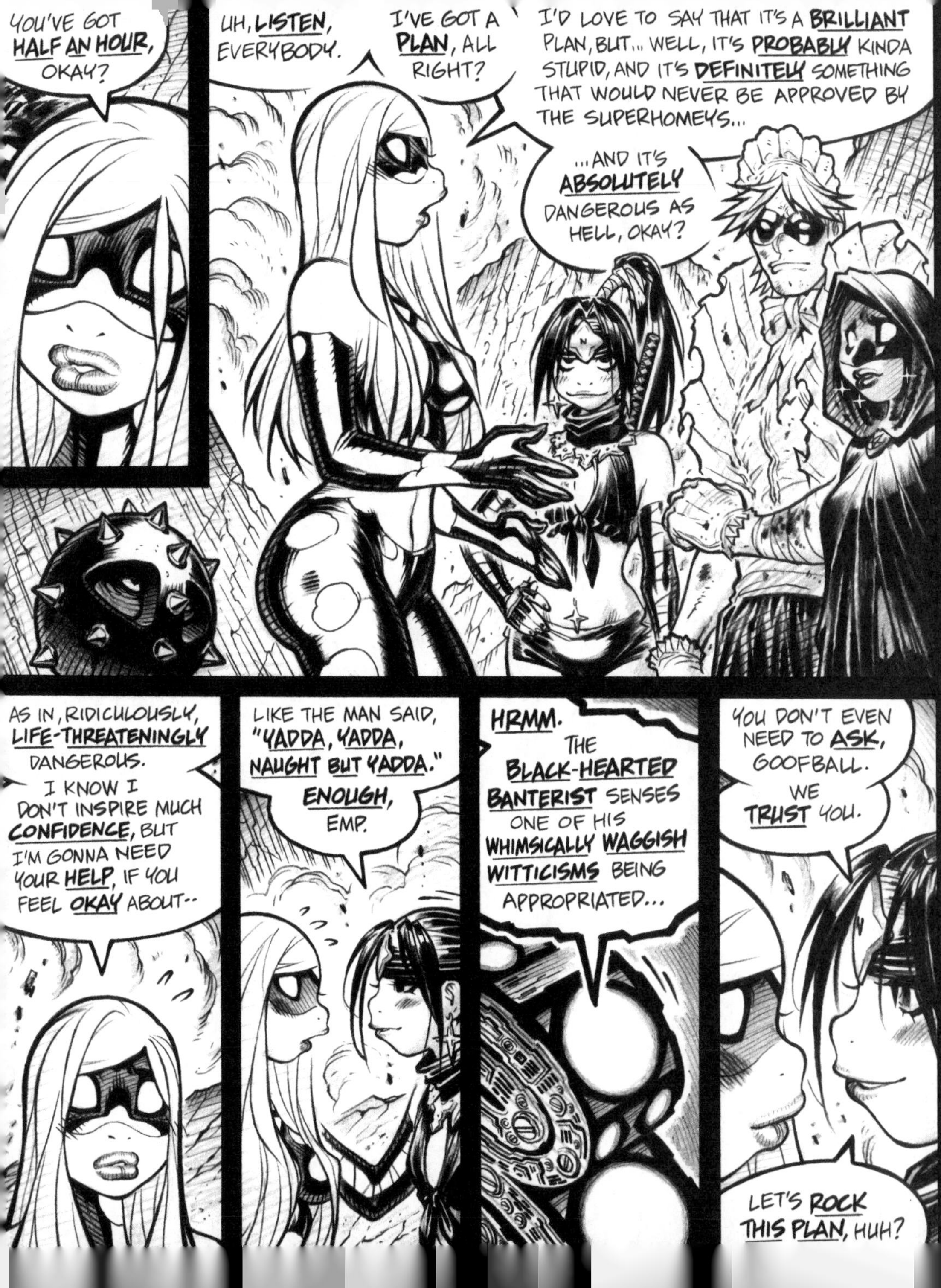
YOU'VE GOT HALF AN HOUR, OKAY?
UH, LISTEN, EVERYBODY.
I'VE GOT A PLAN, ALL RIGHT?
I'D LOVE TO SAY THAT IT'S A BRILLIANT PLAN, BUT... WELL, IT'S PROBABLY KINDA STUPID, AND IT'S DEFINITELY SOMETHING THAT WOULD NEVER BE APPROVED BY THE SUPERHOMEYS...
...AND IT'S ABSOLUTELY DANGEROUS AS HELL, OKAY?
AS IN, RIDICULOUSLY, LIFE-THREATENINGLY DANGEROUS.
I KNOW I DON'T INSPIRE MUCH CONFIDENCE, BUT I'M GONNA NEED YOUR HELP, IF YOU FEEL OKAY ABOUT--
LIKE THE MAN SAID, "YADDA, YADDA, NAUGHT BUT YADDA."
ENOUGH, EMP.
HRMM. THE BLACK-HEARTED BANTERIST SENSES ONE OF HIS WHIMSICALLY WAGGISH WITTICISMS BEING APPROPRIATED...
YOU DON'T EVEN NEED TO ASK, GOOFBALL. WE TRUST YOU.
LET'S ROCK THIS PLAN, HUH?

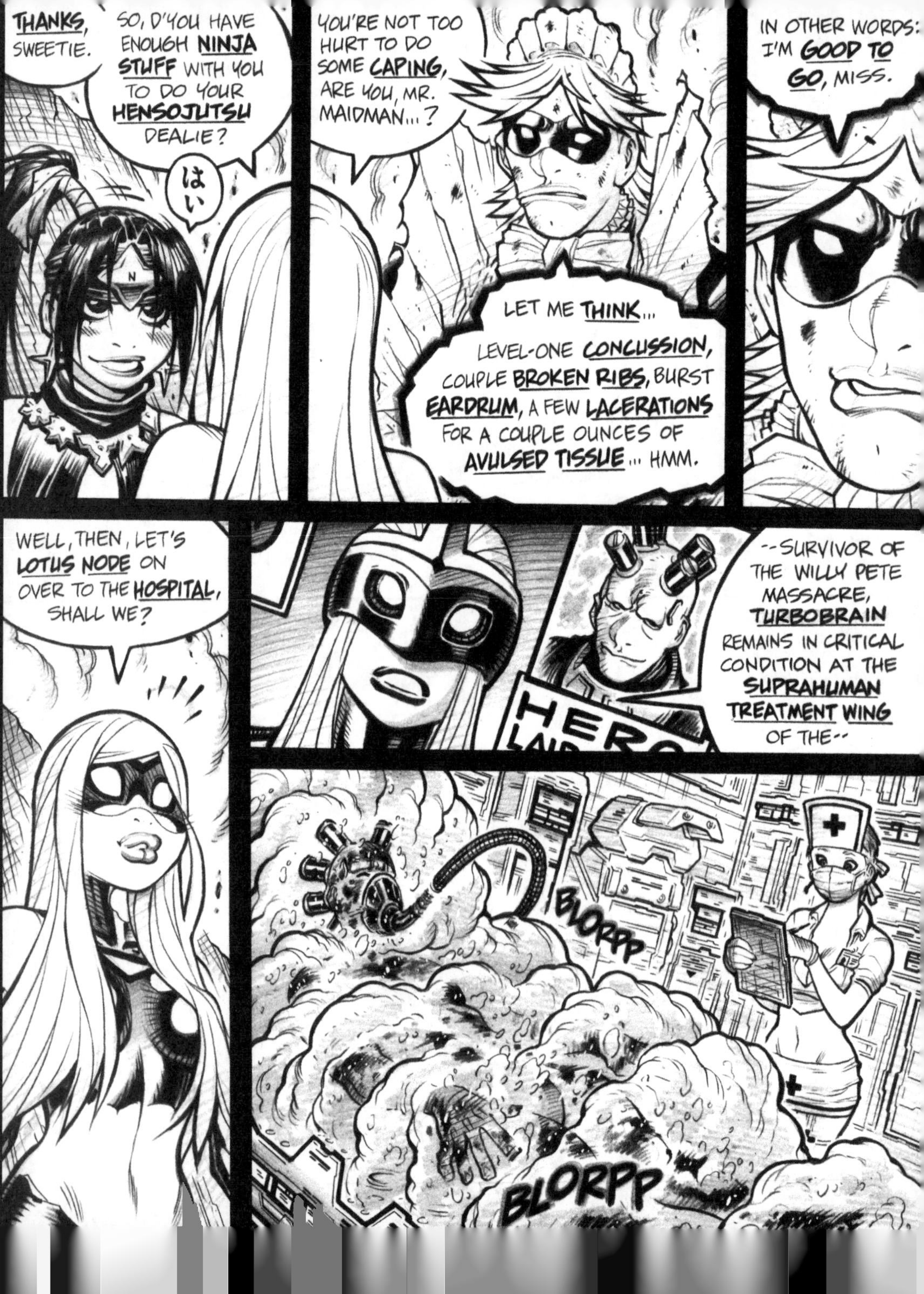
THANKS, SWEETIE.
SO, D'YOU HAVE ENOUGH NINJA STUFF WITH YOU TO DO YOUR HENSOJUTSU DEALIE?
はい
YOU'RE NOT TOO HURT TO DO SOME CAPING, ARE YOU, MR. MAIDMAN...?
LET ME THINK...
LEVEL-ONE CONCUSSION, COUPLE BROKEN RIBS, BURST EARDRUM, A FEW LACERATIONS FOR A COUPLE OUNCES OF AVULSED TISSUE... HMM.
IN OTHER WORDS: I'M GOOD TO GO, MISS.
WELL, THEN, LET'S LOTUS NODE ON OVER TO THE HOSPITAL, SHALL WE?
--SURVIVOR OF THE WILLY PETE MASSACRE, TURBOBRAIN REMAINS IN CRITICAL CONDITION AT THE SUPRAHUMAN TREATMENT WING OF THE--
HERO
BLORPP
BLORPP

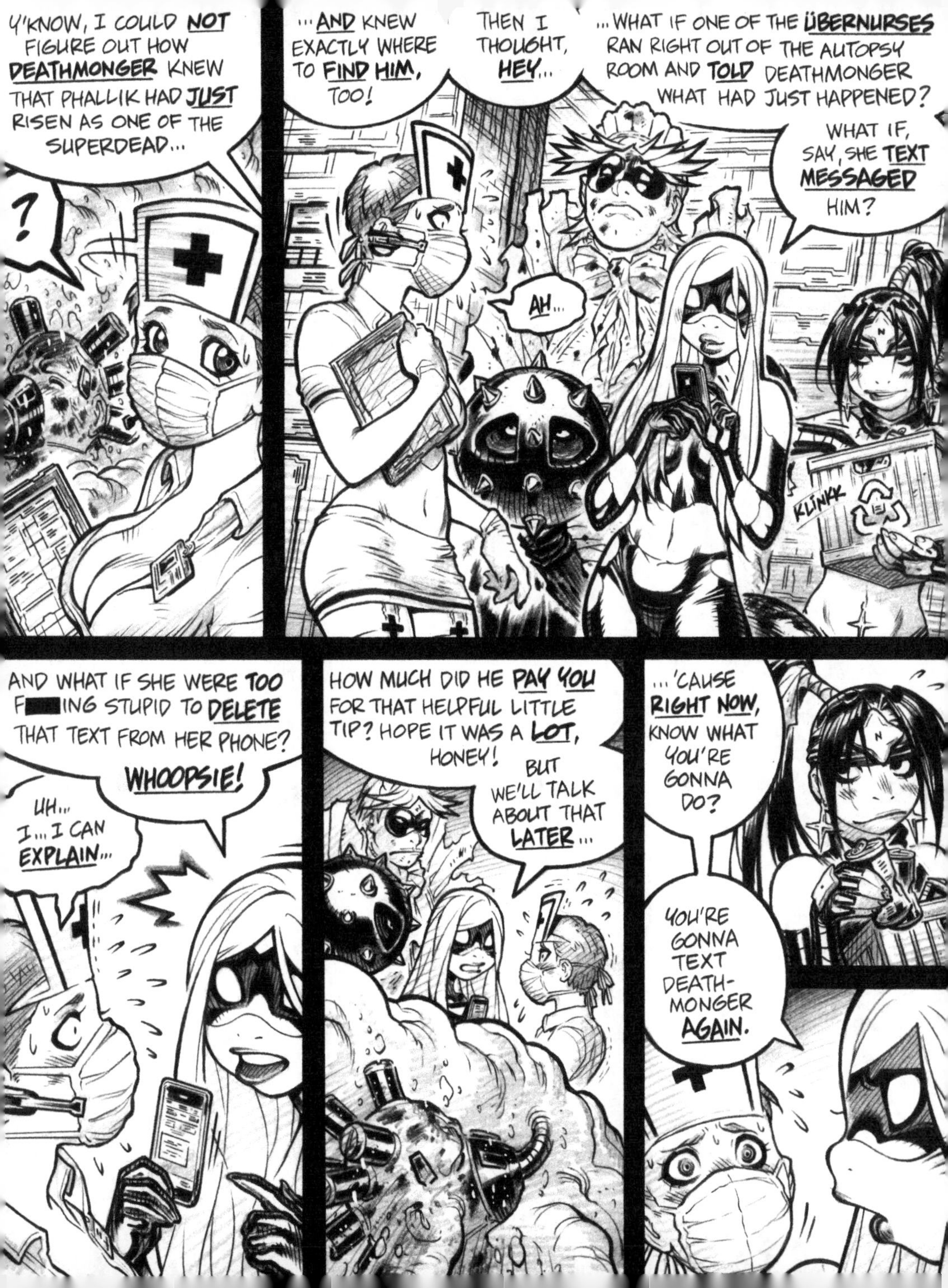
Y'KNOW, I COULD NOT FIGURE OUT HOW DEATHMONGER KNEW THAT PHALLIK HAD JUST RISEN AS ONE OF THE SUPERDEAD...
?
...AND KNEW EXACTLY WHERE TO FIND HIM, TOO!
THEN I THOUGHT, HEY...
...WHAT IF ONE OF THE ÜBERNURSES RAN RIGHT OUT OF THE AUTOPSY ROOM AND TOLD DEATHMONGER WHAT HAD JUST HAPPENED?
WHAT IF, SAY, SHE TEXT MESSAGED HIM?
AH...
KLINKK
AND WHAT IF SHE WERE TOO F[redacted]ING STUPID TO DELETE THAT TEXT FROM HER PHONE?
WHOOPSIE!
UH... I... I CAN EXPLAIN...
HOW MUCH DID HE PAY YOU FOR THAT HELPFUL LITTLE TIP? HOPE IT WAS A LOT, HONEY!
BUT WE'LL TALK ABOUT THAT LATER...
...'CAUSE RIGHT NOW, KNOW WHAT YOU'RE GONNA DO?
YOU'RE GONNA TEXT DEATH-MONGER AGAIN.

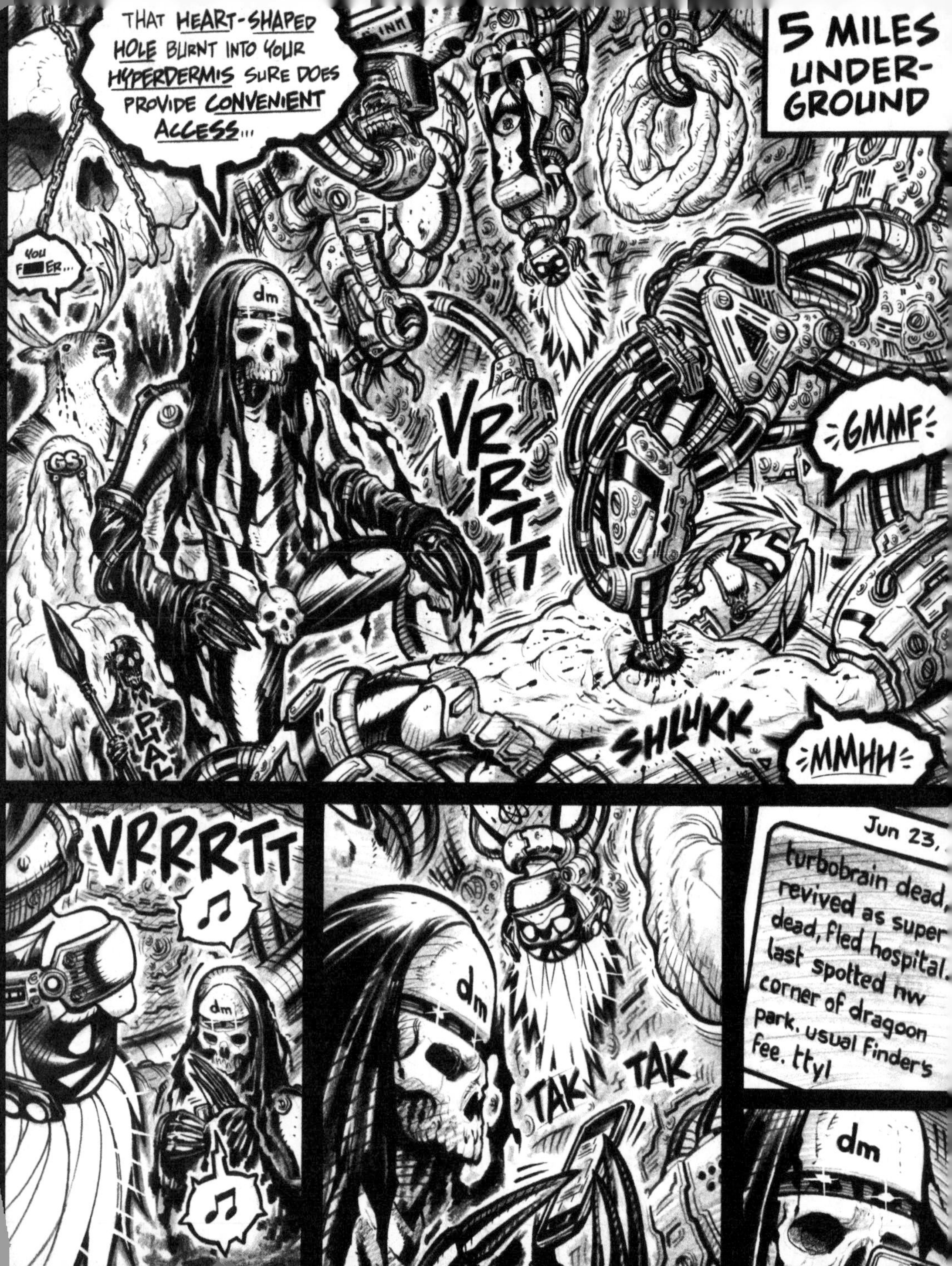
THAT HEART-SHAPED HOLE BURNT INTO YOUR HYPERDERMIS SURE DOES PROVIDE CONVENIENT ACCESS...
5 MILES UNDER-GROUND
YOU F[redacted]ER...
VRRRTT
GMMF
SHLUKK
MMHH
VRRRTT
TAK TAK
Jun 23,
turbobrain dead, revived as super dead, fled hospital. last spotted nw corner of dragoon park. usual finder's fee. ttyl
dm

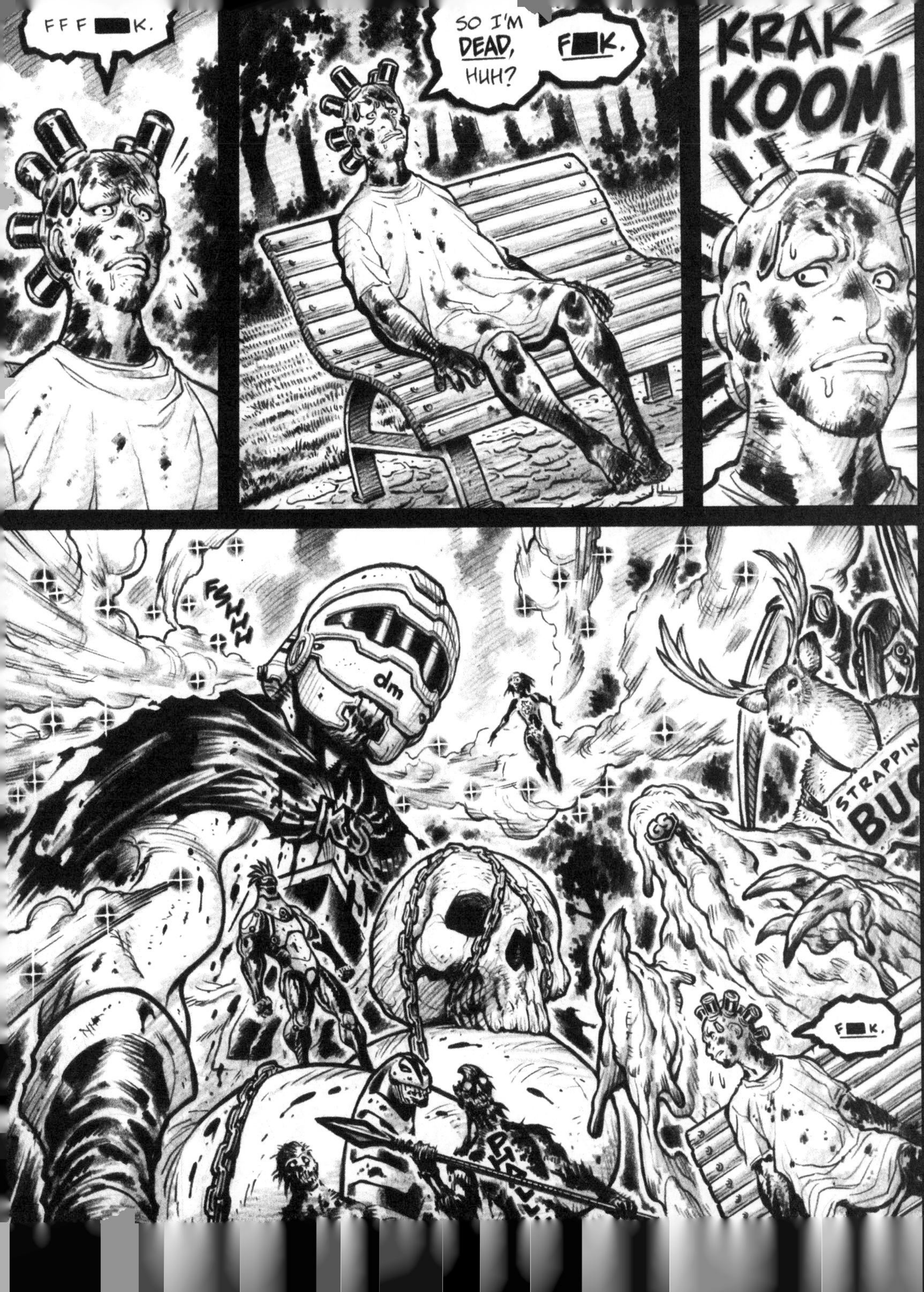
FFF[redacted]K.
SO I'M DEAD, HUH?
F[redacted]K.
KRAK KOOM
FSHHH
dm
STRAPPIN
F[redacted]K.

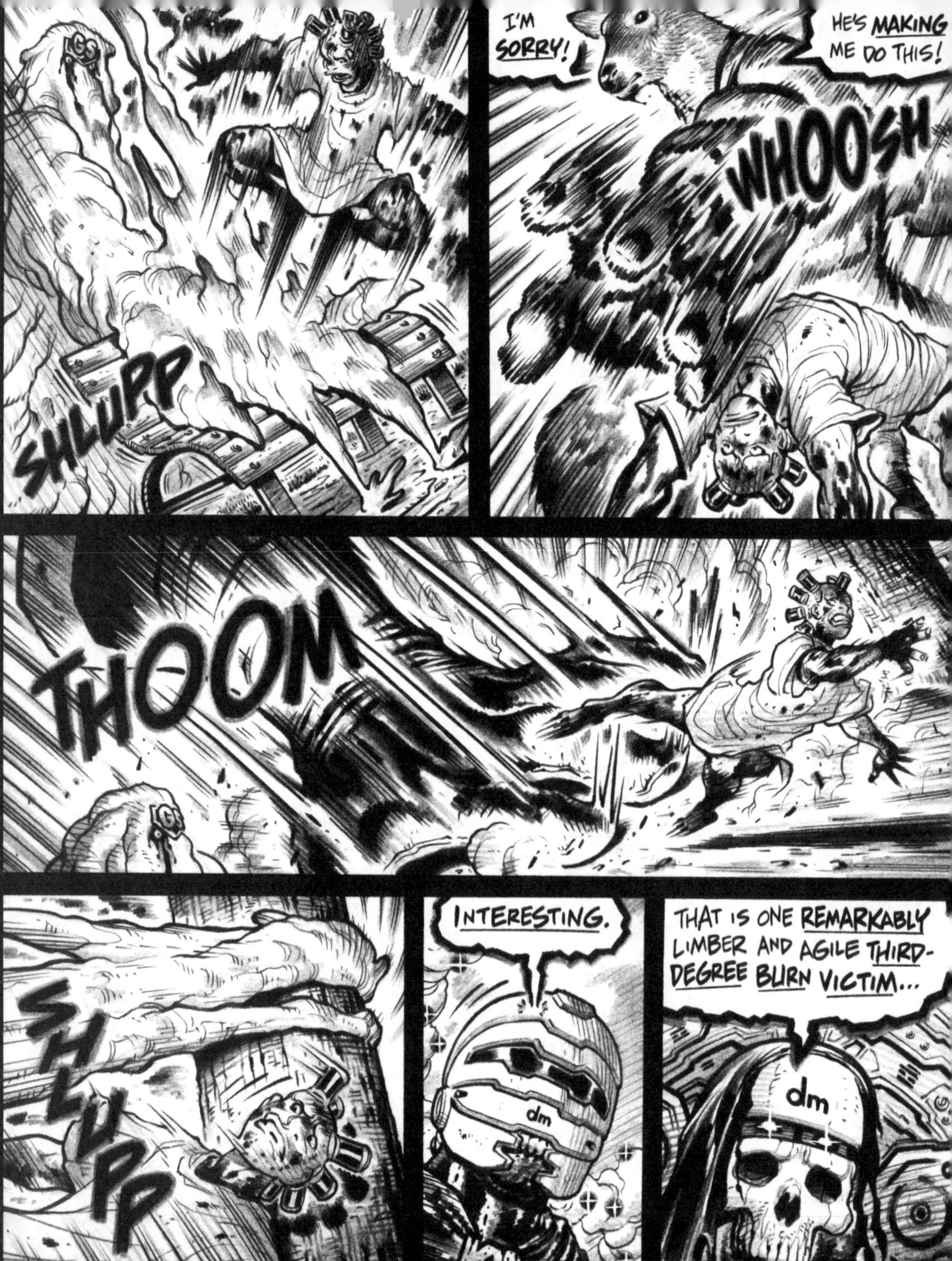
SHLUPP
I'M SORRY!
HE'S MAKING ME DO THIS!
WHOOSH
THOOM
SHLUPP
INTERESTING.
THAT IS ONE REMARKABLY LIMBER AND AGILE THIRD-DEGREE BURN VICTIM...

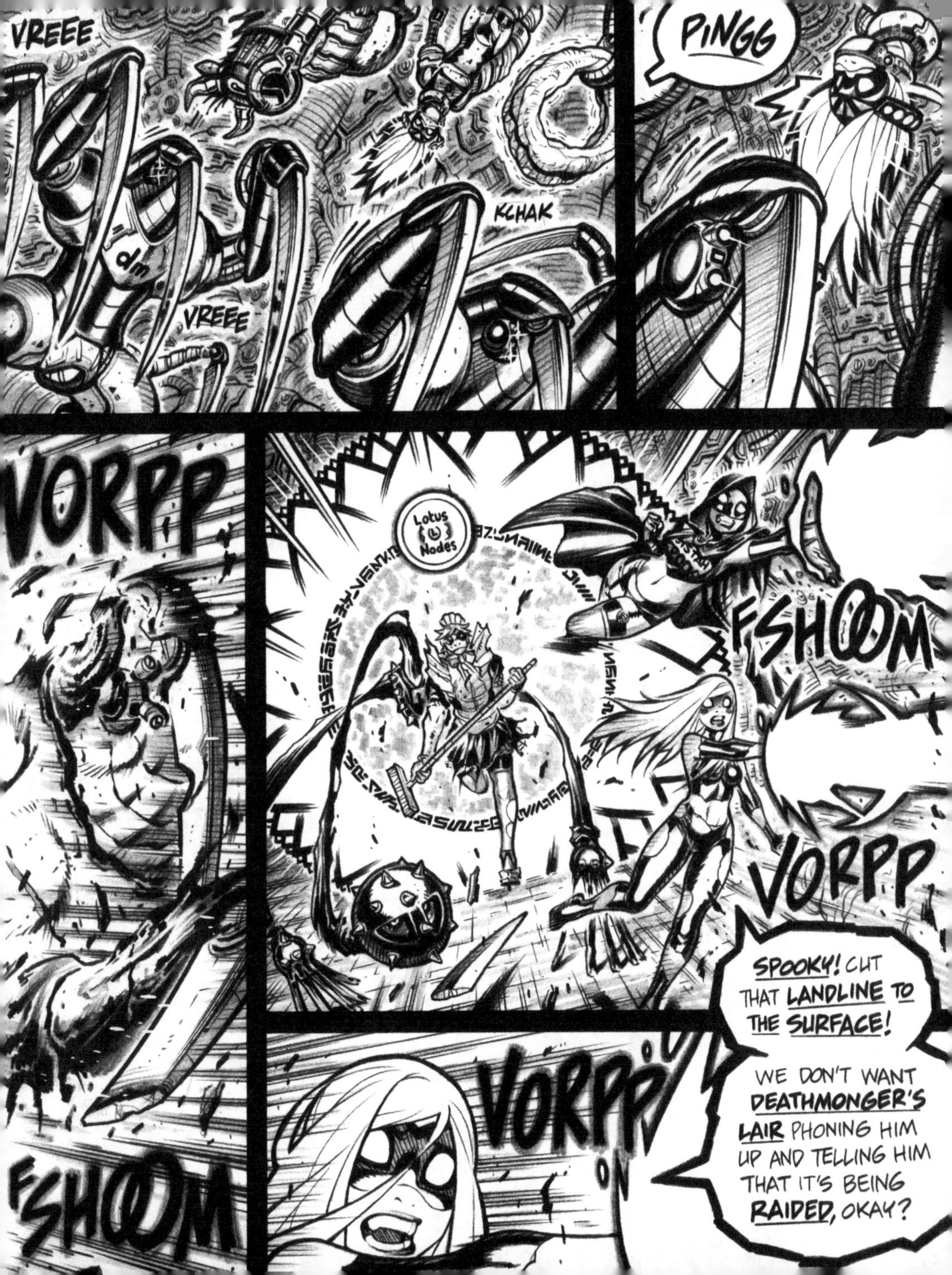
VREEE
VREEE
KCHAK
PINGG
VORPP
Lotus Nodes
FSHOOM
VORPP
SPOOKY! CUT THAT LANDLINE TO THE SURFACE!
WE DON'T WANT DEATHMONGER'S LAIR PHONING HIM UP AND TELLING HIM THAT IT'S BEING RAIDED, OKAY?
VORPP
FSHOOM

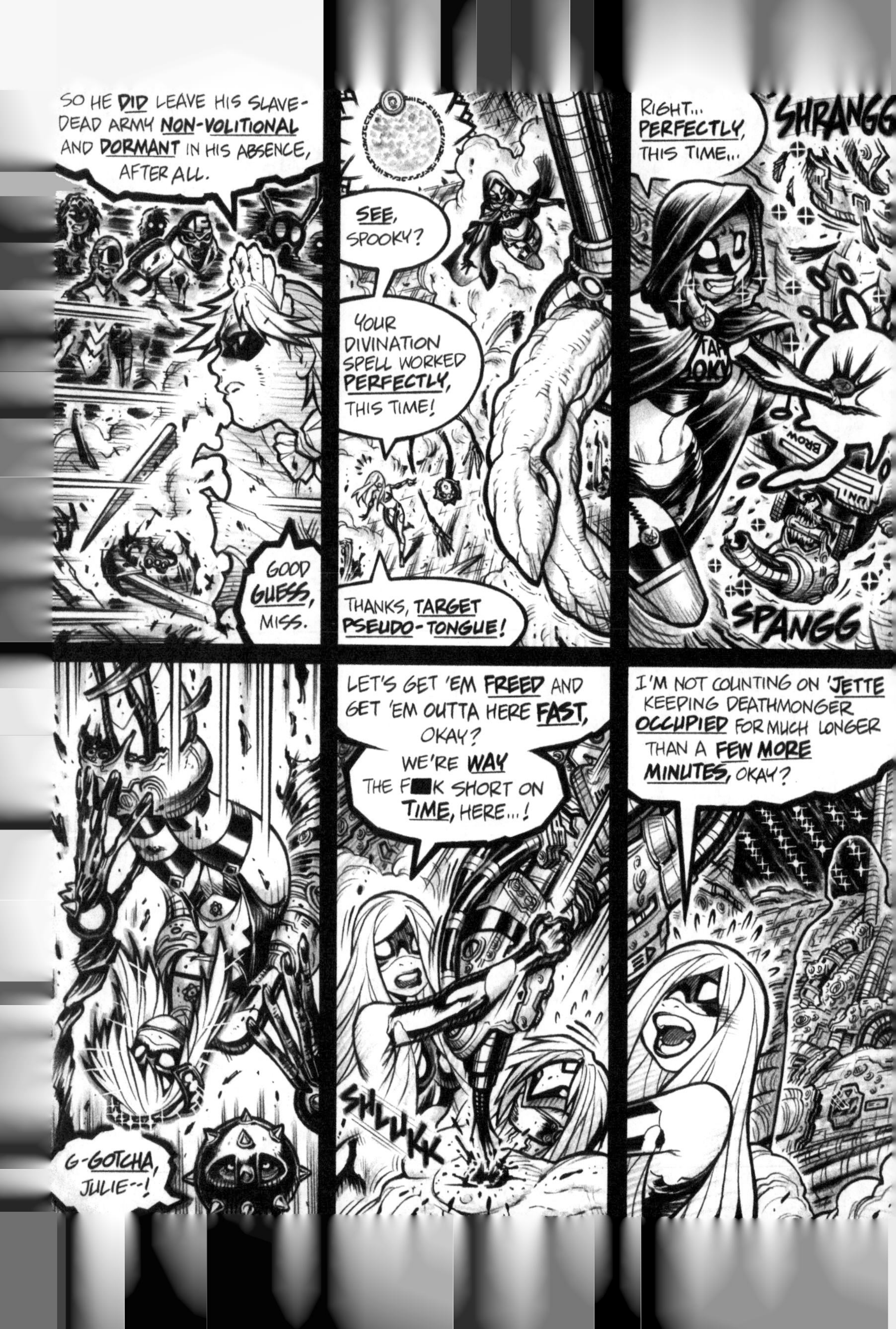

SO HE DID LEAVE HIS SLAVE-DEAD ARMY NON-VOLITIONAL AND DORMANT IN HIS ABSENCE, AFTER ALL.
GOOD GUESS, MISS.
SEE, SPOOKY?
YOUR DIVINATION SPELL WORKED PERFECTLY, THIS TIME!
THANKS, TARGET PSEUDO-TONGUE!
RIGHT... PERFECTLY, THIS TIME...
SHRANGG
SPANGG
G-GOTCHA, JULIE--!
LET'S GET 'EM FREED AND GET 'EM OUTTA HERE FAST, OKAY?
WE'RE WAY THE F[redacted]K SHORT ON TIME, HERE...!
SHLUKK
I'M NOT COUNTING ON 'JETTE KEEPING DEATHMONGER OCCUPIED FOR MUCH LONGER THAN A FEW MORE MINUTES, OKAY?

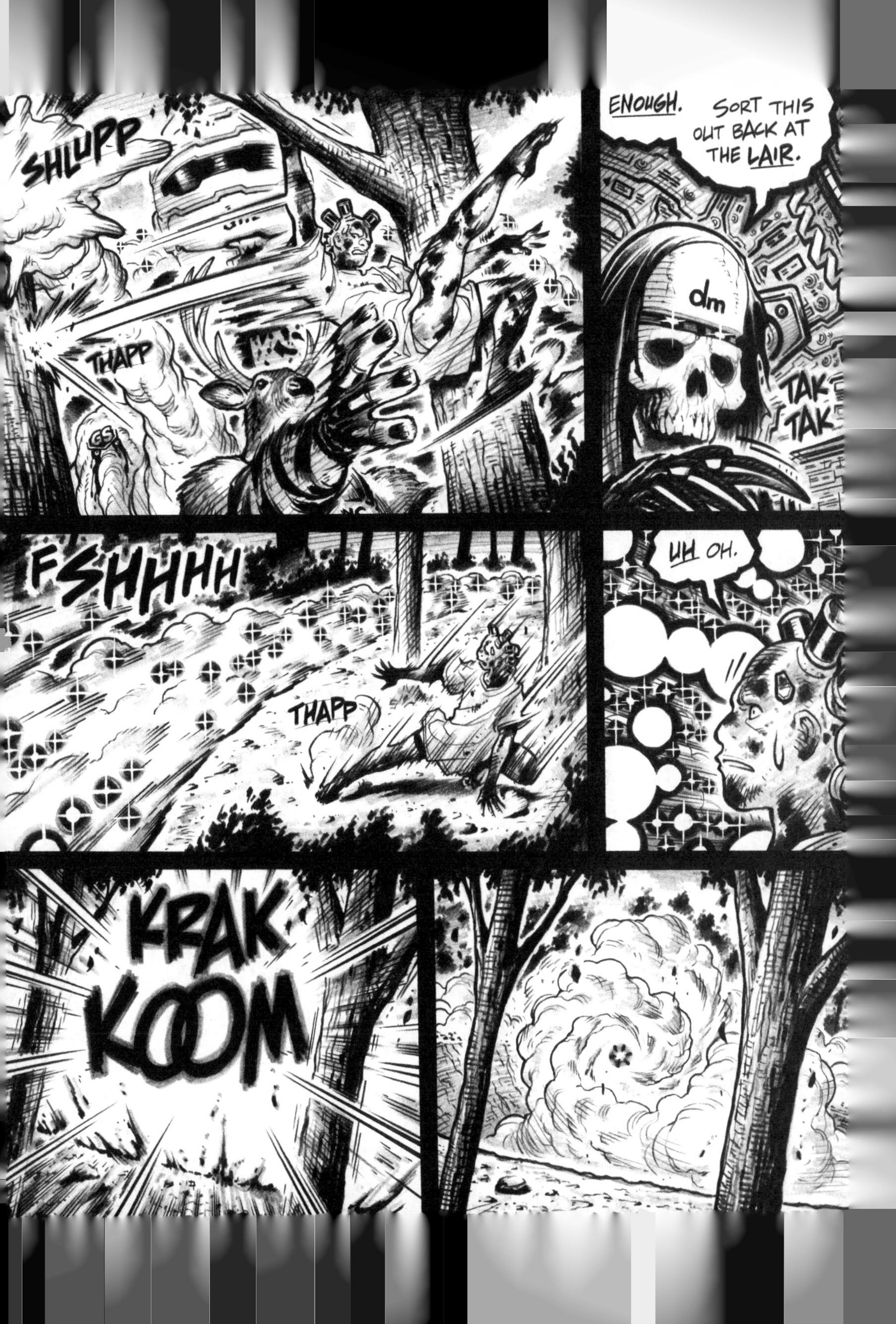
SHLUPP
THAPP
ENOUGH. SORT THIS OUT BACK AT THE LAIR.
TAK TAK
FSHHHH
THAPP
UH OH.
KRAK KOOM

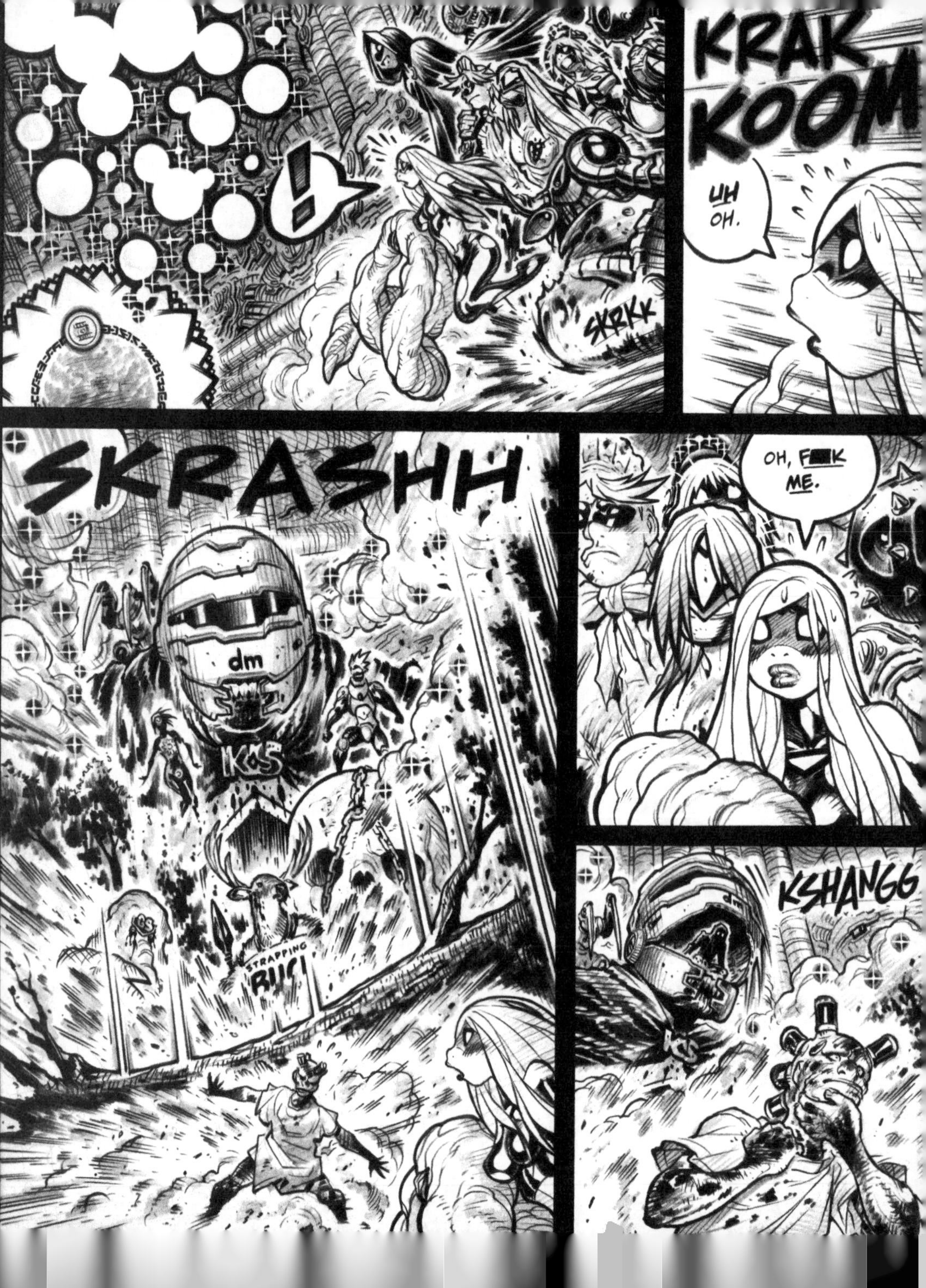
!
SKRKK
KRAK KOOM
UH OH.
SKRASHH
OH, F[redacted]K ME.
KSHANGG

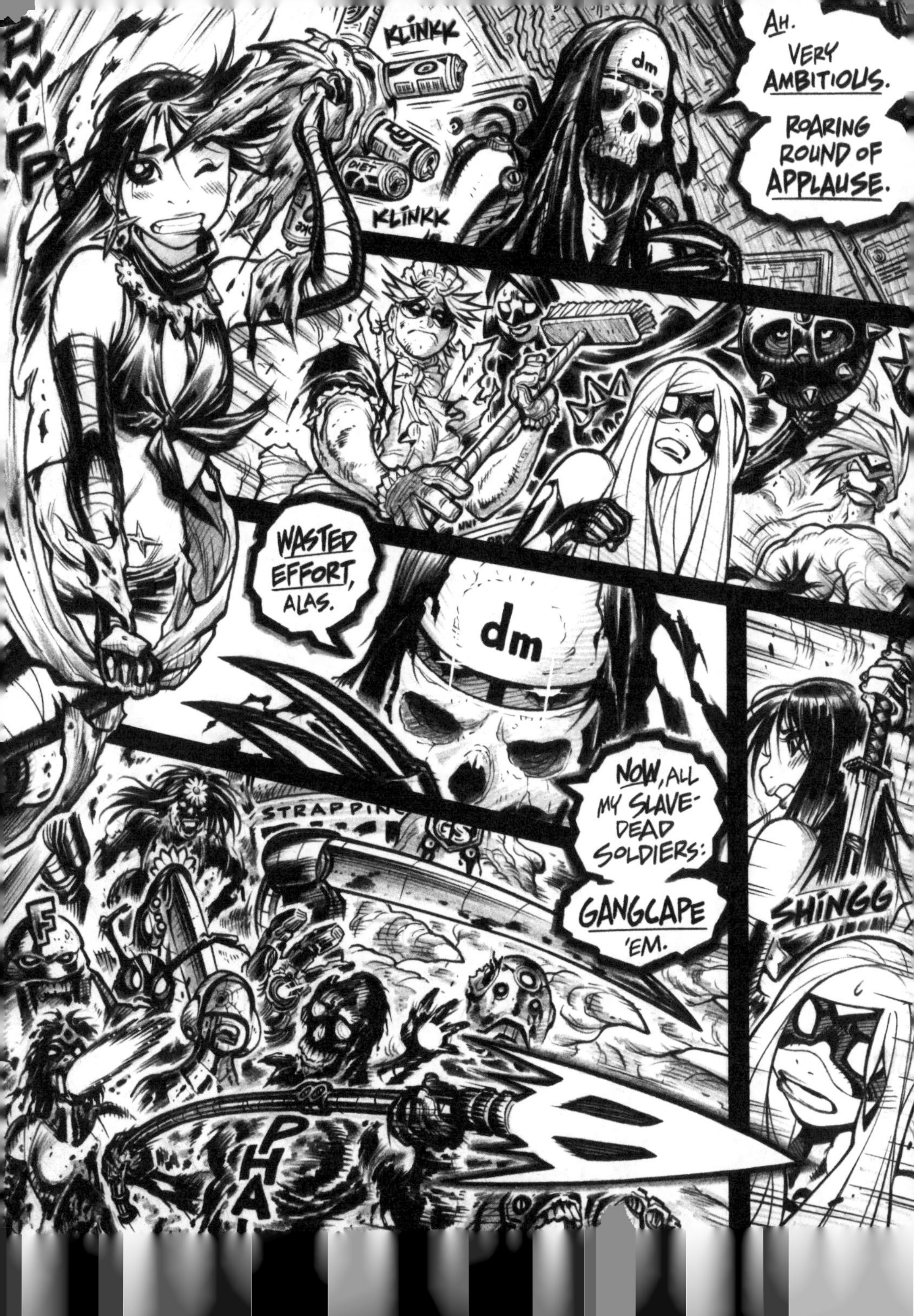
PWIPP
KLINKK
KLINKK
AH.
VERY AMBITIOUS.
ROARING ROUND OF APPLAUSE.
WASTED EFFORT, ALAS.
dm
NOW, ALL MY SLAVE-DEAD SOLDIERS:
GANGCAPE 'EM.
SHINGG
PHA

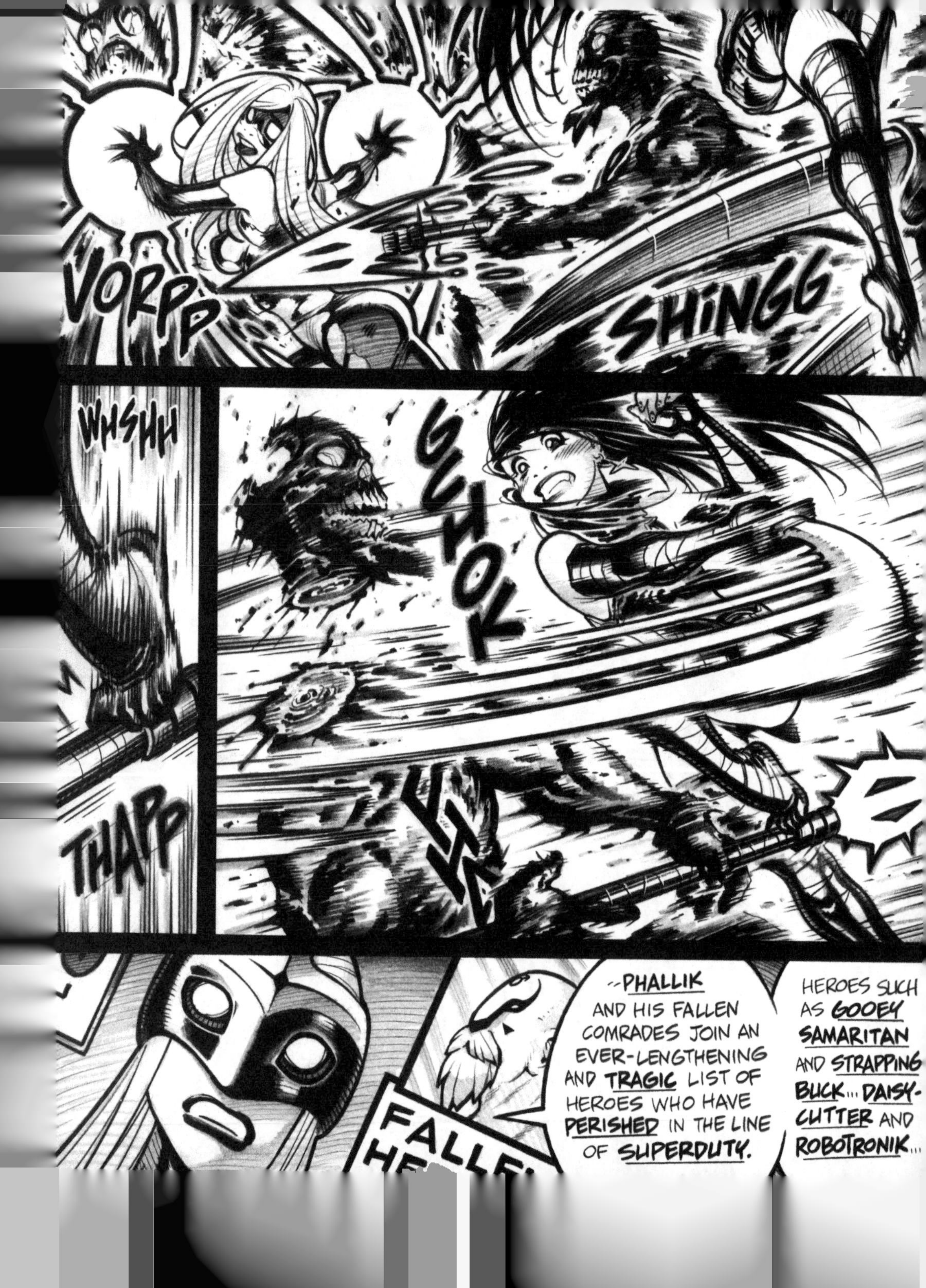

VORPP
SHINGG
WHSHH
THAPP
--PHALLIK AND HIS FALLEN COMRADES JOIN AN EVER-LENGTHENING AND TRAGIC LIST OF HEROES WHO HAVE PERISHED IN THE LINE OF SUPERDUTY.
HEROES SUCH AS GOOEY SAMARITAN AND STRAPPING BUCK... DAISY-CUTTER AND ROBOTRONIK...

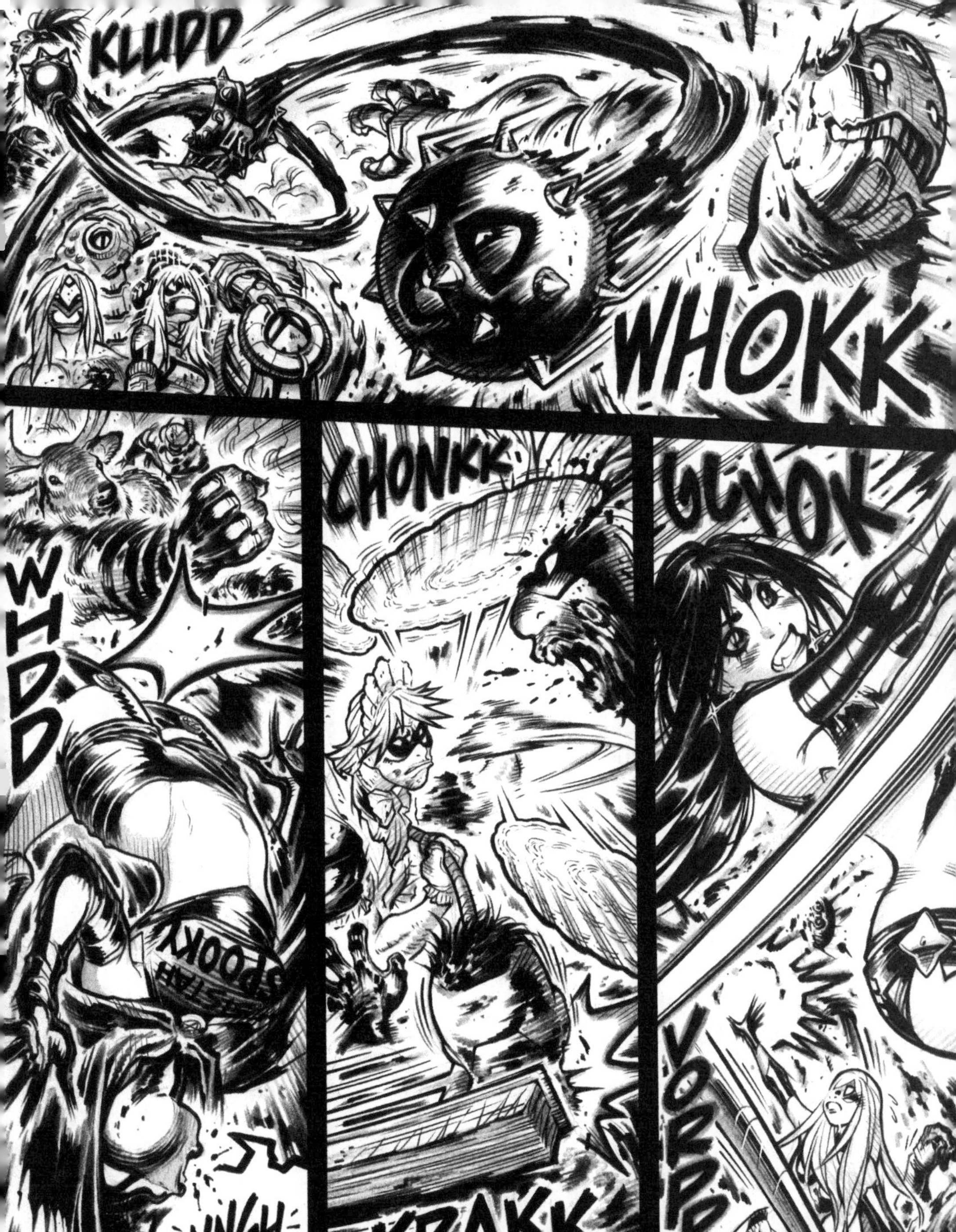
KLUDD
WHOKK
WHDD
SPOOKY
NNGH
CHONKK
KRAKK

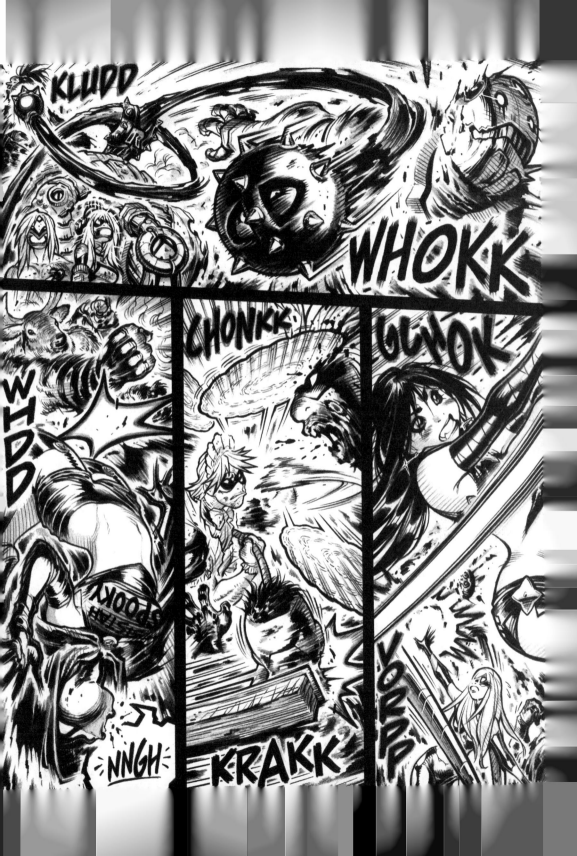

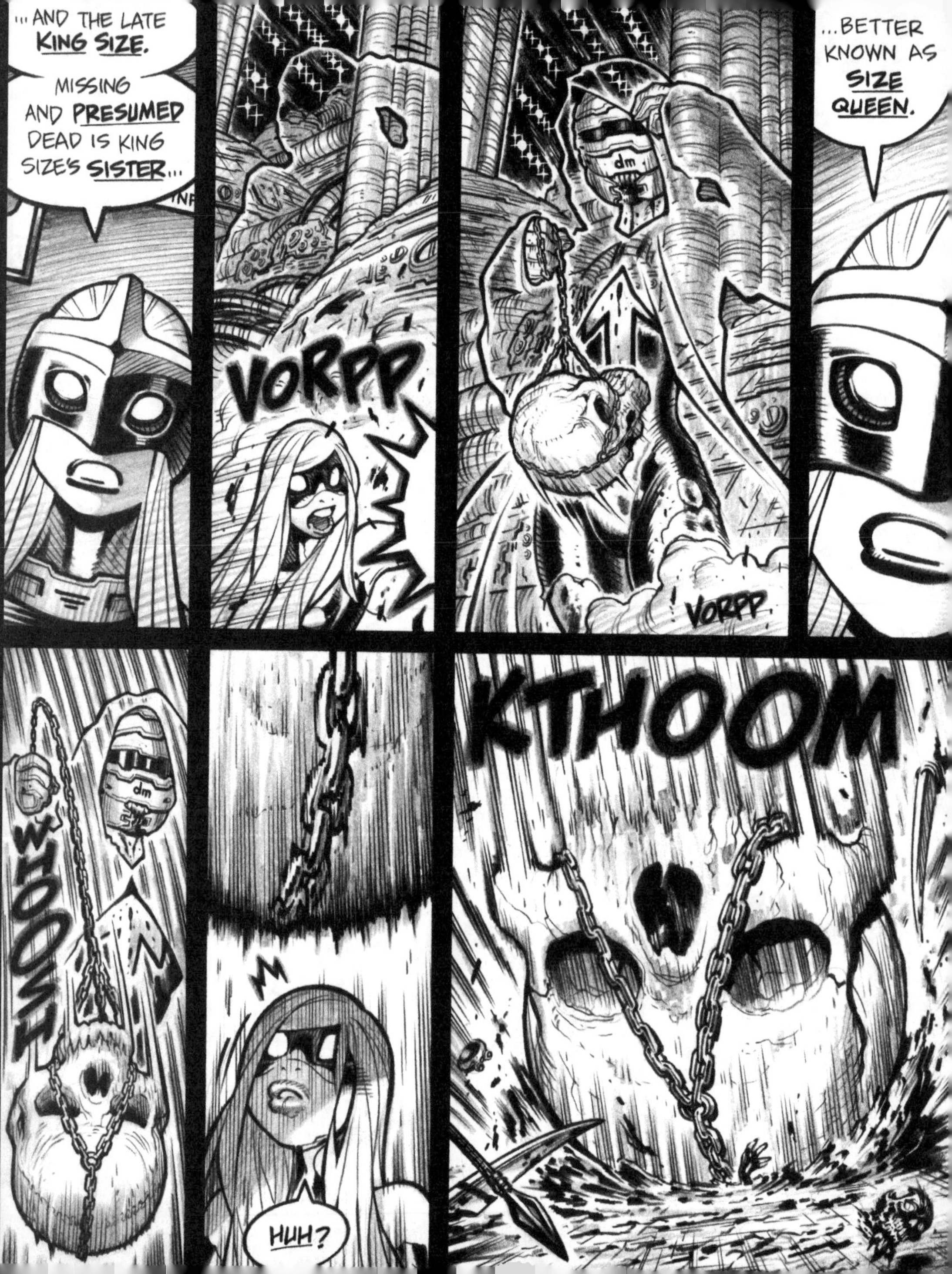
...AND THE LATE KING SIZE.
MISSING AND PRESUMED DEAD IS KING SIZE'S SISTER...
VORPP
VORPP
...BETTER KNOWN AS SIZE QUEEN.
WHOOSH
HUH?
KTHOOM

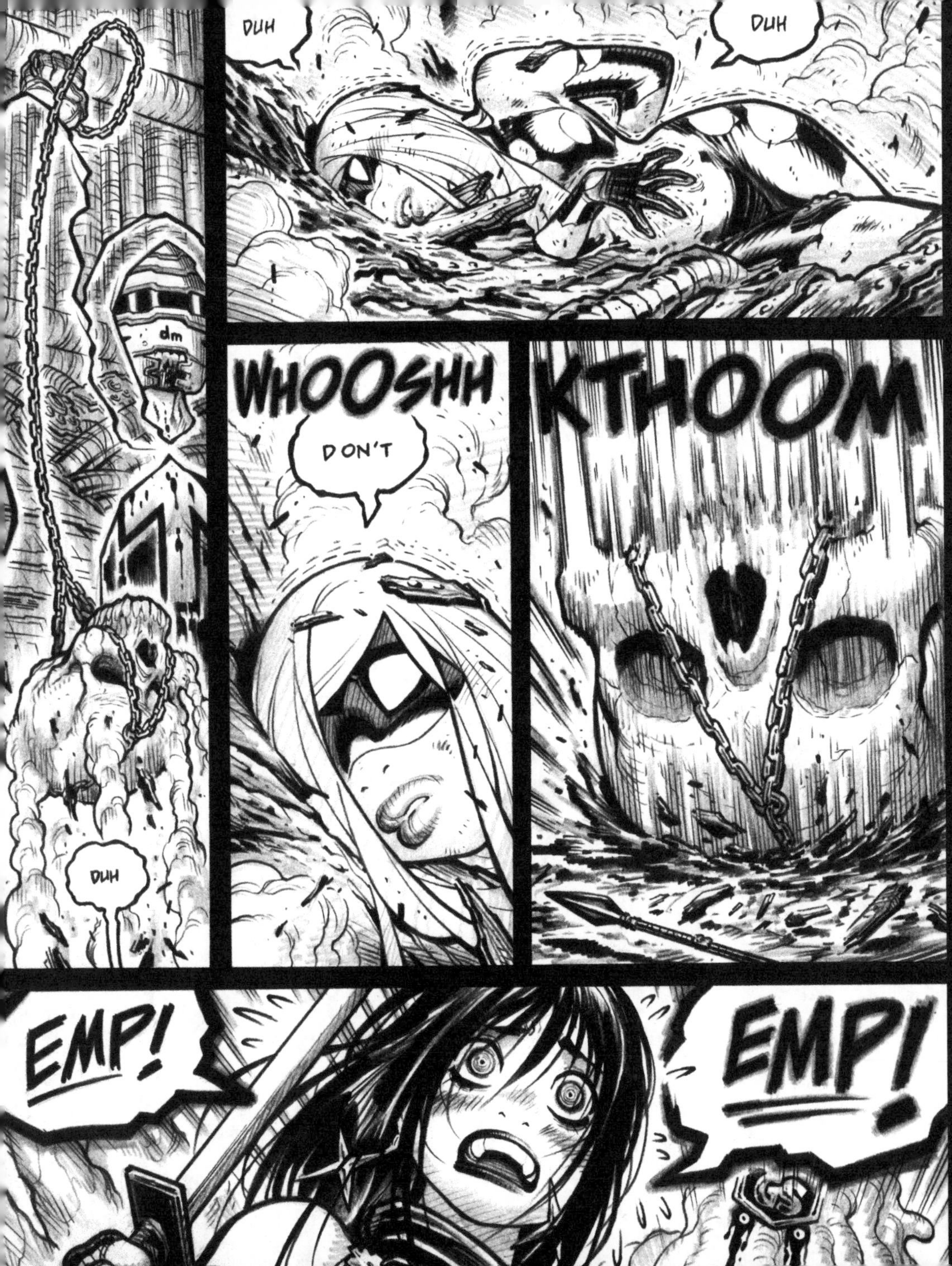
DUH
DUH
DUH
dm
WHOOSHH
DON'T
KTHOOM
EMP!
EMP!

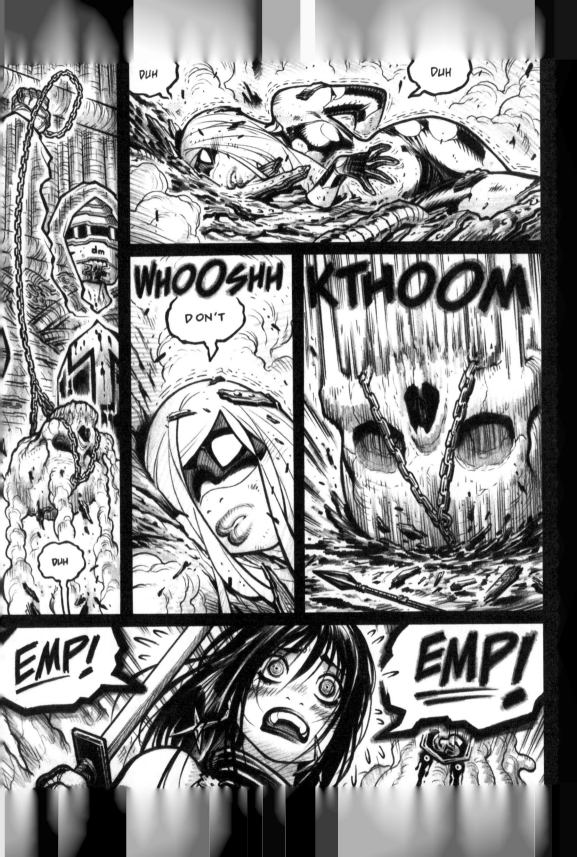

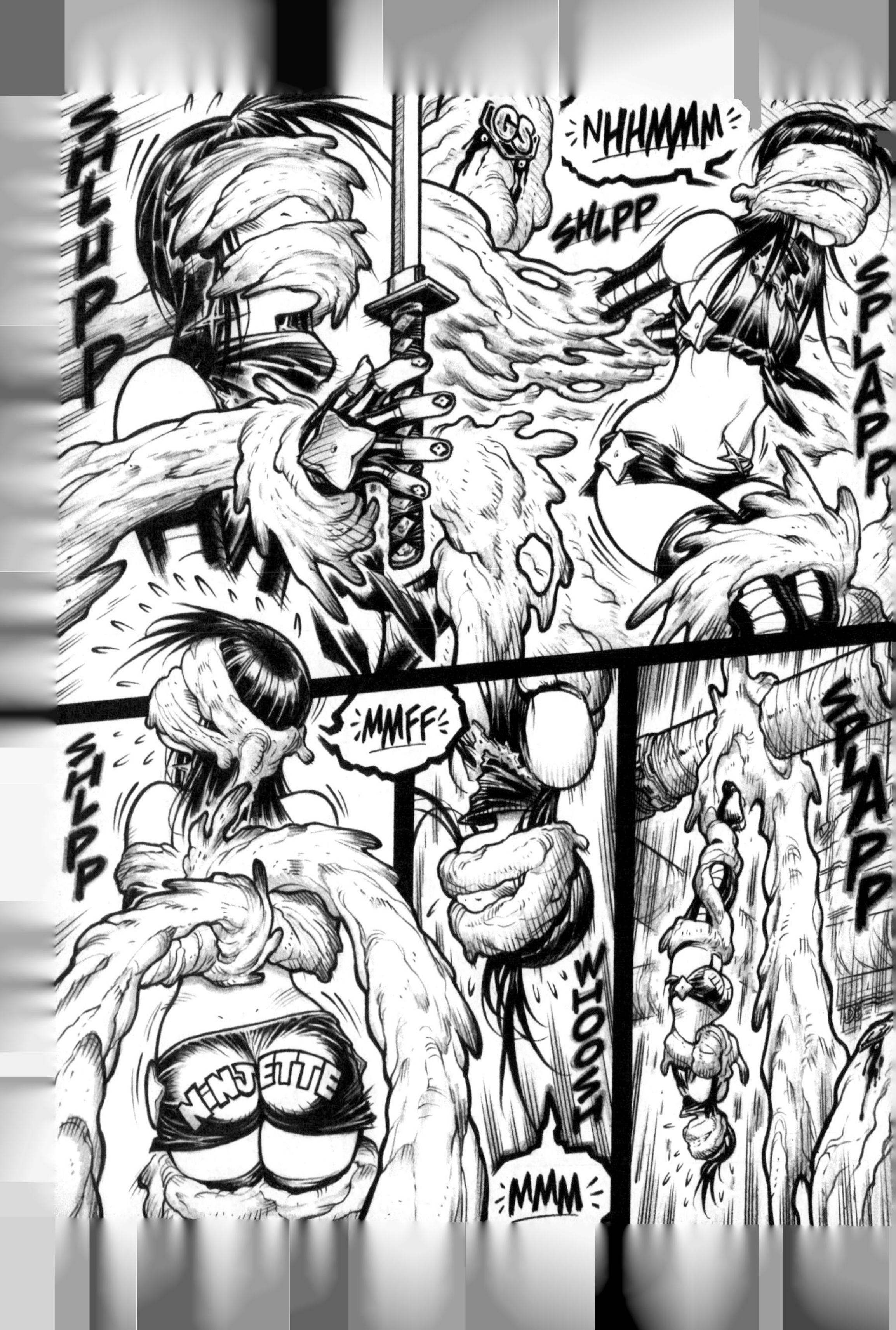
SHLUPP
NHHMMM
SHLPP
SPLAPP
SHLPP
MMFF
NINJETTE
WHOOOSH
MMM
SPLAPP

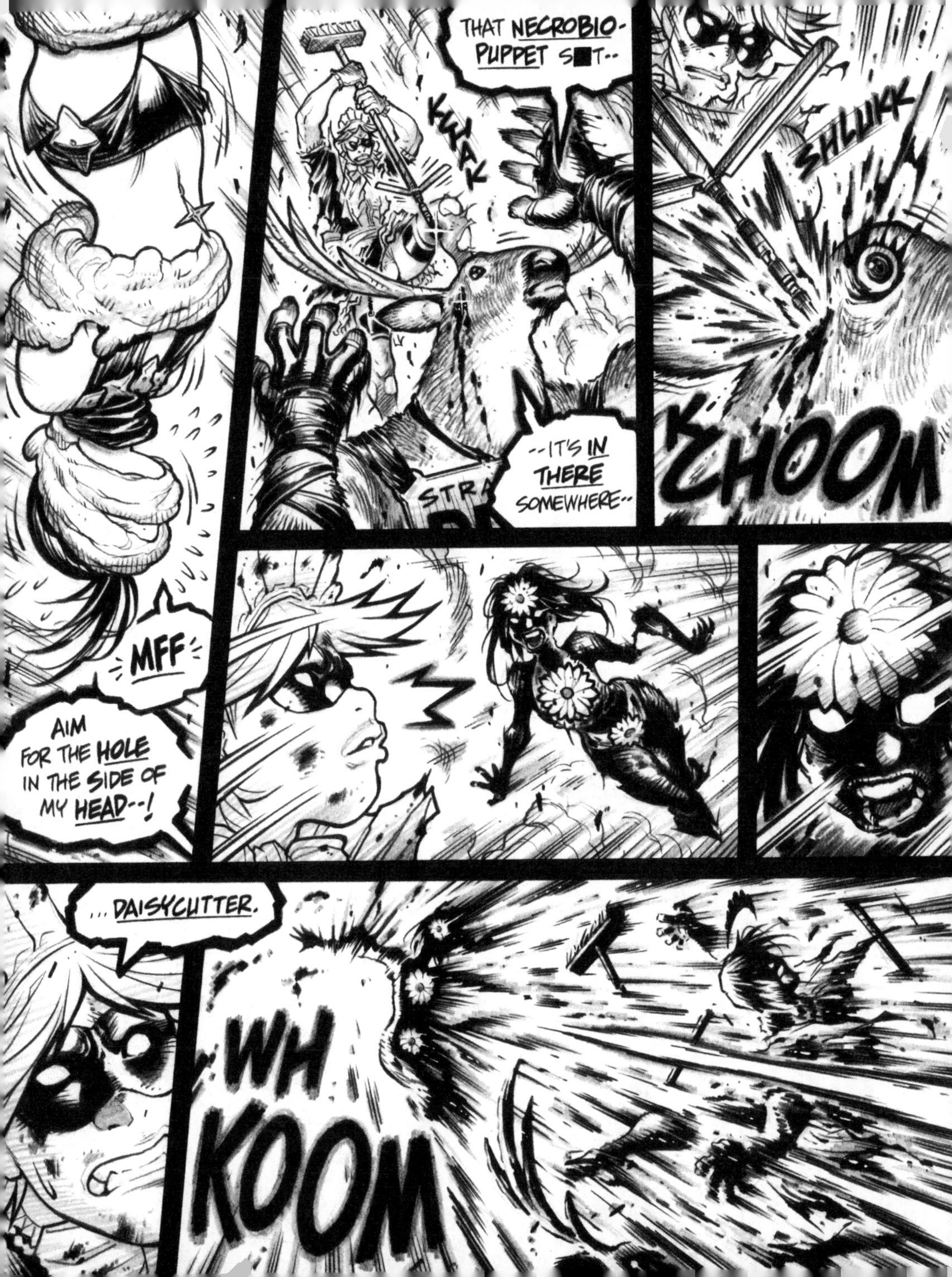
MFF
AIM FOR THE HOLE IN THE SIDE OF MY HEAD--!
KEHAK
THAT NECROBIO-PUPPET S[redacted]T--
--IT'S IN THERE SOMEWHERE--
STRA
SHLUKK
K CHOOM
...DAISYCUTTER.
WH KOOM

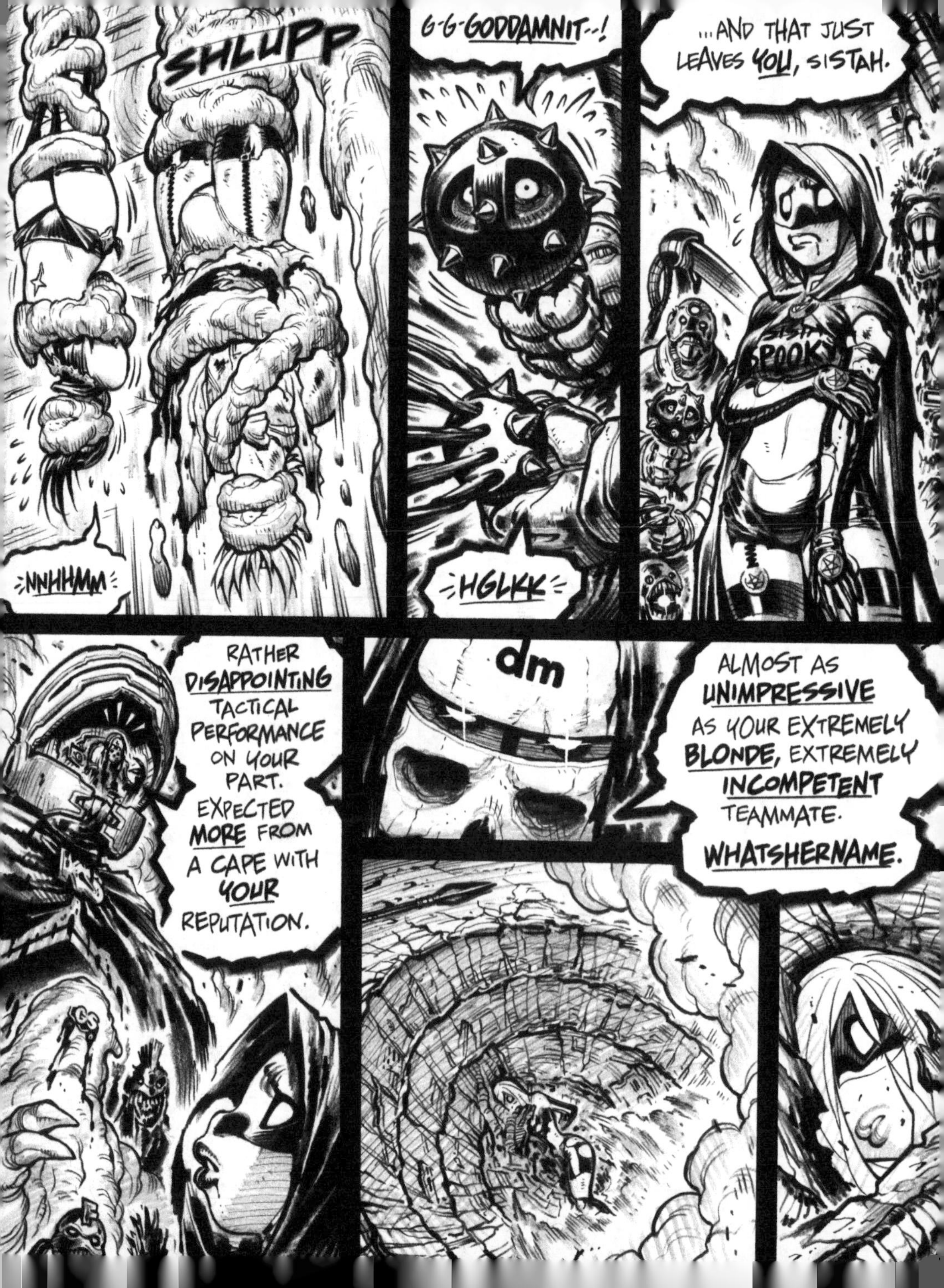
SHLUPP
NNHHMM
G-G-GODDAMNIT--!
HGLKK
...AND THAT JUST LEAVES YOU, SISTAH.
SPOOKY
RATHER DISAPPOINTING TACTICAL PERFORMANCE ON YOUR PART. EXPECTED MORE FROM A CAPE WITH YOUR REPUTATION.
dm
ALMOST AS UNIMPRESSIVE AS YOUR EXTREMELY BLONDE, EXTREMELY INCOMPETENT TEAMMATE.
WHATSHERNAME.

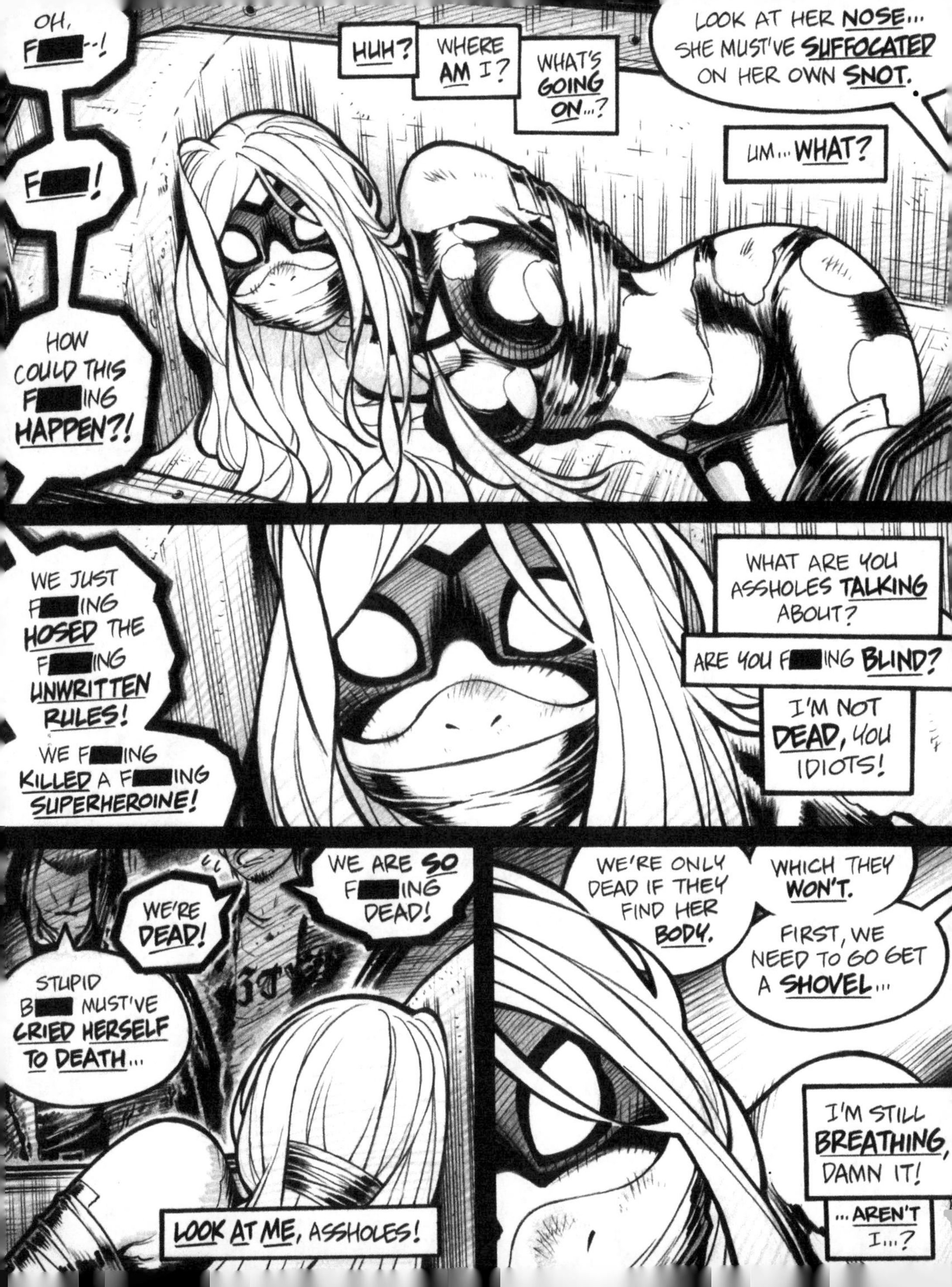
OH, F[redacted]-!
F[redacted]!
HOW COULD THIS F[redacted]ING HAPPEN?!
HUH?
WHERE AM I?
WHAT'S GOING ON...?
LOOK AT HER NOSE... SHE MUST'VE SUFFOCATED ON HER OWN SNOT...
UM... WHAT?
WE JUST F[redacted]ING HOSED THE F[redacted]ING UNWRITTEN RULES!
WE F[redacted]ING KILLED A F[redacted]ING SUPERHEROINE!
WHAT ARE YOU ASSHOLES TALKING ABOUT?
ARE YOU F[redacted]ING BLIND?
I'M NOT DEAD, YOU IDIOTS!
WE'RE DEAD!
WE ARE SO F[redacted]ING DEAD!
STUPID B[redacted] MUST'VE CRIED HERSELF TO DEATH...
LOOK AT ME, ASSHOLES!
WE'RE ONLY DEAD IF THEY FIND HER BODY.
WHICH THEY WON'T.
FIRST, WE NEED TO GO GET A SHOVEL...
I'M STILL BREATHING, DAMN IT!
...AREN'T I...?

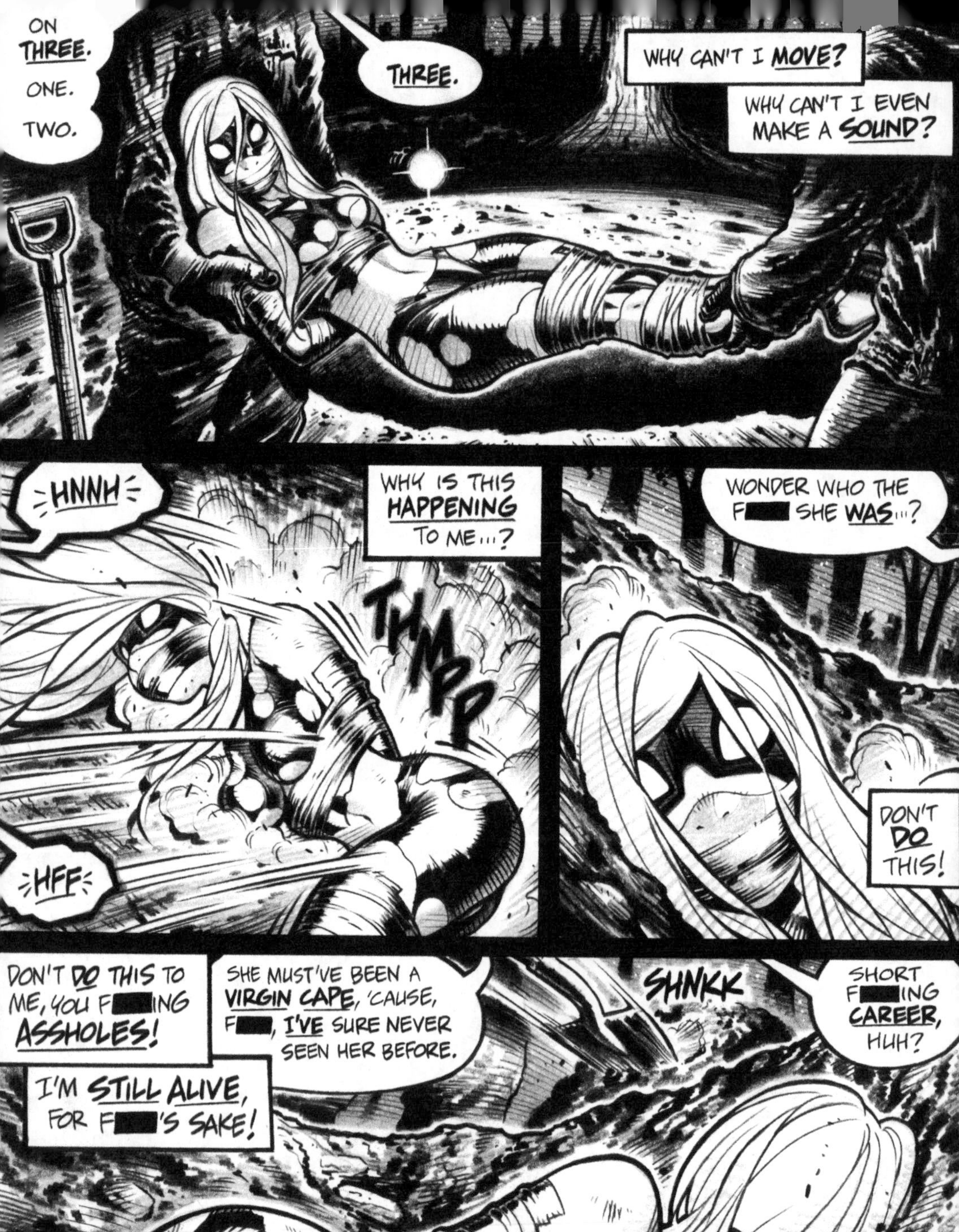
ON THREE. ONE. TWO.
THREE.
WHY CAN'T I MOVE?
WHY CAN'T I EVEN MAKE A SOUND?
HNNH
WHY IS THIS HAPPENING TO ME...?
THMPP
HFF
WONDER WHO THE F[redacted] SHE WAS...?
DON'T DO THIS!
DON'T DO THIS TO ME, YOU F[redacted]ING ASSHOLES!
SHE MUST'VE BEEN A VIRGIN CAPE, 'CAUSE, F[redacted], I'VE SURE NEVER SEEN HER BEFORE.
I'M STILL ALIVE, FOR F[redacted]'S SAKE!
SHNKK
SHORT F[redacted]ING CAREER, HUH?

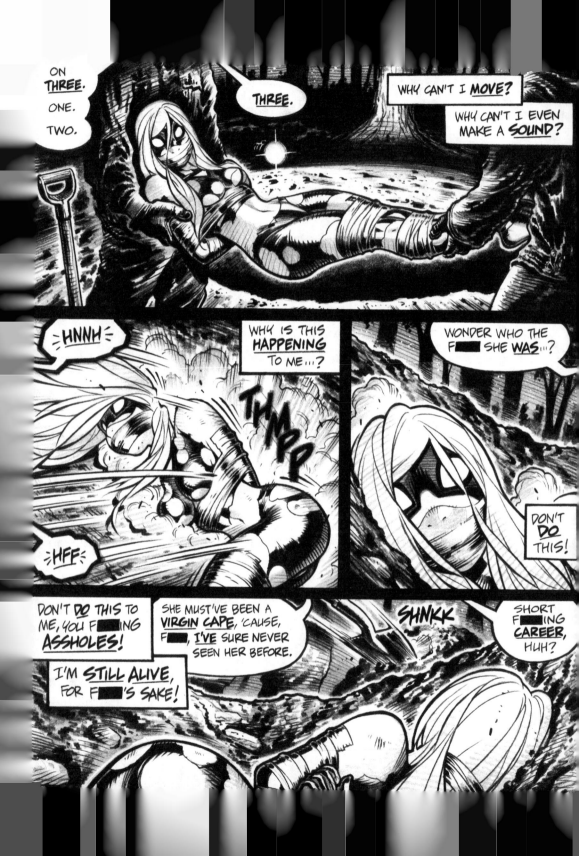

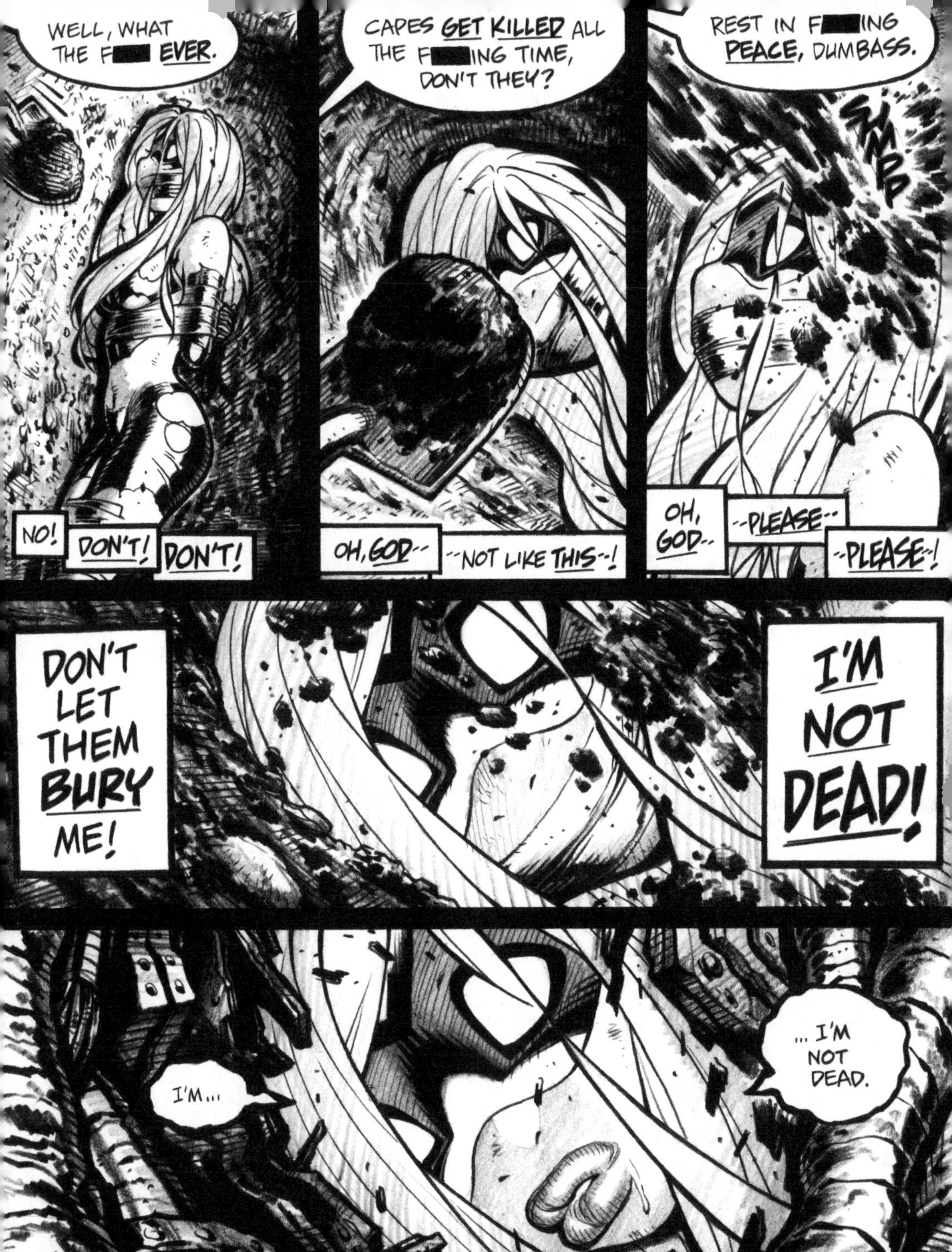

WELL, WHAT THE F[redacted] EVER.
NO!
DON'T!
DON'T!
CAPES GET KILLED ALL THE F[redacted]ING TIME, DON'T THEY?
OH, GOD--
--NOT LIKE THIS--!
REST IN F[redacted]ING PEACE, DUMBASS.
OH, GOD--
--PLEASE--
--PLEASE--!
DON'T LET THEM BURY ME!
I'M NOT DEAD!
I'M...
... I'M NOT DEAD.

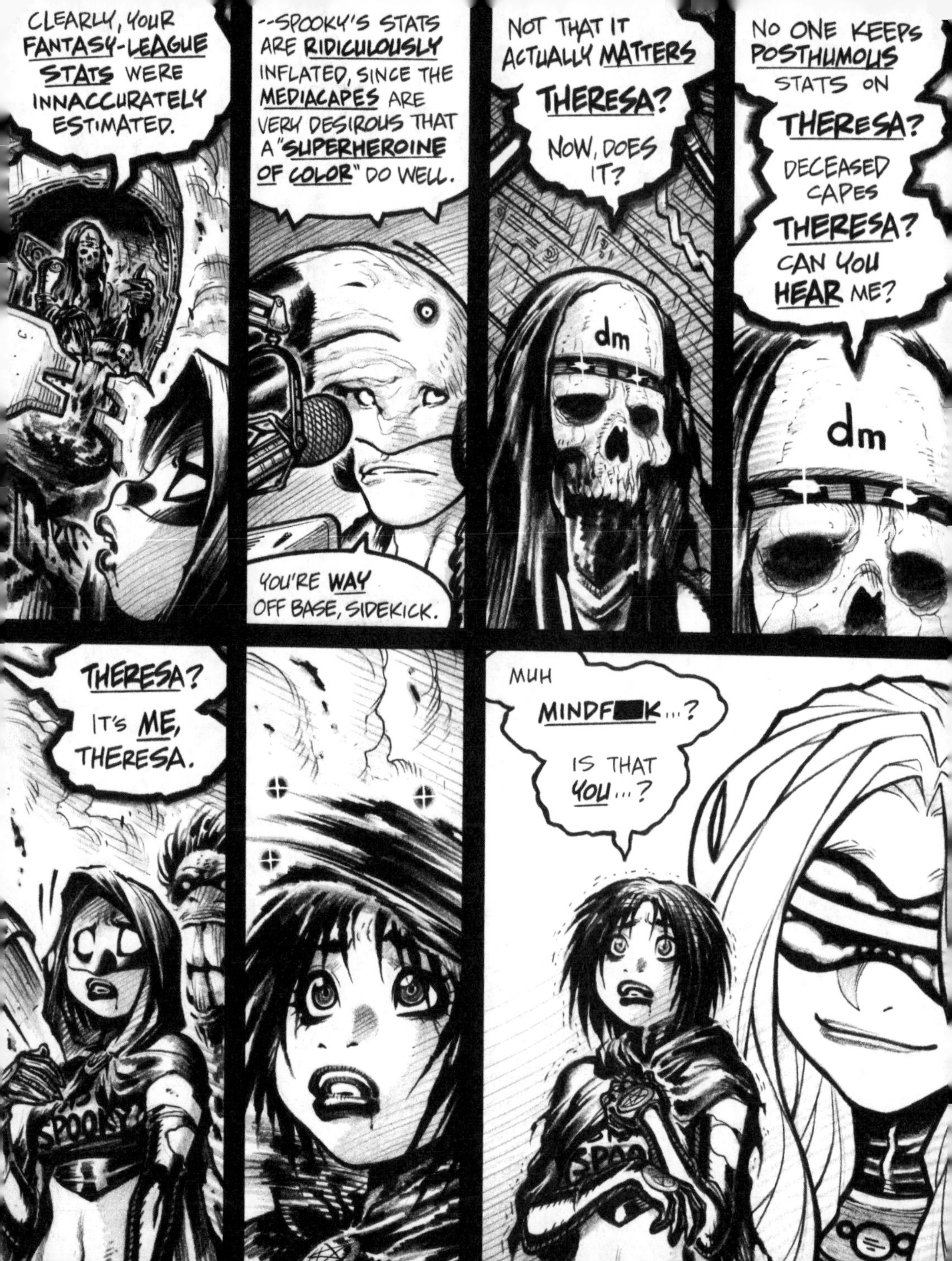
CLEARLY, YOUR FANTASY-LEAGUE STATS WERE INNACCURATELY ESTIMATED.
--SPOOKY'S STATS ARE RIDICULOUSLY INFLATED, SINCE THE MEDIACAPES ARE VERY DESIROUS THAT A "SUPERHEROINE OF COLOR" DO WELL.
YOU'RE WAY OFF BASE, SIDEKICK.
NOT THAT IT ACTUALLY MATTERS
THERESA?
NOW, DOES IT?
NO ONE KEEPS POSTHUMOUS STATS ON
THERESA?
DECEASED CAPES
THERESA?
CAN YOU HEAR ME?
THERESA?
IT'S ME, THERESA.
MUH
MINDF[redacted]K...?
IS THAT YOU...?

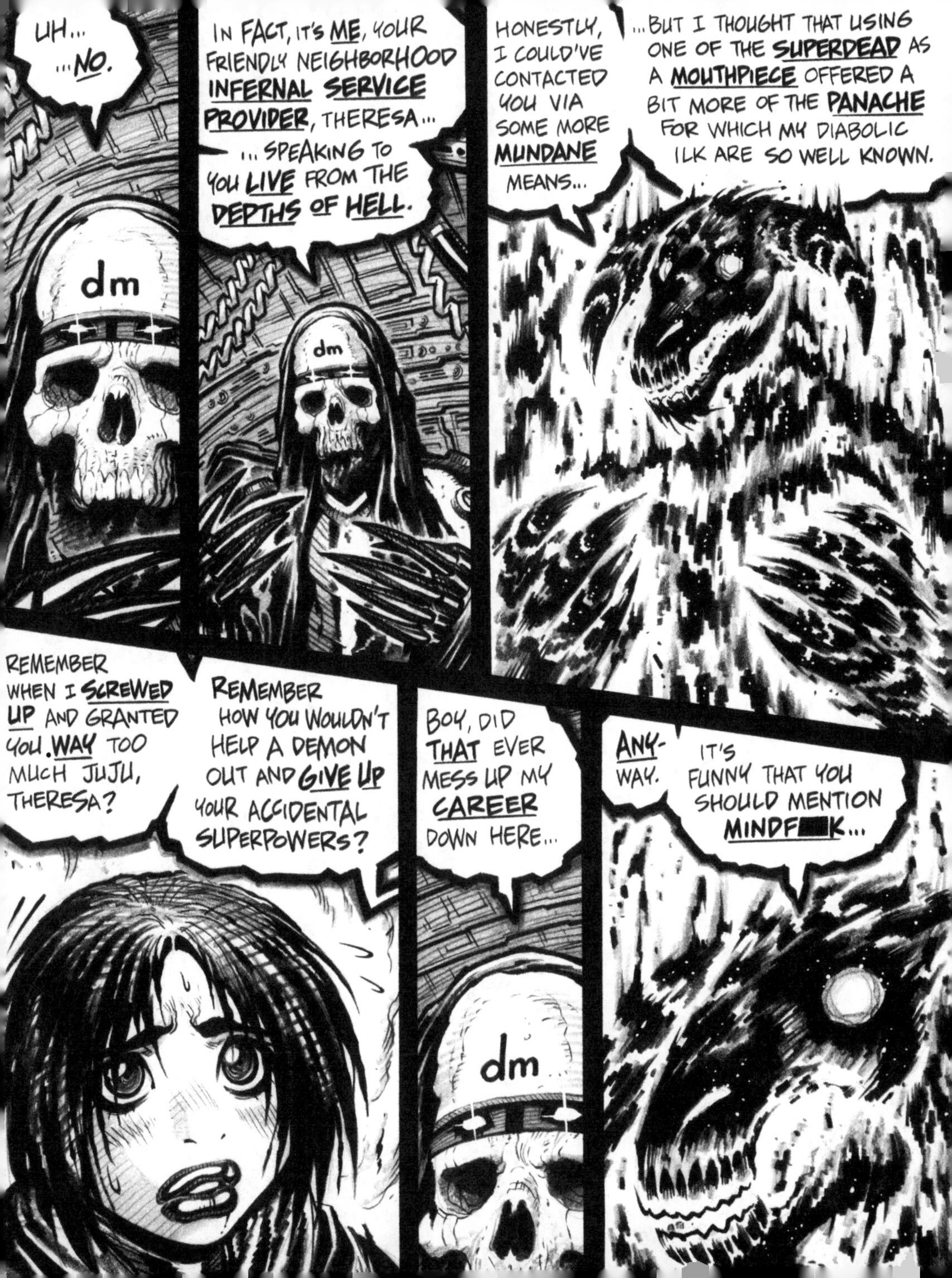
UH... ...NO.
dm
IN FACT, IT'S ME, YOUR FRIENDLY NEIGHBORHOOD INFERNAL SERVICE PROVIDER, THERESA...
... SPEAKING TO YOU LIVE FROM THE DEPTHS OF HELL.
dm
HONESTLY, I COULD'VE CONTACTED YOU VIA SOME MORE MUNDANE MEANS...
...BUT I THOUGHT THAT USING ONE OF THE SUPERDEAD AS A MOUTHPIECE OFFERED A BIT MORE OF THE PANACHE FOR WHICH MY DIABOLIC ILK ARE SO WELL KNOWN.
REMEMBER WHEN I SCREWED UP AND GRANTED YOU WAY TOO MUCH JUJU, THERESA?
REMEMBER HOW YOU WOULDN'T HELP A DEMON OUT AND GIVE UP YOUR ACCIDENTAL SUPERPOWERS?
BOY, DID THAT EVER MESS UP MY CAREER DOWN HERE...
dm
ANY- WAY.
IT'S FUNNY THAT YOU SHOULD MENTION MINDF[redacted]K...

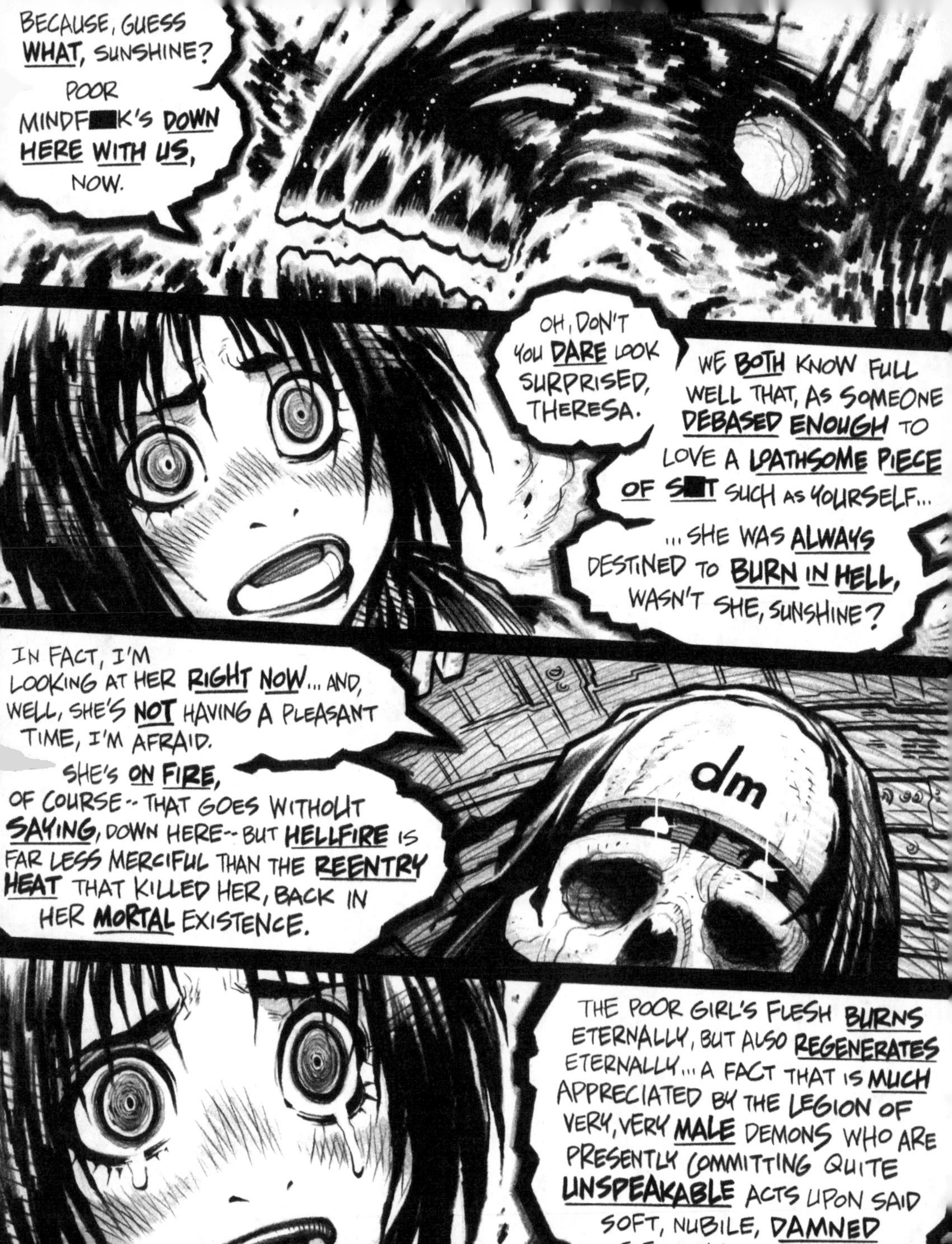
BECAUSE, GUESS WHAT, SUNSHINE? POOR MINDF[redacted]K'S DOWN HERE WITH US, NOW.
OH, DON'T YOU DARE LOOK SURPRISED, THERESA.
WE BOTH KNOW FULL WELL THAT, AS SOMEONE DEBASED ENOUGH TO LOVE A LOATHSOME PIECE OF S[redacted]T SUCH AS YOURSELF...
...SHE WAS ALWAYS DESTINED TO BURN IN HELL, WASN'T SHE, SUNSHINE?
IN FACT, I'M LOOKING AT HER RIGHT NOW... AND, WELL, SHE'S NOT HAVING A PLEASANT TIME, I'M AFRAID.
SHE'S ON FIRE, OF COURSE-- THAT GOES WITHOUT SAYING, DOWN HERE-- BUT HELLFIRE IS FAR LESS MERCIFUL THAN THE REENTRY HEAT THAT KILLED HER, BACK IN HER MORTAL EXISTENCE.
dm
THE POOR GIRL'S FLESH BURNS ETERNALLY, BUT ALSO REGENERATES ETERNALLY... A FACT THAT IS MUCH APPRECIATED BY THE LEGION OF VERY, VERY MALE DEMONS WHO ARE PRESENTLY COMMITTING QUITE UNSPEAKABLE ACTS UPON SAID SOFT, NUBILE, DAMNED FLESH, I'M AFRAID.

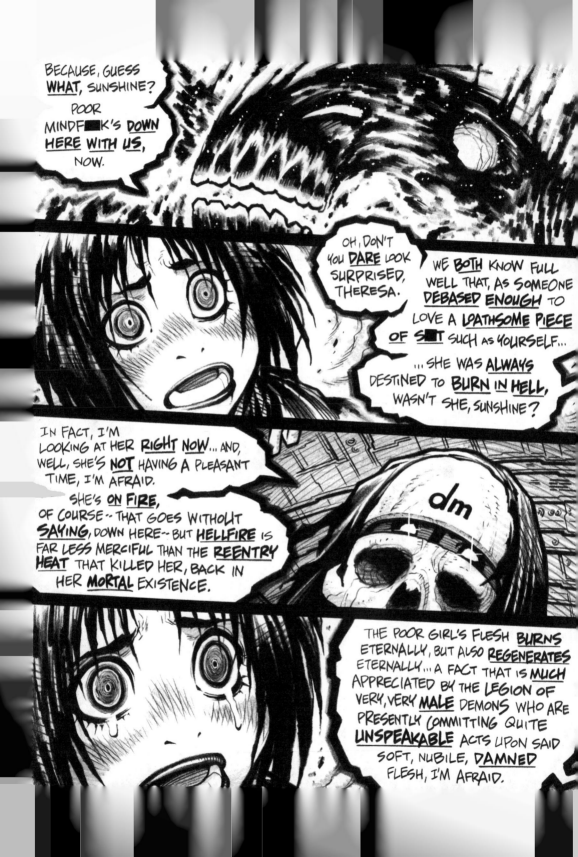

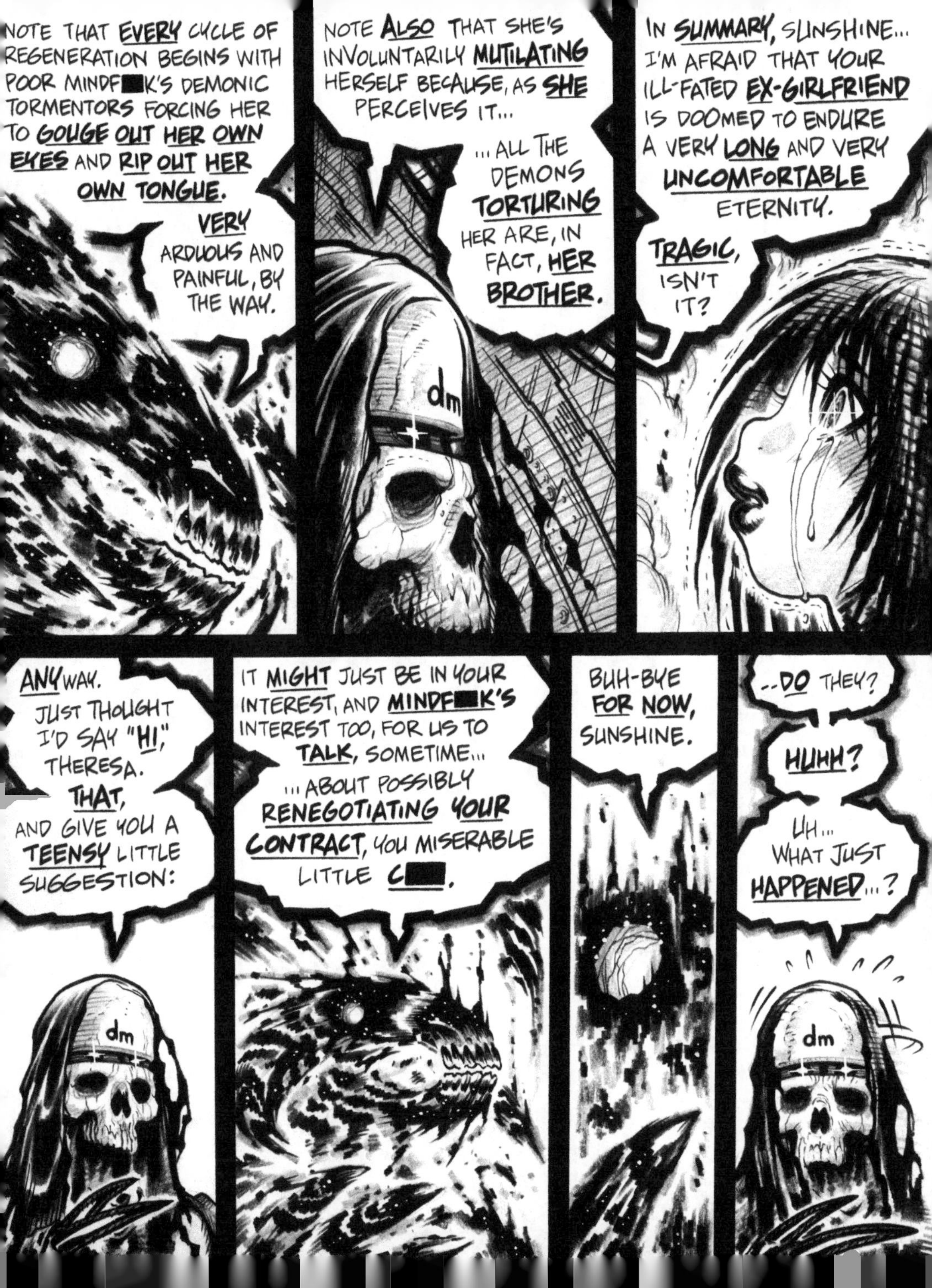
NOTE THAT EVERY CYCLE OF REGENERATION BEGINS WITH POOR MINDF[redacted]K'S DEMONIC TORMENTORS FORCING HER TO GOUGE OUT HER OWN EYES AND RIP OUT HER OWN TONGUE.
VERY ARDUOUS AND PAINFUL, BY THE WAY.
NOTE ALSO THAT SHE'S INVOLUNTARILY MUTILATING HERSELF BECAUSE, AS SHE PERCEIVES IT...
...ALL THE DEMONS TORTURING HER ARE, IN FACT, HER BROTHER.
IN SUMMARY, SUNSHINE... I'M AFRAID THAT YOUR ILL-FATED EX-GIRLFRIEND IS DOOMED TO ENDURE A VERY LONG AND VERY UNCOMFORTABLE ETERNITY.
TRAGIC, ISN'T IT?
ANYWAY. JUST THOUGHT I'D SAY "HI," THERESA.
THAT, AND GIVE YOU A TEENSY LITTLE SUGGESTION:
IT MIGHT JUST BE IN YOUR INTEREST, AND MINDF[redacted]K'S INTEREST TOO, FOR US TO TALK, SOMETIME...
...ABOUT POSSIBLY RENEGOTIATING YOUR CONTRACT, YOU MISERABLE LITTLE C[redacted].
BUH-BYE FOR NOW, SUNSHINE.
--DO THEY?
HUHH?
UH... WHAT JUST HAPPENED...?

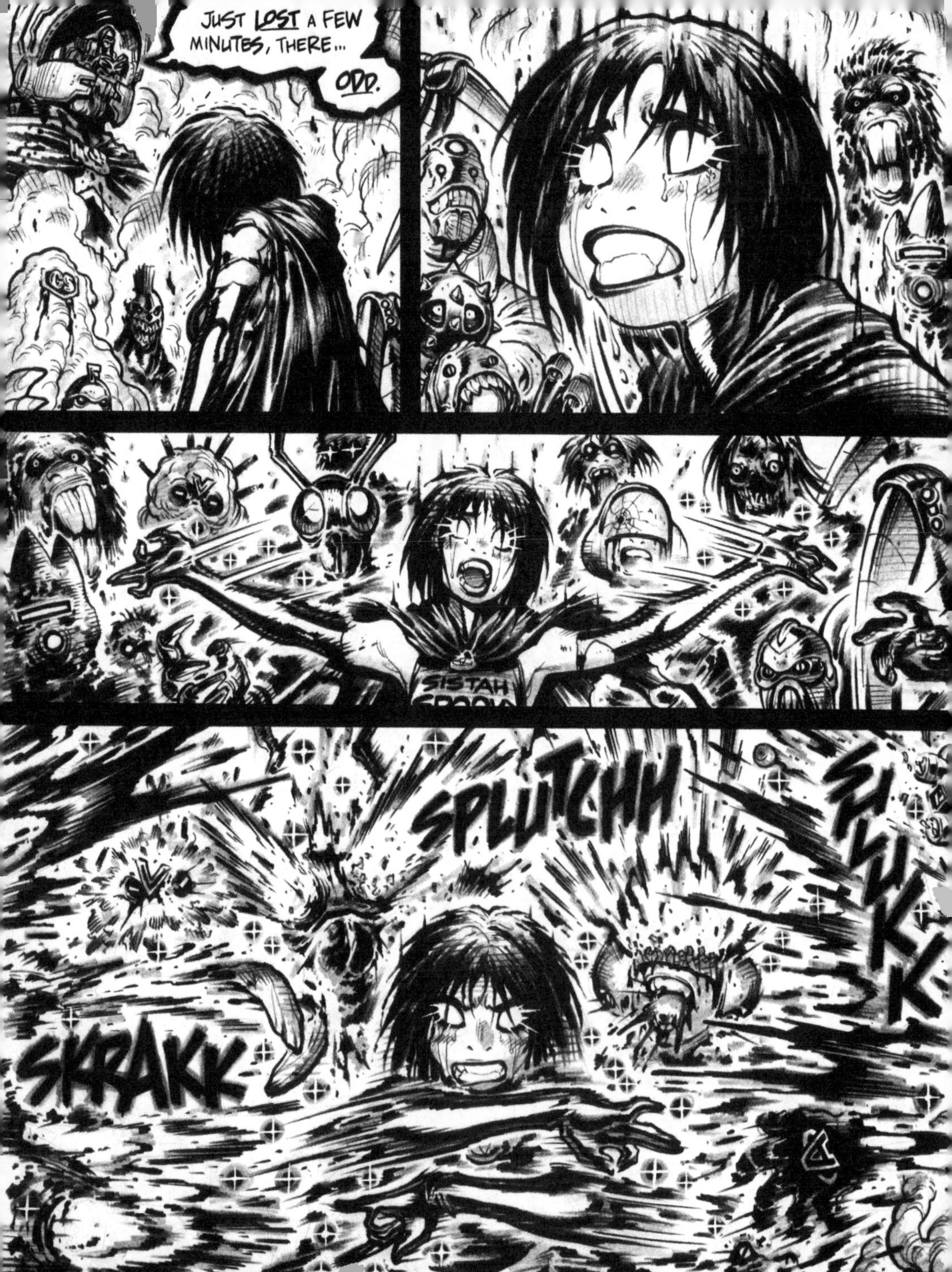
JUST LOST A FEW MINUTES, THERE...
ODD.
SISTAH
SPLUTCHH
SKRAKK

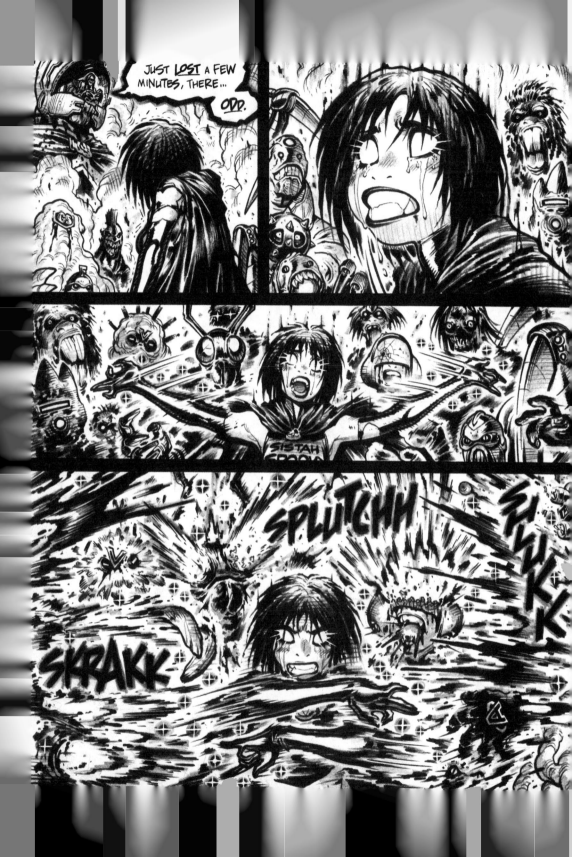

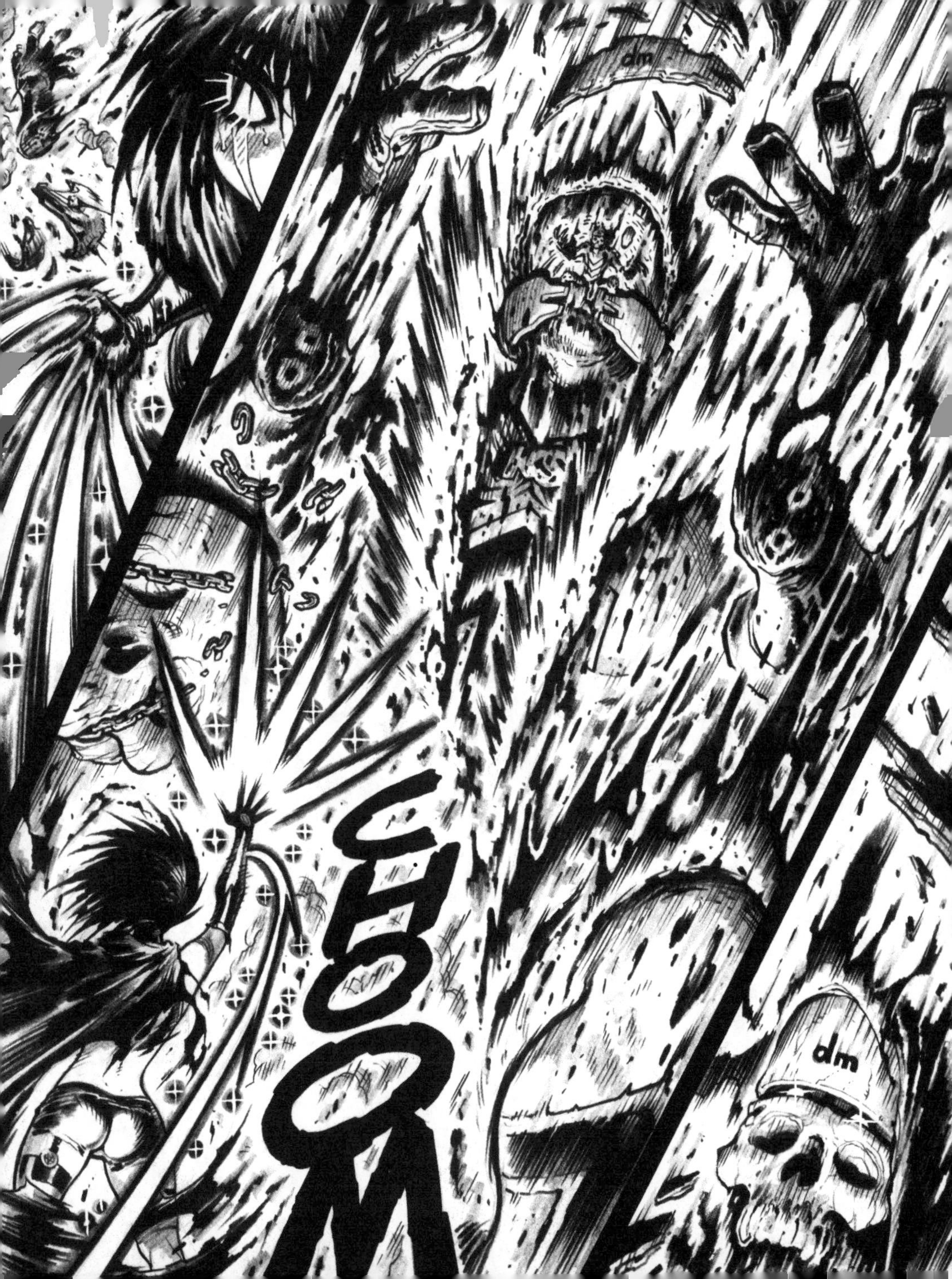
CHOOM
dm
dm

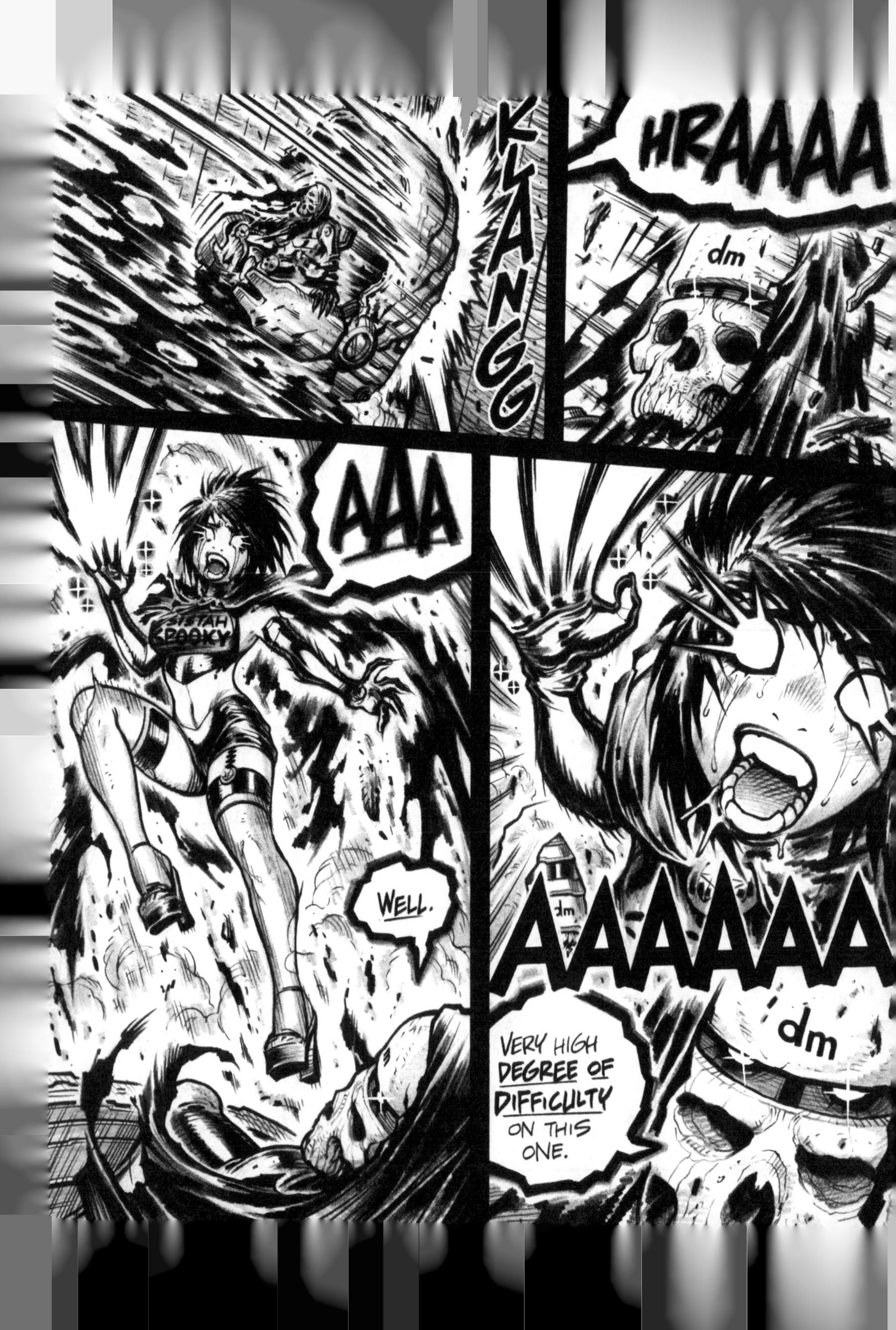
KLANGG
HRAAAA
dm
AAA
WELL.
AAAAAA
dm
dm
VERY HIGH DEGREE OF DIFFICULTY ON THIS ONE.

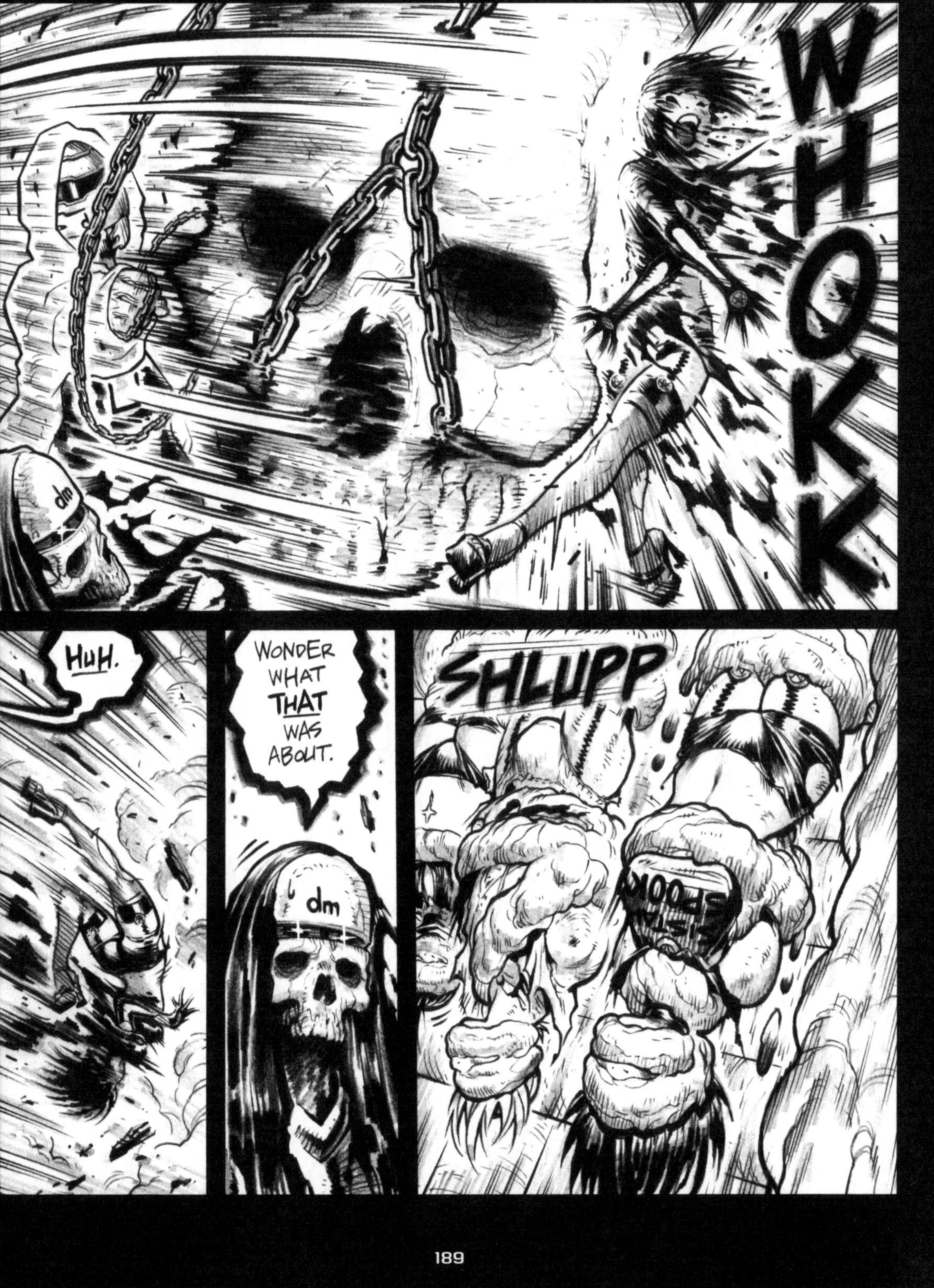
WHOKK
HuH.
WONDER WHAT THAT WAS ABOUT.
SHLUPP

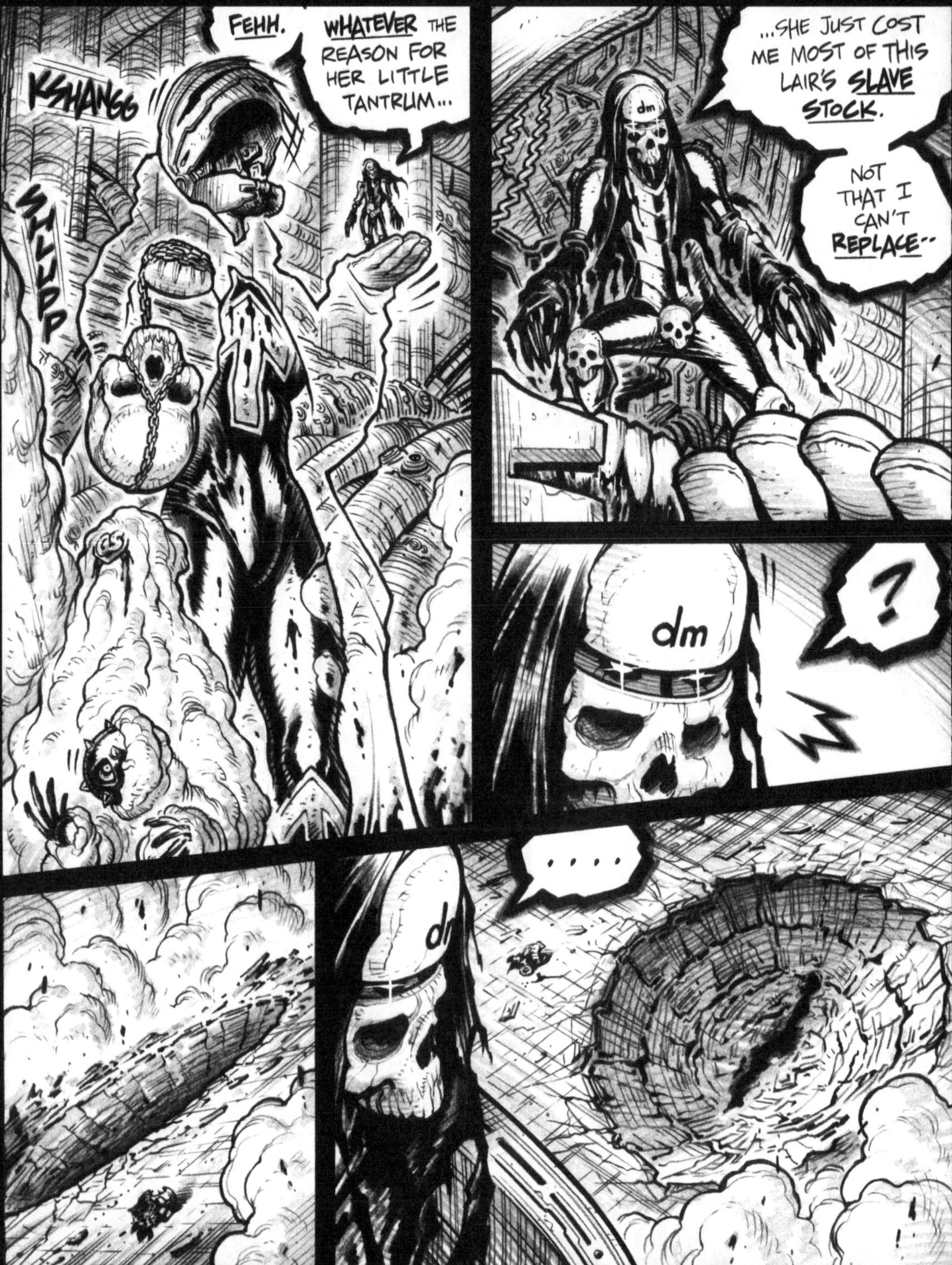
FEHH.
WHATEVER THE REASON FOR HER LITTLE TANTRUM...
KSHANGG
SHLUPP
...SHE JUST COST ME MOST OF THIS LAIR'S SLAVE STOCK.
NOT THAT I CAN'T REPLACE--
?
....

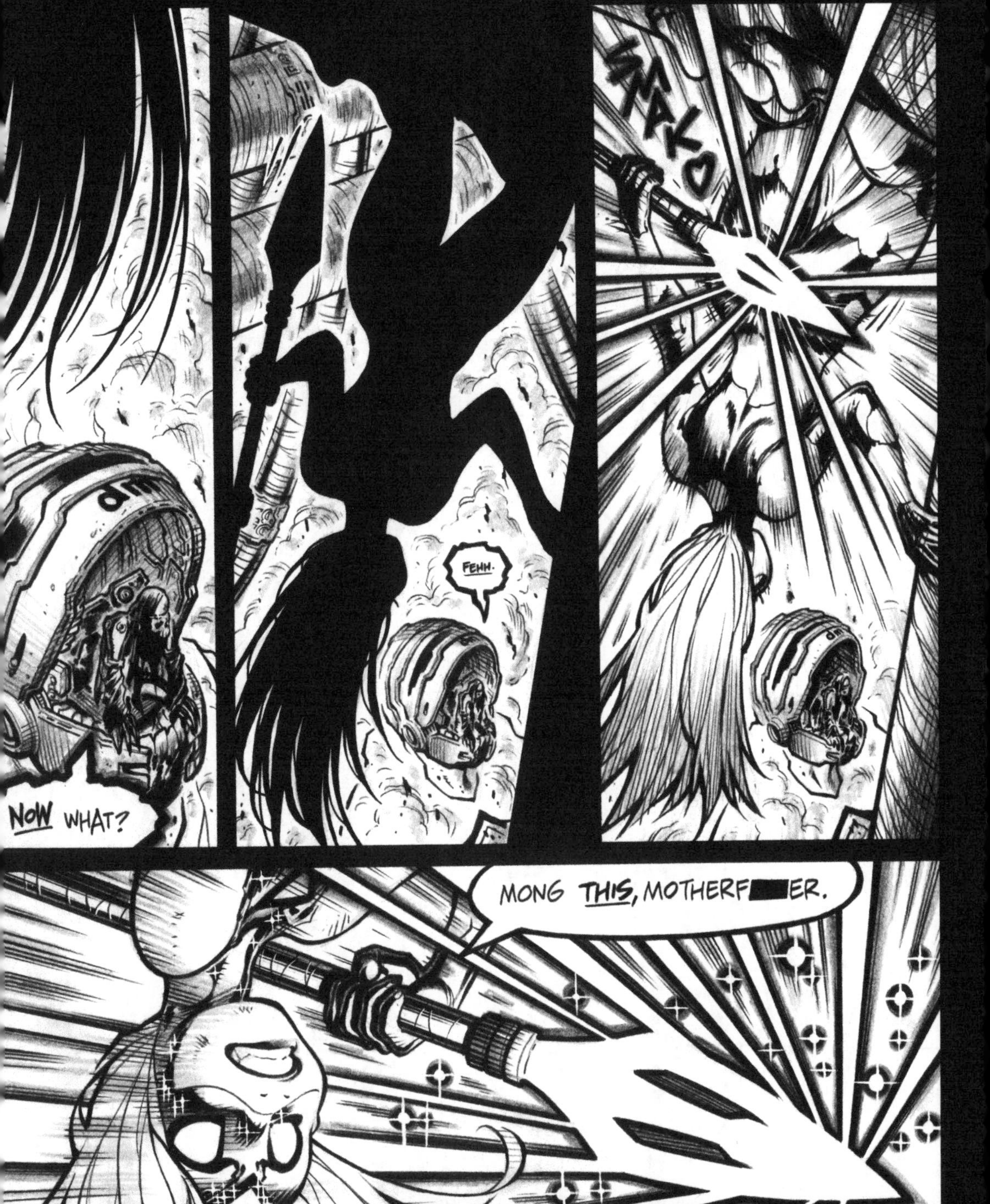
NOW WHAT?
FEHH.
SMAKO
MONG THIS, MOTHERF[redacted]ER.

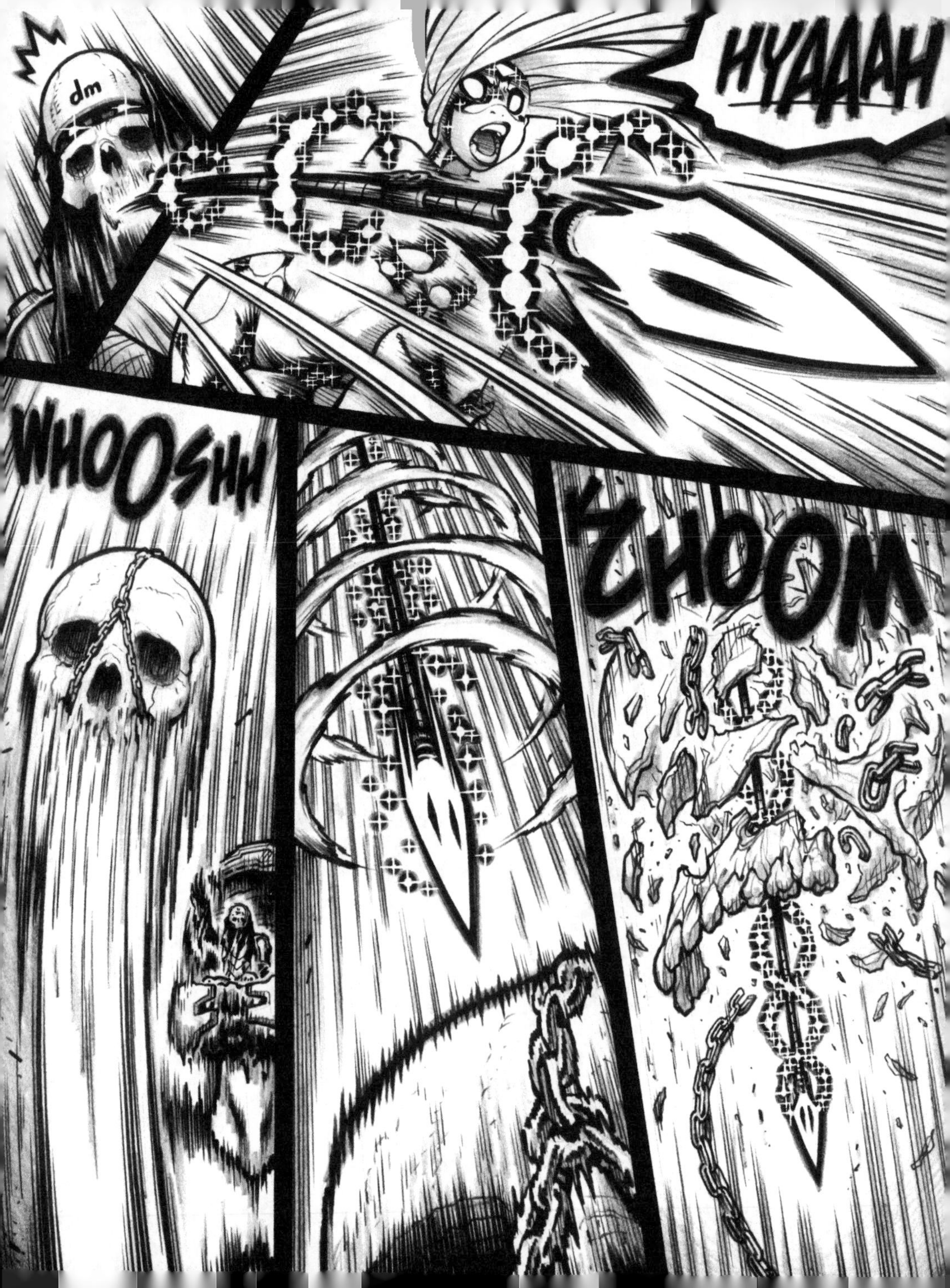
dm
HYAAAH
WHOOSHH
KCHOOM

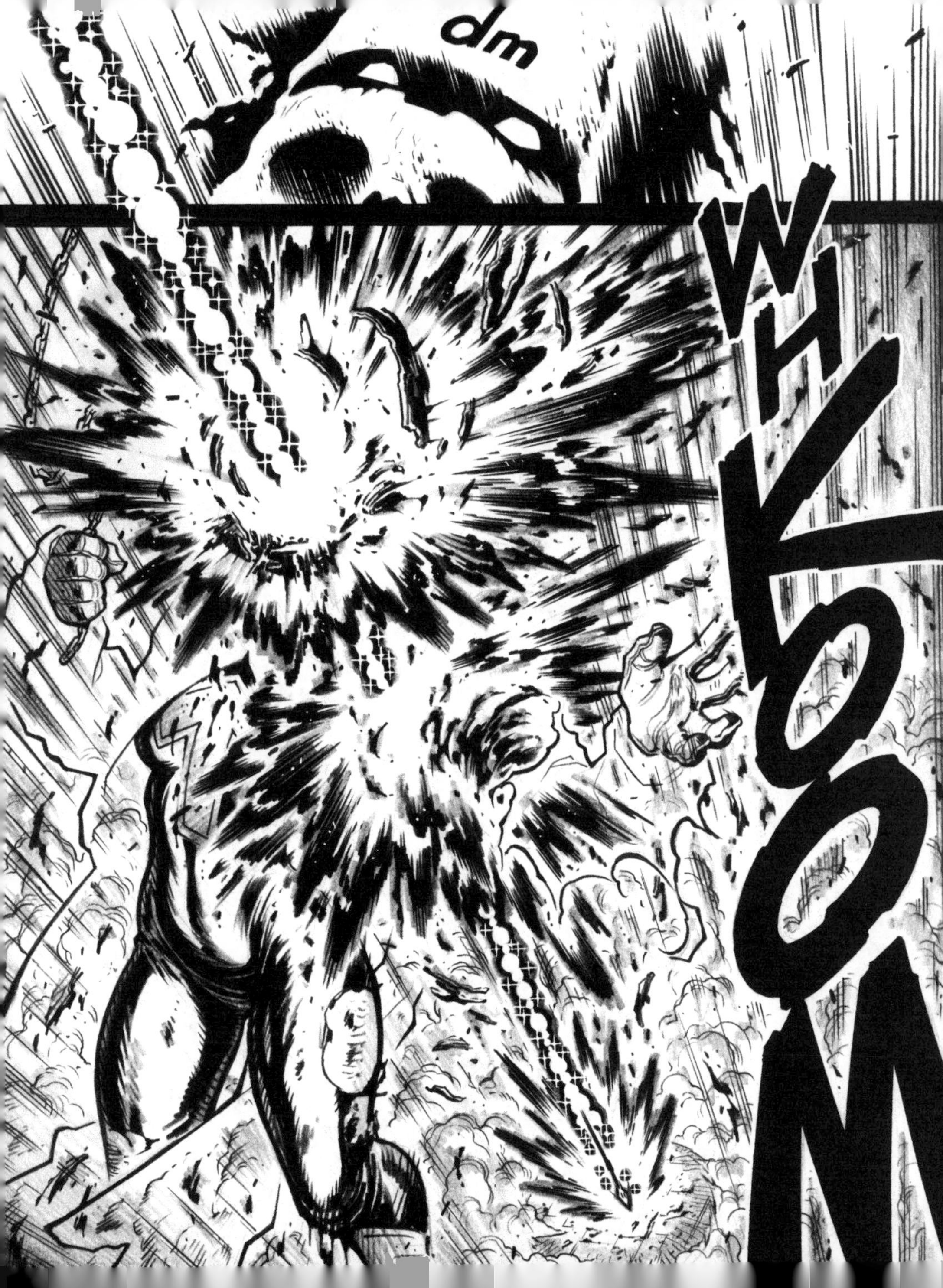
dm
WHOOM

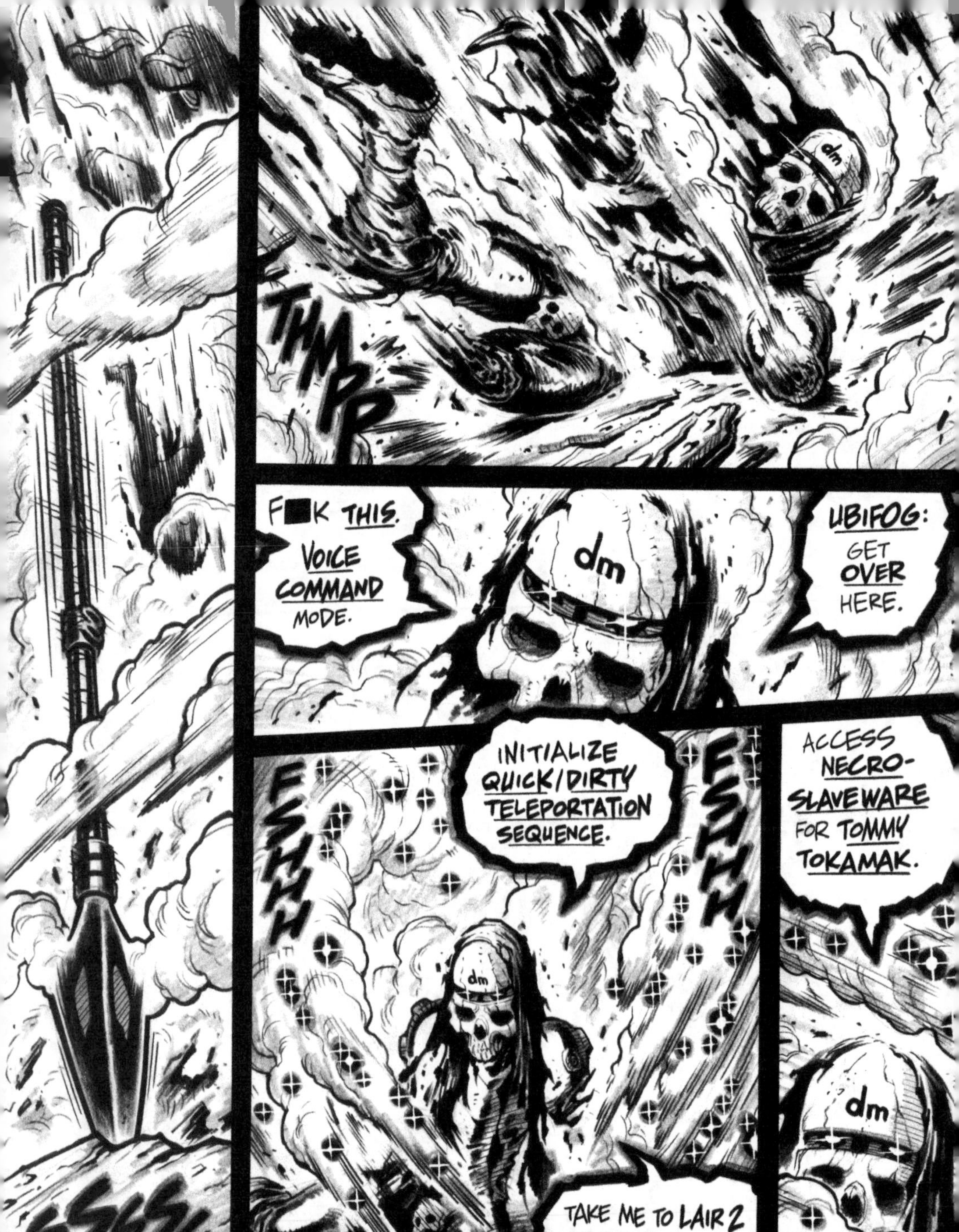
SSSSS
THMPP
F[redacted]K THIS. VOICE COMMAND MODE.
UBIFOG: GET OVER HERE.
FSHHH
INITIALIZE QUICK/DIRTY TELEPORTATION SEQUENCE.
FSHHH
TAKE ME TO LAIR 2 IMMEDIATELY.
ACCESS NECRO-SLAVEWARE FOR TOMMY TOKAMAK.

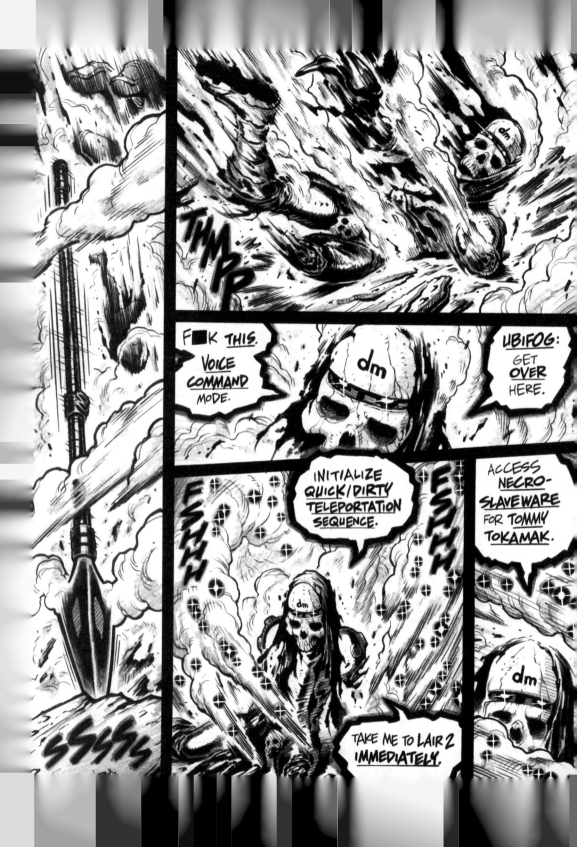

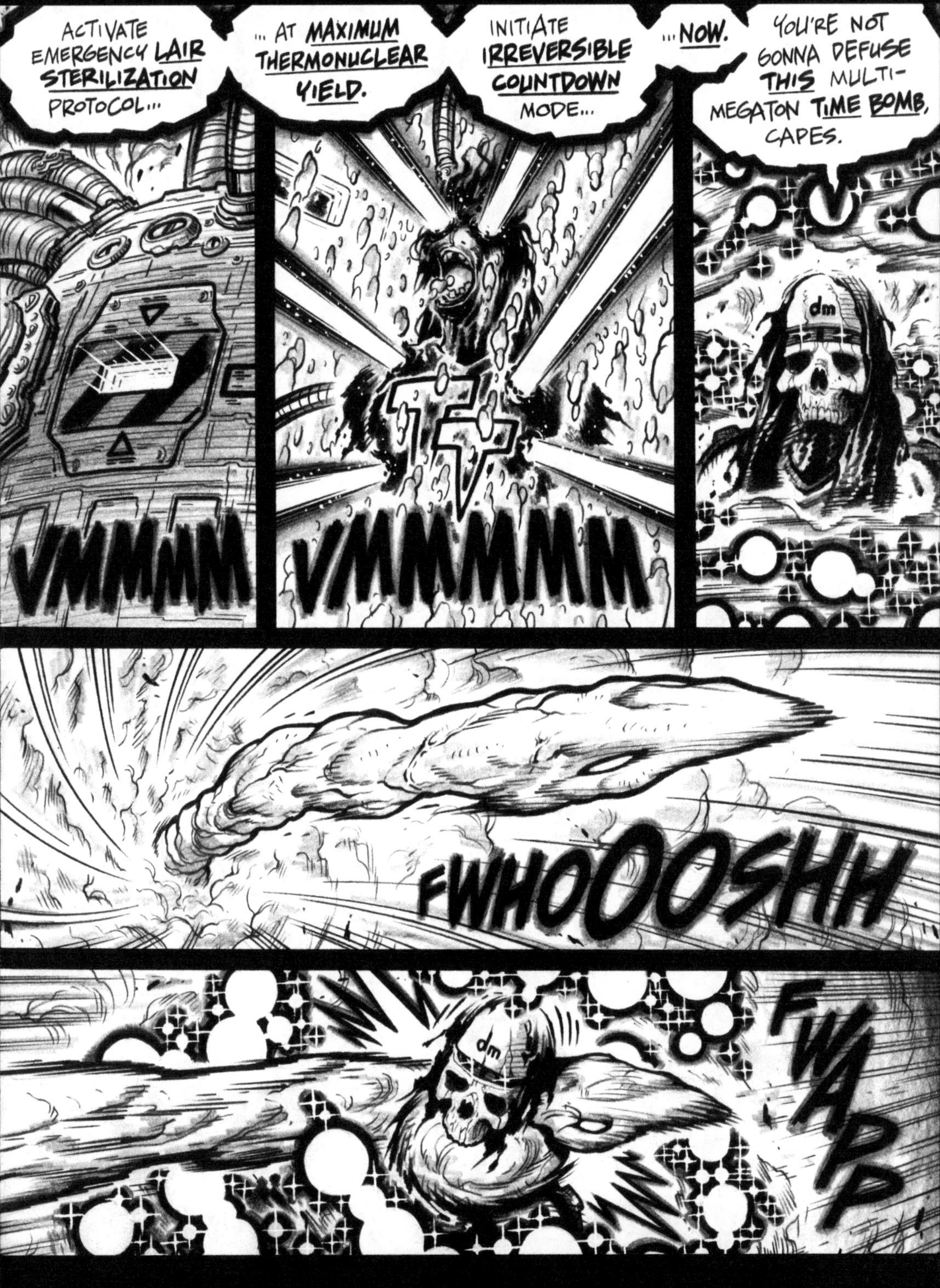
ACTIVATE EMERGENCY LAIR STERILIZATION PROTOCOL...
... AT MAXIMUM THERMONUCLEAR YIELD.
INITIATE IRREVERSIBLE COUNTDOWN MODE...
...NOW.
YOU'RE NOT GONNA DEFUSE THIS MULTI-MEGATON TIME BOMB, CAPES.
VMMMM
VMMMMMM
FWHOOOOSHH
FWAPP

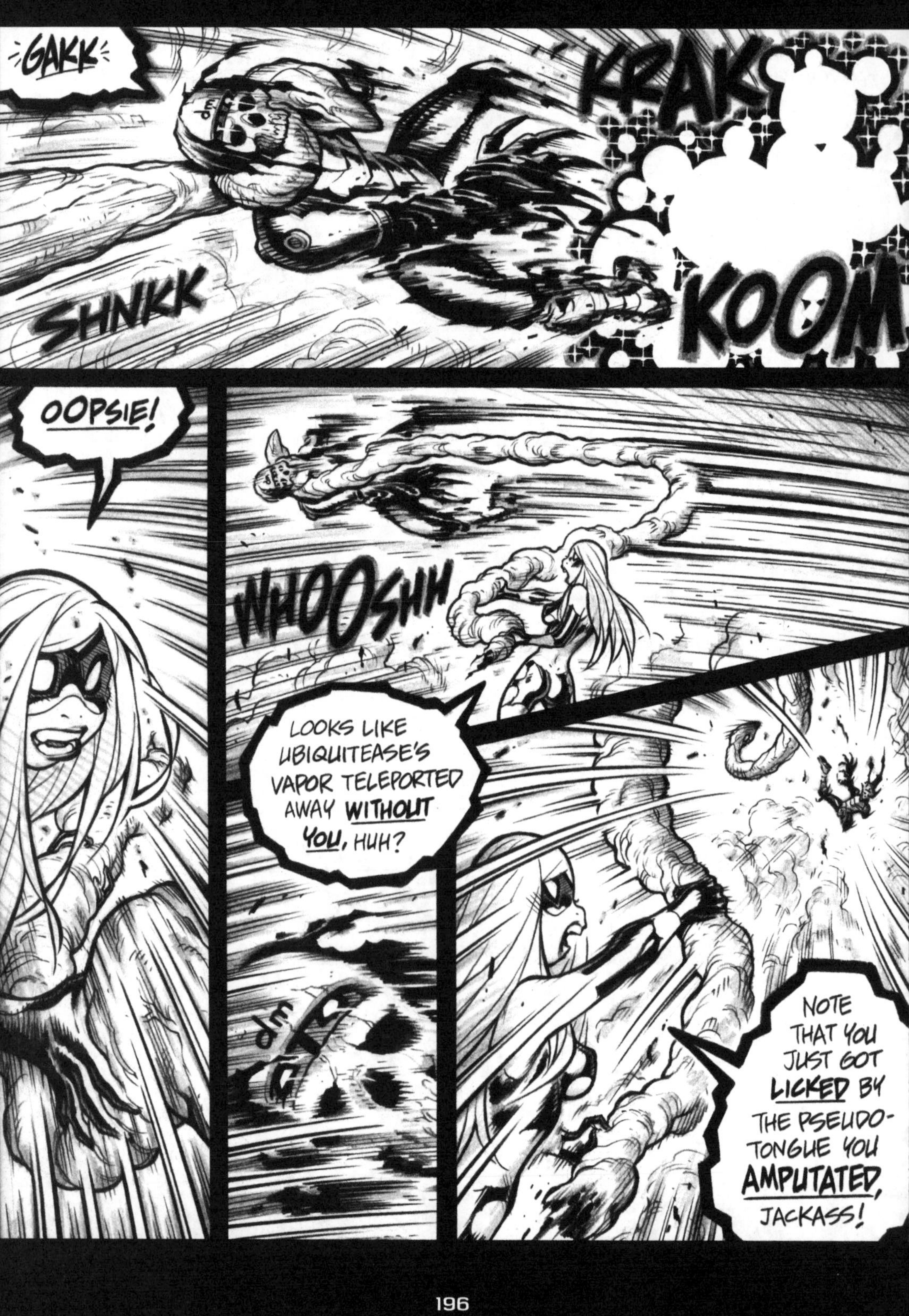
GAKK
KRAK
KOOM
SHNKK
OOPSIE!
WHOOSHH
LOOKS LIKE UBIQUITEASE'S VAPOR TELEPORTED AWAY WITHOUT YOU, HUH?
NOTE THAT YOU JUST GOT LICKED BY THE PSEUDO-TONGUE YOU AMPUTATED, JACKASS!

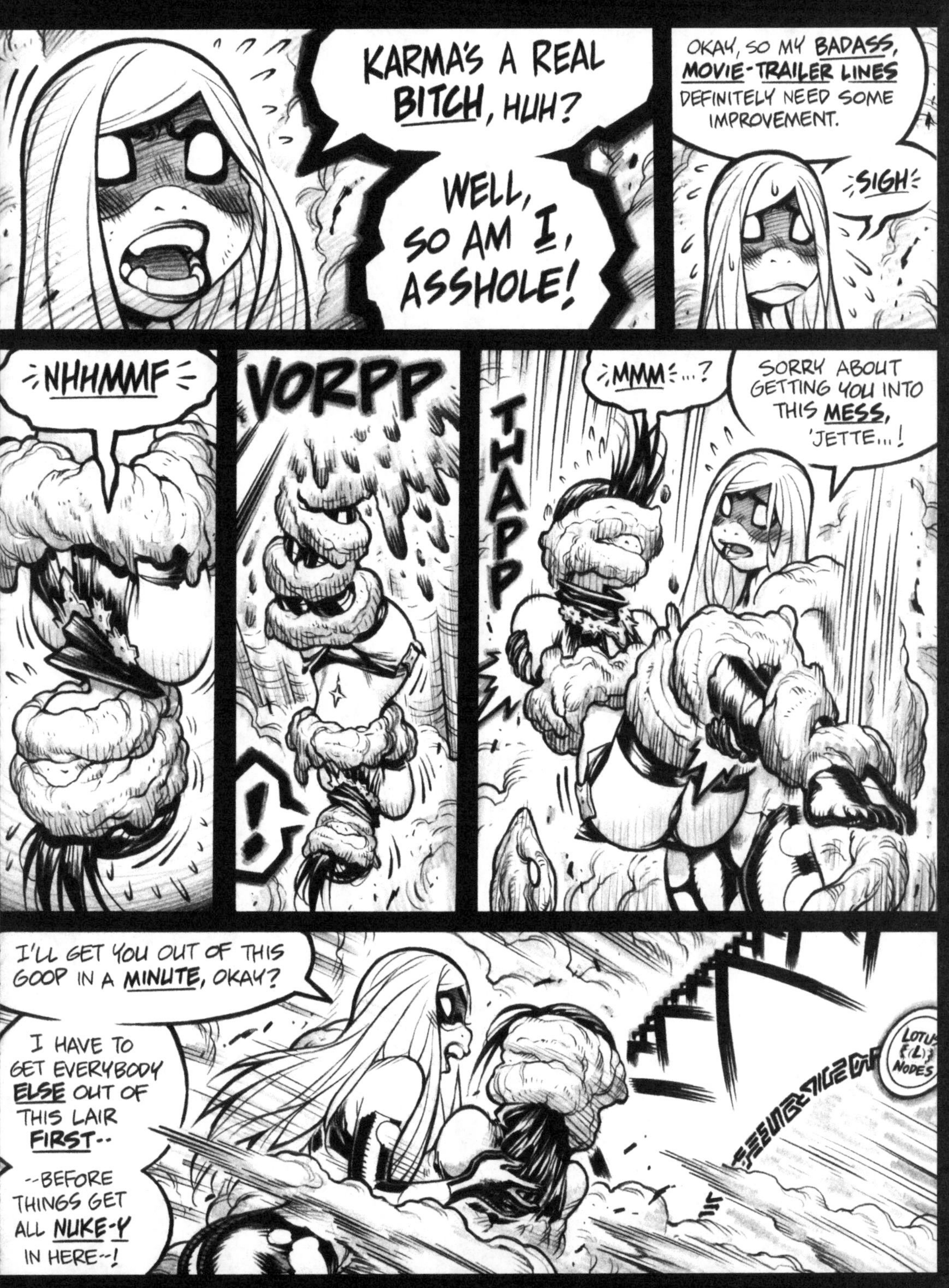
KARMA'S A REAL BITCH, HUH?
WELL, SO AM I, ASSHOLE!
OKAY, SO MY BADASS, MOVIE-TRAILER LINES DEFINITELY NEED SOME IMPROVEMENT.
SIGH
NHHMMF
VORPP
!
THAPP
MMM ...?
SORRY ABOUT GETTING YOU INTO THIS MESS, 'JETTE...!
I'LL GET YOU OUT OF THIS GOOP IN A MINUTE, OKAY?
I HAVE TO GET EVERYBODY ELSE OUT OF THIS LAIR FIRST--
--BEFORE THINGS GET ALL NUKE-Y IN HERE--!
LOTUS (L) NODES

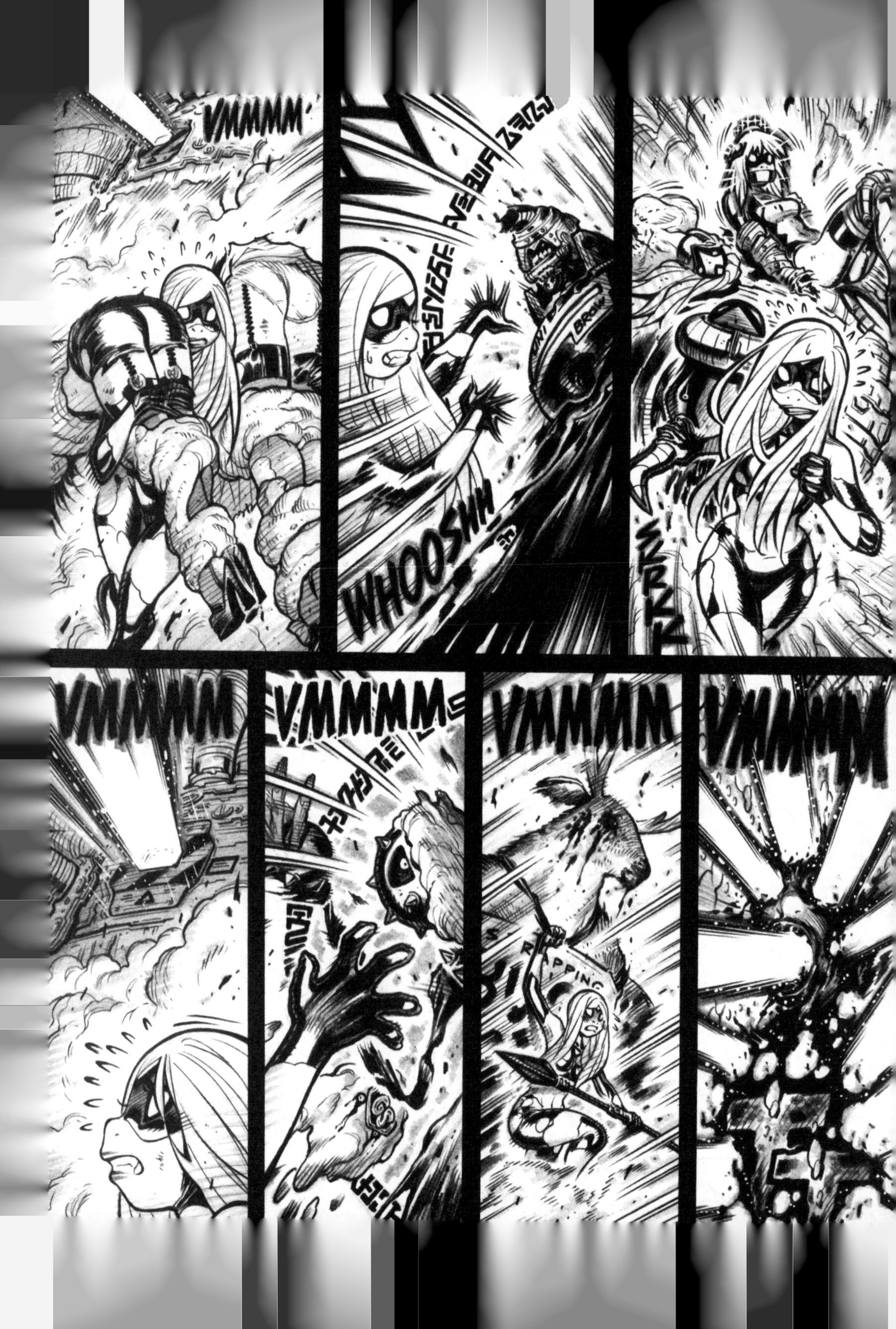
VMMMM
WHOOSHH
SKRKK
VMMMM
VMMMM
VMMMM
S RIPPING
VMMMM

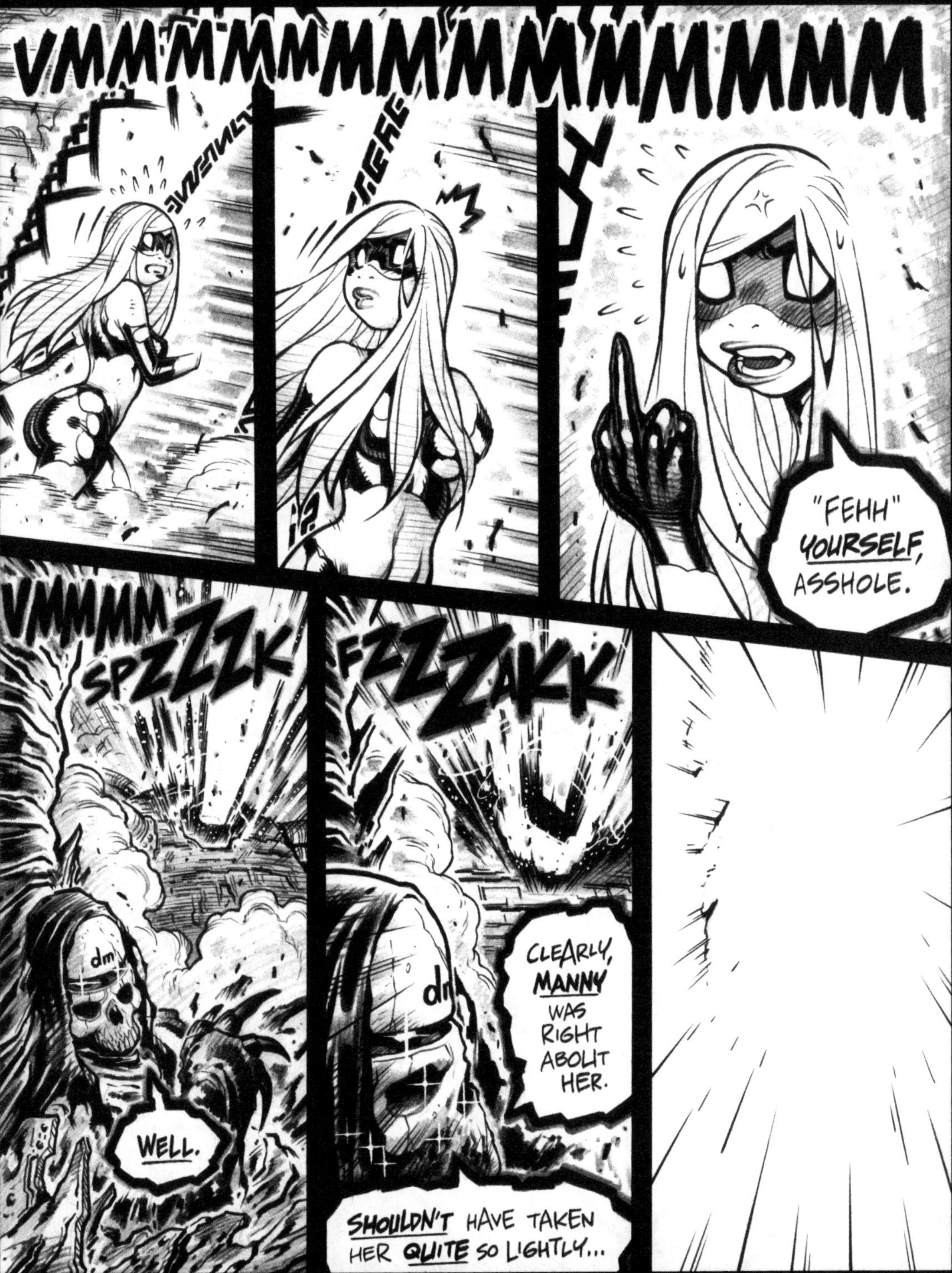
VMMMMMMMMMMMMMMMMMMM
"FEHH" YOURSELF, ASSHOLE.
VMMMM
SPZZZK
FZZZAKK
WELL.
CLEARLY, MANNY WAS RIGHT ABOUT HER.
SHOULDN'T HAVE TAKEN HER QUITE SO LIGHTLY...

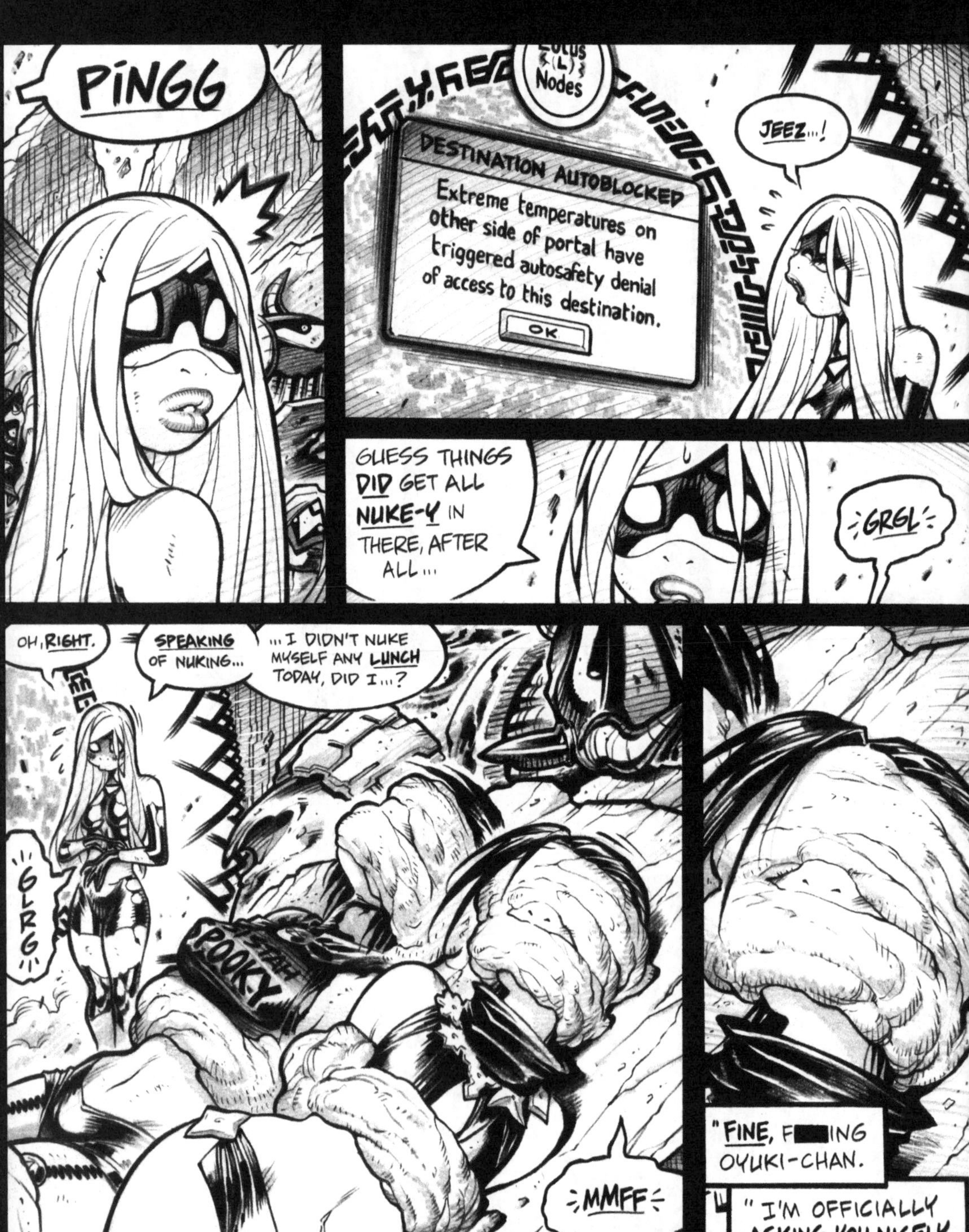
PiNGG
Lotus
{(L)}
Nodes
DESTINATION AUTOBLOCKED
Extreme temperatures on other side of portal have triggered autosafety denial of access to this destination.
OK
JEEZ...!
GUESS THINGS DID GET ALL NUKE-Y IN THERE, AFTER ALL...
GRGL
OH, RIGHT.
SPEAKING OF NUKING...
...I DIDN'T NUKE MYSELF ANY LUNCH TODAY, DID I...?
GLRG
POOKY
MMFF
"FINE, F[redacted]ING OYUKI-CHAN.
"I'M OFFICIALLY ASKING YOU NICELY, ALL RIGHT?"

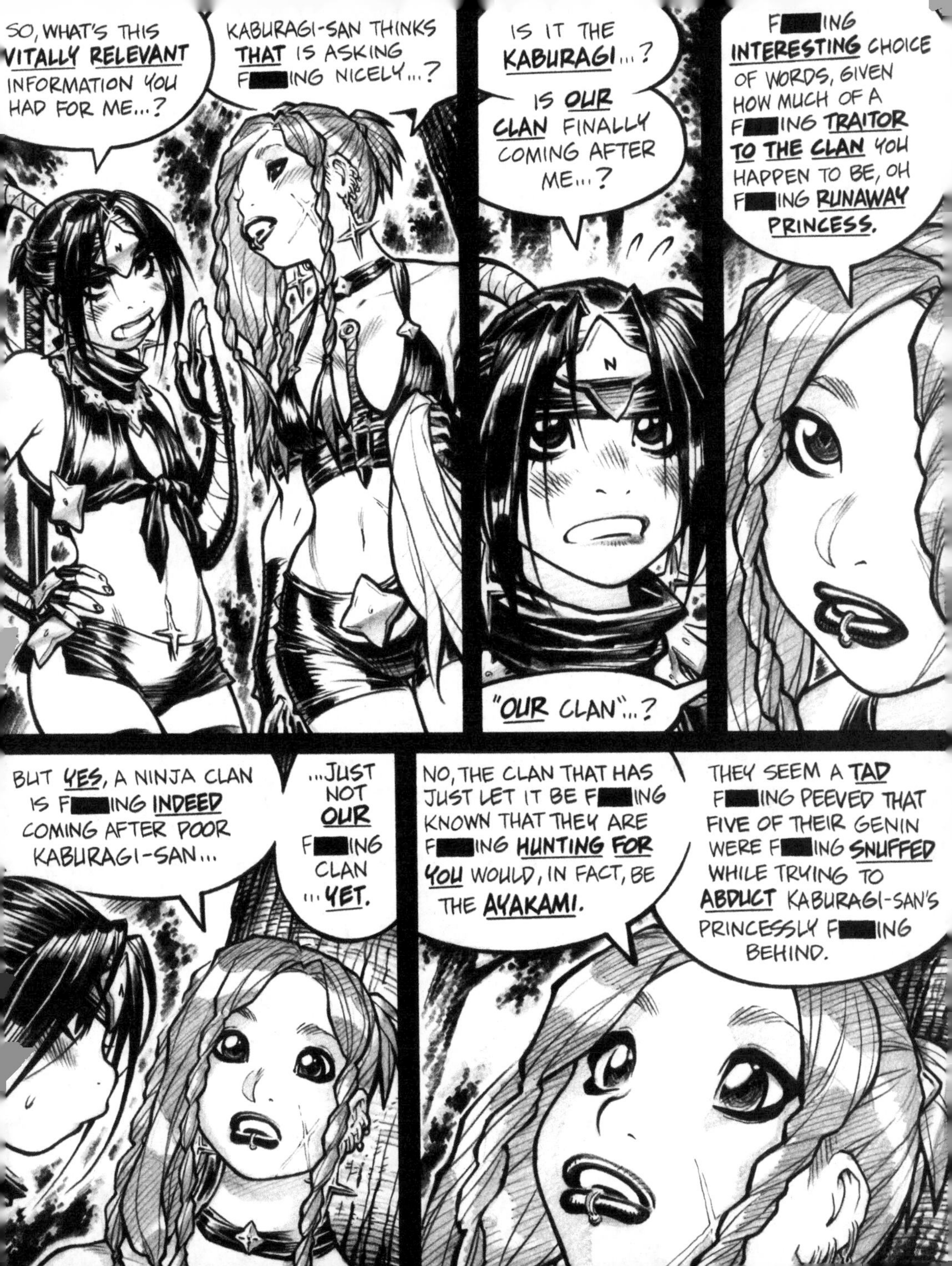
SO, WHAT'S THIS VITALLY RELEVANT INFORMATION YOU HAD FOR ME...?
KABURAGI-SAN THINKS THAT IS ASKING F[redacted]ING NICELY...?
IS IT THE KABURAGI...?
IS OUR CLAN FINALLY COMING AFTER ME...?
"OUR CLAN"...?
F[redacted]ING INTERESTING CHOICE OF WORDS, GIVEN HOW MUCH OF A F[redacted]ING TRAITOR TO THE CLAN YOU HAPPEN TO BE, OH F[redacted]ING RUNAWAY PRINCESS.
BUT YES, A NINJA CLAN IS F[redacted]ING INDEED COMING AFTER POOR KABURAGI-SAN...
...JUST NOT OUR F[redacted]ING CLAN ...YET.
NO, THE CLAN THAT HAS JUST LET IT BE F[redacted]ING KNOWN THAT THEY ARE F[redacted]ING HUNTING FOR YOU WOULD, IN FACT, BE THE AYAKAMI.
THEY SEEM A TAD F[redacted]ING PEEVED THAT FIVE OF THEIR GENIN WERE F[redacted]ING SNUFFED WHILE TRYING TO ABDUCT KABURAGI-SAN'S PRINCESSLY F[redacted]ING BEHIND.

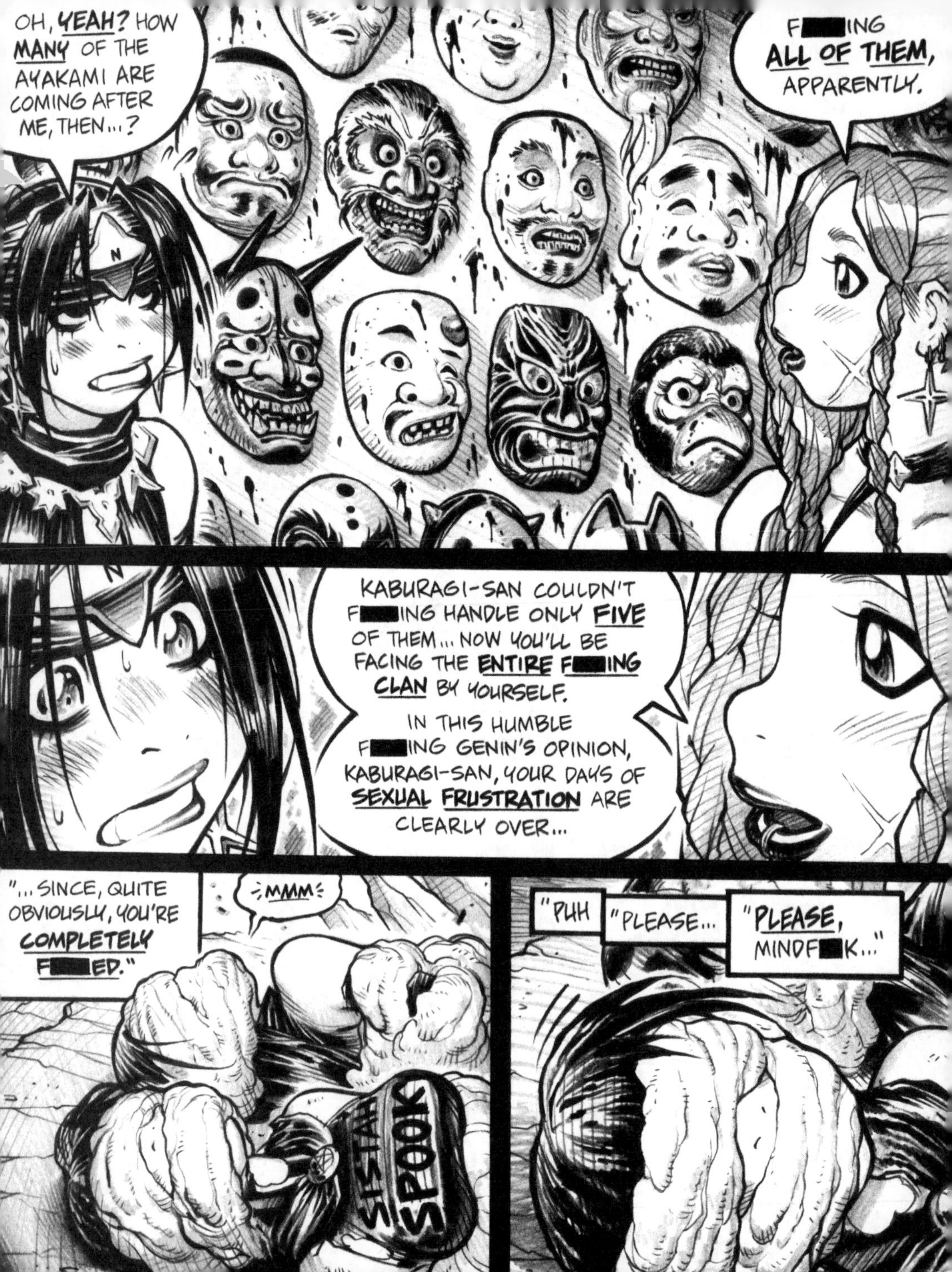
OH, **YEAH?** HOW **MANY** OF THE AYAKAMI ARE COMING AFTER ME, THEN...?
F[redacted]ING **ALL OF THEM,** APPARENTLY.
KABURAGI-SAN COULDN'T F[redacted]ING HANDLE ONLY **FIVE** OF THEM... NOW YOU'LL BE FACING THE **ENTIRE F[redacted]ING CLAN** BY YOURSELF.
IN THIS HUMBLE F[redacted]ING GENIN'S OPINION, KABURAGI-SAN, YOUR DAYS OF **SEXUAL FRUSTRATION** ARE CLEARLY OVER...
"...SINCE, QUITE OBVIOUSLY, YOU'RE **COMPLETELY F[redacted]ED.**"
MMM
SISTAH SPOOK
"PUH
"PLEASE...
"**PLEASE,** MINDF[redacted]K..."

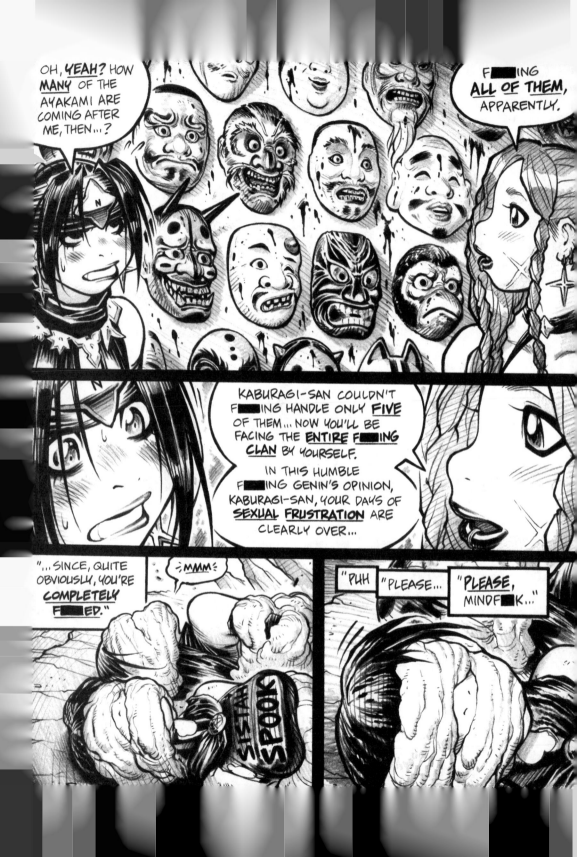

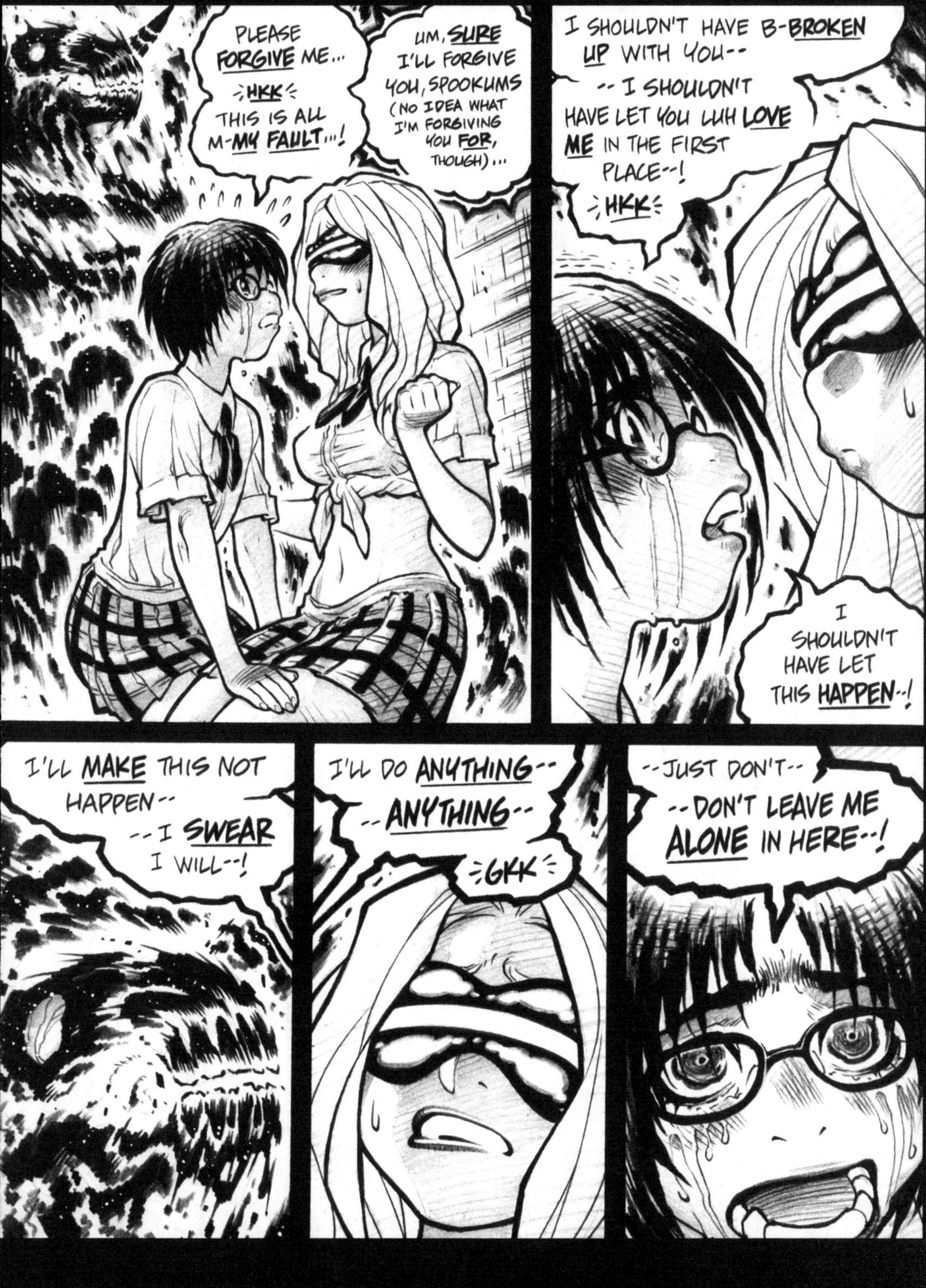
PLEASE FORGIVE ME...
HKK
THIS IS ALL M-MY FAULT...!
UM, SURE I'LL FORGIVE YOU, SPOOKUMS (NO IDEA WHAT I'M FORGIVING YOU FOR, THOUGH)...
I SHOULDN'T HAVE B-BROKEN UP WITH YOU--
--I SHOULDN'T HAVE LET YOU LUH LOVE ME IN THE FIRST PLACE--!
HKK
I SHOULDN'T HAVE LET THIS HAPPEN--!
I'LL MAKE THIS NOT HAPPEN--
--I SWEAR I WILL--!
I'LL DO ANYTHING--
--ANYTHING--
GKK
--JUST DON'T--
--DON'T LEAVE ME ALONE IN HERE--!

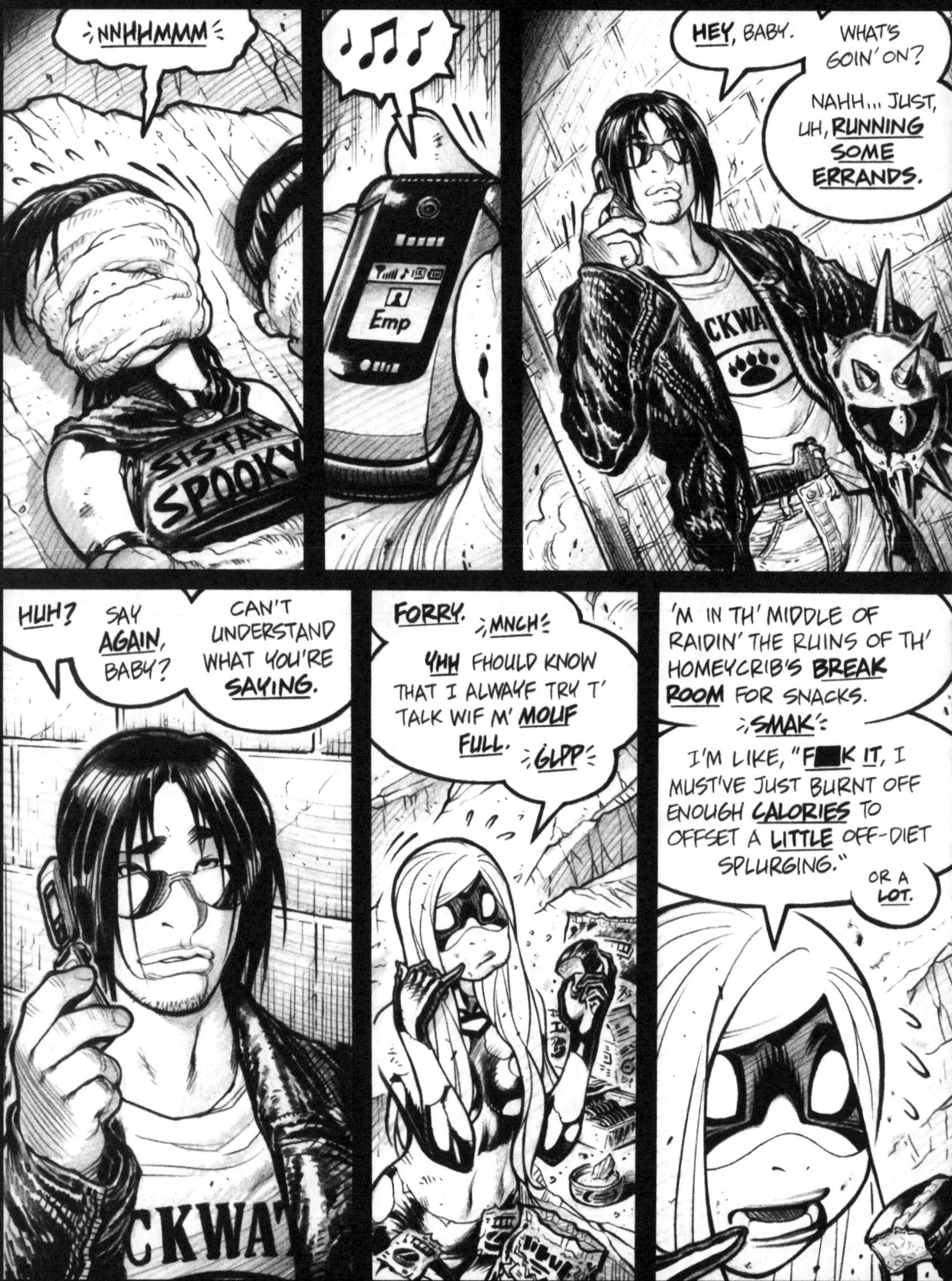
NNHHMMMM
Emp
HEY, BABY. WHAT'S GOIN' ON?
NAHH... JUST, UH, RUNNING SOME ERRANDS.
SISTAH SPOOKY
HUH? SAY AGAIN, BABY? CAN'T UNDERSTAND WHAT YOU'RE SAYING.
FORRY. MNCH
YHH FHOULD KNOW THAT I ALWAYF TRY T' TALK WIF M' MOUF FULL. GLPP
'M IN TH' MIDDLE OF RAIDIN' THE RUINS OF TH' HOMEYCRIB'S BREAK ROOM FOR SNACKS.
SMAK
I'M LIKE, "F[redacted]K IT, I MUST'VE JUST BURNT OFF ENOUGH CALORIES TO OFFSET A LITTLE OFF-DIET SPLURGING."
OR A LOT.

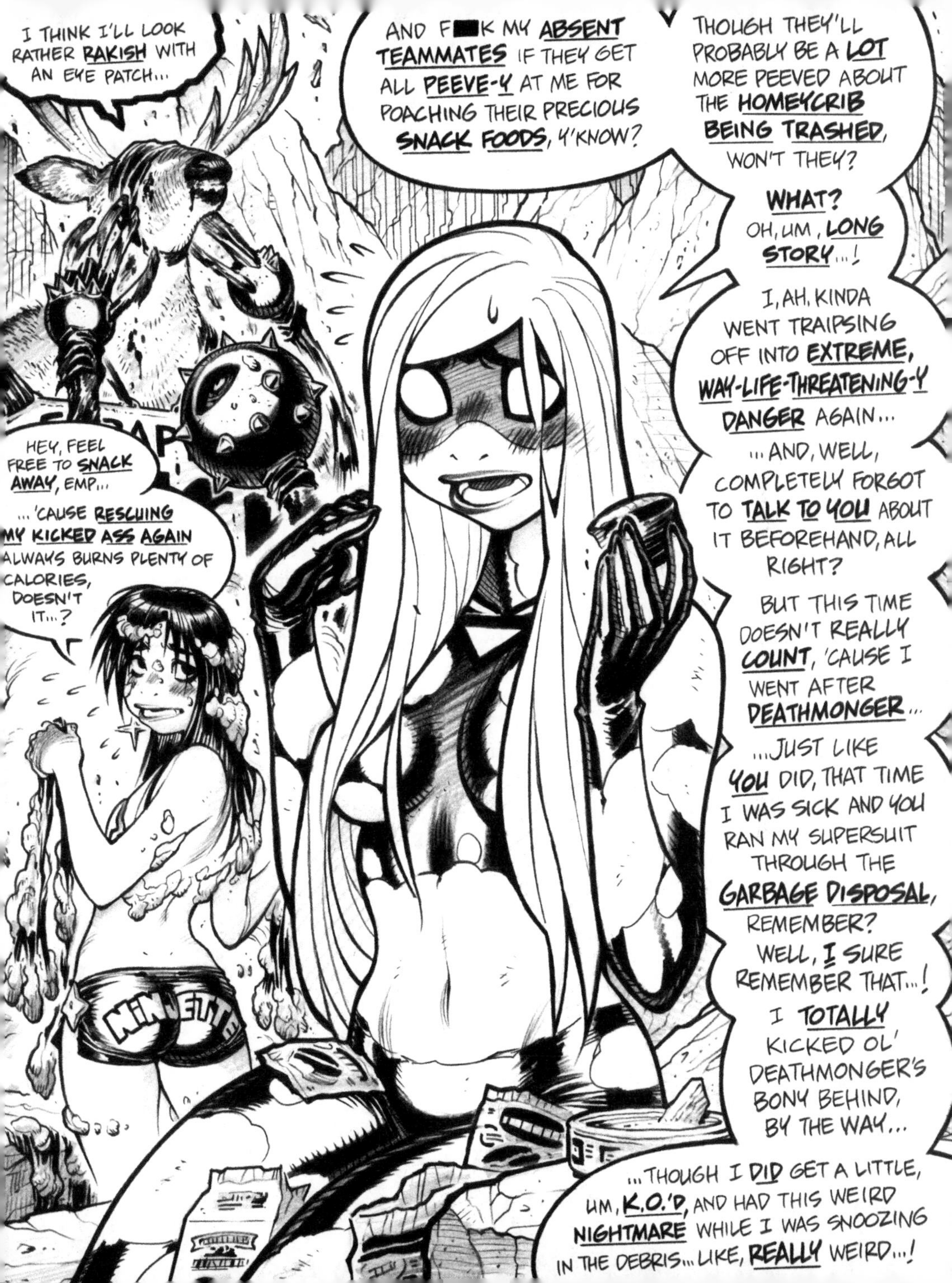

I THINK I'LL LOOK RATHER RAKISH WITH AN EYE PATCH...
AND F[redacted]K MY ABSENT TEAMMATES IF THEY GET ALL PEEVE-Y AT ME FOR POACHING THEIR PRECIOUS SNACK FOODS, Y'KNOW?
THOUGH THEY'LL PROBABLY BE A LOT MORE PEEVED ABOUT THE HOMEYCRIB BEING TRASHED, WON'T THEY?
WHAT? OH, UM, LONG STORY...!
HEY, FEEL FREE TO SNACK AWAY, EMP...
...'CAUSE RESCUING MY KICKED ASS AGAIN ALWAYS BURNS PLENTY OF CALORIES, DOESN'T IT...?
I, AH, KINDA WENT TRAIPSING OFF INTO EXTREME, WAY-LIFE-THREATENING-Y DANGER AGAIN...
...AND, WELL, COMPLETELY FORGOT TO TALK TO YOU ABOUT IT BEFOREHAND, ALL RIGHT?
BUT THIS TIME DOESN'T REALLY COUNT, 'CAUSE I WENT AFTER DEATHMONGER...
...JUST LIKE YOU DID, THAT TIME I WAS SICK AND YOU RAN MY SUPERSUIT THROUGH THE GARBAGE DISPOSAL, REMEMBER?
WELL, I SURE REMEMBER THAT...!
I TOTALLY KICKED OL' DEATHMONGER'S BONY BEHIND, BY THE WAY...
...THOUGH I DID GET A LITTLE, UM, K.O.'D, AND HAD THIS WEIRD NIGHTMARE WHILE I WAS SNOOZING IN THE DEBRIS... LIKE, REALLY WEIRD...!
NINJETTE

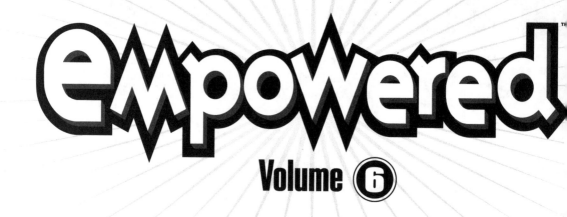

empowered

Volume 6

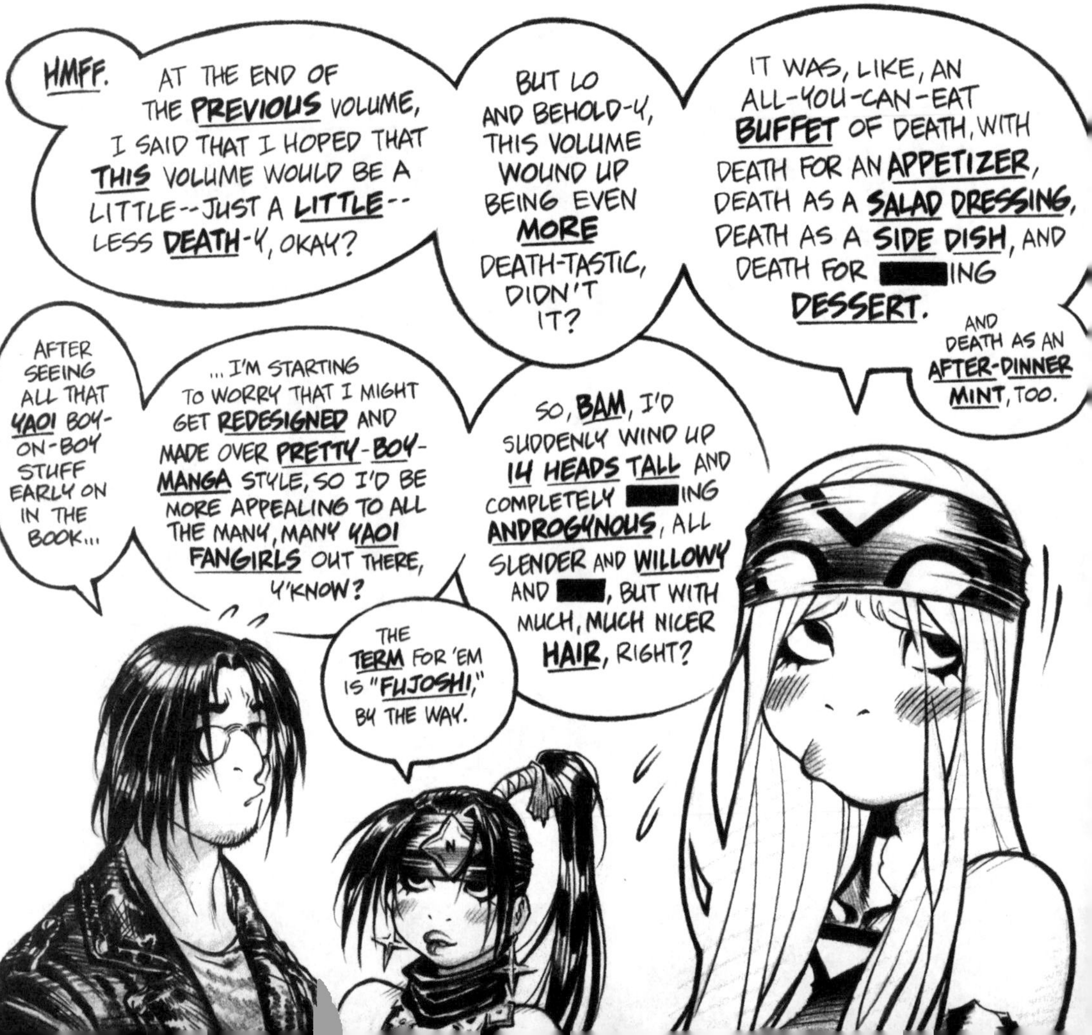
HMFF. AT THE END OF THE PREVIOUS VOLUME, I SAID THAT I HOPED THAT THIS VOLUME WOULD BE A LITTLE--JUST A LITTLE--LESS DEATH-Y, OKAY?
BUT LO AND BEHOLD-Y, THIS VOLUME WOUND UP BEING EVEN MORE DEATH-TASTIC, DIDN'T IT?
IT WAS, LIKE, AN ALL-YOU-CAN-EAT BUFFET OF DEATH, WITH DEATH FOR AN APPETIZER, DEATH AS A SALAD DRESSING, DEATH AS A SIDE DISH, AND DEATH FOR [redacted]ING DESSERT.
AND DEATH AS AN AFTER-DINNER MINT, TOO.
AFTER SEEING ALL THAT YAOI BOY-ON-BOY STUFF EARLY ON IN THE BOOK...
...I'M STARTING TO WORRY THAT I MIGHT GET REDESIGNED AND MADE OVER PRETTY-BOY-MANGA STYLE, SO I'D BE MORE APPEALING TO ALL THE MANY, MANY YAOI FANGIRLS OUT THERE, Y'KNOW?
SO, BAM, I'D SUDDENLY WIND UP 14 HEADS TALL AND COMPLETELY [redacted]ING ANDROGYNOUS, ALL SLENDER AND WILLOWY AND [redacted], BUT WITH MUCH, MUCH NICER HAIR, RIGHT?
THE TERM FOR 'EM IS "FUJOSHI," BY THE WAY.

The End.

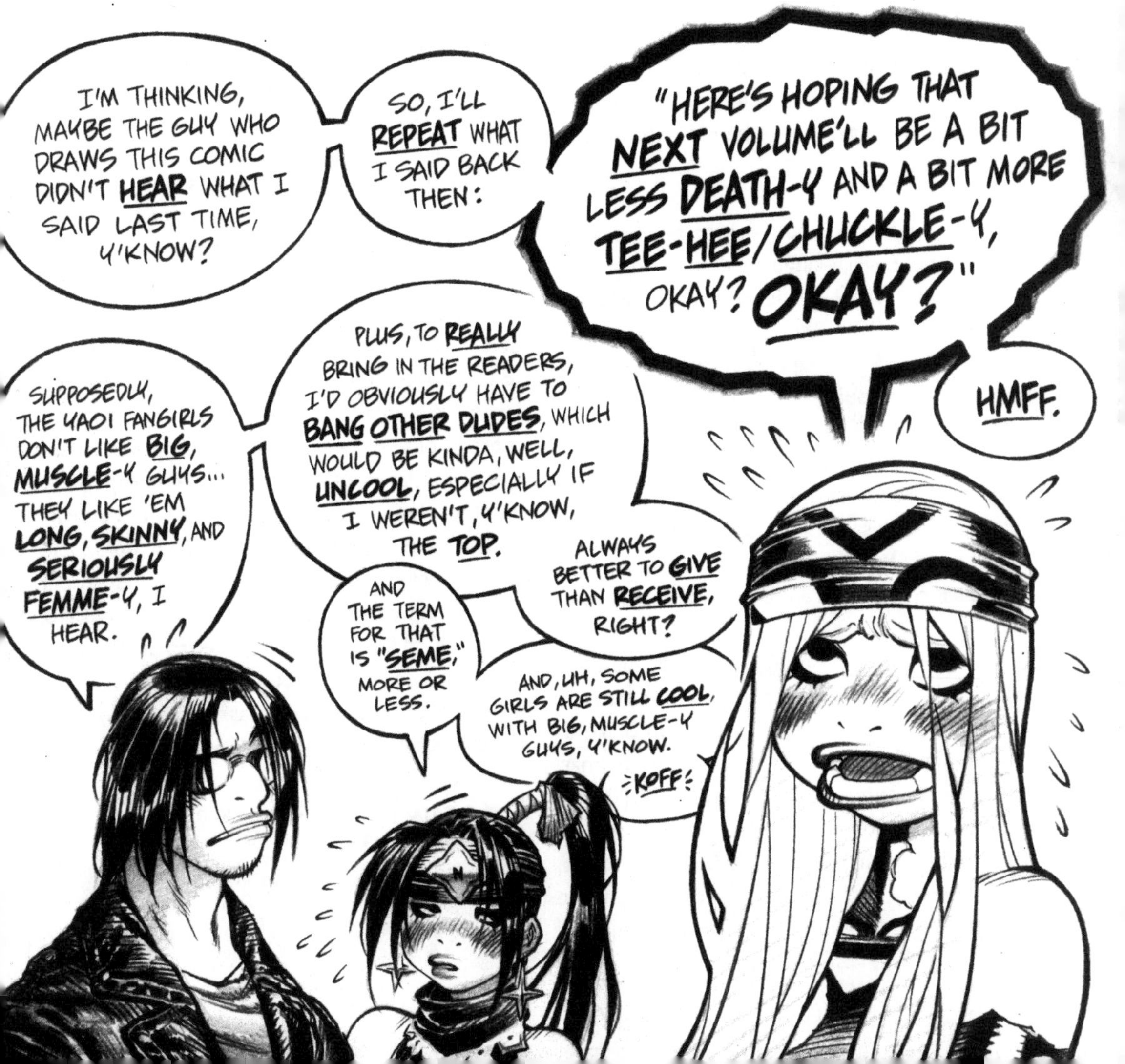

I'M THINKING, MAYBE THE GUY WHO DRAWS THIS COMIC DIDN'T HEAR WHAT I SAID LAST TIME, Y'KNOW?
SO, I'LL REPEAT WHAT I SAID BACK THEN:
"HERE'S HOPING THAT NEXT VOLUME'LL BE A BIT LESS DEATH-Y AND A BIT MORE TEE-HEE/CHUCKLE-Y, OKAY? OKAY?"
HMFF.
SUPPOSEDLY, THE YAOI FANGIRLS DON'T LIKE BIG, MUSCLE-Y GUYS... THEY LIKE 'EM LONG, SKINNY, AND SERIOUSLY FEMME-Y, I HEAR.
PLUS, TO REALLY BRING IN THE READERS, I'D OBVIOUSLY HAVE TO BANG OTHER DUDES, WHICH WOULD BE KINDA, WELL, UNCOOL, ESPECIALLY IF I WEREN'T, Y'KNOW, THE TOP.
ALWAYS BETTER TO GIVE THAN RECEIVE, RIGHT?
AND THE TERM FOR THAT IS "SEME," MORE OR LESS.
AND, UH, SOME GIRLS ARE STILL COOL WITH BIG, MUSCLE-Y GUYS, Y'KNOW.
KOFF

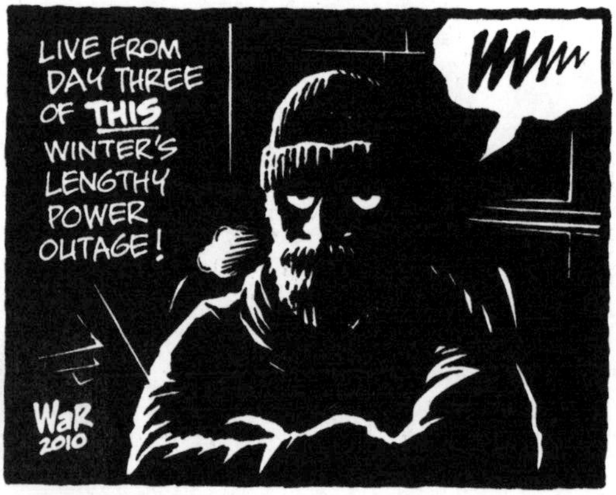
LIVE FROM DAY THREE OF THIS WINTER'S LENGTHY POWER OUTAGE!
WWW
WaR 2010

ADAM WARREN was one of the first writer/artists in the American comics field to integrate the artistic and storytelling techniques of Japanese comics into his work. Yep, he was definitely a manga-influenced pioneer, even going so far as to ride around in a covered wagon and fire his six-shooters in the air while bellowing "Yee-Haw," pioneer style. Okay, maybe he *didn't* actually go that far.

Off and on since 1988, he's written and drawn an idiosyncratic, English-language comics adaptation of the popular Japanese science-fiction characters known as *The Dirty Pair*, who first appeared in novels by award-winning author Haruka Takachiho and were popularized in a varying series of anime incarnations. The six *Dirty Pair* miniseries Adam worked on were known for their purty, purty artwork, future-shockalicious SF concepts, and obnoxiously satirical sense of humor . . . and at least one of them might be available as a trade-paperback collection from Dark Horse. (Or not.)

The rest of Adam's ripped and toned body of comics-related work ranges from forays into the teen-superhero, pop-culture saturation of Wildstorm/DC's *Gen 13*, to a DC prestige-format, far-future iteration of the Teen Titans (*Titans: Scissors, Paper, Stone*), and even a take on old-school anime with a *Bubblegum Crisis* miniseries. More recently, he's created and written the CosmicÜberChica-with-issues project *Galacta: Daughter of Galactus* and the mecha-superteam title *Livewires* for Marvel Comics, along with the miniseries *Iron Man: Hypervelocity*.

Beyond the comics field, he's dabbled in artistic miscellanea such as a dōjinshi "sketchbook" published in Japan and illustrations for magazines such as *Spin*, *GamePro*, *PSM*, *Wizard*, and *Stuff*, not to mention several (very) short-lived stabs into the fields of video games, CD-cover artwork, and TV animation. Currently, he's engaged in an epic, almost mythic feat of what might (very) loosely be described as "home repair"—indeed, the ordeal is remarkably akin to Hercules cleaning the Augean stables, but, alas, featuring a rather less impressive specimen of bearded manhood.

Adam lives a thrillingly reclusive lifestyle somewhere off in the deep woods, where hunting rifles boom, FedEx trucks get stuck in the mud, and grey squirrels the size of Labrador retrievers run up and down the sides of houses all ****ing day long, like the world's loudest and furriest ninja. His hobbies include: pegging himself in the eye with the snapped-off tip from a 4B pencil lead, dosing up with No-Doz®, dosing down with quality microbrews, reading an average of four to eight books per week, bailing over to the local Barnes & Noble to get an average of four to eight more books per week (whilst grinding his teeth at this particular store's repeated, maddening failure to stock *Empowered*), bitching about the truly critical issues of the day (such as death, taxes, and the correct pronunciation of Rajon Rondo's first name), and damaging what's left of his hearing with an iPod full of songs that are far, far too lame to admit listening to in public. His favorite colors are black and blue, which is almost certainly symbolic of something profoundly negative.

Find out more about Adam and his work on **DeviantART**:
http://adamwarren.deviantart.com